THE GERMAN ELEMENT IN ST. LOUIS

A Translation from German
of Ernst D. Kargau's
*St. Louis in Former Years: A Commemorative
History of the German Element*

edited by
Don Heinrich Tolzmann

translated by
William G. Bek

CLEARFIELD

German-Language edition
originally published
St. Louis, 1893

Reprinted from an unpublished manuscript
by William G. Bek, translator (1943)
with the permission of
Western Historical Manuscript Collection-Columbia
University of Missouri/State Historical Society of Missouri

Additional material by Don Heinrich Tolzmann
Copyright © 2000
All Rights Reserved.

Printed for
Clearfield Company, Inc. by
Genealogical Publishing Co., Inc.
Baltimore, Maryland
2000

Reprinted for
Clearfield Company, Inc. by
Genealogical Publishing Co., Inc.
Baltimore, Maryland
2001

International Standard Book Number: 0-8063-4950-6
Made in the United States of America

Table of Contents

Editor's Introduction v

Notes vii

Foreword and Dedication ix

I. A Guide to St. Louis 1
   1. Main Street 3
   2. South Second Street 8
   3. North Second Street 20
   4. North Third Street 23
   5. Former Broadway and New Bremen 30
   6. South Third Street 36
   7. South Fourth Street 42
   8. North Fourth Street 50
   9. South Fifth Street 57
   10. North Fifth Street 64
   11. Sixth Street 73
   12. Franklin Avenue 75
   13. Washington Avenue 80
   14. Locust Street 84
   15. Olive Street 87
   16. Pine Street 94
   17. Chestnut Street and Court House 97
   18. Market Street 108
   19. Frenchtown 123
   20. South Seventh Street 141

II. German-American Life 147
   21. Public Gardens 149
   22. Instrumental Music and Song 154
   23. The German Theater 177
   24. German Physicians 188
   25. The Independent Protestant Congregations 194
   26. The Oldest German Church Organizations 200
   27. The German Immigration Society of St. Louis 206

    28. The Free Congregation of North St. Louis 211
    29. The Turner Societies 216

III. Business and Industry 231
    30. The Levee and River Traffic 233
    31. The Omnibus Period   The First Street-railways 237
    32. The Mail Service 255
    33. German-American Industries of St. Louis 259

IV. Selective Bibliography 333

V. Index 339

Editor's Introduction

In the course of the 19th century, St. Louis came to form one of the corners of the famed "German Triangle" along with Milwaukee and Cincinnati. This work provides a basic guide to St. Louis at the threshold of the 20th century with particular emphasis on the German-American dimension of the city. As it was published somewhat more than a century ago, it now amounts to an historical guide to the city and its German element.

Although the 1893 German-language edition, *St. Louis in früheren Jahren: ein Gedenkbuch für das deutsche Element*, had been translated by William G. Bek in the 1940s, it had never been published. However, it definitely merited publication in the editor's view due to the wealth of information it provides on the German heritage of St. Louis.[1] In editing the work, a number of textual and organizational changes were undertaken to enhance and improve the text, including the arrangement into parts and chapters.

Ernst D. Kargau (1832-1907) was uniquely qualified to write this historical guide to St. Louis. Born in Grünberg in the German province of Silesia, Kargau had attended private schools and then business schools in Berlin before coming to America. From 1860 onwards, he found employment with the German-American press of St. Louis. He first worked at the *St. Louis Tages-Chronik* and then later at the *Anzeiger des Westens* and the *Westliche Post* until the loss of sight in 1888.[2]

Kargau had not only edited German-American newspapers but had become a noteworthy journalist, essayist, and author. Indeed, an 1893 anthology of German-American literature included a selection of his works.[3] Shortly before his death, he published an article on the history of the Missouri River. An examination of the German-American press of St. Louis would most likely reveal a selection of his historical and literary work, most of which, of course, focuses on St. Louis and the surrounding region.

Published more than a century ago, Kargau's survey of St. Louis now takes on the character of an historical guide to the city and its German element and as such serves to illuminate the community in the period before the First World War. Of course, the world wars of the 20th century did much harm to the German-American heritage in general, so that this work takes on special importance with regard to the pre-world wars period.[4]

Since the celebration of the American Bicentennial in 1976, German-Americans have experienced an ethnic heritage and roots revival, as have other ethnic groups in the U.S. This has also been reflected in the emergence of German-American Studies as an academic field of study. This new edition of Kargau's work may be seen as a reflection of this growing interest in the German-American heritage and its significance for understanding American history.[5]

A special word of gratitude is due to the University of Missouri-Columbia's Western History Collection, for permission to publish Bek's translation of Kargau's work, and also to Steven Rowan, University of Missouri-St. Louis, for his assistance in general on the topic of the German heritage of St. Louis. Finally, gratitude is herewith expressed to Dorothy Young, Department of Germanic Languages and Literatures, University of Cincinnati, for the preparation of the manuscript of this work.

Notes

1. The German-language edition appeared as: Ernst D. Kargau, *St. Louis in früheren Jahren: ein Gedenkbuch für das deutsche Element*. (St. Louis: Druck der A. Wiebusch & Sohn Print. Co., 1893).

2. For bio-bibliographical information on Kargau, see Robert E. Ward, *A Bio-Bibliography of German-American Writers, 1670-1970*. (White Plains, N.Y.: Kraus, 1985).

3. See Gustav A. Zimmermann, *Deutsch in Amerika. Beiträge zur Geschichte der Deutsch-Amerikanischen Literatur*. (Chicago: Ackermann & Eyller, 1892).

4. Regarding the anti-German hysteria and sentiment of the world wars, see Don Heinrich Tolzmann, ed., *German-Americans and the World Wars*. (München: K. G. Saur, 1995-97).

5. For an up-to-date German-American history, see Don Heinrich Tolzmann, *The German-American Experience*. (New York, NY: The Humanities Press 1999).

Foreword and Dedication

Having been requested by many persons to publish, in book form, my account of St. Louis in former years, I comply with pleasure. The reminiscences which are recorded in this volume may be regarded as a contribution to the history of the German element of our city, even though it, by no means, makes claim to completeness. The idea of completeness is extremely flexible. What appears complete to one may seem to be the opposite to another. Nevertheless these reminiscences will awaken in the older readers recollections of many things they have experienced themselves. They will recall to memory many fond pictures of the past, many joys and sorrows of days long passed, present again the forms of many friends and contemporaries, who no longer dwell among the living-- in a word they will transfix them to the earlier times with their work and striving, their toil and anxiety--but also their successes. To the younger generation these pages will give knowledge of the life and activity, the work customs and manners of former years, and will show the prominent part which the older generation has had in the most varied fields in the development of our city.

By dedicating this book to the German element of St. Louis I wish to express my gratitude for the kind reception which this element gave me thirty-three years ago, and the good will which it has shown since then. Especial thanks are due those who by valuable oral and written communication have facilitated the task of preparing this book. Such a task is not an easy one under ordinary circumstances, and which was particularly difficult for one who for the last five years has been deprived of the sense of sight. Now I hope that *St. Louis in Former Years* may fulfill the indicated purpose and may be received with approbation.

E.D. Kargau
St. Louis
August 1893

The German Element in St. Louis

I. A Guide to St. Louis

The German Element in St. Louis

1. Main Street

Former residents of St. Louis who left the city twenty-five or twenty years ago, and who since then have not been here, would, if they returned, scarcely recognize Main Street, in spite of the fact that structurally it has been changed but little. They would look in vain for many names which they were formerly accustomed to see on the door plates. Many of the old firms do not exist anymore. Some have passed out of existence during the years, having succumbed finally after a more or less severe struggle with keen competitors. Others followed the motto: "Westward the star of empire takes its course," and are now located on streets farther to the west. Still others have entered undertakings which necessitated their removal from Main Street. Finally there are some businessmen of that day who are in the fortunate financial situation that they could retire to private life.

Up to the time when these changes took place, Main Street could justly be regarded as the center of local wholesale business. One wholesale house joined upon another. There was no branch of business that was not represented here. Life and activity in this street was the most animated imaginable. There was no end to the loading and unloading of goods from morning till evening. Bales, boxes and barrels barred the sidewalks, so that one had difficulty getting through. In crossing the street one had to be in a hurry to dodge the many vehicles if he expected to reach the other side safely. But it was not the maddening haste that characterizes the present time. Business had not yet assumed such a feverish character.

Only in exceptional cases did orders arrive by telegraph. Customers in the country were content to use the mail. Orders did not have to be filled with such great speed. A large part of the shipments was sent by steamboat and some of the steamboat companies dispatched their boats only every other day or every third day. The number of freight trains that were dispatched during a single day from this side of the river, or, for that matter, from East St. Louis, was very small compared with today. Before the completion of Eads Bridge and the tunnel only three railroads had their tracks here and on the other side of the Mississippi there were only four lines. The network of rails which in later years was spread so rapidly over Missouri and neighboring states, providing thousands of cities and villages with rail-connection was in the process of developing, or had not even been planned. Commercial travelers, provided with their sample cases, traveled with horse and wagon to see their customers. Sometimes the roads were so terrible that the horses could not go any further. In bad weather the smallest village inn was still better than the country road. The drummer of that day did not have to be as economical in the use of time as now. He knew that his customers would wait for him if he should arrive a few days late. He did not have to fear that his competitor would get ahead of him by jumping on the caboose of a freight, beat him to a couple of stations and take his customers away from him.

The old Merchants Exchange on the east side of Main Street, between Market and Walnut, which at present looks insignificant, was in those days considered imposing and an ornament to the city. The bourse was large enough for the business of the period, although on some days it was rather crowded. The noise of the wheat-pit was reserved for a later time, and the madness of speculation had not yet reached those heights which exceed all bounds of reasonable daring. People did not expect to get rich in a day, and consequently they did not become poor with the twist of a wrist either. Still there were exciting times, too. At the outbreak of the Civil War there were some stormy scenes at the bourse. A part of the members sided with the secessionists for business reasons, or they held that the cotton barons had a perfect right to withdraw from the Union, if they so desired. The majority of the members where loyal to the Union. This difference of viewpoint led to a break. The members that sided with the North withdrew. They leased suitable rooms in a new building on North Third Street next to the post office. Here they opened a second bourse which they named Union Merchant Exchange. Those who sided with the South continued to support the Chamber of Commerce on Main Street. This break lasted for a whole year. The reunion took place in November, 1862. With it the old harmony was happily and permanently restored.

North of the entrance of the old exchange building was the Franklin Savings Institution. This bank was organized in 1857. Among the founders are to be mentioned: Charles F. Meyer, Charles Taussig, John C. Nuelsen, Charles A. Cuno, John C. H. D. Block, H. J. Spaunhorst, A. C. Cordes and William D'Oench. The latter was the first president. Francis Ringeling served as cashier during the twenty years of the life of this bank. It discontinued business in 1877. In the same building as the bank was the office of the Franklin Fire Insurance Co. For many years Louis Duestrow was the secretary and business manager of this concern. Another German bank--the German Savings Institution-had its place on the southeast corner of Market Street, therefore, in the same Exchange block. This bank was organized in 1853. Among its first directors were William Palm, Louis C. Hirschberg, Franz Saler, C. R. Stinde, Wayman Crow, Edward Eggers, Felix Coste and Robert Barth. The latter served as president till 1875. Since that time F. W. Meister has held this post. When the bank was first organized it was located on the east side of Main Street between Chestnut and Pine. The first cashier was Isaac Rosenfeld, Jr. From 1856 to 1864 Charles Enslin was cashier, and since then Richard Hospes has served in this capacity. After the crash of the National Bank of the State of Missouri (whose president was James H. Britton), the German Savings Institution occupied its rooms in the new Exchange Building, corner of Third and Pine.

Under the roof of the Exchange Building on Main Street was located the Corn Exchange Bank, which existed for only a short while. Also the Union Savings Association, moreover, the office of Taussig, Livingston and Co., the mill-owners H. A. Homeyer and Co., the hardware business of Rashcoe, Mense and Co., and the Commission House of Wattenberg, Busch and Co. About the middle of the sixties Ernest Wattenberg went to New York, where he became one of the most important importers of hops. His successors, Adolphus Busch & Co., were mainly interested in malt, hops and brewery utensils. Presently the Bavaria Brewery--E. Anheuser & Co.--claimed Busch's entire activity. Charles Ehlermann, a nephew of Wattenberg, as a very young man, had worked for his uncle and had become thoroughly acquainted with the business. He now took over the commission house and continued it with brilliant success. With him was associated as a partner, Charles Rueppele, who had been the bookkeeper of the old firm. Opposite the Exchange Building there was, since the beginning of the sixties, the office and display rooms of the St. Louis Woodenware Works (owners Jacob Tamm, Theodore Tamm and Charles Everts). These Works had belonged to Jacob Tamm and Henry P. Meyer during the fifties. Their office was on North Main Street near Chestnut. Also opposite the Bourse there was, during the sixties, the toy and hardware business of Wolf (or Wolff) & Hoppe. Their successors were

Neuhaus, Krite & Co. Later this concern became H. R. Krite & Co. Their place of business has for years been on North Main between Vine Street and Washington Ave.

For the convenience of those who had business on the Exchange there was a restaurant on the first floor of the Exchange Building, also accessible from Commercial Alley. Between twelve and two o'clock, at noon, it was often difficult to find a seat. Close by there was also a saloon, which did an extremely lively business.

Immediately behind the Exchange Building on Commercial Alley, which is now called Commercial Street, was located the banking business of Angelrodt & Barth. Angelrodt was the consul of Prussia, Bavaria, Hessia and a few other German states. Upon Angelrodt's return to Germany, Robert Barth succeeded him as consul. The Swiss consulate was close by. It was in charge of Paul Guye of the firm of Laue & Guye. The consul for the free imperial city of Frankfort was F. A. Reusz, who in company with Constantine Peipers had a commission and banking business on Main near Walnut Street. The consul for Norway was John G. Schuetze. The drug business of Schuetze & Eggers was located in the block north of the Exchange. The gentlemen of the diplomatic corps were, therefore, rather close together.

Of the best known German firms which belonged to the most outstanding of this street, the following have long ceased to exist: Cuno, Mense & Meyer; Suesz, Singer & Co. J. Weil & Brother, (dry goods), Wolf & Hoppe (toys and hardware, Lackmann & Busch (notions); F. Dings & Co. (stockings, notions, and brushes), and their successors Ziock & Lenz, respectively. William Ziock & Co., who now supply the United States with stockings from Rockford, Illinois. Flohr, Meier & Weil; Kramer & Loth (hardware); Johannes Ludwig (hats and caps); C. W. Gausz & Co. (W. F. Giesecke, partner); C. R. Stinde (shoes and boots); Bender & Etzel (toys and hardware); whose long time bookkeeper, Ernst von Wilucky, died some time ago; Bunding & Voigt (window glass). Heinecke & Estel, and Westermann & Meier were at that time the most important importers of porcelain, glass and earthenware. Today this sort of business is handled by the firms E. F. W. Meier & Co., and H. Westermann & Co. Some years ago they moved to Washington Avenue, near Lindell Hotel, but after some time returned to Main Street. The old firm of L. and C. Speck & Co.

(clocks, hardware and toys, German yarn and stockings) transferred their place of business to Washington Avenue after John F. Zisemann left the firm and after the death of Louis Ritterskamp. Their location was between Seventh and Eighth Streets. After Charles Speck withdrew to private life, the successors in the business discontinued the old firm name.

When Bernhard Goldschmidt retired from business the firm of Goldschmidt, Fink & Co. became the well established firm of Fink & Nasse. The senior member was the former steamboat captain Conrad Fink. August Nasse, his son-in-law, was after 1866, one of the partners. One of the oldest and most respected business houses was that of Adolphus Meier & Co. Adolphus Meier was president of the Exchange and for a long time one of its directors. Also for many years he was vice president of the Boatmen's Savings Institution. He represented business frequently at commercial conventions. He was one of the main supporters of the construction of several western railroads, and in general was one of the most public spirited citizens. His business partner (and brother-in-law) John C. Rust, was a member of the city council during the later part of the sixties. Then he severed his connection with the firm and returned to his native city of Bremen. For a number of years this firm dealt in hardware, being located on the corner of Main and Chestnut. Later it gave up the hardware business and devoted itself to the export of tobacco and cotton.

Another hardware business, that of Bremermann & Co. (later Julius Meyer & Co.) was located on the corner of Market Street. South of Walnut Street were the grocery and commission houses of Hammerstein & Schild; R. and W. Heinrichshofen; A. Schneider; Mauntel & Bulte, whose specialty was flour; H. Bohn, as well as the Teichmann commission firm, whose owners, at the beginning, were Charles H. Teichmann, Charles Hoppe and Andrew Einstmann. Later this firm became the Charles H. Teichmann Commission Co., whose president was Charles H. Teichmann. Teichmann's son, Otto L. was secretary and treasurer and his brother-in-law, Adolph Bang was vice president.

There was also the firm of Carpenter & Wahl which firm later became John Wahl & Co.

Another German firm, that of Nedderhuth was at first located on Commercial Alley, but in 1865 moved to Main Street, where it operated as a Pickle and Provision concern (Nedderhuth Packing & Provision Co.).

On Commercial Alley, respectively, South Levee, were the firms of G. Woltmann & Co., Hunicke & Wist, Haenschen & Orthwein, and on North Levee was the still existing business of A. Krieckhaus & Co.

The now great business of Peters Saddlery Co. at that time had ample room in a small building with three windows, located between Market and Chestnut Streets. Rothhan & Straus Brothers, which is today one of the largest concerns of this line--the Straus Saddlery Co.--at that time had their office and storerooms between Locust & Vine Streets. On North Main Street was located during the sixties the blacksmith shop of P. J. Pauli (or Pauly), which specialized in work for the steamboats. From it developed the great establishment of P. J. Pauli (or Pauly) & Brother.

2. South Second Street

The business part of a growing American metropolis, as was already indicated in the previous chapter, undergoes changes from time to time, which sometimes come near to complete transformation. Some streets, however, seem to be more or less untouched by such changes. South Second Street of St. Louis is one of these. As far as the general character of the street is concerned, it has not changed much in forty years and more. With the exception of a few new buildings it looks today as it appeared many years ago, even though it has lost some of its former activity.

During the first half of this century this street, like the other streets running parallel to it between Seventh Street and the river, was predominantly inhabited by Frenchmen. With the German mass-immigration, which began in 1848, Second Street changed its appearance. A large part of the immigrants of that time came by way of New Orleans and then on Mississippi steamboats. Those that landed in New York and Baltimore also made use of water transportation from Pittsburgh or Louisville for their travel farther west. It was, therefore, quite natural, that the new arrivals, no matter if they remained here or wished to go farther west, at the outset looked for shelter and accommodation near the landing place. Second Street satisfied these requirements sufficiently. Beside the already existing hotels and boarding houses many new ones sprang up. The French *Hotelier* (for so he called himself, even though he disposed of only a half dozen rooms) found keen competition in the German *Wirt* on whose houses one could read: Zum Darmstaedter Hof, Zur Stadt Basel, Zur Stadt Offenburg, Rastatter Hof, Zuden drei Eidgenossen, Der Gasthof zum gruenen Baum, Der Eichendranz, Stadt Mainz, Der Pfaelzer Hof, etc. The pension franchise by and by gave way to the German hotel and boarding house. Gradually the *boulanger* was replaced by the German baker, the *charcutier* by the German butcher and sausage maker. In the place of the cafe, in which, by the way, much less coffee than red wine and absynthe was drunk, came the beer hall. The spice shop yielded to the German grocer.

In the nearby Main Street business was exclusively devoted to wholesale trade. In Second Street, from Walnut Street south, retail business prevailed. Craftsmen and shopkeepers of every sort pursued their business peacefully and industriously from early to late. And so it is still in this region, even though the lively trade of former days has lessened. There was a time that one who passed through this street could imagine himself transplanted to Germany, for one heard only German spoken here. This continued till the growing generation brought English home from the school. In spite of that the German mother tongue is even today predominant in commerce there.

In the fifties and sixties the Rheinische Weinhalla (Rhenish Wine Hall) was regarded the best German hotel in the city. After Gustav Heinrichs had sold out to Louis Wolf the house became celebrated for its excellent kitchen, which reputation it has continued to maintain till this day under the splendid management of Mrs. Dorthea Wolf. Only a few rooms were rented by the month to some not-too-old bachelors. The demand of strangers made this restriction necessary. German merchants from Missouri and Illinois, who came here to do their buying, and representatives of eastern firms liked to lodge in this hotel because it was so close to Main Street which at that time was the main business street for almost all kinds of goods. Moreover, one could be sure to meet many a friend among the noonday guests. One dined splendidly and between twelve and half-past two o'clock a seat was rarely vacant in the dining room. Many of those who in those years came here are no longer in our midst. Among these are to be named Charles F. Meyer, John F. Zisemann, Charles DeGreck (who as also his intellectual, young wife did so much for the entertainment in the Germania club, as in later years was done by Dr.

Kolbenheyer, Leopold Methudi (or Methudy) and A. F. Straszburger), the jovial Henry Gildehaus, George Bender, Fritz Etzel, Charles Hobicht, F. Samesreuther, the jolly singer Anton Roesler, who on a hot summer afternoon was overcome by the heat and died on the corner of Fifth and Market Streets, the loveable Dick Wist (of the firm of Hunicke & Wist), Dick Addicks, who as cabin boy and sailor on Bremen ships had sailed the seas, and then, after all, had decided to settle on solid land, where he had advanced from the position of an employee to that of a partner in the firm of Smith and Co., dealers in groceries and tobacco. Among the merry guests, moreover, was to be seen Louis Lemke who even today is a stately figure. Formerly he was called the handsome Lemke. There was also Franz Scharwitz who at that time worked for L. and C. Speck Co. Also the very young Dr. Lingenfelder who took part in the war as army surgeon, and many others.

The years of the war provided a unique activity for the Rhenish Wine Hall. It was the favorite stopping place of officers of the Union army who came to St. Louis for a longer or shorter stay. Some of them who were on detached service, spent weeks and months there. Among these were Captain Indes, Major Poten, Major Hansen, Major Conrad and Lieutenant Grenzenbach. Also Prince Salm Salm, who had so faithfully remained with the unfortunate Archduke Emperor Maximilian in Mexico, was a guest here at that time. After the battle of Pea Ridge, in the spring of 1862, young Lieutenant Hermann Tuerk, (who at the beginning of the war had given up a position in one of the local business houses), was brought back here. An enemy bomb that had exploded close before him had destroyed his eyesight. The blind man received the best of care in Wolf's house for months. Later he was returned to his native city of Luebeck and to his parents. Through the efforts of local friends Congress allowed him a pension by a special legislative act.

Continuous ill health, due, in part to the enervating work in the hotel, compelled Louis Wolf to give up the hotel business. The Rhenish Wine Hall passed into the hands of Charles Leinberger, who up to that time had operated a hotel bearing his name in the Oak Hall Building on South Fourth Street between Washington Avenue and Lucas Avenue (at that time called Green Street).

It would be difficult to find two men as different as Wolf and his successor. The former was a very substantial man, serious and taciturn. Leinberger, on the other hand, was a man of the world, who had more interest in the thoroughbred horses that he liked to drive than in the case of his guests. He was a great talker and had no difficulty in holding his own with half a dozen wine drummers whose tongues were pivoted in the middle. In his hotel on Fourth Street everything was very elegant. During the first two years of the war things were very lively there. --Older readers will perhaps recall Colonel de Ahna about whom appeared many items in the local newspapers long after that time. This former Bavarian officer lived here for a long time as a recruiting officer. He had his headquarters in this hotel. It attracted not a little attention that as long as the colonel lodged here two sentinels always stood guard before the hotel entrance. The colonel was a handsome man who never appeared on the street except in full uniform. It was whispered at that time that he did not lack gallant adventures.

After the end of the war the uniforms disappeared from the Rhenish Wine Hall. The rattle of the saber was no longer heard, but on that account it was no less lively. The sons of Mars had gone away, and the messengers of Mercury (vulgarly called drummers) came in still greater numbers. But also artists took their quarters at Leinberger's place. Among these are to be mentioned Otto von Hoym, the long-time director of the New York Municipal Theater. He lived here when he filled his engagement as guest artist. There was also Antonie Becker-Grahn, who celebrated well-deserved triumph here. Also the bass singer, Carl (or Karl) Formes, as well L'Arronge and his young wife preferred this small German hotel to the large American hotels.

Of the later owners of this hotel should be mentioned: Henry Schweickhardt, Henry Bodemann, the former owner of Bodemann's Grove, and Osthoff Nau.

In the same block and on the same side of the street was a German restaurant such as does not exist in our midst now-a-days. It was owned by Hippo (more correctly, Louis) Krug. In those days it was the gathering place of the German business men. In the forenoon for the morning draught, and still more in the evening, after business hours, they were accustomed to gather here. Between six and seven o'clock it was difficult to find a seat at one of the many small tables. Much beer was drunk and much politics was discussed. Hippo liked to join in the conversation and the discussions. He was an extraordinarily well-read man and he was not inclined to hide his opinion. At the time of the morning draught it was particularly lively when the discussions turned to war and peace, state affairs and to learned topics. Participating in the discussions were Daniel Hertle, (of the *Westliche Post*); Doctor Hillgaertner (of the *Anzeiger*); (and later of the *Neue Zeit*); Adalbert Loehr (of the *Tages Chronik*); "Stout" Wolf, who published the French weekly *Revue de l'Ouest*; Papa Anheuser, the apothecary Enno Sander, Charles Eggers and others. When things became really animated one could be sure that Ferdinand Fuchs and Doctor Hammer were among the disputants. As Mr. Fuchs was a member of the firm Nedderhuth & Fuchs, importers of European products, and to distinguish him from other Fuchses he was called "Delicatessen" Fuchs. for a long time he has now been living in Mannheim.

Another of the regular guests was Ferdinand Lingenau, who died during the strike in the summer of 1877. In his testament he named the socialists of the world as his heirs. At the time of which I am writing, he was not yet thirsting for the blood of monarchs but was satisfied with red Aszmannshaeuser wine or plain claret. Moreover, he was at that time not the plain citizen but on the contrary an epicure, and by no means an admirer of the Spartan mode of living. "Bring me an anchovy sandwich," was accustomed to say to the waiter,--"a lot of bread, a lot of butter and a lot of anchovy." (Anchovy is a species of small fish).

The reputation of this excellent restaurant was fully maintained when it passed into the hands of F. L. Schmid, who managed it for several years, It was, without doubt, the most frequented restaurant in the city. Schmid insisted upon strict order, and was busy from early till late hours. When he sold it because of declining health, and went to Germany for some years, the business was in a flourishing condition. His successor, August Korn, died after a few years. Later Henry Schweickhardt again took the place over, but the time of its earlier splendor was gone.

Of the three German book stores, which at the end of the fifties and the beginning of the sixties deserved this designation, two were located on South Second Street. They were owned by William Meylert and Conrad Witter respectively. The brains of the Meylert store was Julius Helmich.

He was also the guiding spirit under the management of Bandissin, then under Rashcoe, and still later under Thalmann, successively successors of Meylert. Julius Helmich was a personified book catalog. He had been the owner of a large book concern in Bielefeld, had participated in the uprising of 1848, and when the reaction set in had sought a new home on this side of the ocean. Helmich did not have to refer to Hinrich's book catalog. He had the information completely in his head. He knew where and when a book had been published, in how many editions it had appeared, and in many instances he could tell you the contents. In Meylert's store another book man was employed who formerly had had a bookstore of his own-- Florentine Schuster. He was a very large man who looked like a giant beside the mercurial Helmich.

Until the time when the Witter bookstore was transferred to Fourth Street, it was located on the corner of Walnut and Second Streets. Meticulous neatness obtained in this store. The spacious place was well lighted, and in this regard was in marked contrast to Meylert's shop in which semi-darkness prevailed. Conrad Witter himself returned to Germany more than two decades ago, leaving to his two nephews the business, which even then was quite extensive.

At that time the Barnum Hotel, which only recently went out of business, was regarded as the first hotel of the city. It occupied the greater part along Walnut Street between Second Street and Main. The Lindell and Southern hotels were not yet built, and neither the Planters House nor the Virginia Hotel (Corner of Main and Green Streets) could compare with the Barnum in regard to equipment. It bore the name of its owner--Theron Barnum, who was the brother of the famous circus and menagerie man, Phineas T. Barnum, whom he resembled in a striking way. --During the fair week of 1860 this hotel entertained the then eighteen year old Prince of Wales, who, with a numerous retinue, spent four days in St. Louis.

The corner of Barnum's hotel was occupied by Enno Sander's drugstore. The shop adjoining was Hermann Limberg's men's clothing store. Opposite the hotel, on the south side of Walnut Street, Charles F. Schneider had a restaurant, which was very popular. Immediately at the outbreak of the war he sold out to Volkmann in order to join the army. After he suffered the loss of his left arm he returned, and a bit later established himself on the southwest corner of Second and Chestnut Streets.

Volkmann sold out to Louis P. Eber in 1861. Eber enlarged the Café National considerably by adding the space which was behind Heitz' safe factory.

Two of the most important German firms of that time were situated on the west side of the block between Market and Walnut Streets. The house on the corner of the alley was occupied by the druggists D'Oench, Rives & Co., later William D'Oench & Co. An explosion of a vessel filled with naphtha caused a great fire in 1868, which destroyed the four-story building and its entire content. After rebuilding, the place was occupied by the wholesale grocers, Meyer & Meister, who up to that time had done business in an adjoining building. Mr. F. W. Meyer, the present president of the German Savings Institution, severed his connection with the firm many years ago. From then on the concern was known as Charles F. Meyer & Co., which went out of business after a short time.

The original site of Lemp's brewery, which now occupies several blocks in the south-western part of the city, was on the east side of Second Street, between Walnut and Elm Streets. Here it was where Adam Lemp, the father of the founder of the present brewery, fifty years ago brewed the first real St. Louis lager beer. This beer was brewed in a large copper kettle. In this old building the first story is preserved in its original condition and is still used as a saloon. Opposite this place the watch maker John Bolland and the cigar makers Nauer & Co. (H. N. Nauer & Guido Kalb) had their places of business. The latter firm later occupied the corner of Second and Market Streets.

John Schiffmann and Ferdinand Krueger for many years were established as successful merchant tailors on South Second Street. Both became owners of restaurants. Schiffmann's place was at the corner of Fifth and Elm Streets, while Krueger's was in the Apollo Theater where he was the partner of Louis Schiller. Krueger also devoted considerable time to providing costumes for the theater. Mr. Schiffmann was a rich man at one time. He lost his property because he endorsed the notes of other people, who then left him in the lurch.

For many years Philipp Dauernheim had a real German tavern on the northwest corner of Second and Elm Streets. His place was orderly and quiet which was a source of much satisfaction for the skat players who were accustomed to meet here in the evening. As in all of America so also in St. Louis very few people played the game of Skat. The immigrants from Germany were not familiar with the game, unless they came from Saxony or Thuringia. Then came Karl Monelius who, with the assistance of the dentist Steck and some former Heidelberg students and some Forty-Eighters, instructed their friends in the secrets of this game of cards.

Dauernheim closed his tavern at midnight or a bit earlier. But for those who did not care to go home at that hour there were other places to visit. For example there was the tavern that had the attractive name: "Die ewige Lampe" (The eternal lamp). On eight or ten rather narrow steps one ascended to a very large garden in the rear of which was the tavern which in addition to other things also had a billiard table.

Julius Stange was for many years the jovial host of this tavern. He was a typical Berliner whose spicy language and witty expressions were a delight to hear. His successor was the easygoing Alsatian Louis Thannberger. In spite of the fact that he was good-natured, he could at times be a man of action. For example, two young Americans, whom one could call "dudes" came to his place on a Sunday morning and asked for good brandy. He served them with his accustomed politeness, filling the glasses with the best cognac. Then he saw how one of the young men spat out the contents of his glass, and intentionally did this right in front of the bar. In the next moment Thannberger had him by the coat collar and shoved him through the open door to the above-mentioned steps. There he gave his customer a vigorous kick on the rear, so that he landed on the street below before he knew what had happened. When the other one started to remonstrate, Thannberger disposed of him also without much ado, and also threw him down the steps. Then with a French accent he called after them: "Au revoir, you come again to my place!" Then he mopped his moist forehead with a dark red silk handkerchief and accepted the compliment of the other assembled and highly amused customers.

Each forenoon he served roast beef for lunch. He insisted on doing the carving himself. With the greatest satisfaction he cut the thin slices and with inimitable grace laid them on the bread for his customers. When the roast was particularly tender and juicy he would say: "Exquisite, Messieurs, Exquisite!" But he did not only serve delicious roast beef, but also the finest coffee. When he later on opened a second place of business, south of the Rhenish Hall, this place was crowded each afternoon with coffee drinkers. --Since we are here dealing with historical matters, I might add that this house maintained its reputation for good coffee under the management of Thannberger's successor, Frederick Kluender. The latter had been a printer before he took over the restaurant.

Of the "Ewige Lampe" every trace has disappeared. The site on which it stood and the garden have been leveled a long time ago.

In the same block was also Bernard Schweickhardt's wine room (Zur Traube-grape) with its enormous round-table. Each evening a number of good friends gathered around this table and discussed the best interests of the city and let the events of the world pass in review.

Henry Schweickhardt, the brother of Bernhard, had, to the middle of the sixties, managed a tavern in East St. Louis, opposite the landing place of the ferry boats. On Sundays and holidays hundreds of ladies and gentlemen from St. Louis visited this place. After he moved to St. Louis he became an associate with Moritz Schuster, the importer of German wines. The cellars of the firm of Schuster and Schweickhardt were on the corner of Walnut and Main Streets, under the old Merchants Exchange building. Their sample rooms were, however, in the Tavern on Second Street. Every time when a new shipment had arrived from the other side, there was a great wine sampling around the giant round table. Every variety--Rhenish, Morel and Palatinate wine--was subjected to a thorough test, and the judgment of this areopagus was considered final. To this set of belonged, for example, the well known wine connoisseur, Dr. Philipp Weigel. Usually he acted as presiding officer. Other experts were the druggist Enno Sander and Dr. Lips, who owned the drugstore on the corner of Myrtle Street.

Many a one who did not know the life and activity which is here depicted might believe that at that time that nothing but eating and drinking happened on Second Street. That would be entirely wrong. It is true that there were ample opportunities to quench one's thirst without resorting to Mississippi river water. There were an unusually large number of hotels and restaurants that were concentrated in a small area, and each had a tavern adjoining it. However, this did not in any way impede the diligence of the inhabitants. The greatest activity prevailed in the shops and stores from early till late. If it happened that one or the other imbibed a bit too much and became quarrelsome, the innkeeper simply evicted him without calling the police. In very rare cases a heated dispute ended in blows. Occasionally such differences were brought before the justice of the peace. One did not have to go far, for his office was on the first floor of the Barnum Hotel. Both parties to a dispute willingly submitted to the verdict of the squire or to that of a jury of neighbors. After such a hearing the accuser and the accused, together with the witnesses, the jury, the judge and the constable joined in a glass of reconciliation in a nearby tavern.

The west side of Second Street seems to have been predestined to supply the means for man's liquid spirituous food. At the place where once had stood the giant round table, mentioned above, in later years Charles Wetzler had his wine store, and on the spot where once the "Ewige Lampe" shone, Charles Rebstocky Co. had their whiskey store. Later the latter firm moved to Main Street, and now the old site is occupied by the Isidor Bush Wine & Liquor Co.

The laboratory of Enno Sander was in the same block but around the corner of Myrtle Street, and was later transferred to the south side of the latter. His drug store, as already stated, occupied the corner of the Barnum Hotel. Before coming into the sole possession of Sander it had been the drug store of the Doctors Behr and Hammer, who had the location adjoining the tavern "Zur Traube."

There was no lack of German drug stores on Second Street. Lips' drug store occupied the south-east corner of Second and Myrtle. Theodore Kalb's drug business was on the south-east corner of Second and Poplar. Druggist Tschirpe, in whose store F. W. Sennewald served as pharmaceutical chemist, had given up the business in the middle of the fifties. Dr. Behr lived opposite his apothecary shop, Dr. Karl Hanck, two doors below Walnut Street, Dr. Roesch on Third, not far from Elm, Dr. Lips on Myrtle near Third, and Dr. Rose on Second, south of Lombard (now Papin) Street. The German immigrants were, therefore, amply provided with doctors and druggists.

On the southeast corner of Elm Street, Volkening & Oebicke had their grocery store. A few houses farther south was the store and workshop of tin-smith Cajacob, who among other repair work understood how to keep the then popular German study lamp in order. Here, too, was the sewing machine store of S. Bartmann. The Gruene Baum (Green Tree) and Griesmayer's Hotel offered the most spacious accommodations for strangers. They took care of a large number of travelers, and also a great many of boarders who stayed the year around. The Gruene Baum was particularly popular when George Diesz was the owner. Two of his daughters married Joseph Schneider and Max Feuerbacher. Schneider opened the Chouteau Avenue brewery, and Feuerbacher became the partner of Abe McHose in the Green Tree brewery, which at that time was located approximately on the site where now the Iron Mountain railroad crosses Second and Third Streets as it enters the Chouteau Avenue depot. In the later part of the sixties the present Green Tree brewery was organized by Feuerbacher and Louis Schloszstein, which today is one of the largest in our city. The Green Tree later came into the hands of John Zimmerer, who has operated the hotel for many years with success.

A very well known personality in those years was Jacob Blankenhorn, the owner of the barber shop adjoining Lips' drugstore. Whoever wanted to know what was happening within a radius of many, many blocks could be sure to obtain information from him. After his death his widow, also a very talkative person, continued the business for awhile, whereupon she retired to private life under comfortable circumstances.

In the earlier years Charles Hoffer had the reputation of making the best sausage in all of St. Louis. He was a man who embarrassed no one by excessive politeness, but in the matter of supplying the finest meats he was surpassed by none of his contemporaries. He was the predecessor of John Boepple.

On the northwest corner of Spruce Street was located the grocery business of A. C. L. Haase, whose pickled herring were famous far and wide. Later he devoted himself exclusively to the fish business. He founded the Haase Fish Company, one of the largest business concerns in the whole west.

Ignaz and Conrad Benzinger owned a picture and picture frame business near Spruce Street, which for its time was very extensive. They also had a large collection of books.

One of the most important businesses on the street was that of the copper smith, Charles Wetzel. His competitor, William Rose, gave up his lucrative business and devoted himself to politics. A clever copper smith became a poor politician whose loose tongue put him for a few weeks in 1861 in the Gratiot Street prison. (This prison was formerly McDowell's College.) Democratic Bill, as he was generally called, was really not a bad fellow, but unfortunately he forgot the old adage, Shoemaker stick to your last.

Two substantial wine shops were operated by Adam Guerdan and Bernard Franz. The latter called his place Zum Vater Rhein.

The distillery of Dreyer & Ulrici was an extensive affair. It was situated on the east side of Second Street between Cedar and Mulberry. It also furnished swill for hundreds of cows, since at that time, the sale of milk was not yet under the control of the bureau of health.

Ruedy's amusement park and popular theater were situated on the west side, two doors below Mulberry Street. The entrance to the park was on the latter street. The theater had a rather large stage. In summer and autumn on Sunday afternoons and evenings the place was attended by many people. This continued for many years. By and by the taste of the public changed, and though John Ruedy made every effort to reawaken interest in his place, he could not accomplish it. In 1861 a regiment of house guards was quartered here. In the large dance hall it looked like barracks and the park was a military camp. Ruedy himself joined the army as a captain. During his absence and as a consequence of the war, his establishment, like so many others of this type in St. Louis, as also in other cities, failed.

Diagonally across, on the east side, there was during the fifties and sixties the livery stable and the furniture store of Charles Eberle, who at that time was one of the best known German citizens of St. Louis.

In the sixties Gerhard (or Gerhardt) H. Timmermann located his machine shop on Chouteau Avenue between Main and Second Streets. In the course of time this enterprise was greatly enlarged, and under the name of St. Louis Iron and Machine Works, managed by G. H. and John H. Timmermann and Hermann Krutsch became one of the largest concerns of this kind.

Below Convent Street was the packing plant and smokehouse of Mathias Steitz. The hams that he prepared had at that time as fine a reputation as Whitacker's enjoy at this time. Steitz was one of the most respected German citizens and had the confidence of everyone. During the later years of the fifties he had a seat in the city council, and in the sixties he was a county commissioner.

3. North Second Street

The location of banks furnishes the best proof of the change which the business part of St. Louis underwent in the last thirty-five years. At this time there are twelve banks on North Fourth Street, beginning on the south side of Chestnut and extending to the north side of Franklin Avenue. If one includes the Merchants National Bank in the Laclede building, whose entrance, to be sure, is on Olive Street, and the Third National and the Bank of Commerce, the National Bank of St. Louis, and the banks on Third Street, then one has seventeen banks within a space of only twelve blocks. In former years the banks were more widely distributed. On Main Street was the Bank of the State of Missouri, generally known as the Old State Bank, and the State Saving Association, the German Savings Institution, the Franklin Savings, the Traders and Merchants Bank. Today none of these are to be found anymore in those localities, and on North Second Street there are also none. Formerly between Chestnut and Olive there were five public banks and four private banking firms, and on Main Street several more of the latter type were to be found.

In 1891 the Boatmen's Bank moved into its new fortress-like building on Washington Avenue and Fourth Street, but for four decades it had been on the northeast corner of Second and Pine. Adjoining the later site was the St. Louis Building and Savings Association. For many years this concern had Charles Enslin as its circumspect financier. When the association became the Bank of Commerce the new banking firm lost Enslin's services all too soon in his death. The building on the southwest corner housed the Southern Bank and the still flourishing Mechanics. A few years ago the latter moved to Fourth and Pine Streets. The Third National Bank had its location in the same block on Second Street. In the immediate vicinity were also the following banking firms: Loker Brothers, R. S. Ladue, Tessone & Danjen, and Allen, Copp & Nisbet. The head of the latter firm was Thomas Allen who for many years was president of the Iron Mountain Railway Co. He also rebuilt the Southern Hotel. He died in Washington while he was serving as a member of the House of

Representatives. The former sites of banking institutions now serve as the office and storage plants of the Hermann Eisenhardt Soap and Washing Soda Company.

Close beside the Buildings and Savings Institution, whose president was Felix Coste, there was as early as the sixties, the well-known firm of Stracke & Caesar, wholesale dealers in spirituous liquors. Opposite this site was the old firm of William Koenig & Co. with its storerooms for agricultural machinery. Later this firm moved to South Eighth Street near Clark Avenue. The head of this concern for many years served with distinction as a member of the public school board. The main difference between South Second and North Second Streets was, and is to this day, that the former serves retail business almost completely, while the latter is exclusively devoted to wholesale business, largely grocery and produce. Among the oldest grocery firms is to be named Spaunhorst & Hackmann. Before moving to Second Street they had their business for many years on Main Street, opposite the Virginia Hotel. Another firm, just as old, was that of Erfort & Petring, southwest corner of Washington Avenue, which did an enormous business, particularly before the war. Grant and Keiser, to which firm belonged George W. Keiser, who later joined the steamboat captain John P. Keiser in a commission business (now located on North Levee). Near the end of the sixties the firm of Schulter & Mette was changed to the wholesale wine and liquor business of Mette & Kanne (Louis Mette and George Kanne) formerly on Second, now on Main Street. The large building situated some distance back of the street immediately behind the Jacoby House, was occupied by H. Gildehaus & Co. After the death of Henry Gildehaus his former partners, Wulfind & Dieckeriede, continued to do business there for many years until they were in need of more space. Up to the time of their transfer to Locust and Sixth Streets, C. Conrad & Co. had their wine business in the basement of the same building in which H. Gildehaus & Co. were located. For several decades the wine and liquor store of Gustav Hoeber was located on North Second. Later he moved to South Fifth between Market and Walnut. Weinhagen & Hornbostel, dealers in fancy groceries were also on North Second. Farther north Wiszmann & Senden for many years had their wholesale wine, liquor, tobacco and cigar business. There was also the firm of Imbs, Meyer & Fusz who had an extensive flour business. On the corner of Washington

Avenue was the brass foundry of Kupferle & Rosewell (Missouri Brass Foundry), which later became the very extensive Kupferle Manufacturing Co., and which is still located on the same site. A few houses to the north was the Eagel Bell and Brass Foundry of Kupferle & Bosselier. In the immediate neighborhood there was during the sixties the storage plant of the Pittsburgh iron and nail firm of Graff, Bennett & Co. Later they moved north of Franklin Avenue. The manager of this firm was for three decades M. J. Lippmann.

One of the much patronized German hotels of those days was the Friederich Haus, named after its owner, and located on the southeast corner and Vine Street. Although it did not contain as many rooms as the Monroe House it was no less elegant. The Monroe House later became the Olive Street Hotel. The Monroe House (corner of Second and Olive Streets) was the first local hotel that introduced the European plan, that is, allowed the guest to take their meals in the hotel or anywhere else, and charged only for the meals that were actually eaten there. The number of taverns on North Second was much smaller than on South Second. Nevertheless no one needed to famish. Captain Schreiner had a genuine German tavern on the northeast corner of Chestnut. (In later years John Bamberger owned this place.) Dominoes and chess were diligently played in a small room in the rear of the building. Jacoby & Feikert enjoyed an enthusiastic patronage, particularly by the Americans. At their place of business no beer was served, but the finest brandies and whiskies, procured from Kentucky or imported from France, could be had. The sherry, port and Madeira offered here could have been served at any princely table. As one entered this place for the first time, he was impressed with the quiet that reigned here. The two owners were of a rather taciturn nature and were not accustomed to speak with their customers unless the latter began the conversation. Most of the guests tarried no longer than the purpose of their coming required. The four or five small tables on the east wall of the place were usually unoccupied. Men came, drank and went away. Among those who did this with punctuality were Colonel George and Colonel John Knapp, the publishers of the *Missouri Republican*, Nathaniel Paschall, the highly intelligent editor of the paper, Captain Daniel G. Taylor (who was the mayor of the city from 1861 to 1863), Colonel John G. Priest and other prominent, for the most part good democratic politicians. The proximity of the *Republican* building made it very convenient. They even remained faithful to this practice after the *Republican* had moved into its new house on the corner of Third Street. With the exception of Colonel Priest none of the above-named are now living. For more than four decades this place was operated by Jacoby & Feikert.

4. North Third Street

Perhaps it was only by chance, but it is worth mentioning, that from the middle of the fifties to the middle of the sixties, three different concerns within the space of two blocks on North Third were selling patent medicines. At the same time there was also an herb doctor in that same part of town. This man had formerly owned a wine shop in Berlin, and, no doubt, been more of an honor to his early profession than to the profession of medicine. Having failed in business abroad he had emigrated to America and established himself on the northwest corner of Third and Market. Presently a small name plate, bearing this inscription appeared:
--Dr. Louis Drucker, Herb Doctor--
under one of his windows.

It is to be assumed that he had not earned the title of doctor under a medical faculty, but at that time no state or city board troubled itself about the actual existence of the genuineness of a diploma. Therefore, this one-time Berlin wine merchant could mix his herbs unhindered. This much may be said, that there were no reports current that they had caused any mischief.

On the west wall of the building opposite (a building that later was changed into an hotel which had the name Prescott House) giant letters announced that there was located the office and store rooms of Blakesly's celebrated liniment. A narrow, shaky wooden stairway on the outside of the building led to the second story where the liniment store was. The inventor of this remedy was a quiet, modest man, who became excited only if one addressed him as "doctor." He emphatically refused to have this title.

A few doors away Blakesly had a German rival, John Schuetze, who made an ointment with which he did a good business for many years. On the corner of Chestnut Street, where later the *Republican* building was erected, was a small two-story house in which Ezra Easterly had a store where he sold patent medicines, some made by himself and some made by others. A block farther north, on the corner of Pine Street, "Doctor" James H. McLean had his little shop, where he sold his fever medicine and liver pills.

Between Market and Chestnut, Heidsick & Moll had their fine grocery store. Adolph Moll, the grocery king of Franklin Avenue was the founder of this business. During the sixties this store went into the hands of the present owner, Julius Vogeler, who, therefore, has operated it over a quarter of a century.

Nearby, a Hollander, who also spoke German rather fluently, had a small lunch room. Every evening he closed it promptly at nine o'clock, because he opened it again at three o'clock in the morning. The carriers of the morning papers, which at that time were all printed within a few blocks of each other, arrived there at the above hour in order to strengthen themselves with a usually frugal meal. The coffee, which was served by the Hollander, was no tribute to the colonial possessions of his fatherland. No trace of Java was to be found in it. But it was hot at all times, and therefore, on cold winter nights, it was welcome to the newsboys and other night guests.

The tavern situated under the *Anzeiger* building was usually open till after midnight. Henry Boernstein, who personally had no use for taverns, was nevertheless the owner of three taverns. The one mentioned above he opened in the first place because he did not need the room for newspaper purposes, and secondly, because he was of the opinion that the tavern, managed in German manner, in which the customers could enjoy instrumental and vocal music, as well as other entertainment, would be an effective and valuable factor in the social life of German countrymen. As his first partner he chose the excellent Frederick Schaefer, who later became the Lieutenant Colonel in Boernstein's Second Missouri Volunteer Regiment. This tavern soon became one of the favorite gathering places for of the German citizens. The concerts had just as much drawing force as the beer which was obtained from Eimer's brewery in Belleville. On Sundays in the afternoon and evening a great many people came. Schaefer's successor was Louis Schiller. He rented the property. The musical and other forms of entertainment had ceased some time before.

Rich and interesting recollections are associated with the *Anzeiger des Westens* with Henry Boernstein's journalistic and other varied activity in St. Louis, which, as is well known came to an end at the outbreak of the Civil War, or rather, with his appointment as consul at Bremen. His co-editor, Carl Ludwig Bernays had at the same time gone to Zuerick as consul. Dr. George Hillgaertner, who continued the editorial work for a while discontinued the publication in the following March because of difference that arose during the congressional election in the autumn of 1862. In July publication was resumed under the management of Carl Daenzer. The old ramshackle building which no longer met the requirement was nevertheless kept in use till 1872, when it was replaced by a suitable new one.

Directly opposite the *Anzeiger* building Ferdinand Meszmer had his modest workshop as locksmith. During the latter sixties he moved to Market Street between Fifth and Sixth Streets. Here he began to manufacture the brass stopcocks for beer kegs. Since then an entire factory had to be erected in the southern part of the city for the manufacture of this article.

The building opposite the *Anzeiger* building and which belonged to the Board of Education, during the sixties, bore a number of inscriptions that attracted the attention of passers-by. Its front wall was covered from top to bottom with sayings of Thomas Jefferson, which dealt with the right person has to own a part of the earth, that is the right to own some real estate. Charles Peteler, who rented this building as a storehouse for his stock of leather, wanted to express his displeasure over difficulties he had in regard to real estate. The quotations did not disappear from the front wall till he transferred his business to South Third Street. Peteler was not a radical, though he was a faithful adherent to the principles of socialism.

Under the name, The Monkeys, there existed at that time three taverns that were owned by John Behringer. One of these was on the place where the front of the *Republican* building ended on Third Street. The peculiar name which Behringer gave his saloons was due to the fact that he kept a number of monkeys of various size and kind in his places of business and in the display windows. A special kind of punch served there was called monkey punch, and an extract for the preparation of this drink was sold by the bottle for family use. This drink could be drunk hot or cold.

For many years the workshop of gunsmith, Duenkel, a clever mechanic, stood next to the above building.

During the later part of the sixties Stamm & Moller's wine and liquor business was located on the east side between Chestnut and Pine. Hermann Stamm was associated with Christoph Moller. The latter had formerly had his place of business on South Seventh Street, opposite Center Market, where he sold Catawa Bitters. This beverage was first made in Hermann, Missouri. After dissolving the partnership, Moller was associated with Adolph Ehlers, who a short while before had been the county jailor. The business was given up a few years later.

Where the imposing front of the Exchange building now stands there were formerly four or five unpretentious two-story houses. Only on the corner of Pine Street there stood a massive four-story red brick building. Originally the federal customs office was located here. For this reason the Old Customs House was retained. The corner shop was occupied by a pawn broker. In the second story were the offices of a few of the most outstanding legal firms. Among these was that of Kribben & Kehr (Christian Kribben and Edward C. Kehr). After the death of the former the firm was that of Woerner & Kehr. This combination was dissolved when J. G. Woerner became probate judge. The notary Adolph Kehr, the father of the lawyer, was one of the first Germans to come to Missouri, He also had his office in this building for several years.

The fourth story of the Old Customs building, which had a second stairway on the Pine Street side, was called Mahler's Hall. At the beginning of the fifties Monsieur Xaupi, with whom the grandfathers and grandmothers of the present generation had learned to dance, had in Albert Mahler a very energetic competitor who also lured away many American customers. Xaupi, who passed away a short time ago, enjoyed the best of health, even in his advanced years. He walked with elastic step and straight as a candle. In his movements and manner he was the model of a dancing master of the old school. His appearance was quite different from that of "Professor" Mahler, who was only a few years younger. Mahler was not very tall, and, moreover, he did not enjoy the best of health. The latter fact, however, did not hinder him in the performance of his calling. With admirable perseverance and tenacity he gave instruction in various parts of the city, and sometimes gave instruction in dancing during a large part of the night. He organized an orchestra which in the early sixties had no equal in playing dance music. When in the winter of 1864 the original Lindell Hotel was opened with one of the most elegant balls that ever took place here, Mahler's orchestra played the dance music while Mahler himself directed the dances. At the beginning of the program August Waldauer gave a concert, and also played the music for the promenade.

At that time St. Louis lacked suitable dance halls, and Mahler's Hall for several years was very much in demand. In addition to the balls which he gave himself, it was used as a place of amusement by many societies and lodges. All this in spite of the fact that the hall was by no means beautiful, the ceiling rather low and the adjoining rooms inadequate. Moreover, the dining room, situated on the floor below was very modest.

(The Lindell Hotel mentioned above was a few years later destroyed by fire.)

Mahler Hall later passed into other hands. It became an ordinary dance hall which derived its patronage from young men and women who were more or less well acquainted with the police, and who found it perfectly natural that after the "ball" they were brought by uniformed escorts to the police station on Chestnut Street.

In one of the above-mentioned two-story houses was the confectionary of W. Dorsten. The owner came from Holland and the proverbial Dutch cleanliness reigned everywhere in his shop and his bakery. He served a good cup of coffee and a large piece of cake for ten cents. This price he also maintained during the years of the war.

In the house adjoining Robert Fuchs had his cigar store, to which he added a small beer room. In the next block, four doors north of Pine on the west side of Third Street, Henry Heuer had a large tavern. The arrangement was for that time a most elegant one. In the middle of the wide room was a fine fountain, which made the place cool in the summer. The tables were supplied with marble tops, and the quality of the beverages was in keeping with the equipment of the place. During the Know-nothing riots Heuer was struck on the forehead with a stone, which left a deep scar, a memorial of those stormy days.

Opposite this place Fritz Lawall had a tavern. The second story of this place was leased by a society which in 1865 developed into the Germania Club. Lawall's successor was Rudolph Wagner, who formerly had operated a shoe shop on Pine Street. He added a restaurant to his tavern. For many years he was the president of the reform society for innkeepers. When the erection on modern business houses took his place on Third Street, he built a handsome place on Jefferson Avenue, close to Benton Park. Here he continued to manage a tavern till his death.

In a building on Third Street adjoining the houses above described, Attorney Henry C. Brockmeyer had his office during the sixties. Later he became Lieutenant Governor of the state. His place of business was later occupied by the *St. Louis Times* and still later by the German evening paper *Courier*.

For many years the Jefferson Mutual Fire Insurance Co. had its office between Pine and Olive Streets. It was organized in March, 1861 by the election of the following officers and directors: Louis Bach, then city treasurer, was chosen president; C. R. Fritsch, secretary; and F. W. Biebinger, treasurer. Moreover, the following were seated as directors: L. Schneider; Rudolph Weszling; H. Kortkamp; H. Eisenhardt; C. Schulz; Adam Conrad; Casper Stolle; Julius Thamer; and G. O. Kalb. On May 1 the company began business. A week later secretary Fritsch was sworn in the United States Reserve Corps, with the result that the office of the insurance company was closed most of the time. But even without this incident there would have been but little to do, for all business was stalled during the first years of the war. During the following months there was practically no income, so that the question was discussed in September whether the business be liquidated or continued. It was decided to do the latter, even though it was only for the purpose of meeting obligations assumed. Progress continued, though slowly. Now the Jefferson Fire Insurance Company has for many years been one of our soundest insurance companies.

The great activity which formerly prevailed in this part of Third Streets, was closely associated with the traffic which the post office brought. At that time there were no mail carriers and no branch post offices, indeed only a few mail boxes in the city. Banks, bankers, businessmen and lawyers, in general all who had a rather extensive correspondence, rented mail boxes for a fixed price. In the post office on Third Street there were more than four thousand such boxes. These businessmen went or sent messengers to the post office two or three times a day (except on Sundays) for their mail. Those who had no mail box got their letters at the general delivery.

For a long time there were also special windows for ladies. From morning till evening people came and went so that the steps to the building and the corridors were always crowded. In those days the papers printed each day the list of letters that had arrived for delivery, and not only once a week as is done now. On days when German mail arrived a small migration came to the post office from French Town and New Bremen. On Sundays the place teemed with business men and politicians even before ten o'clock and at the stroke of twelve all rushed for their letters. This continued till one o'clock, when at Third and Olive Sunday quiet also set in.

North Third Street had during the sixties some claim to be called the Wall Street of St. Louis, and even twenty years ago one could say that it was entitled to this name. Between Vine and Pine were crowded together the Bank of St. Louis, The Exchange Bank, the Second and the Fourth National Bank, the National Banking and Insurance Co., the Citizens Savings, the Real Estate Bank, the Central Savings Bank, the Continental Bank, the Valley, and the Merchants National Bank, surely a stately number, and more than sufficient to justify the appellation of Wall Street. However, by and by most of these institutions changed location, and Wall Street illusion was past.

For awhile this street was greatly preferred by bankers and brokers. When the speculation fever in mining stocks raged, broker offices sprang up like mushrooms. The solid ones came to stay while others were of the fly-by-night type and soon disappeared from view. This same part of the city also had the tendency to become a sort of newspaper row or printing house square.

On the southeast corner of Locust Street stood a fire engine house with a tower and a large fire bell. After the organization of the paid fire fighters this building was vacant for a considerable time. Then it was changed to suit the purposes of the newspaper *Dispatch*. The above was not the only fire engine house in that neighborhood. Another was located close to the St. Louis Theater which occupied the site on which later the post office building was erected on the corner of Olive Street.

A few of the most prominent German firms were located on North Third Street. Between Locust and Vine were the distillers Nuelsen & Meersmann (later Nuelsen & Raszfeld.) John C. Nuelsen later turned to other undertakings, while Joseph Meersmann was compelled to retire more than three decades ago because of the loss of his eyesight. He died in 1891.

The extensive grocery business of Block, Evers & Co. was between Vine and Washington Avenue. This firm originally consisted of J. C. H. D. Block, John H. Evers and Charles Nohl. When the latter severed his connection the firm was continued under the name of Block & Evers. Later Block also left the firm to become president of the Fourth National Bank. He held this position there till he died in 1891. Evers later organized the Evers Stove Co. of which he was president, Hermann Lenz vice president and Henry Evers secretary. This firm does not exist anymore.

On the northwest corner of Vine Street, opposite the old City Hotel, was located Heckelmann's drug store. In front of it was a large garden.

On the east side of the block near Washington Avenue there was in the sixties the saddle firm of Hotze, Meyer & Co., later Homann & Hotze which became the firm of the Homann Saddlery Co. (President, William Homann).

In 1864 there was organized the Fourth National Bank by Joseph Meersmann, J. C. H. D. Block, F. E. Schmieding, Francis Cornet, Christian Peper, Casper Stolle, C. L. Buschmann and J. H. Kaiser. This bank was located on the northwest corner of Washington Avenue and Broadway. At the time of organization Meersmann was chosen president, F. W. Biebinger cashier, G. A. W. Augst assistant cashier. Because of eye trouble Meersmann had to give up his position as president. Block became his successor. In 1873 the bank moved to the corner of Fourth Street and Washington Avenue, and for years has been one of the strongest banks of the west. Now Biebinger holds the office of president and Augst that of cashier.

5. Former Broadway and New Bremen

From Green Street (later Christy and now Lucus Avenue) on North Third Street was called Broadway. As early as the fifties there were a few very large German business concerns located there. Among these was the iron and steel business of F. E. Schmieding and Co., which was later continued by Ernest and F. A. Witte and Guido D'Oench, and which became the Witte Hardware Co. There were also the dry goods firm of Torlina & Jorgensen, Diamant's millinery business, Marx & Schoen's dry goods and groceries, which upon moving to main Street became the firm of Marx & Haas, and where they operate an extensive jeans business. They were located in the Lindell Hotel block. Schuetze's drug store was on the corner of Morgan Street. Across the street, on the east side was the retail and wholesale drug business of Adolph Harlesz & Co. (H. A. Varrelmann was the partner). A little farther north were the produce, grocery and commission firms of Cornet & Co., Buschmann & Co., Haake & Brother, and others. On the corner of O'Fallon Street there was in the fifties the wholesale liquor business of J. H. Rottman & Co. After the death of Henry Obermoeller the business was continued by Rottman alone. It is now located on Fourth Street near Morgan. The former firm of Heidsich, Zell & Co. was changed to the Zell Bros. Commission Co., which for nearly a quarter of a century has carried on an extensive business.

Amid numerous provisions and commission houses was Keevil's hat store, announcing its wares by means of a giant red-painted hat. But still more effective was the system of announcements which Keevil, the Hatter, made use of in the newspapers. From beginning of the year to its end he announced his goods in English and German newspapers. He was the first local businessman who really understood and valued printer's ink. Before him no one had made such extensive use of advertising space in the St. Louis newspapers.

Close by there was, extending over a number of stores, the Bowery Theater. It was quite inviting on the outside and inside. For the most part blood and thunder plays were here presented. As a variation vocal concerts and dances were given. The approval of the audience was always manifested by terrible whistling, as is often heard even in respectable theaters in this country. From the gallery the bootblacks and newspapers boys gave expression to their overflowing enthusiasm when the villain was slain and innocence was rescued.

On an October night in 1865, which fortunately was calm, fire broke out shortly after a performance and made an end of the Bowery Theater. Art did not suffer a loss by the destruction of this theater and the shopkeepers in that neighborhood were glad that that fire hazard was removed.

The great activity which was seen on Broadway from O'Fallon Street on, during the latter part of the fifties and after that, was due to the fact that the city market house was located there till 1869. It stood in the middle of the street, and was so wide that vehicular travel between Green and Morgan Streets was very difficult during market hours. During the forenoon and on Saturdays, also in the afternoon and evening, there was an indescribable congestion here. On the south and north sides of the building steps led to the basement where the vegetable market was established. A walk through this room, in which, of necessity all sorts of vegetables lay in gay confusion, was, particularly on hot summer days, a real trial for ones olfactory sense. If anyone hurried out on the south side to get a breath of fresh air, he was sorely disappointed, for there he ran into odors of the fish market. In the first story were the stands where meat was sold. Among the owners of these stands were some very wealthy men. The organization of meat market men had its origin in the city market. The battle between the market butchers and the meatshop men was a very hot one. The meetings of the butchers were held in the upper story of Philipp Krieger's tavern.

As long as the market house was in that locality there were many large and small dry goods and millinery stores, stores for clothing, and hats, porcelain, and hardware in that neighborhood. When the market house was removed, most of these businesses disappeared. The removal of the unsightly market house improved the appearance of the street a great deal. This improvement, however, was increased still more by the removal of the houses on the west side of the street and the leveling of the ground in preparation for the construction of approaches to the Eads bridge which was presently built.

A part of Broadway, situated farther to the north underwent a radical change by the removal of the mounds, a heap of earth one hundred and twenty feet high. It was between Florida and Webster streets and its eastern slope extended to Main Street. The scholars are not yet agreed, whether the "Big Mound" was the work of human hands, that is made by the Indians, or if it was created by mother nature. Proof that could have supported the first assumption was rather meager, and today the view prevails that the redskins were not responsible for the presence of the hill. Be that as it may, no sensible person could consider it an ornament, although it would have been inexpensive and rather easy to have changed it into a promenade by means of terraces and suitable plantings. For the children it was a very welcome playground. Here they played to their hearts' content during the pleasant seasons, and in the winter, when there were ice and snow, slid down the slopes on sleds. On sunny days the hill also served for the drying of clothes, and it was not a picturesque and highly esthetic sight to see red flannel shirts, long stockings and intimate articles of wardrobe flutter in the airy height.

At the junction of Broadway and Seventh Streets was the Mound Market, a private undertaking, the result of demands of the neighborhood. The necessary money was raised by subscription. Till the erection of city market house on Broadway and O'Fallon, and the establishment of Biddle's market, the butchers who did business here, and the farmers who sold their produce, did a very good business. The upper story was made into a hall, in which meetings of various kinds and balls of the best society were held. The fire company, named after the mound, also had its station in this building. For political gatherings, Lohmann's Hall on the corner of Jefferson Street was frequently used. This hall was also a popular dance and entertainment locale, in which frequently festivals of German societies, balls and masquerade balls, as also concerts were held. One of the most frequented German taverns on Broadway was that of Dietrich Sommerfruechte. Many blocks farther north an old German by the name of Blumentritt had a primitive public garden restaurant, where one could get an excellent evening meal.

A part of the present North St. Louis was originally, just like Carondelet, a town by itself, and was called Bremen. Even now the region north of Cass Avenue is popularly known as New Bremen. This is due to the fact that here predominantly the immigrants had settled who came from northern Germany. Even now pure Low German is spoken here in all its varied dialects, such as Westphalian, Hannovarian and Oldenburgian, just as it is spoken in Bremen and in Mecklenburg. By this we do not mean that the purest High German was not heard. The proverbial industry of the North German, his perseverance, his economy, and the simplicity of his mode of living, which are peculiar to him, no matter where he resides, were quickly noted in our New Bremen. In a shorter time than anywhere else in the city, large and small factories of every sort sprang up here, and also the most varied industrial establishments. Thus for example the Jefferson Mill, owned by the Sessinghaus Brothers, the workshops of Louis Espenschied and John Cook (who in spite of his name was a German) who during the war made thousands of wagons for the army. The large furniture factories and chair factories, as for example those of Heller & Hoffmann, Conrades, Logemann and others. To these were added at a later date those of Peters, Petersen, Prufrock, Prang, Vornbrock, Hanpeter & Eckhof, etc. There was the Manewall & Lange cracker factory. Woodyards and sawmills were there in large number. The firms of Schulenburg & Boeckler, and Philipp Gruner & Brother were among the most outstanding in this branch. There were great tanneries, stove foundries, meat packing houses that chose North St. Louis as the site for their businesses. The only two glass factories which existed here at that time were on Broadway. Also a goodly number of breweries, which, of course, can not be compared with the breweries of today, were in New Bremen. Among those that have gone out of business a long time ago were the Broadway Brewery, those of Angelbeck, Hannemann and Christian Koch. On the other hand the following still exist: the Bremen Brewery founded by Tobias Spengel, and now managed by William Schreiber; the City Brewery, built shortly before the war by Charles G. Stifel; Forster's Hyde Park Brewery; Liberty Brewery (Heidbreder); and the one established by Brickwirth & Griesediek and which has now been operated by Brickwirth & Nolker.

The large number of all these undertakings, in which thousands of people have employment, has given this part of the city the stamp of an extremely busy manufacturing city, in which things are astir throughout the year as in a beehive. Especially to be mentioned are the Niedringhaus factories of Florida Street where pressed and enameled tin ware is made, which is shipped to all parts of America and to other parts of the world. Farther north are the great rolling mills where the tin is prepared for the factory. Also the Mallinckrodt chemical works, one of the largest, whose products are sent to all parts of the Union and to South America, was located here.

The enormous trade in horses and mules was also concentrated on Broadway. The animals were shipped by the thousands on the Mississippi, as in fact it is done even at this time. During the war, block upon block was converted into a single, huge horse and mule market. Here the army bought most of its horses for the cavalry and artillery, and mules for the transportation trains.

At that time no streets were paved with granite blocks. The limestone used for paving caused the streets to be terribly dusty. The fine dust lay in thick layers on the street and in the houses. The inhabitants on Broadway suffered greatly, since hundreds and hundreds of animals were driven past their houses daily, stirring up great clouds of dust which covered everything in shops and dwellings.

The extremely active business in this part of the city and the distance to the banks in the center of the city offered an inviting field for banking institutions in this locality. The Tenth Ward Savings Association on the southeast corner of Broadway and Jefferson, with Henry Overstolz as president and Theodore Kochn, as cashier, did a flourishing business for a number of years, but later ran into difficulty. It was absorbed by the Fifth National Bank, which derived an ignoble advantage from the failure of its predecessor.

One of the oldest and well known businesses of the city was the iron and steel business of Rubelmann, founded by George A. and John G. Rubelmann. In time two businesses developed from this. The Rubelmann-Lucas Hardware Co., whose president is John G. Rubelmann, located on Broadway and Tyler, and the George A. Rubelmann Hardware Co., on Sixth Street near Franklin Avenue.

There was also no lack of livery stables in North St. Louis. As early as the fifties Jacob Gauger had such a stable on Broadway near Clinton, and John Amend had his barn on Ninth Street.

One of the best known persons in New Bremen as elsewhere was Judge Philipp Stremmel. Several times he served as justice of the peace. For a while he was county judge. As a member of the school board he rendered good service. He took a great interest in lodges such as the Odd Fellows, and held important lodge offices. He may be designated as one of the outstanding representatives of the German element.

Just as great popularity was enjoyed by the justice of the peace, Nacke, who was one of the best known German citizens of New Bremen.

Social life developed slowly among the Germans of North St. Louis. Consistent with the seriousness of the North German character, the people first thought of the practical side of making a living and only then they thought of amusement. In the course of time singing societies and Turner societies were also formed north of Cass Avenue. These added much to sociability.

The Free Congregation is to be considered as the center of the intellectual life of the Germans in this part of the city. Not only in the matter of questions of faith but also in the preservation and dissemination of liberal ideas and principles this congregation is active. Most of the founders of this congregation do not dwell among the living any more, but their successors continue faithfully in their footsteps.

Because of the great expansion of our city it was but natural that the inhabitants of the different regions moved more or less within the limits of their own part of town. Before the time when cable-cars and electric railway had been invented it was indeed a journey to go from North St. Louis to South St. Louis, or when a man from Frenchtown wanted to visit a friend in New Bremen. The interests of various districts were also not always identical. Then, too, there was no lack of jealousy. But on great occasions these secondary considerations disappeared and there was no more talk of geographic boundaries, nor of this side and that side of Market Street. This was shown most brilliantly at the Schiller celebration in 1859, at the German festival during the French-German war, and at the Turner and song festivals.

6. South Third Street

During the fifties and sixties the row of eight or nine, entirely uniform, two-story houses on the east side of Third Street between Market and Walnut was called Bishop's Row. These houses stand on the ground of the cathedral and are the property of the diocese. On the northeast corner of the row was for many years the Catholic book concern of Patrick Fox. This was the only thing in Bishop's Row that had anything to do with the church. The upper stories of the buildings were for the most part occupied by the families of the shop owners. In one of these shops "Baby" Welker had his tinshop. He was called "Baby" because of his stately size. He was the brother of Fritz Welker who was a clever cartoonist. Fritz Welker died much too young. A furniture store which was quite imposing for that time was that of John Ellermann, who occupied the adjoining property. Nearby in Bishop's Row was the well-known printing business of Julius Buechel, which is still there at this time, though the business has greatly expanded.

The four houses in the middle of the block, on the west side, belonged to an old Spaniard whose name was Florenz. In his younger years he laid the foundation of a considerable fortune as a pirate in South American waters. It was hard to believe that the dapper gentleman with the silk high hat and old fashioned stand-up collar was a former buccaneer.

In one of the houses, belonging to the old Spaniard, Ernest Schmidt had his wood turner's shop. Because he had an artistically-carved elephant in his display window his friends called him the "Elephant" Schmidt. Nearby was the baggage room of the Ohio and Mississippi railroad. The wine and liquor business of Philipp Bardenheier was, during the sixties, two doors south of their present location. The Frenchman, Jean Michel, had his liquor deposit in the lower story of the house at the northwest corner of the block, which is now occupied by the cotton factory of Senter & Co. On the northeast corner of Third and Walnut was, during the early sixties, the provision and grocery business of Henry W. Kuhs. On the southeast corner stood three unimposing brick buildings. In one of these, during the forties, the brothers William and Christian Schotten made the conceivably smallest beginning for their later so extensive business. They did not even have a shop. In one room in the second story, one of the brothers ground the mustard seeds in a coffee mill, mixed them with vinegar and put the mixture in small bottles. The other brother, armed with a large basket sold this "Duesseldorfer" mustard in the whole city. From the beginning this mustard was of excellent quality. The firm is now operating an extensive business on Second and Walnut Streets, and sends its product over the entire west. At the place where stood the three unimposing brick buildings there was erected a large building in which Steinwender and Sellner had their wholesale wine and liquor business for a long time. Close by was the commission business of Haws, Hadnett & Co., in which Peter J. Schroth was employed during the sixties.

Washington Hall and still more, the Washington Garden, passed through their palmy period in those years. Tony Niederwieser, Bernhard

Laibold, Frank Boehnz, and particularly the combination of Boehm and Felsing made this establishment one of the best amusement places. It had its origin in Washington Brewery. There had been a demand for a place where dances and other festivals could be given. So the company built Washington Hall. In the sixties there was rarely a Saturday evening during the winter season without a party being staged by some society. Then, too, the owners frequently arranged balls and masquerades, which were attended by large numbers. There was also dancing on Sundays. While Niederwieser was still actively interested in the Garden, musical and declamatory entertainments were arranged here. Tony appeared as a singer of comical songs and Lieder. He was always enthusiastically received. Boehm's Band (later known as the Knight Templars Band) conducted by Frank Boehm, played concerts in the summer as well as winter to large audiences. During several seasons a summer theater, under various directors, was staged here, and played before capacity houses. On the Fourth of July the Garden was always brilliantly illuminated. And whenever the Duerkheimer sausage-market was observed, there was much activity in Washington Garden for two days. It is not known whether Frank Boehm was the one who inaugurated the idea of playing the march of the druids, from the opera *Norma*, as the signal that the banquet was ready to be served, or if somewhere, before him this custom was established. The fact remains that for several decades, at the hour of midnight, the dancers of St. Louis repaired to the banquet hall accompanied by the above named march. Thousands of St. Louisans who have never heard of the opera *Norma*, nor of its composer, Bellini, have marched to this tune, and know it merely by the name of Supper-March.

Until moving to Fiftieth Street, the "Washington" fire company had its station next to Washington Hall. The station was a two-story building and before the introduction of paid fire fighters the Washington volunteer company had its headquarters here.

Two doors from this place was the German Institute, a school for boys which had been organized by a number of local Germans. It was a splendid school. For many years Franz Sigel taught here. John Eyser, who died in Denver in 1891, conducted the school for a number of years. Many young German Americans secured a good education here.

The German Element in St. Louis

Most probably it is known to but few of my readers that St. Louis at one time had journalist's inn. This name was, of course, current only in duly initiated circles, and was applicable only during the years from 1865 to 1870. A somewhat gloomy appearing, two-story house on the west side of Third Street, three doors below Myrtle, served as quarters for these newspaper writers. These were poetically-gifted Udo Brachvogel, the practical Joseph Pulitzer, and the critical Johannes Rittig, or in other words, a classicist, a practical man (respectively a politician) and a critic. Aesthetes, as one can see, was in the majority in this trifolium. Brachvogel and Rittig were enthusiastic for art, and their pens were ever ready when it was a question of furthering the interest of the German stage. While they sat in the theater in the capacity of art critics, the third member attended ward meetings or organized them. After the toil of the day the three assembled under the common roof and spent hours in lively and interesting exchange of ideas. For a while these three journalists were joined by two others, Harry Rubens (a brother-in-law of Joseph Keppler) and Frederick Herold, who were also employed by local papers. This region seems to have had an attraction for literati, for on the northwest corner of the two streets just mentioned, during the fifties and early sixties, Otto Ruppius resided. Ruppius had been called by Henry Boernstein to edit the Sunday supplement to the *Anzeiger*. From his pen came a number of novels, three of which bear the titles: *Between Two Worlds, The Peddlar, The Bequest of a Peddlar*.

At that time we did not have such elegant Russian and Turkish vapor baths as we now have. For that reason the very modestly appointed bathing establishment of "Doctor" John Fisch, located on the east side of Third Street, had a good deal of patronage although the neighbors wished that he were in Halifax because of his sulphur baths.

On the northeast corner of Spruce Street stood a spacious warehouse in which was located the commission business of Elon G. Smith & Co. They dealt in smoked meat, ham and lard. The city government consisted at that time of two branches. Smith was for some time a member of the upper house and for a while served as its chairman. On various occasions he represented the mayor. If he had had his way there would be no railroad tracks on Poplar Street at this time. In 1862 the Iron Mountain Railroad had been allowed, for military reasons, to lay a track on Poplar Street to secure rail connection with the station of the Pacific Railway. When, after the war, the property owners and residents of the entire southern part of the city urged the removal of the tracks, the railroad company persistently refused. So Elon G. Smith, while he, for a while, functioned as mayor, in the absence of Mayor Thomas, took the initiative. One afternoon at five o'clock he betook himself under the protection of some policemen and with a dozen workers of the street department, who were provided with pickaxes and crowbars, to the corner of Main and Poplar, and caused the rails around the curve to be removed in his presence. Then he posted policemen there with orders to prevent the replacement of the rails, if need be, by force of arms. That was on a Saturday. On the following Monday the railroad company caused to be served a temporary injunction forbidding the city authorities and the police from interfering with the operation of this connection track. The monopoly won over the citizens. The temporary injunction was made a permanent injunction. and now, after thirty years, this injury and damage to property still exists as a flagrant volition of right and justice.

The brewer George Rusch established a garden on the southwest corner of Third and Plum Street, and operated it during the fifties and sixties. Some called it Busch's Garden though it was better known by the name of Beuna Vista Garden. This was the gathering place of large crowds, consisting mostly of German families. The chief attraction of this Garden was the excellent concerts that were presented here on several evenings during the week and also on Sundays in the afternoon. The orchestra was under the direction of Severin Robert Sauter who employed only good musicians. He himself was an excellent violinist. In the selection of the programs he showed very fine taste. A modest admission fee was charged. The Garden had a number of beautiful shade trees and also a fountain.

Where today the Dodson-Hils Packing Co. is located, on Third and Cedar Streets, was formerly the old Pacific Mill, and on the southeast corner Shotten & Brothers operated their business, which was mentioned earlier.

The south half of the block was the property of the St. Mary's congregation. Except for the St. Joseph's congregation this was the oldest German Catholic congregation of St. Louis. In the course of years various reconstructions and additions were made. When at the beginning of the seventies more room was required for school purposes, the vacant space south of the church was assigned to the Sisters of St. Mary. The hospital of this order, situated on Papin near Sixteenth Street, and the cloister on Arsenal Street are situated on land which Mrs. Anna Schiller dedicated to the sisterhood. Mrs. Schiller's husband had for many years an inn on South Main Street.

At that time the Reverend Melcher was pastor of St. Mary's Church. He continued in this capacity till he was called as bishop to Green Bay, Wisconsin. Vicar-general Melcher was a very tolerant and highly educated clergyman. He was assisted by the Reverend Muehlsiepen, who succeeded Melcher in the pastorate as well as vicariate. After a few years Muehlsiepen resigned his position to devote himself to the office of vicar general and the supreme management of the Ursuline Academy. His successor at St. Mary's was the Reverent Faerber. Bernhard Neumann served as organist and teacher at St. Mary's for nearly forty years.

On the northwest corner of Third and Lombard Streets was, at that time, John Kern's wagon-maker's shop. On the southwest corner was Palm's foundry. This was, however, not merely a foundry but an extensive machine construction plant. Among other things, the first locomotive of the Ohio and Mississippi railroad was built here. William Palm was one of the most representative men of the German element. Not only was he an expert technician but an all around educated man, thoroughly informed on economic problems, widely read and a great friend of the arts. In the interest of art he left St. Louis in the sixties to spend several years in Rome. Our Washington University had in him a strong advocate, and he bequeathed a sum of fifty thousand dollars to this institution.

Till 1865 the Evangelical Lutheran Trinity congregation had its church on Lombard Street between Third and Fourth. Then they moved to their new and splendid church on Eighth and Lafayette Avenue. The old church passed into the possession of Leonhardt and Schuricht, the owners of the mill situated across the street. In Palm's former foundry is now located the well known buggy factory of Bauer and Walter.

The Tyrolian House on the corner of Third and Convent Streets contained for a long time the only large public hall in this part of the city. The hall, situated in the second story, was used for dances and other festivals. Moreover, theatrical performances in the French and Bohemian language were given here. Then, too, the hall served for political gatherings, and at some of the ward meetings the sessions were very spirited and sometimes violent. The Tyrolian Hall was built by Franz Saler. His bookstore occupied a part of the lower floor. It was at that time the only Catholic book store in St. Louis, and so did a very lively business. Good old Papa Saler was one of the best known personalities in the city. He passed away in 1893. Until his end he published each year his calendar--Der hinkende Bote am Mississippi (the lame Messenger on the Mississippi). Till 1863 Saler also operated a lumber yard. This lumber yard was on the east side of Third (at that time Jackson Street) below Rutger. In 1863 it passed into the hands of Fleitz & Ganahl. (Peter J. Fleitz, who soon thereafter moved to Saginaw, Michigan, and John J. Ganahl, the present owner of the most extensive business in South St. Louis.)-

7. South Fourth Street

The free space at the junction of Fourth and Fifth Streets had on the south side the market house of the French and Convent market. A bit closer to Fifth Street stood a two-story brick building which belonged to the city and which served as the police station of the southern police district. The front faced the river. The lower story consisted of a single, large room in which was the office. In the second story, which was reached by an outside stairway at the rear of the building, was the jail.

Where the Iron Mountain Railroad now has its station for its local trains between St. Louis and Carondelet there formerly stood a one-story frame structure in which a wainwright and wheelwright had their shops. On the east side of the block of Fourth Street, between Chouteau and Lombard (now Papin) Streets was August Leisse's woodyard, who moved to the northwest corner of Sixth and Chouteau Avenue during the late sixties to get more room for his buildings. Since then the furniture and carpet business of the Mueller Brothers and the shoe business of Charles Stumpf are located here. After the discontinuance of the Iron Mountain Bank (in the corner house) Phillip Mueller opened a saddle shop there. Close to the woodyard John C. Tiemeyer had a retail tobacco and cigar business. Later he operated a wholesale leaf tobacco business on Walnut

Street. The opposite corner was occupied by the O'Fallon Mill, which extended from Fourth to Fifth Street. It was partially destroyed by fire on several occasions. At last it was converted into a cracker factory. After it had stood empty for some time it was bought by the Iron Mountain Railroad, which planned to use the ground for a spur of their tracks to connect with the Union Depot, but permission to lay this track has not yet been granted. Heitkamp's Hotel was managed by jovial Fritz Heitkamp himself, while his energetic, pretty wife supervised the kitchen and dining room. This place has long ago gone into other hands.

Separated by the narrow Lombard Street from Heitkamp's place was the workshop of the coppersmith Albrecht Leisse. Under the same roof Caspar Claes manufactured show cases on a small scale, and here laid the foundation for the manufacturing concern of Claes & Lehnbeuter. In 1860 John Engelke and Frank Feiner began the operation of the large Southern Mills, which were situated a bit farther north. Toward the end of the fifties Henry Rachow opened his tavern on the corner of Gratiot Street. In this place a special room was reserved for the game of scat. On the east side of the street between Lombard and Mulberry (now Gratiot) was a large court, belonging to Heitkamp's Hotel. It was intended for vehicles of every kind. Now August C. Stiefel's stove and tinware business, and John Mueller's shoe store have occupied this site for decades.

On the northeast corner of Mulberry Street, Justice of the Peace Keating had his office. Peter Berger, a Creole, functioned as constable and sometimes as lawyer's clerk, practicing without license. Squire Keating was very popular, as is attested by his repeated election to office. (For many years he had his office in *Westliche Post* building.) Popularly he was generally called Supreme Judge. Indeed he sat on his elevated seat with an earnestness and dignity which would have done honor to any supreme judge. "Pete" Berger saw to it that order and quiet reigned during court sessions. In this court the then-still-young attorney Cornelius often astonished his audience by his oratorical achievements. The well-known German justice of the peace, Anton Michel, had his office in the same block at that time but on the west side. He did not enjoy the popularity which was that of his colleague, Keating.

In the early sixties Franz Mols had a drug store on the southeast corner of Cedar Street. He sold it to Ernest Riecker who transferred it to the northeast corner.

At the place where at this time the elevated railway passes over Fourth Street from the Merchants Bridge to the Union Depot was situated a large lawn behind which stood the Gamble mansion, which in the sixties was occupied by the Coste family. Later it was used as an annex of the Laclede school, and indeed as a kindergarten. The Laclede school was on the corner of Fifth and Poplar Streets.

On the southeast corner of Plum Street, in the same block, Louis Visseur had an inn during the sixties. Later Theodore Pfau acquired it and operated it under the name of Flora Garden. Pfau had been educated as a gardener and was a great friend of flowers. He changed the previously neglected plot on the side of his house into a pretty garden with baskets, bowers and artistic flower beds, and a fountain. During the summer evenings a good orchestra gave concerts here. When in the winter of 1868-69 Marie Seebach, with her German company, played for two weeks, some admirers of art, headed by Udo Brachvogel and Joseph Keppler, arranged a supper in her honor in Pfau's restaurant.

The above mentioned concerts gave Charles Thiet, whose tavern was near Pfau's place, occasion to announce in the newspaper that his friendly neighbor was also furnishing musical entertainment for the customers in his place.

Pfau was also the founder and secretary of the society of fancy gardeners, which unfortunately does not exist any more. In its time this society arranged a splendid floral exhibition, at which such gardeners as Beyer, Schray and Michel exhibited a most beautiful display of flowers.

In 1859 August Wiebusch built a house in which were located the print shop and bindery of August Wiebusch and Son. The older Wiebusch had immigrated from Osnabrueck in 1849. In 1881 he died and the extensive business is now managed by Henry Wiebusch, who for so many years was the partner of his father. From 1854 to 1860 the elder Wiebusch had his printshop in the basement of Trinity Church on Lombard Street. The typesetter, Bernhard Bellstedt, who had worked in the same office with A. Wiebusch in Germany, came here thirty-four years ago and since then has been working in that business without interruption. He is still actively engaged in spite of his seventy-nine years. Christian Wolf entered the business as an apprentice twenty-seven years ago, and Cornelius Mueller about fifteen years ago. Both are now stockholders. Also a few other persons have been active in the business for a long time, as, for example, Louis Meyrer, who began seventeen years ago.

Until the Lutheran Synod of Missouri and the Evangelical Synod of North America established their own publishing houses, Wiebusch took care of all their publications. Moreover, a German Bible, known as the Altenburg edition, was published by Mr. Wiebusch. He issued it in three imperial volumes. Later this edition of the Bible was taken over by the local German Bible Society. Many other publications have come from this publishing house in the forty years of its existence. To mention just one-- the *Illustrated Christian Paper for Children*, which was bought by Mr. Wiebusch from C. G. Witte twenty-years ago. Then it had but few subscribers. From a monthly publication Mr. Wiebusch changed it to a bi-weekly and raised the number of subscribers to nearly, 50,000. Some years ago the Evangelical Synod took over the publication of this paper.

The Apollo Garden had a great attractive force at that time because of the concerts that were given there. At first these concerts were given by Mr. Derlitz and later Waldauer and Vogel conducted the band. The winter theater had not yet been built, therefore the garden was still large, and the concerts were attended by the best citizens. Moreover, the programs were not interfered with passing trains as happened often in later years and in such annoying a manner at theatrical performances. The garden was situated several feet higher than the street and the tavern. On the side of the street there was no door, indeed nothing on the outside indicated that there was anything to drink behind the high windows. For the visitors of the garden a separate entrance was provided near Poplar Street. With the building of the winter theater, (not the present one, but the one erected in 1868) the size of the garden was very much reduced, and attendance fell off correspondingly. The theater performances were not suspended during the summer months, for the walls on the north and south sides of the auditorium could be removed in hot weather. If it happened that during a performance a thunderstorm broke, the spectators near the walls had to flee to the parquet to escape the deluge.

In February of 1869 the first and last German press ball was staged in the Apollo theater. The preparations for this event were the most elaborate. The whole parquet was resplendent with a rich display of foliage plants and flowers. Great palms occupied the corners. Garlands were wound around the white columns that supported the gallery. The stage had been converted into a garden of flowers. Above the whole stage, small gas flames were arranged to spell: "Welcome to the German Press Ball." In the gallery opposite the stage a band of twenty-four of the best local musicians under the direction of Benjamin Vogel played the best dance music. Charley Leinberger furnished the supper at a cost of four hundred dollars. The committee in charge consisting of the local editors of the *Anzeiger*, the *Westliche Post*, and the *Missouri Staatszeitung*, would have been very much embarrassed if Dr. Preetorius had not agreed to underwrite the agreement with Leinberger. In spite of the fact that the tickets cost five dollars each, the cost exceeded the income by eighty dollars, which deficit was covered by one of the men who gave the ball, with the firm resolve never to arrange a German press ball again.

At the other corner of Poplar Street, Adolph William and Karl Reisse, in two adjoining stores, had a wallpaper and toy business. In the story above these stores was Louis Rohrer's business school. This was later handled for a short while by "Professor" Bemisch. The latter was a popular singer, and also wrote verses. After he gave up the school he became a life insurance agent.

On the site where today Drummond's tobacco factory and its accessory buildings stand, stood formerly the Mulanphy Hospital, managed by Catholic sisters. The hospital was named for its founder who donated the land on which it stood, and who also contributed a considerable amount of money for its erection. It was a very gloomy appearing, three-story building, whose front faced Spruce Street. It was set a few feet back from the street. It was surrounded by a poorly-kept lawn and by a low, iron fence. On Fourth Street a wide gate admitted one to the yard, in the southeast corner of which was the room for dead bodies. Usually when the double door was opened it was for the purpose of carrying a casket out. Even today that part of Fourth Street cannot be considered attractive. With the removal of the hospital from this part of town, the street assumed a more pleasing appearance, but still there are on the west side of this block, as also in the next block to the south, many houses that should have been replaced by new structures long ago.

At the beginning of the sixties William Beckmann had a merchant tailor shop, where Mueller's confectionary is now located. Then he opened a tavern on the corner of Spruce. Close by were the grocery and commission businesses of Edward Beckmann & Co.

On the northwest corner of Myrtle Street where, at one time, Richardson's drug store stood, till it was destroyed by fire, and where then the Meyer Brothers & Co. established their drug business, there stood in the early sixties, the house of Edward J. Gay, one of the most prominent and wealthiest businessmen in the city. His family was one of the last to leave South Fourth Street. In the forties and fifties this had been considered one of the most fashionable residential districts. Gay's house was situated some distance from the street. Rather high stone steps led up to it. Adjoining the north side of the house was a large garden. During the latter part of the sixties the dancing master, Fischer, had his dancing school here. The "Professor" did a good business for a number of years. His dance evenings, and in the summer, also his restaurant in the garden, were well attended. Not content with this, he added a small annex to the front of the house where he opened a small confectionary shop, café and ice cream parlor. Finally he disappeared, leaving his creditors in the lurch.

The building on the southeast corner of Elm Street, in which Schraubstaedler and St. John had their type foundry, had in its two upper stories the club rooms of a society, known as "Arion of the West." This organization which occupied these rooms for a number of years staged some of the most successful carnivals. Here was also held the banquet in honor of Hans Balatka, who came from Baltimore as director of music. On that occasion Dr. Spiegelhalter presided as toastmaster. In these rooms were also held the carnival sessions at which Adolph Harlesz, Doctor Otto Greiner and others celebrated their greatest triumphs.

This building had been built the later part of the sixties. The basement was especially constructed for the firm of Isidor Busch & Co., who in time transferred their office and wine storage plant from the corner of Main and Walnut to Fourth and Elm Streets. Isidor Busch had been treasurer of the Bluffton Wine Co., at the head of which George Husmann, the owner of a nursery in Hermann, Missouri, presided. In spite of the efforts of their chemist, Frings, to improve the quality of the Bluffton wine, the company found it advisable to give up the business, and to dispose of its supplies at public auction. At this sale Busch outbid Karl Conrad. Since that time Busch has worked ceaselessly to improve our native vineculture. He also exported many Missouri grape vines to France where they brought excellent results. The fire which on Christmas Eve 1881, destroyed Cupple's broom factory on Elm Street, also destroyed the property of Busch & Co. After a brief interim this company moved to its own building on Second Street below Elm. The hotel which is now called the Continental Hotel, was, for many years, known as Koetter's Hotel. It was originally the residence of Archibald Gamble, a brother of former Governor Hamilton R. Gamble. In time this structure has undergone many changes. When Tony Niederwiesser, in the latter fifties, opened the "Tivoli," the house occupied only about a half of the lot on the Third Street side. The front half was a garden and as such, one of the most popular places of entertainment that St. Louis had at that time. On Sundays, Sauter's orchestra and also Vogel's orchestra, regularly gave concerts there. After the first rebuilding, a large hall was provided in which concerts were also given in the winter. A broad stairway, under a pavilion, which was erected for the musicians in the middle of the hall, led to the basement in which six or even more billiard tables were set up. This billiard hall, also had an entrance from the Elm Street side. Especially on Sundays this place teemed with players and lookers-on.

Niederwieser's successor, after 1865, was George Wollbrecht, who served a term in the legislature. Tony was content with the opportunity to serve in the city council. He was elected to this honor when he was the owner of the "Walhalla." The dwelling of General Harney, situated between Market and Walnut Streets (which was later owned by Gregory Wintergarten), was changed by him into a restaurant and tavern. This place had a hall that was large enough for dramatic presentations. After the National Theater burned, its director, William Koser, gave his performances in the "Walhalla." Antonie Becker-Grahn and Otto von Hoym appeared on this stage as guest artists.

Two houses north of the Tivoli, Charles Buehler had an elegant restaurant during the later part of the sixties. It was located in the second story of the house. Buehler was a first class cook. The epicures of our community frequented the place, but there must not have been enough of their number, for in spite of the excellent roasts and steaks, the establishment had to close its doors rather soon.

Directly opposite the Tivoli was a two-story house. The upper story had a glassed-in veranda, which was a part of the dining hall of the "Casino." Under this name Louis Loos operated a tavern and restaurant in 1865. He was one of the first victims of the cholera in the above year. The business later passed into the hands of August Dorguth. Subsequently the place was rebuilt and operated by the Swiss, Arb.

In later years this corner was occupied by Buff & Kuhl's mineral water store (later Buff & Rau), and Ullman's small cigar store.

The foundation for the first Southern Hotel was begun in 1860. Because of the war, its construction was interrupted, and was not resumed till some years later. During the night of April 11, 1877 the first Southern Hotel was destroyed by fire. This hotel was rebuilt by Thomas Allen. Formerly this site from Fourth Street and the then existing alley had been occupied by a woodyard and three or four rather unimposing dwellings.

On the southeast corner of Walnut Street, Moritz Schuster at one time had a well-patronized wine cellar. A few doors east of this place the gun smith, Linzel, had his workshop. For many years he has been in business in Little Rock, Arkansas.

At the northeast corner, which later was occupied by the "Cap Horn," there was for a time the office of the paper *Puck* and later the office of the dentist, Roemich.

Beside General Harney's house, on the spot where, for years, Dickmann has had his birdshop, Edward Buehler had a German book store and circulating library, till he moved to Chicago in 1864. In his manner and appearance, Buehler would have been a credit to any chancellory prior to '48. He understood his business and was as thoroughly acquainted with German and French literature as any old bookdealer in Leipzig. Later the book dealer, Frederick Roeslein, owned this store.

A few doors north, Charles T. Lolmann sold pictures, picture frames and mirrors. Adjoining was the store of H. Moeller who dealt in fancy knitwear and toys. Mrs. Moeller, who was busy from early to late was the soul of this business.

David Nicholson's grocery business, which even at that time was quite extensive, was located on the west side of South Fourth, between Walnut and Market. He occupied two buildings. Later he moved to Sixth Street. The toy store of Rudolf Ulrici was a bit farther to the north. Ulrici has now been living in Dresden for a long time. At the corner of Market Street, where now the imposing granite structure stands, which the Tyler heirs built, there was formerly a ramshackle, shingle-covered, two-story house. In the corner room Horwitz & Cohn had their tailoring business. Immediately above them was a dentist's office. In this building Franz Ruff had his workshop in which he made umbrellas. His umbrellas and parasols were regarded the best in the city.

The Ruff family lived in the story above the shop, and when their daughters, who were accomplished choir and concert singers, sang and played the piano in the evening, with the windows open, passers by often stopped to listen. If the young ladies should now display their talent at the same place, their voices and their piano would be drowned by the noise of the electric street railway and the cable cars that run on both sides of the site where the house stood.

In the granite building, with its hundred offices for lawyers and other businessmen, the elevator travels up and down, and everywhere typewriters click. To the ears of the realistic generation of today this perhaps sounds just as good as fine music.

8. North Fourth Street

Without regard for the feelings of the builder, the unsightly tower at the northeast corner of Fourth and Market Streets is called the pill tower. This designation has offended Doctor McLean deeply to the end of this life, for he was very proud of the structure, the plans for which he had drawn with his own hands. The tower looks much too clumsy for the building which bears it. This corner looked much better before the bizarre taste of the owner marred it.

Formerly a plain building occupied this site. In its upper story was a photographic gallery. In the shop on the ground floor E. Kuchn had his hat business. In the basement there was, during the later fifties and early sixties, a tavern of doubtful reputation. It was managed by women.

A few doors farther north was Louis Steller's candy shop and restaurant. In the upper rooms of this building there was an elegantly appointed dance hall, which was more in demand for small parties than any other place of this kind. In 1866 Steller gave up his business and devoted himself to viniculture on his farm in St. Louis county. He continued this work until his death which occurred a few years ago.

About in the middle of the block Robert C. Pate had a barroom, that was open day and night. It was not a very large place. The space behind it, a long and wide room in the lower story was for years the most frequented keno-house in all of St. Louis. It earned for its owner enough money to allow him to own expensive race horses and live a luxurious life. The ordinance forbidding the keno game did not trouble him much. If the police raided the place, which happened often, and arrested players and employees, Pate bailed them out, and in half an hour the whole crowd was free again. Also the confiscation of the gaming devices by the police did not have any effect. Hardly had the police carted them away when a new supply was brought from its hiding place and installed, so that after a brief interruption the games were resumed. But finally Pate had to succumb, for the police raided his place night after night and so put the keno out of business.

A couple of doors farther, August Darguth had a restaurant on the second floor. On the ground floor, Georg Bamberger for years had his saloon.

The building which is now occupied by the International Bank and the adjoining store were, before the reconstruction of the place, one single large store. A gold star, visible from a great distance, and giant letters announced that there William Keiler had his Star Clothing Store. For a long time business was very good. The owner lived extremely well. He had the fastest race horses in the city. Then the star began to fade, and in spite of many vain efforts to bring back its former luster, it went out entirely.

The west half of the present exchange block, or in other words, the east side of Fourth between Chestnut and Pine, today does not contain a single building that occupied that site twenty years ago. None of the many railroad ticket offices, which are located there now, existed. Most of the buildings were two-story structures. Only a few had a third story. On the corner of Chestnut, where the ticket office of the Vandalia line is now located, there was the International Saloon, a tavern whose interior arrangements must have cost thousands of dollars. Two doors from it the photographer Bernhard Kielholz had his place of business. He was a bit hypochondriacal at times. City life did not please him, so he bought himself a farm in Wisconsin or Minnesota and settled there.

A little farther on one could find the photographers Boehl and Koenig who, for the last few decades, have operated a branch business in Carondelet. This firm made a specialty of photographs of buildings, street scenes, parks, etc.

In the second half of the sixties the Frenchman, Bonnet, had a tavern in this row of buildings. It was located in the real part of the building, to which a narrow passage led. There was a very large room, in which, even in the daytime, a semi-dusk prevailed. This was due to the fact that the two windows opened on a narrow court that was surrounded by a high wall. So much the more cheerful and pleasant was the very large dining hall, at whose small tables intended only for two guests, one could, at all times enjoy Bonnet's celebrated art of cooking. The gourmands were agreed that one could nowhere else find better food than here. The service, as it was handled under Bonnet's supervision, could hold its own in any restaurant of the city today. When the buildings in this part of the city were reconstructed, Bonnet's place also underwent some changes. A small barroom replaced the former large one, and a very large dining room took the place of the old one. Unfortunately a fire destroyed this part of town a few years later, and so also wiped out Bonnet's business. This loss was a severe shock to Bonnet, who was not in good health. He died soon thereafter. In this fire the dealer in hats, M. J. Steinberg, whose store occupied the front part of this building, also suffered considerable damage.

The Planters House which had been in use for fifty-six years, was torn down in 1892 to make room for a building that was in keeping with the times. The Planters House ended its most successful period in the middle sixties, when Lindell Hotel and the Southern Hotel were opened. Up to this time there were only two other large, first class hotels, which could compete with the Planters House, namely the Virginia Hotel and Barnum's Hotel. But neither of the two had the patronage of the former. Benjamin Stickney, who was the manager of the Planters House for a quarter of a century, became a rich man. His house enjoyed the patronage of the traveling public from one end of the year to the other. Travelers were glad to pay high prices if they could be assured comfortable lodging and excellent service, such as the Planters House offered. Its kitchen was known everywhere for its excellence. In earlier years the cotton barons of the south were accustomed to come to St. Louis each year, often accompanied by their families, and stayed for weeks. The Planters House was their preferred hotel, where some of them took quarters for months. Until recently when reconstructions were made, the rather small office was located on the second floor. So much the larger was the bar, which was located to the rear, and which occupied the entire middle of the lower story. From Fourth Street one passed through a cigar store into the barroom. From the second story, a narrow, somewhat dark stairway also led into it. The bar itself was so long that between thirty and forty customers could be served at the same time. For the lessee this barroom was a veritable gold mine. This room in a certain sense took the place of a rotunda or lobby, which this hotel lacked, and which today is the rendezvous of the business world and guests in every large hotel. When the waves of politics ran high the owner of the Planters was accustomed to dispose of twice as much old bourbon than ordinarily. Toward the end of the sixties there was a second tobacco and cigar store in the basement of the Planters House. The owners of this store, Mueller and Schlueter, had a real bonanza, especially during the years of the war, when the sales of tobacco and cigars were greater than ever before.

The oldest local music store, Balmer and Weber, was for more than three decades in a two-story building between Pine and Olive Streets. Early in its existence the firm added to their trade in music and instruments an establishment for printing music. In time this became very extensive. The engraving of the usually artistic title pages was attended to by the copper engraver, John Scharr. He was employed by the firm for nearly twenty years, when he established himself independently. The note printery was in the upper story. The lower floor was used as sales room. Although the latter was regarded as quite spacious, one had to wind his way between pianos put on display, if one wished to reach the back of the store, or to the bookkeeper of the firm, Charles G. Weber. The latter maintained his poise and composure at all times. The lively and very motile Charles

Balmer looked after the sales and the printing of music. As he was a musician and music enthusiast in every fiber, one may justly call him the center of the local musical life in the earlier years. Of this we shall, however, speak in a later chapter in greater detail. In Balmer and Weber's store not only the local musicians and teachers of music met daily, but also the friends of music, for in the rear room one could often hear excellent piano playing and beautiful singing. No virtuoso who gave concerts here failed to come to this store and become acquainted with Charles Balmer. The sales of tickets for concerts, the opera and larger musical undertakings took place here. On special occasions, as for example for the sale of seats for Grover's German and Strakosch's Italian operas, as also concerts by Patti, Parepa, Rosa, and Thomas the place proved too small to accommodate the crowd of buyers. At the end of the sixties the firm moved to Fifth Street, first into a large building on the east side, between Pine and Olive, and later next to the Mercantile Library, where there was also much space available, but in time returned again to Fourth Street. In the same block there was also located, in the later sixties, the piano and music business of Compton and Endres, who for a time handled the sales for the St. Louis Piano Manufacturing Co.

On the northeast corner of Pine Street and Fourth there stood till 1864 a long, narrow, low building, in which Lippincott, who later became the manufacturer of soda water, had a candy and sweetmeats shop together with a restaurant that specialized in oysters. This restaurant was open till after midnight. At the end of performances in the adjoining Ben de Bar's Theater, the Lippincott place was crowded with people. (The site of the Lippincott place was till 1892 occupied by a building which the *Globe-Democrat* erected there.) The most elegantly furnished drug store of that time was that of Alexander Leitch, at the northeast corner of Olive Street. In the adjoining building was the oldest jewelry business of St. Louis, that of Eugene Jaccard. The Everett House was in those years one of the high class hotels. Its dining room was on the first floor and the kitchen was in the basement. After a fire, which did considerable damage to the dining room and also to the part of the upper story, the interior of the hotel was considerably changed, and the two upper stories over the stores as far as Locust Street were added. Later the north half of the Everett House was leased by John H. Hurst, and operated separately as the Hurst Hotel.

If one compared the imposing building, Odd Fellows Hall, which was erected a few years ago on the southeast corner of Ninth and Olive Street, with the building which stood on the northwest corner of Fourth and Locust Street, and which for four decades was known as Odd Fellows Hall, then the change that has taken place during the intervening years becomes very evident. And yet that site was for many years considered one of the best and most lively corners in the business part of the city, when in the first half of the sixties, D. C. Jaccard and Co. opened their business in the lower story of the old Odd Fellows Hall. Out of the concern grew the firm of Mermod, Jaccard and Co. which is one of the most outstanding businesses of this kind. Of the four participants, D. C. Jaccard, August S. Mermod and C. F. Mathey had held responsible positions in the house of Eugene Jaccard. The business founded by them grew from year to year, and even before their move to Broadway was one of the points of attraction in our city. The five or six buildings which were on the north end of the block, and since then have been replaced by new structures, were named after their owner: Glasgow Row. In the two buildings next to the corner was the dry goods business of Vandervoort, McClelland and Co., whose successors are Scruggs, Vandervoort and Barney. Two other buildings in the Row were occupied by the dry goods firm of Ubsdell, Pierson and Co. Out of this concern grew that of Barr, Duncan and Co., which in the first half of the sixties moved into a large building between Vine and St. Charles Street. A few years later this firm was known as William Barr and Co.

On the southeast corner of Vine Street was Hafkemeier's carpet store, and adjoining it was the wholesale millinery business of Strausz and Loewenstein. In the sixties this became two separate firms. Glasgow Row was completely rebuilt near the end of the sixties, while the business houses to the north of it, between St. Charles Street and Washington Avenue were not modernized till many years later. Until that time a broad veranda, extending over the entire sidewalk, had darkened the shops under it to a greater or lesser extent, but in the hot summer months had given protection from the burning rays of the sun. In the event of a sudden shower it offered a welcome refuge for the feminine world.

The rooms located over these shops were known as Veranda Hall, and later, when the National guard established quarters here, it was known as Armory Hall. Before the sons of Mars held their entrance there, the large hall, together with its adjoining rooms, was used by German and non-German societies for balls and festivals of every kind. So for example the Orpheus and Social Singing choirs had several of their most delightful masquerade balls here. For a long time also all greater concerts were held here. The first Viennese Ladies Orchestra which had come over the ocean from the beautiful, blue Danube, and so was the real thing, attracted full houses there for a whole week. Mrs. Inez Fabri-Mulder, who for many years was the most popular teacher of voice in San Francisco, sang in this hall on one of her concert tours through the United States. In the spring of 1877 Hermann Linde gave his readings in this hall. On one occasion this place was used for an exhibition of fowl. Faber's talking machines were shown here. Tom Thumb, the dwarf, displayed himself here. Then, too, political conventions and assemblies convened in this hall.

On the corner of Washington Avenue the Fourth National Bank had its establishment for nearly a quarter of a century, (before it moved into its new quarters at the southeast corner of Fourth and Olive Streets.) Prior to that the Oak Hall Clothing House of the Keiler Brothers occupied the site on Washington Avenue, and opposite to it, where now the Boatmen's Bank stands, was the establishment of Ticknor, Robbins and Co., the predecessors of Edwin Ticknor and Co. These two firms were the first to introduce the one-price system here, and the practice of supplying a clear label on every piece of clothing was also started by them. At that time there were no banks on Fourth Street. The first such institution was the North St. Louis Savings Bank, which in 1865 occupied the southeast corner of Morgan Street. The directors of the "Woodenshoe Bank," as it was popularly known, were almost exclusively business men from north of Washington Avenue, solid Low Germans. At the cornerstone laying of the new bank building Westphalia, Hanover, and the-then-free imperial city of Bremen were numerously represented. Nearby Ringen had his stove business, and Ganahl and Schallert had their leather business. Opposite the bank was Kunsemueller's drapery store. Diagonally across from this site, on the northeast corner, was Frederick Steigerwalt's tavern. A few doors farther north A. Dunker and Co. had their dry goods business (J. H. Trorlicht was a member of this firm), and although the store extended from Fourth to Third Street, it proved, even in the sixties, to be too small. Therefore, the firm, which was now changed to Trorlicht and Dunker, occupied the large building on the southwest corner of Christy Avenue, where it added a carpet department to their dry goods. Upon moving to the block between Washington Avenue and St. Charles Street the firm confined itself to the sale of carpets, drapes. During the middle sixties Leonhard Roos established a fur store two doors south of Christy Avenue on the west side of Fourth Street. It developed into the largest concern of this kind in our city. It continued to do business on Fourth Street till it moved to Locust Street near the Mercantile Library. On the west side, between Morgan Street and Franklin Avenue, Louis Volkening had his bookstore near the close of the sixties. Then he transferred his business to Fifth Street near Walnut. Farther to the north J. P. Haas had his leather business, which is now on Lucas Avenue near Fourth Street. On North Fourth Street, as is evident from the above, the retail business had been concentrated, and the largest businesses of this kind existed for decades beside smaller concerns, till the exodus to the streets farther west began. With that the street began to change its appearance. Then came a transitional period which is still in progress. One of the results is the new, colossal buildings that are already completed or that are now in the process of construction, and the many banks which during recent years have been built on Fourth Street.

9. South Fifth Street

In the second half of the fifties one could still read in the advertising columns of the *Missouri Republican* and the *St. Louis Herald* with whom one could deal in buying and selling slaves. At that time only a few firms handled this horrible trade, and one of the "dealers in human flesh" was a German whose name was Anton Wisemann. His "place of business" was a stable on the southeast corner of Third and Walnut Streets. There he kept the Negroes and mules, with which he carried on a remunerative business. In the winter of 1860-61 only one such business remained in St. Louis. The owner was B. M. Lynch, and the house in which he kept his "wares" behind lock and bolt stood on the northeast corner of Fifth and Myrtle Streets. It was a few feet above the street paving and was set rather far back from the street. On the Myrtle Street side the place was enclosed by an eight-foot fence. It and the iron-barred windows were supposed to prevent or at least make difficult any attempt at flight. The men and women who were sold to the south were taken to the levee and on the boat locked to a long and heavy chain. In the same manner the slaves that arrived here were transported to the "nigger pen," as the gloomy looking house was called. Lynch's office and residence were on Locust Street near Fourth Street. His slave trade ended in 1861. In this year an attractive two-story house was built close to the corner. For a time this house was used as military headquarters. Until the time when McDowell's College was changed into a military prison, the building on Myrtle Street was used for such a purpose.

Today but few houses on South Fifth Street show that at one time many of the wealthiest families lived here, and yet such is the case. The houses on the northwest corner of Fifth and Gratiot Streets were, during the sixties, occupied by Gustavus W. Dryer, Rudolph Ulrici, D. C. Jaccard, Amade Valle and other equally outstanding families. When the rich real estate agent, Byrne, occupied the three-story house, built by himself, on the east side, near Cerre, it was considered, according to the standards of that time, an elegant home. In the seventies this house was occupied by Doctor Hammer. Equally elegant were the two houses on the opposite side of the street where for several years was located Helmkampf's German private school.

When in 1866 the cholera again came to St. Louis several persons in this block fell victim to it a few days after its appearance. Among these were the well-known wine dealer, Haquett and his wife, as also the parents of the equally well-known, Philipp Haquett.

The long row of houses on the east side of Fifth between Cerre and Poplar, known as Walsh's Row, netted, even in the sixties, a high rent. The same was true of the next block, whose north corner was occupied by Doctor Wislizenus until a few years before his death.

None of these houses now show that only a few decades ago they were considered fashionable. The corner house on Elm Street, in which the brothers Gruen have now had their wine room for many years, was, in 1861, still occupied by George R. Taylor, who at that time was the president of the Pacific Railway Co. On Myrtle Street, between Fifth and Sixth Streets was the residence of Eberhard Anheuser, and on the west side of Fifth, between Walnut and Market Streets resided Adolphus Busch and Dr. Philipp Weigel.

The German Element in St. Louis

My readers who have lived in St. Louis for a quarter of a century, or who have known our city that long, will scarcely believe that in 1865 the site not occupied by the Olympic Theater was still an unoccupied place, which extended almost to the alley that leads from Walnut to Elm Street. This space served as a yard for the inhabitants of a two-story tenement, whose front faced the above-mentioned alley. Passers by could see the yard hung with washing on almost every weekday, between and under which a dozen of unwashed, ragged children made a horrible noise while playing. Guests who occupied rooms in the Southern Hotel on the Fifth Street side must been greatly edified by this vis-a-vis. Also the sisters who managed the St. Philomena School for Girls in this neighborhood must have been very much annoyed. This school was in the corner building on Walnut. On Sundays and on holy days one could see a long procession of teachers and students going to services in the Cathedral. At present the St. James Hotel occupies the site on Walnut Street.

At the beginning of the sixties the St. Philomena school abandoned the building. In its place there came a fair-sized hotel, the Paschall House. This and the Smizer farm soon became one of the main prizes of a lottery which was organized with the sanction of the authorities. At that time Lottery in Missouri was not yet under the ban. During the period when Frederick Muench, Gert Goebel, Emil Preetorius, Isidor Busch, Henry J. Spaunhorst, Anthony Ittner, August Koch and others made the laws, one did not commit a crime by buying chances in a lottery. The Paschall House Lottery, as it was called, in 1868, had an enormous number of participants. State and city officials, judges and lawyers, clergymen, men from the exchange, teachers and pupils, craftsmen and day laborers, housewives and their maid servants, seamstresses and bootblacks, in other words, everybody, took chances. For the sake of completeness it may be mentioned that none profited by the transaction.

In the fall of 1865 the construction of the Olympic Theater was begun. Originally and primarily it was intended for four-legged artists. When, in the following spring, it was opened, its interior arrangement was that of a circus, and one of the best equestrian troupes in the country gave an exhibition. That was something new here. Circus riders had up to that time been seen only under the canvas tents, and the charm of novelty contributed to make the undertaking a success. However, it was apparent that a change would have to be made the undertaking a success. The performances were well attended. However, it was apparent that a change would have to be made soon, for such performances could not attract permanently. For two years a variety theater succeeded. Then the interior was rebuilt and every trace of the circus disappeared. The winter season of 1869-70 was the first in which the Olympic could justly lay claim to being a first class theater. The companies that have since then appeared, have, with few exceptions, represented the legitimate theater. Tragedies, comedies, and farces were presented. Nor should we forget the opera which played every winter for a few weeks. The London director, Mapleson (Her Majesty's Opera) preferred the Olympic to the other local theaters. With the exception of one season his company always appeared on this stage. Adelina Patti, Companini, Etelka Gerster, Marcella Sembrich did excellent work here in the Italian opera. Then, too, our own German opera, under the direction of Theodore Habelmann played for several weeks during the winter. German as well as non-German music-lovers still recall these events with pleasure.

The repertory of the Habelmann company was a very extensive one. In the course of time of three or four weeks the following operas were performed: *Czar und Zimmermann, The White Lady, Faust, The Jewess, Martha, Lucretia Borgia, The Merry Wives of Windsor, Lucia di Lammermore, Traviata, Troubadour* and others. In the old Olympic, which was torn down in the middle seventies and replaced by the present structure, one performance of Flotow's *Stradella* was given by German amateurs. The German theatrical performances on Sunday evenings, under various directors, were for many years the gathering place for the local German element.

Fifth Street between Walnut and Market seems, for a long time, to have been destined to care for the inner man. In the first half of the sixties Mr. and Mrs. Porcher had on the west side of this block, a restaurant with real French cuisine. A few years later Charles F. Schneider opened a German restaurant just south of the *Westliche Post* building. On the east side of the block, Schilling and Schneider later had their Wintergarden restaurant adjoining the brewery. On the southeast corner of Fifth and Market one could get from Cafferatta, and Italian salad or a glass of Maraschina. On this corner there was till 1866 a one-story house, in which Angelo Cafferatta had a remunerative retail trade in southern fruits. Except during the cold winter months, the shop, which was provided with a far projecting roof, was almost completely open on both street fronts, by the letting down of all the windows. Piles of golden Messina Oranges, bright yellow lemons, pineapples, heaps of cocoanuts, malaga grapes, and bunches of bananas, suspended from the ceiling, formed an attractive sight that caused the mouths of passers by to water. The store was a long room, and on Fifth Street it had a side room where one could get coffee, chocolate and a cold lunch, in the summer also lemonade and ice cream. About the middle of the block, Theodore Plate had a private German school in 1864, which was in a two-story duplex house set some distance back of the street. During the war the Porchers, mentioned above, opened their Restaurant de Paris opposite their former place of business, five doors north of Walnut Street. Their cuisine was of superior quality.

In the three-story building in which August Froebel at one time had a restaurant for ladies adjoining his tavern, L. Baumann & Co. had a watch and jewelry store during the seventies. Directly in front of the Froebel's place the Brothers Kunkel had their music store and the display rooms for Steinway pianos. In the upper story they conducted a music school.

The site which is now occupied by the Temple Building, northwest corner of Fifth and Walnut, was, till 1869, occupied by the Second Presbyterian Church. It was a stately structure. Along its entire front were sixteen or more gray-sandstone steps. Eight tall and correspondingly massive Doric columns constituted an imposing facade. The interior of the church was suitably lighted by tall arched windows on the Walnut Street side and by sky-lights in the ceiling and in the frieze on the Market Street side. The basement contained the rooms for the Sunday school and the home of the caretaker. The very rich congregation was one of the first to transfer its church to a part of the city farther to the west. It built a fine new church at Lucas Place, corner of Seventeenth Street. The old church was sold to David Nicholson. Of the front walls only the one on the west side was designed to stay, and of this only about two-thirds of the original height. While tearing down the upper third a considerable part fell off and buried several workers under the ruins. Two of these were severely hurt. They were carried into Sander's drug store, where first aid was given. A hastily summoned physician was unable to help one of the men who died shortly after. A reporter of an English morning paper insisted in his efforts to ascertain from what county in Ireland the man had come, and plagued the dying man with questions. Enno Sander put an end to this senseless performance by grabbing the reporter by the coat collar and hoisting him to the middle of Walnut Street, much to the satisfaction of all eyewitnesses.

The two upper stories of the Temple Building were originally intended for theatrical performances and concerts. Conforming to this purpose they formed a single wide and spacious hall. There were about five hundred seats on the lower floor, and there was also an extensive gallery. The rather central location, and the pleasing arrangement of the building assured the Temple of great popularity. Many concerts, lectures and other programs were given here. One of the programs, at which every seat was taken, was the musical-dramatic evening entertainment which was arranged by police judge, Cullen, who was known as "the terrible judge." The program was given for the benefit of the home of the homeless. The judge himself recited scenes from *Hamlet*, *Macbeth* and other Shakespearean dramas. Mrs. Eugene Karst, better known by her maiden name of Julia Bogy, the only daughter of federal senator, Lewis V. Bogy, sang. She was a most excellent and charming singer. Charles and Jacob Kunkel were the piano virtuosos of the evening. Kiselhorst played the flute, and a local journalist filled the rest of the program with humoristic recitals.

A young woman of St. Louis, Carrie Goldsticker, who went to Europe for training on the operatic stage, was given a benefit performance in the Temple before she started on her journey. On this evening she sang the great role of the gipsy, Acuzena, from Verdi's *Trovatore*. About twelve years later she sang the role of Ortrud in *Lohengrin* in the New York German Opera. This role she also sang in 1886 at the Saengerfest in Milwaukee. In Halle on the Saar, where she was for a long time engaged as a singer, she married a rich merchant.

Also a wrestling match was at one time staged in the Temple. Julius Schroeder, the owner of a popular restaurant on Fifth and Myrtle had accepted the challenge which an itinerant wrestler, who called himself "The German Oak," had issued. It was a very hot summer evening, when the two very stout men appeared on the stage dressed in trunks. After the customary preliminary formalities had been attended to, the wrestling began. Even in a less sultry atmosphere, they could have done their work only in the sweat of their brows. But at the temperature that prevailed in the hall, they must have felt as if they were sitting in a Russian steam bath. There was no lack of enthusiastic cheers on the part of the audience to inspire the wrestlers to ever greater zeal. The contest lasted a long time. The St. Louisan, who followed the sport only as an amateur, pleased his many friends by his performance against the more skilled opponent, but finally had to take the count. For a long time he was the hero of that occasion.

Immediately after completion of the Temple Building, Henry Fleischmann opened a Viennese coffee shop, and in connection with it he established in the basement a Viennese bakery. The latter is still being operated by Fleischmann's successors on Seventh and Walnut Streets. Fleischmann's coffee shop was built L-shaped and had one entrance on Fifth Street and another on Walnut. The latter led into a smoking and reading room which could satisfy the most pampered taste. It was the first of this sort of establishment in St. Louis, but, unfortunately did not draw the patronage which it deserved. When, after some years, Fleischmann opened a still more elegant place between Pine and Olive Streets, in which he invested heavily, he did not have the desired success either.

The Temple Building was after some years completely remodeled. The great hall, in which prior to elections many political meetings took place, was changed into two stories which the Frisco Railroad Co. used as its offices of administration. Also the other stories where changed. The main entrance was put on Fifth Street. Several smaller stores were made of the former, large store. In one of these the Elleard Nursery, whose manager is Statius Kehrmann, had been located for many years. The upper stories were made into offices for insurance companies, architects, lawyers, as for example Kehr & Tittmann; Chas. P. & John D. Johnson.

In the spring of 1874 the *Westliche Post* moved into the building which it now occupies. The publishers had bought it some years earlier. The sum of eighty thousand dollars, which was paid for the property, was considered a high price, but today, because of its location on Broadway and Market, it is considered still much more valuable. To the time of moving the newspaper into this building, it was mainly used as an office building for lawyers, notaries, doctors, etc. Our old fellow-citizen, Rudolph Schulenburg, who can still be found there, opened his office in that building in 1865. Other lawyers whom we can mention in this connection are Gustav von Deutsch, Joseph Jecko, Gustav Hospes, Doctor Dudly, a bachelor, had his coroner's office there. On the corner Jones & Sibley had their drug store. Mrs. O'Sullivan had her millinery shop on Fifth Street. In the basement, under the drug store and the millinery shop was a tavern which was noted because it had feminine bartenders. At the head of these Ganymedes was Mollie Fitzgerald, a young Irish woman, who often literally fought with customers and with the police, and so frequently was put behind lock and bolt. When a city ordinance was passed in the sixties, forbidding the employment of women in taverns, robust Mollie tried to play a trick on the law, by becoming the nominal owner of the place, however, her constant conflict with the authorities finally led to the closing of the tavern. Several years later the basement was reconstructed for the use of boilers, steam engines, and printing presses, and today the *Westliche Post* occupies almost all the rooms of the whole, big building for newspaper purposes. In time extensive remodeling took place to suit this purpose. Where, for more than four decades, except for a single interruption, had been a drug store, there is now the splendidly equipped business office of the newspaper. An Edison dynamo in the machine room produces the electricity for the illumination of the whole building and two Perfecting presses of the most modern construction--one of the wonders of our times--print, cut, glue and fold the papers, which an army of carriers on foot and with horse and cart distribute in the early hours of the morning from the Des Peres River to Baden and from East St. Louis far beyond Forest Park, while morning trains carry them to all parts of the world. Things change with the passing of time and the modern newspaper shows this plainer than anything else.

10. North Fifth Street

No street in the business part of our city has undergone such great changes in the last three decades as North Fifth Street. Most of the buildings that stood on it have disappeared, to make room for more modern structures. Only very few businesses which were located between Market Street and Washington Avenue thirty or even twenty years ago are there anymore and many have gone out of existence entirely. For example, in the block opposite the court house there is not a single business that was there in the fifties and sixties. On the northwest corner of Fifth and Market, where Thomas Allen erected the present building twenty years ago, which for a long time served as an office building for the Iron Mountain Railroad, there formerly stood an unpretentious two-story house. In this building Hermann Eisenhardt, the present owner of Eisenhardt's soap factory, and the president of the Jefferson Fire Insurance Co., had a grocery store for many years. On the north wall of this building a narrow wooden outside stairway led to the upper story, where was located a doctor's office and the photograph gallery of John A. Eibert.

The next three or four buildings were set a few feet back from the street, and about five feet above the street level. From 1865 to 1867 the Hotel Garni, owned by Arnold & Lang, was located in two of these structures. Lang has now been a member of the police department as police sergeant for some time, he is Arnold's son-in-law. Originally they used only one of the buildings as a wine room, which was managed entirely after the German pattern and so was generously patronized by the German businessmen. In September of 1865 they opened the hotel, and for that purpose acquired the second story of the adjoining building also.

In the above-mentioned wine room a meeting of the most prominent German merchants was called in 1865 at which the Germania Club was organized. This club continued to exist for twenty-seven years. As in later years Koetter's was the preferred headquarters of the German artists, so Arnold & Lang enjoyed at that time, the patronage of this group. The first guests of this kind were Edward Hertig and Hedwig Hesse, who in the fall in 1865, were here as guest artists for a considerable time. In the following spring Mr. and Mrs. von Fritsch, or in other words, Ottilie Genee and her husband, who was not an actor, lived here. Later the singer, La Roche, his wife and daughter stopped there, also Louise Haase, who at one time was the director of the Apollo Theater, furthermore, Emil Laszwitz, Johanna Claussen and her first husband, an American by the name of Jarvis, and then also Mr. and Mrs. von Zerboni or Zerbonie. But also non-German artists stopped at this hotel, as for example, the principals of the Grau Italian Opera Company, who sang in the DeBar Theater in 1866. Also the master of the ballet, Sarti, and his Italian dancers stopped here. This company enjoyed a continuous run of six months with the "Black Crook," which they presented during the first season.

In the next buildings, Salo Hirschberg dealt in theatrical equipment and costumes.

On the northwest corner of Fifth and Chestnut Streets, where now the Hauser Building is, the hatter, Albert Fischer, for a long time had a hat and fur business. In the adjoining buildings was, in the first part of the sixties, P. G. Anton's piano store. Later he transferred his stock to the Laclede Hotel, and from there to the middle of the block between Olive and Locust, opposite the Mercantile Library Building. The store which Anton had occupied earlier, between Chestnut and Pine the music dealers, Bollmann & Schatzmann used during the sixties. In time these two men developed the largest business of music and musical instruments in the city, which is now owned by the Bollmann Brothers.

On the northeast corner of the block, where now the Golden Eagle clothing store is, stood at that time the Centenary Methodist Episcopal church. It was a massive structure, whose walls were strong enough to be used when the building was changed into a business structure. A furniture business first occupied the renovated building. Later the auction firm of Whedon & Tyler took possession and were there for many years. The heirs of John J. Roe bought the lot and erected on it the splendid building that adorns it now. At one time John J. Roe owned one of the most extensive packing plants in St. Louis. He was president of the local Exchange and also of the New Orleans Steamboat Line. A stroke took his life on a hot summer day as he was about to attend a meeting of the directors of the steamboat line.

During the sixties there was on the east side of the same block Esher's Varieties, a kind of inferior theater. Later this place was occupied by a tavern without music and ballet. Early in the seventies the clever actor McKee-Rankin had the unfortunate idea of establishing a small but very nicely arranged theater in which only the higher dramas and genteel comedies were to be presented. To this end he leased the second building on Pine Street and spent a considerable sum in its reconstruction. It was a splendid theater, but, unfortunately, it did not have the necessary patronage. After a year Rankin gave up the undertaking. This building and the adjoining one were then torn down, and in their place a large building was erected, which was first occupied by the wholesale dry goods business of Joseph Weil & Co. Later this same building was reconstructed, and has since then been occupied by Mills & Avery. Originally a so called office building had stood on this site, in which, during the sixties, among others, Dr. Comstock, the well-known homoeopathist had his rooms in a part of the second story. He had studied in Vienna for several years, where he had learned to use the German language fluently. He was very enthusiastic about things German. In his living room he had a tile stove that came from Vienna. On the walls were scenes from all parts of Germany. He was very fond of speaking in German, and his German visitors could scarcely believe that he was a real Yankee.

At the northwest corner of Fifth and Pine Streets about fifteen feet back of the street, stood the house which till 1859 had been occupied by an old French family. In the spring of 1861 this house attained a certain degree of notoriety. The Berthold mansion was for many years the gathering place of the elegant society of St. Louis. The very wealthy family entertained much. The arrangement of the spacious mansion was designed to make the stay of the guests who came to the many festive occasions as agreeable as possible. Broad steps led to the first floor. A portico, supported by eight tall columns of dark sandstone, extended along the whole front, which distinguished this house from all its neighbors. To the right and left of a hallway were rooms which now-a-days would be called parlors. In these splendid rooms the "Minute Men" made their headquarters in March, 1861. This was an organization of, for the most part, young men who made no secret of the fact that they sided with the South. In the last days of April they manifested their sympathy with the secessionists by stretching a rope from the roof of the Berthold Mansion to the building on the opposite corner and from it displayed a large secessionist flag over Fifth Street. This flag displayed a lemon yellow crescent on a dark blue field. This act, conceivably, caused great indignation, not only in the center of the city but particularly in Frenchtown and New Bremen. The excitement grew from hour to hour till its removal. It was known that the Minute Men had firearms of every description at their headquarters, and that their leader, Major Shaler, was a hot-headed person who would give the order to use these arms upon the slightest provocation. In the interior of the building it did look like barracks. Most of the two hundred and fifty members remained there also at night. In almost all the rooms mattresses were spread out, and along the walls stood guns. But there was no conflict. The flag was removed when it had been made clear to Major Shaler that the "Dutchmen" would not stand for this sort of thing. There were no further demonstrations of this kind on the part of the Minute Men. Into this same Berthold Mansion, however, the military authorities moved later, and during the recruiting, that had been ordered by President Lincoln, things were very lively. Those who reported for service in the army drew their numbers there, which either incorporated them with the army or set them free, and Doctor Julian Bates, a son of the Attorney General in Lincoln's cabinet, decided in a room of the upper story as to their physical fitness.

Some years later Christian Freund erected a four-story building on this site in which he established the largest confection store, together with a restaurant, in the St. Louis of that time.

Directly opposite there was, during the fifties, a handsome building-to be sure not as large as the one located there now-in which Humphrey had his business. On this corner a Hollander by the name of Pezolt formerly had a confection store. At the opposite corner of the block, the southeast corner of Olive Street, where now the Insurance Building stands, formerly stood a building that attracted attention because of its architecture. The building was used as a restaurant. On the Olive Street side a covered balcony extended along the first story, about eight feet above the level of the street, where the customers ate their meals in the summer. In the space under the balcony a woman sold soda water, oranges and other southern fruits. On the Fifth Street side wide steps led into a hallway, and then one entered to the left into the elegant dining room, and to the right went down six or seven steps into the confection store, which was located in the adjoining building. The second story of the two connected buildings contained a rather large hall that was used for banquets. There were also smaller rooms for private dinner parties. Till the beginning of the sixties Eugene Guendaudon was the manager of this establishment, then Frederick Walter took it over, and his successors were Merkel and Baumgaertner.

At the northeast corner of Fifth and Olive Street there were formerly a number of small buildings. Directly on the corner was the store of the Ravold Brothers who did a fine business in embroidery and patterns. On this site Eugene Jaccard built a building in the latter part of the sixties, and in 1886 the Bank of Commerce Building was erected here. Luyties' homoeopathic drug store was at that time already on the site which it now occupies, but did not indicate that it would expand to its present extent. The wholesale dry goods store of Henry Bell & Sons was on the southeast corner of Locust Street. During the sixties this firm had moved from Main to Fifth Street. The building of the Mercantile Library, opposite the buildings just described, and which was torn down five years ago, differed advantageously in size and in architecture from the buildings around it. The company that built it fifty years ago intended to provide an imposing structure that should be as nearly fire proof as possible. This they accomplished at great cost. The library room was almost one and a half stories high. During the first decades it sufficed all needs. The hall in the uppermost story was the largest concert hall in the city, till the exposition building with the great music hall was erected.

All great concerts were, therefore, given at the Mercantile Library Hall. During the period when Lyceum lectures were popular in America, no winter passed by without lectures being given there. On some of the occasions every seat was taken, as for example when Henry Ward Beecher or Charles Dickens, Gough, the apostle of temperance, or Mark Twain spoke. Equally popular was also the witty Artemus Ward. When the latter had returned from his sojourn in the land of the Mormons, he lectured on Utah and its inhabitants. The admission ticket to this lecture read: "Admit bearer and ONE wife." Once, and only once the hall was used for a baby show. At this show some sixty foolish mothers sat for three hot summer days from ten a.m. till five p.m. with their pitiable offsprings, age six months to two years, each hoping for one of the five or six prizes. The dwarfs Tom Thumb and Minnie Warren were frequently seen here. The corner store of the old building was used by the St. Louis Piano Manufacturing Co. for some years as a sales room. A great part of the lower story was used by the cabinet maker, Bernhard Thole.

Only a few of the founders of the library are still alive. In the course of the years the institution has surpassed by far the expectation of the founders. The building, which was erected on the site of the old one, conforms to the demands of modern time. On the site where formerly three or four business houses stood, Scruggs, Vandervoort & Barney built a giant establishment which is the most elegant that St. Louis has at this time. By this structure the entire region has been made more attractive.

The sewing machine millionaire, Singer, built a valuable structure on the northeast corner of Fifth and Locust Streets. Some years ago this was bought by the American Central Fire Insurance Company. At the beginning of the sixties this site was occupied by the United Presbyterian Church. One day the sewing machine monopolist came here, ostensibly to see St. Louis, in reality to select a suitable building site for a structure that should house a branch office and at the same time should be a good business investment. Till then his sales rooms had been on Fourth Street in the Everett Block, under the management of Edwin Dean.

For a long time after the above mentioned church disappeared, there stood private houses on the site now occupied by Mermod, Jaccard & Co. In the private houses the lower stories were changed into shops. In the upper stories dressmakers, barbers, and chiropodists established themselves. The buildings were torn down in the later sixties and in their place appeared large business houses. The corner building was occupied by Chase & Cabot, wholesale drygoods. Later they were burned out. Beside them was the hat firm of Gausz, Hunicke & Co., as well as other firms that formerly had been on Main Street. On the north end of this block (St. Charles Street) where at a later time Emil Bessehl had a branch of his tavern, there was, during the years of the war, the office of the Provost-Marshal, who occupied the room in the second story which formerly had served as headquarters for the National Guard. Soon after the war Gustav F. Vogtmann had his pasteboard factory here.

Formerly a one-story frame building, which was used by a joiner, occupied the northwest corner on St. Charles Street. There Ely Walker & Co. erected their large drygoods store, which they occupied till they moved to Washington Avenue. At this time Crow's Drygoods Store is at the St. Charles Street site. A few paces farther to the north a sign painter had his shop in a wooden shack. Then came an unoccupied space, and then a two-story building that was used for offices. On the corner of Washington Avenue, on the site where today the Frank Building stands, there was a long, wooden shed in which tombstones were made. It was a singular fact, that on the northwest corner a similar business was being operated. The result was that on both sides of the avenue, throughout the year, monuments of the most varied kind were on display on the sidewalk. This shows better than anything else what an enormous change has taken place, for there are but very few places in the business part of our city where real estate is as valuable as on these two corners. On one of these now stands the Mammuth Building in which Samuel C. Davis & Co. have their dry goods business. In 1885 this company celebrated its fiftieth anniversary. On the southeast corner where Nugent's Drygoods Palace stands at this time, Hermann H. Niemann formerly had an elegant tavern, which he later transferred to the corner of Third Street and Washington Avenue.

Where today Brandt's shoe store is situated, on the corner of what was formerly Green Street, there was at an earlier time "The Clipper," a whiskey saloon, as uninviting on the outside as on the inside. It was operated by a certain Jack Looney, who had been a prize fighter. A large room behind the bar-room was the gathering place of those who follow low types of sport. Not only were prize fights staged here at late hours of the night, but often also dog-fights and cock-fights, and on Saturday evenings there was a mass murder of rats by dogs especially trained for this purpose. Of course wagers of small or large amounts were placed on the outcome of the events. Frequently there were bloody altercations at the conclusion of such a program, and occasionally gunplay. The police closed both eyes when it came to Jack Looney's doings, because, it was rumored, the latter gave the police important tips that led to the discovery and apprehension of many a criminal. It is said of Looney, that in spite of his daily association with crooks of every kind, he never abetted them. In the middle of the sixties he built five or six houses west of "The Clipper" on Green Street, near Sixth. Here he had a dance hall and also a theater of inferior grade.

Where the Market Hall now stands and in fact as far as Morgan Street there was a row of shacks, that seemed ready to collapse. A cheap eating place, a couple of shops in which used furniture was sold, represented the business interests here. In the midst of these humble surroundings Squire John M. Young, as one of the most popular justices of the peace, enjoyed far greater patronage in his shack here than in later years on Chestnut, between Second and Third. The earnestness and dignity which he displayed at hearings, settling a dispute among neighbors and deciding the ownership of a stolen fat goose, were not in keeping with his real nature. Everyone who knew him well, knew that he had a wonderful sense of humor. The present Market House can not be called a beautiful structure, but in comparison with the old Market House the former represented a great improvement.

The west side of Fifth Street, between Morgan and Franklin underwent many radical changes. There was formerly located William Bechtner's Summer Garden and Theater (Bechtner's Varieties). In the fifties this place was well patronized. In 1861 it served one of our Home Guard regiments as quarters, and looked very warlike. A rather high, massive wall surrounded the Garden on the Fifth Street side. Two sentinels guarded the narrow entrance. In the south-western part the guard drilled, and at the opposite end was the mess kitchen. During the war the Garden ceased to serve as such. The site was built up with small houses, which later were removed to make room for a large building which in 1891 was destroyed by fire. At the corner of Franklin Avenue, where Penney and Gentles now have their fashion shop, was formerly a tavern and oyster saloon.

Until 1864 a Christian Church stood on Fifth between Franklin Avenue and Wash Street. This building was then changed to a theater, which, however, existed for only a short while, in spite of the fact that the performances were not bad at all. A few doors to the north, Louis Schneider operated the only confection shop in this region. Schneider was very popular in German musical circles.

Dr. Joseph Spiegelhalter participated in the war as a physician. Upon his return he was twice elected to the office of coroner. He had his office in a building on the east side of the street between Franklin Avenue and Wash Street. This was very convenient for the newspaper reporters, since they could stop at the coroner's office on their way to the station house of the third police district. The furniture factory and store of Martin Lammert was originally on the corner of Wash Street. Now his sales department is on the corner of Locust Street, while his manufacturing plant and storage is still at the old site.

During the war and long thereafter horses and mules were sold at auction on the corner of Fifth and Carr Streets. These animals were brought there in great herds. For a number of years, John Finn was the owner of this extensive business. Later he became the sheriff. For a long time he was one of the most outstanding representatives of the Irish element and of the Democratic Party in St. Louis.

The office of the third police district was in the early sixties in one-story building between Biddle and O'Fallon Streets. In the next block Patrick Driscoll worked in his blacksmith shop, and incidentally played local politics so successfully that on various occasions he was elected to represent his ward (it was at that time the ninth), in the city council where "the learned blacksmith," endowed with sound native wit, often hit the nail on the head.

11. Sixth Street

In former years Sixth Street seems to have been particularly preferred for churches. On the west side between Franklin Avenue and Wash Street was the Union Baptist Church. Its doors and windows were Gothic in design. Between Franklin Avenue and Morgan Street the Fell Methodists had a church, and on the southeast corner of Sixth, and St. Charles Streets, was situated the First Universalist Church. On the southwest corner of Sixth and Locust (a part of Barr's drygoods establishment now occupies a part of this site), was the Second Baptist Church. It was a massive structure which could have served its purpose for a long time, if the wealthy congregation had not preferred to move to the west end. On Twenty-seventh and Locust it built a magnificent church, which, however, was destroyed by fire during the later seventies.

Between Locust and St. Charles Streets on Sixth Street was the Benton School, which in the first half of the sixties was moved to the corner of Ninth and Locust Streets. The old school, which was named after the celebrated Missouri statesman, was only a two-story structure, and contained no more than eight rooms, two of which were used for high school purposes, until on Fifteenth and Olive Streets a separate building was erected for high school students. Next to the school house the Temple of the United Hebrew Congregation was built in 1859, which was used till the later seventies when the congregation moved to its new building on the corner of Twenty-first and Olive Streets. Beside the old Temple on Sixth Street was for a long time George Deagle's Variety Theater, which was later converted into a livery-stable. On the west side of the block there stood as late as the first half of the sixties a number of private houses, in which some of the most prominent families of the city lived, as for example, Mayor Oliver D. Filley, to whom the third house south of St. Charles Street belonged. A few years after his death, the property passed into other hands, and a restaurant was opened here. However, the latter was only a pretext and a blind for a real gambling den. The houses on the northwest corner of Sixth and Locust Streets were bought by Charles H. Peck, the president of the St. Louis Mutual Life Insurance Co. After removing the old building Peck had his brother-in-law, the architect Barnett build the imposing structure, which next to the conscienceless management of the above company caused the shameful failure, by which many thousands, predominantly Germans, a large number of widows and orphans, were deprived of the investment they had made in insurance. Prior to its failure the company had twice changed its name.

On the southwest corner of Sixth and Pine Streets, where the new Glove-Democrat Building now stands, there was Kendel's steam bakery. At the other end of the block, on Chestnut Street, was the office of the city health officer. On Sixth Street was the city dispensary. Wedged in between these two buildings was--a whiskey saloon. The Department of Health of the city had been transferred here when in 1864 the city authorities leased a part of the courthouse from the county, and housed its bureaus in it. This location was most unsuitable for the Board of Health, and justly gave cause for much ridicule and criticism of the health authorities. When soon after the war, Dr. Hammer became the head of the department, he secured suitable rooms by transferring the dispensary and health offices to a practically new building on the east side of Sixth, five doors north of Chestnut Street.

To the time when the Four Courts were completed, the county jail was on the southeast corner of Chestnut and Sixth Streets. The building which contained the cells was in a yard, free on three sides, while on the Market Street side there was a high wall. On the Sixth Street side there was a rather high wall, through which a low door led directly into the office of the jailor. This office, a small one-story building, stood exactly on the spot where now the ladies' entrance to the Laclede Hotel is situated. On the Chestnut side the jailyard was in part enclosed by a three story building that served as police lock-up and was generally known as the calaboose.

Between Market and Walnut Streets there was, during the sixties, on the site where now the *Chronicle* Building stands, Wisemann's "Nigger Pen," that is a kind of stable in which the Negroes were held, with whom he carried on an extensive trade. Wisemann lived for a long time on the opposite side of the street. On the southeast corner of Sixth and Spruce Streets was the St. John's Episcopal Church. In 1867 this was bought by the local Italians and converted into a Catholic Church. But disagreement in the congregation and financial difficulties caused this body to dissolve after a few years. The building was sold, and for some time now has been used as a billiard hall.

On the southeast corner of Sixth and Cerre Streets, the Bohemian Jewish congregation built a Temple during the fifties. In 1875 this congregation moved to its present Temple on Chouteau Avenue and Eleventh Street. The old church they sold to a Negro congregation. Now agricultural machinery is manufactured there.

The large building on the southwest corner of Gratiot Street, which for many years served as a malt house for the Forster brewery, was in former years used for the same purpose by Hunicke & Wist. In the sixties also Marquard Forster's vinegar factory was transferred here. Formerly it had been at Fourteenth and Spruce Streets.

Only one single house of worship of the many that had been erected on Sixth Street, has remained untouched by the change of time. This is the church of the Annunciation on the corner of LaSalle (formerly Labadie) Street. In which Archbishop Ryan (Philadelphia) and after him Vicar General Brady served as pastors for many years. Both were very tolerant and humane men. Brady died in March 1893.

12. Franklin Avenue

Franklin Avenue may still claim to be one of the main streets for retail trade. And yet it is not by far as it was in former years. In the forties and fifties and even later there was in this street such a lively business that many an unimposing store, with a relatively small stock of goods, was a real gold mine for its owner. If one wanted to see real activity he need only go, or rather let himself be pushed by the crowd, along Franklin Avenue on a Saturday. This surging to and fro lasted till almost midnight. Most of the businesses at that time, and for that matter, even today were and are in the hands of Germans, and most of the inhabitants on this street are Germans. Because of this reason Franklin Avenue was always in the foreground when great German festivals were observed. No street was more richly decorated at the Schiller festival in 1859, as also at the ratification of German unity in 1870, and again at the festival of song and the German Day in 1889 and 1890, and on the occasion of celebrations of German lodges that had their halls along Franklin Avenue.

The Citizens Railway, which is a cable line, was one of the first of the local street-car lines. From the outset it was one of the best paying investments. It was also a great benefit for the Avenue and for the entire west end north of Morgan Street. Originally the street-car extended only about a half block beyond Grand Avenue, the extension via Elleardsville

(Café Brillante) to Rinkelville, and the branch to the fair grounds came somewhat later. Not only the inhabitants of this part of the city but also the mules of the citizens Railway Co. must have rejoiced when the cable line was established. The Society for the Prevention of Cruelty to Animals would have had ample opportunity to prefer charges against the drivers of the mule-drawn street cars, particularly during fair week, when the poor quadrupeds could scarcely move the over-crowded cars.

The former Cherry Street, which runs from the levee to Third Street, has of late been called Franklin Avenue, which in a sense is justified, since it is an extension of this street. John F. Tolle's mill, which has made him a rich man, and the City Brewery were the main buildings on this short street. Charles G. Stifel, in the fifties, built a new brewery on Howard, between Fourteenth and Fifteenth Street. In 1861 this was the headquarters of the regiment commanded by Stifel.

One of the above-mentioned lodge halls, Nies Hall, on the north-west corner of Fourth Street, was built during the late sixties. Immediately several lodges took quarters there. Somewhat farther toward Fifth Street was for many years the toy store of Henry P. Fabricius and the liquor business of Adolph Wippern. In the same block there was, at the beginning of the sixties, the office of the justice of the peace, Grether, who in 1865 and 1866 was chairman of the City Council. Later he became associated with Adam Boeck in the real estate business under the firm name of Grether & Boeck.

The southeast corner of the Fifth Street of that time (now Broadway) was owned by Nugent, where his dry goods business was located, which at this time is one of the largest in St. Louis. At that time it was only a small store, and yet the Crawfords would have given almost anything for it, for the buildings on both sides of the corner were already in their hands. As they did not have enough room for their business, they looked forward to the day when they could obtain the corner. This day finally came when the lawyer, Albert Todd, built two large structures on the west side of Fifth, between Morgan Street and Franklin Avenue, of which Nugent occupied the one farthest to the south. Hergesell, who was one of the organizers of the Social Saengerchor, for many years had his little book store on the south side of Franklin Avenue, between Fifth and Sixth Streets. Later he transferred his business to the corner of Sixth Street, that is, to the outer wall of Rethwilm's place of business. Edward F. Rethwilm is one of the oldest German merchant tailors. The same was true of Henry Trieselmann, one of the best known citizens and supporter of German societies. He died in 1891.

Among the well known persons we must mention the jeweler, Kortkamp, and his brother, the tin smith, William E. Kortkamp, who during the later sixties was a member of the City Council. Almost four decades ago the well known druggist, O. W. Heyer, occupied the same place of business where he can be found today. The same is true of the porcelain dealer, Charles F. Lange, in the same neighborhood. In fact, only few changes have taken place in this block during the last fifty years. Among such changes are to be mentioned the transfer of Brandt's shoe store to Broadway and the burning of Plant's mill. Quite close to the northeast corner on Sixth Street was the photograph gallery of G. V. Brecht, and his factory that produced implements for butchers, which latter business has for a long time been one of the most extensive in the entire west. The Franklin Avenue Bank, now called the Franklin Bank, was for a long time located on the northwest corner of Sixth Street. A few doors to the west was a German confection shop. From a relatively small beginning in 1865, A. Moll built up an extensive grocery business, which is situated on the south side of Franklin Avenue between Sixth and Seventh Streets. The tavern on the northwest corner of Franklin Avenue and Seventh Street was managed for more than a quarter of a century by John Meis. Meis was a loyal adherent of the Republican party, and his sonorous voice was effectively heard in ward meetings.

Motte & Specht, who have made the firm "Famous" celebrated, were, during the sixties, located on South Fifth, between Hickory and Rutgers Streets. There they had a very small store. From their first location they moved to Franklin Avenue. On the south side of the Avenue, between Seventh and Eighth Streets they sold boots, shoes and clothing on the first floor of a small building. In order to attract attention to their store they had a Negro, wearing a soldiers mantel, walk to and fro from morning till evening in front of their place of business. In the course of a few years they were in a position to move to a building diagonally across the street, and fill its stories with their goods. Extensive advertising brought "Famous" much patronage. The business grew still more and increased still more after moving to the corner of Fifth and Morgan Street.

Theodore Trauernicht, who entered the army soon after the beginning of the war, will be remembered by the older musicians of our city, for he imported all sorts of musical instruments from Europe. At that time one was dependent on German and French manufacturers for brass and string instruments. Now that is no longer the case. One of our oldest German citizens, J. G. Haas had a soap factory, as far back as the fifties, on Eighth and Wash Street. His sales office is still there, while his factory was long ago moved far to the north. His son-in-law, Henry Arnold, is at the head of the business.

At the beginning of the sixties, Rudolph and George Wesseling had a livery stable on the southeast corner was Gauszmann's hat store and on the northwest corner was Adam Wenzel's tavern (Wenzel's Hall) with several lodge rooms in the upper story. Because of lack of club rooms this tavern was, particularly in the early years, a preferred recreation center for a large number of Jewish business men of this neighborhood. With great zeal they devoted themselves to games such as Klabbrias, Sixty-six, and dominos. In this same block was the Waldecker stove business, the carpet store of Joseph Crawford & Sons. Formerly this firm had had a large stock of gas fixtures and lamps in connection with the carpet business, when they were located on Fifth Street between Locust and St. Charles Streets.

Between Ninth and Tenth streets was Charles Zimmer's wallpaper store, and Ernest Witte & Co.'s hardware business. Also the store of Holthaus Brothers (Anton and Arnold), dealers in pictures, picture frames and books was located here till 1866. As proof of the fact that Franklin Avenue was a good business street, the fact may be mentioned here, that on the day before Christmas in 1865 almost six thousand dollars worth of goods were sold by the Holthaus store. Two well-known liquor firms were Reipschlaeger & Thias, and Thiemann & Reipschlaeger. After the death of August Reipschlaeger, Thias continued the business alone, and William Reipschlaeger continued that business alone after the demise of Ernest Thiemann. On the southeast corner of Eleventh Street stood the Evangelical Lutheran (Saxon) Immanuel Church. When in the later sixties this building was badly damaged by fire, the congregation decided to build a new church on Sixteenth and Morgan Streets.

During the fifties and sixties Franklin Avenue could boast of one innkeeper whose popularity extended over all of St. Louis. This was Peter Weber. His tavern together with a summer garden and theater were located on the northeast corner of Tenth Street. Here he built a large building, a part of which was for a long time occupied by the German American Bank, while the tavern (Walhalla) occupied the eastern half of the lower floor. This tavern was later managed by Goerlich and Helfensteller.

On the northwest corner of Tenth Street there were, during the sixties, two names written over a tin shop, behind which there was a still smaller tin workshop. This name has for some time become known throughout all of America and even in Europe. The names of these men are F. G. and William F. Niedringhaus, the owners of this business from which grew the St. Louis Stamping Co., that produced the enameled-ware, which, one may say, has been distributed over the whole civilized world. This company's factory and roller works are among the largest of this type of establishments in the country. By the introduction of this kind of utensil there has been developed a new branch of industry on this side of the ocean, which has made us independent of the English product. Formerly such wares had to be imported to a large extent from England. For some years now there stands a large corner building in which Charles Niedringhaus operates a furniture, stove and tin business.

The building on the southeast corner of Eleventh Street (now called Lightstone Hall) was in former years the Odd Fellows Hall. The tavern adjoining it was managed by H. Wolfarth, a very well-educated man, who, however, was poorly qualified as a tavern keeper and consequently his business did not prosper. One of the oldest livery stables of St. Louis was established by Frederick Laumann during the fifties. After his demise it was continued by Louis Spelbrink. Laumann was one of the best known German citizens and took a lively interest in public life. Three drug stores were located in the same neighborhood for more than three decades. They were owned by William Roepke, Charles Bang, and Gustav A. Klipstein. The latter died in 1892 and his son, Theodore, was his successor. From 1860 to 1868 Henry T. Wilde had a liquor business between Twelfth and Thirteenth Street. Then he gave that up and devoted himself to the improvement of real estate. Older readers will remember Louis Seitz who, in spite of the fact that he manufactured vinegar, never sounded a sour note, but was generally beloved because of his friendliness.

In his younger years Statius Kehrmann, Sr. had a hardware store between Sixteenth and Seventeenth Streets. Formerly he had been a clerk with the well-known firm of Wolff (or Wolf) and Hoppe on Main Street.

During the later sixties he gave up the hardware business and took up fire insurance, in which he was very successful. He always continued to be vitally interested in public affairs.

The extension of the Franklin Avenue streetcar line west of Grand Avenue early in the sixties brought a much needed connection with Café Brilliante and Rinkelville. It is true that it was only a single track with a couple of sidings on which the car had to wait till a car, coming from the opposite direction, passed. But it was better than no streetcar, even though it took very much time to get to the sharpshooter's park, or to Rinkel's or Adam Ofenstein. Now that is, of course, different. Where formerly, on both sides of Eaton Avenue, there were long stretches of unoccupied land, or fields of wheat and corn, there are now splendid residences and well-cared-for gardens, and even still farther out on the St. Charles Rock Road, houses will be close together. The cable car which now convey one quickly to Ofenstein's Grove will extend still farther west, where a new part of the city will arise.

13. Washington Avenue

Of the older streets of our city none have undergone such extensive changes during the last fifteen years as Washington Avenue. Indeed it is only a relatively short time ago when on this avenue, west of Tenth Street, there were only residences. Today commerce and industry have long ago passed this boundary. Some of the largest and most beautiful business houses are beyond Tenth Street, and the chimneys of many factories tower in the air as far as Twenty-third Street. Wholesale trade and industry have actually taken possession of Washington Avenue, and the number of private houses decreases from year to year.

Three decades ago the State Tobacco Warehouse stood on the northeast corner of Sixth Street and Washington Avenue. That is the site where warehouse daily auctions of leaf tobacco were held. The one-and-one half story structure occupied half of the block on the Washington Avenue side and also half of the block on the Sixth Street side. In the rather weather-beaten old building, however, not only tobacco was sold, but it also served for many years as a ball room, and the elegant society of St. Louis have danced through many a night without paying heed to the strong odor of tobacco that issued from the hundreds of casks that were stored here.

Somewhat farther toward Fifth Street stood an elegant residence beyond a small, well-kept garden. In 1862 this was changed into a restaurant. During the presidential campaign in 1868, it served as Democratic headquarters, which no doubt was hard on the fine wall paper and the inlaid floors.

The land on which Lindell Hotel stands belonged to the heirs of Peter Lindell, Sr. after whom this well-known hostelry is named. A corporation, or as we would now say, syndicate, bought this land in the fifties for the purpose of building a hotel on it. However, the structure was not completed till the summer of 1863. On the outside and inside it was a beautiful building. Indeed it was the first really elegant hotel in our city, and its completion was celebrated with enthusiasm. While the building was beautiful, the surroundings on Sixth, Seventh, and what was then Green Street, were deplorably ugly. In the spring of 1867 the hotel burned. The rubbish and ashes were left undisturbed for nearly six years before the construction of the present hotel was begun. It is true that Washington Avenue at that time was in its transitional stage. On the southwest corner of Seventh Street there stood, as late as 1870, a tenement house, inhabited for the most part, by Italians. On the west end of the same block, where today a business building, several stories high, stands, was a so-called marbleyard. The north side between Seventh and Eighth Streets was occupied by one and two-story houses, of which three or four were occupied by Negro families. In front of a tailor shop and cleaning establishment, trousers and coats hung for drying. And in one of the houses lived a recently immigrated Chinese, who made a scant living by selling paper flowers.

West of Seventh Street there was not yet any business house. On the northwest corner of Eighth Street stood the church of the First Methodist Episcopal congregation. The wall on Eighth Street was covered from top to bottom with dark ivy. It was a beautiful sight. When the building was torn down the disappearance of the ivy wall was regretted more than that of the building. In the middle of this block a little back from the street, stood a half-dilapidated house with a wide open passage through it. This passage led into a large yard which was surrounded by one-story small houses, in which whites and blacks lived. Frequently the police had to restore order here. Then came a coal yard, and beside it a sign painter had his shop. Today there are massive six-story buildings there, occupied by some of the most respected wholesale firms. (A. Frankenthal & Brother, Rosenheim, Lewis & Co.)

For half a century the buildings of St. Louis University, which is under the direction of Jesuits, occupied the two blocks between Ninth and Eleventh Streets. Not until the disciples of Loyola had moved to their new college site on Grand Avenue was Tenth Street opened through the old campus site, and thus the barrier to traffic removed. The old College buildings, which had a rather gloomy exterior, were pleasantly arranged on the inside, and the long residence of the Jesuit fathers, and the white curtained boarding house on the north side of the wide campus was a model of neatness. The front side of this latter building was situated on Christy Avenue, and was separated from the street by a small garden. The Xavier Church, on the southwest corner of Ninth Street and Lucas Avenue, which belonged to the University, was one of the largest and most beautiful in the city. For decades it had one of the largest and richest congregations. Many of the old French families, which formerly had belonged to the parish of the cathedral, in which originally all the services were held in the French language, joined the St. Xavier church, because here on one Sunday each month the services were in French. Another church which was in this neighborhood, namely the Trinity Episcopal Church, on the northwest corner of the Eleventh Street and Washington Avenue, at an earlier date had sold its property to commercial interests. It is rather safe to assume that within a period of a few years no churches will be found on Washington Avenue, Locust and Olive Streets east of Grand Avenue.

On the south side of Washington Avenue, at Eleventh Street, there was at the end of the sixties a vacant space, where show companies put up their circus and menagerie tents. No doubt my readers will be surprised that even some years later there were entirely vacant plots between Locust Street and Washington Avenue and on Nineteenth and Twentieth Streets, so that in the middle of the seventies Barnum and Forepaugh could have their circus here.

In 1857 the buildings of Washington University were built on the south side between Seventeenth and Eighteenth Streets, therefore at a time when there were still many building sites available on this part of the street, and the front foot could still be bought for thirty or forty dollars.

Real estate was at that time not yet subject to speculation such as has become evident on this street, particularly during the last fifteen years.

Two decades ago there were still innumerable vacant lots between Twentieth and Twenty-fourth Streets. It is true that the presence of Schaeffer's soap factory may have had more or less to do with this. Now vacant building sites east of Grand Avenue are hard to find, for industry has stretched its arms farther and farther to the west. Here and there between elegant residences of the west end factories make their appearance. And even though such an intrusion is not welcomed by the people residing there, nevertheless, it is only a question of time when such changes take place to an even greater extent.

On the other hand, Washington Avenue underwent hardly any changes in its eastern part, from the Levee to Fourth Street. With the exception of the region which had to be changed, due to the building of the Eads Bridge, which was of great advantage to the avenue, everything is still as of old. The heavily-loaded freight wagons which come from the Levee and from Main and Second Streets still have difficulty getting up Washington Avenue, which is quite steep there, just as they did thirty years ago, only the number of trucks is considerably smaller since the bridge and the tunnel have brought such extensive changes in our entire traffic.

The building of this bridge required all of seven years, namely from 1867 to 1874. It was built under the direction of Captain James B. Eads, who also conceived the idea to construct a bridge over the Mississippi at St. Louis. As chief engineer he supervised in every detail the execution of the plans drawn up by himself and his assistants. As his first assistant he had Colonel Henry Flad, who later, for sixteen years, was the chairman of the board for city improvements. The mathematical calculations for this giant structure were the work of Flad and of Engineer Carl Pfeifer, who later became commissioner of Streets and Harbor. The financial part of the undertaking was, from the outset, in the hands of Dr. William Taussig, the chairman of the Executive Committee. On July 4, 1874 the bridge was opened for traffic with appropriate ceremonies. Two hundred years before, in 1674, Marquette had discovered the Father of Rivers, and one hundred and ten before the dedication of the bridge, in 1764, Pierre Laclede had raised the first log house, which constituted the beginning of present day St. Louis.

14. Locust Street

On the north side of Locust Street at the end of the fifties and beginning of the sixties, the office of the *Missouri Democrat*. This paper was the forerunner of the present *Globe Democrat*. No one thought of applying the name "Democrat Building" to the structure. It was a dilapidated affair. Each of its three stories contained only two rooms, and they were not large rooms. A narrow, steep and shaky stairway led directly from the street to the second floor. On the ground-floor the business office was located on the right side and the press on the left. A wooden barrier divided the counting room. Here were the desks of the chief owner of the paper, Billy McKee, and Dan Houser, who were at their post from early in the morning until late at night. Houser was bookkeeper and cashier. He received advertisements and also help, if necessary, with the distribution of the paper. The space before the barrier was so small that there was scarcely room for six persons. If one had successfully climbed the above-mentioned stairs, then he stood in a narrow hallway which separated the editorial room from the local department. The equipment of the former was limited to two worm-eaten desks and the chairs that went with them, and three or four chairs for probable visitors. At one of the desks worked Peter L. Foy, the editor-in-chief, whom President Lincoln appointed postmaster to succeed John Hogan, who held the position under Buchanan. At the second desk sat George W. Fishback, the second editor and part owner of the paper. The room of the local editor and of the one reporter that was assigned to him served also as a storeroom for the printing paper, which was piled almost to the ceiling. To reach the two small desks, at which the local news was written and compiled, one had to wind his way through these stacks of supplies. The typesetters room was on the third floor. On the evening of the capture of Camp Jackson things were lively here. In addition to the typesetters a number of well armed, loyal Union men were there, who intended to protect the office of *The Democrat* in the event of an attack on the part of the secessionists. The paper had advocated the abolition of slavery zealously, and made its whole influence felt for the election of Lincoln, and had done everything in its power for the preservation of the Union. Because of this it had now to deal with the enmity of those who favored the South. On the evening of May 10, 1861 feeling ran very high. Inciting speeches by Uriel Wright and others, delivered from the balcony of the Planters House, contributed much to the excitement. An angry mob moved down Locust Street with avowed intention of destroying the type and the press of the *Missouri Democrat*, and thus to prevent its appearance at least for the time being. The chief of police, McDonough, owed his appointment to the police commission which had recently been named by Governor Claiborne F. Jackson, and so favored the secessionists. However, fearing the possible results if the mob was allowed to proceed, he faced it with a considerable number of policemen. He furthermore informed the mob that the office of the *Democrat* was occupied by a company of volunteers from the arsenal which would meet the attackers with rifle fire. This announcement brought even the most rabid monster to his senses. The crowd dispersed and was not seen again.

McKeen was fond of a good drop of liquor and he did not have to go far to find it. A few steps from his office, Billy Baumeister had the Merchant Saloon in the basement of the corner building on Main Street. This was famous because of its fine liquors. And opposite the *Democrat* was William Gundelfinger's tavern, well known for its lunches. At that time there was also the extensive liquor business of P. G. Gerhart in the next block. Gerhart sat in the city council for awhile, and later was interested in real estate.

Opposite this place of business, George Casper had his shoemaker's shop. Whoever wanted to have well-fitting shoes in those days had Casper take his measurement. A shoemaker who did fine work need not fear competition. Among the disciples of Saint Crispin who enjoyed a good trade, were a few well-known Germans, as for example, Stumpf at French Market, old man Heckler on Walnut Street, opposite the Barnum Hotel, John Henn on Fourth, near Pine Street, and the latter's bosom friend, George Schumacher.

The latter was the father of Bertha Ricci whom Max Strakosch had educated for the opera. Later she sang the roles of Siebel (Faust), Genoro (Lucretia Borgia), Acuzena (Trovatore), etc. in her native city, and was well received.

The Western Union Telegraph Company, which for its local operation aside from its many branch offices, has now for more than twenty-five years required all the rooms of a four-story building, needed at the beginning of the sixties only three or four rooms. These were situated on the south side of Locust between Third and Fourth Streets.

Between Fifth and Sixth Streets the artistic joiners, Seidel and Winklee, had their place of business for a quarter of a century.

At the end of the sixties the region west of Sixth Street was occupied by residences. Due to this fact this street formerly had so many churches. In addition to the church site on the corner of Fifth and Sixth Streets, which has been previously mentioned, there was in the north side between Seventh and Eighth the St. George Episcopal church.

The first site mentioned in the above paragraph is now occupied by the Singer Building. The St. George Episcopal Church was changed to a furniture store during the sixties. Prior to this change advocates of women's suffrage held a convention in this church.

The Central Presbyterian church was situated on the northwest corner of Eighth and Locust Streets. On the corner of Tenth Street was the First Congregation Church, and on the Eleventh, the Union Presbyterian Church. From the latter, two of the best-known St. Louisans were carried to their last resting place in the Bellefontaine cemetery, namely, Nathaniel Paschall, for many years editor of the *Missouri Republican*, and General Frank P. Blair. In the political arena these two men fought out many a bitter feud.

As is seen from the above, this street had from the outset many churches, and so it is to this very day. One might call it the street of churches, since it exceeds all other streets in this respect.

Formerly the Missouri Park was situated on Fourteenth Street. It does not exist anymore. West of Fourteenth Street, Locust Street was called Lucas Place, while beyond Jefferson Avenue it resumed the name Locust again. Even in the fifties Lucas Place was one of the most beautiful residential sections of the city. Only elegant houses, for the most part surrounded by beautiful gardens, were seen here. One of these was Mary Institute. Before it was transferred to the west end, it stood not far from Doctor Nelson's church. The site of Doctor Nelson's church is now occupied by the Germania Theater. The building of the Historical Society of Missouri, on the southwest corner of Sixteenth Street and Lucas Place is another of these formerly elegant residences.

15. Olive Street

While at this time that part of Olive Street which lies in the extreme western part of the city exhibits many business houses, at the end of the fifties, from Sixth Street on, was occupied almost entirely by residences. Indeed the oldest and wealthiest families of St. Louis lived here. Some drug stores, a few candy shops, ice cream parlors and fruit stands had crept in. The owners of these establishments were looked upon as intruders, who had no right among the private homes. During the forties Olive Street, quicker than any other street, had been built up with residences which at that time were considered elegant. Most of these residences were occupied by the owners themselves, so that there were but few changes of occupants. The streetcar line was not constructed till the middle of the fifties. Even today one would rather live in a house past which no street car runs. In these early days people were even more averse to have a car track in front of their house. The street car was a principle reason for the exodus that by and by followed. Many of the residences were converted into business houses. For many of my readers it may be difficult to believe that Olive Street was one of the most fashionable residential parts of our city a relatively short while ago.

In 1851 the federal government bought the St. Louis Theater on the southeast corner of Third and Olive Street, in which plays had been given for fourteen years. On the site it built a post office and customs building. This structure served this purpose for thirty years.

The above-named theater was built in better taste than any of the present theaters in the city. The money for the building had been raised by subscription, and two veterans of the American stage, N. M. Lodlow and Solon Smith, had leased it. Mark Smith, the son of Solon Smith, was a most excellent actor. Unfortunately he died much too young.

The change of the location of the post office from Second and Chestnut proved to be of great commercial advantage to the neighborhood at the new site. Several banking houses moved in from Main Street. When in the early sixties the first national banks were organized, the St. Louis National Bank was established on the northeast corner of Third and Olive Street, the Union National Bank on Olive Street, directly below the post office building, and the Second National Bank near the latter on Third Street in a building erected by Frank P. Blair, in which for some years the inland revenue office was located.

In the basement under the Union Bank, east of the post office, the Napa & Sonoma Wine Company had its place of business. It was managed by E. C. Prieber and Aloys Thomann.

On the south side of Olive Street, between the Third and Fourth Street, the Peoples Theater was erected in 1852. It was in operation only for a few years. On the site where the dramatic muse had held sway, then "Professor" George Matthews devoted himself to his art--that is to the dying, cleaning and repairing of men's clothing. A couple of trousers and vests, which were hung before the door, announced from afar, where the "Professor" rendered useful service to the masculine world. Nearby the master shoemaker, John H. Schneeberger had his shop. The Gast Banknote and Lithographing Company is one of the most thriving concerns of this kind in the United States. It was founded in the fifties by the brothers Leopold and August Gast. At first they had their place of business on South Fourth, then on North Fourth and later on the corner of Third and Olive. Here Leopold severed his connection with the firm while August Gast continued as head of the concern till Louis J. Wall took over the management of the establishment. At the west end of the block (corner of Fourth Street) Pollack's men's clothing store was situated during the fifties.

The main owner of the four establishments that are known as Delicatessen is Charles C. Sprague. He began his career in the restaurant business on the north side of Olive, near fourth Street. The firm of Sprague and Butler operated a small restaurant in the lower part of a small two-story building. The room was not large, the ceiling was low, and the nearness of the kitchen at times made itself felt unpleasantly. The great patronage soon made an enlargement of the place of business imperative. It was one of the most frequented restaurants in the business part of the city. The customers at the noon hour were merchants, clerks, lawyers, bank employees, post office employees and such. The place was never closed for it had a certain patronage even during the night. As long as the Ben de Bar's theater was on Pine Street, many theater-goers frequented this restaurant after the performance, particularly during the oyster season. From the near-by telegraph office employees came during all hours of the night. About twelve o'clock a half dozen or more newspaper men arrived. Attorney Britton A. Hill, who died a few years ago, came almost every night. He lived on the corner of Third and Pine, therefore, close by, and was accustomed to arrive at the restaurant at about eleven o'clock and stay till about one o'clock. Hill was a heavy eater and a great epicurean. A large platter of tenderloin steak with truffles, or a fried, young duck were for him a snack, which he consumed with half, and often a whole bottle of Bordeaux. His main object was entertainment. He loved to converse and if he found the right company he did not think of going home at all. Also Ben de Bar frequently went there, and if he was in a good humor, and was almost always in good humor, then he related many interesting things of this early years, which he spent in London, where he was educated as an actor. He also contributed many interesting experiences on this side of the ocean. He, as well as Hill, were Shakespeare enthusiasts. When the two ate and drank, having their napkins under their chins, one involuntarily had to think of Falstaff. For many years the young German, Alexander Roman, had the management of the restaurant at night. He was very popular with the customers, who regretted it very much when he gave up his position in order to take over the restaurant on Second and Pine which previously had been operated by Frederick Buesching.

On the northwest corner of Fourth and Olive, where now the Continental Bank stands, was during the sixties the dry goods business of Porter and White. A bit farther, toward Fifth Street, was located the lacemaker, John Helgenberg. Approximately on the site where the Third National Bank now stands, Mrs. Helen Fuchs made her artistic embroidery which was famous throughout the entire west. Major Fuchs, her husband, commanded a battery during the war, and later held the office of city registrar. He passed away some years ago, while his wife still survives in excellent health.

At the beginning of the seventies H. J. Spaunhorst and other prominent Catholics began the publishing of the *Amerika*. It was first edited by Anton Hellmich and Doctor E. Preusz. Upon the latter's retirement Hellmich edited it alone. This paper was for some time published in this block, till it was transferred to Third Street, near Chestnut, where the office is still located.

On the southwest corner of Fifth and Olive stood till 1858 the residence of Attorney John F. Darby. He was a rich man and for a time served as mayor of the city. He spent the last years of his life under very unpleasant circumstances. The Darby Building, erected by him on this corner passed into other hands in the middle of the sixties. It did not bring good returns until it was reconstructed in the interior. The photograph gallery of John A. Scholten was located in the two upper stories of the building on the northwest corner during the later sixties. At that time it was the most elegant of this class of businesses.

On the western corner of the block stood the residence of Jean Baptiste Sarpi, one of the wealthiest old Frenchmen. His family at that time constituted the elite of society. Near the end of the fifties the house was leased by the Missouri-Pacific Railroad, which established its offices in it.

Opposite, where now the splendid Commercial Building stands, were likewise residences, which, at the time in question, were arranged for businesses of various kinds, whereupon tailors, corset makers, dentists, barbers, etc. moved in.

On the south side of the next block the transformation of residences into business houses took place even earlier. Among the first who moved in there were the tailor Zallee, the art dealer B. E. Thonssen, and the real estate agent Kaime.

The building which occupies almost half the block between Olive and Locust, Sixth and Seventh Streets, for which the Barr Dry goods Company annually pays sixty thousand dollars rent, is called Julia Building. It is named after Mrs. Julia Maffitt, the widow of Doctor Maffitt, a sister of Charles P. Chouteau. Before this building was erected during the middle of the sixties, the Chouteaus and Maffitts lived on the corner of Sixth and Olive Streets. The two three-story red brick houses were several feet above the street level, and on Sixth Street was a large garden. The two houses were built in the forties, and were still in the best of condition when they were torn down. Less valuable, and in part poorly preserved houses stood between Eighth and Ninth Streets, and Olive as well as Locust Streets. Nevertheless the United States had to pay a high price for the property in 1877, when it was bought for the erection of a post office and revenue building in the designated block.

On Olive Street there were all sorts of little shops with boarding apartments in the upper stories. On the south side of the street, where now the Fagin Building and the imposing Odd Fellow Hall stand, were tailor and shoemaker shops and a very modestly arranged laundry.

The Unitarian Church which stood on the northwest corner of Ninth and Olive continued to serve church purposes till May 1872. At the last services which were held in this building, Doctor Elliot, the chancellor of Washington University and former pastor of the congregation, as well as Doctor Snyder, his successor, preached. On the next morning the place teemed with workmen who tore down the building in a few days. Thereupon the building of Pope's Theater was begun. With unequaled speed, namely in less than eighty days the structure was built and equipped, so that it could be opened in the following September of that year. The expectations which were entertained by Charles Pope's friends and supporters in this theater project were unfortunately not fulfilled. An initial success was not of continued duration, and the heavily mortgaged building and theater changed owners.

At the corner on Ninth directly across the street, which is now occupied by the Emily Building, was at that time a lawn. Adjoining it was a very spacious house which faced Olive Street. During the sixties Porcher's restaurant was located here. This place was still in operation in 1882, so that Madam Marie Geistinger could have quarters there during the two weeks of the above year, when she appeared here for two weeks as guest artist. The restaurant had no bar room. The initiated, however, knew that even without entering one of the dining rooms, one could get as much to drink as one desired. There was a small room in which the bar was represented by a narrow board, three feet long. In the securely closed cupboards stood whole batteries of flasks from which cognac, Madeira, sherry and old bourbon could be obtained.

Several doors farther was the office of dentist Dr. Dienst. Since the latter's demise this office is occupied by Dr. Roemmich. Nearby was also Fox's photograph gallery, Freund's confection shop, and from 1871 on-- Scholten's establishment.

A row of houses on Olive Street which began at the corner of Eleventh Street and occupied half of the block, was called Dorris' Row. The father of Tom Dorris, who was known for his extravagant mode of living, was a very wealthy man. He had the houses built which for a long time brought in a high rental. His aged widow was murdered one night in the old Dorris mansion by her ill-bred grandson, the son of attorney Brown. The mansion was located near the St. Charles Rock Road.

On the south side in the same block were also elegant houses, among them that of Mr. Yeatman.

Now one can hardly recognize this region, which, as it were, has become the center of the piano business. Connected with the piano business are extensive furniture businesses.

In Twelfth Street, from Olive to Chestnut, there stood in the seventies the two Market Houses. These were called the Lucus Market, two large barrack-like structures, which for many years disfigured the street which sooner or later will be one of the broadest and prettiest business streets of St. Louis. When the city council finally decided to dispose of the Lucas Market, and the two long sheds were torn down, it was said that shade trees would be planted along the street and convert it into a splendid boulevard, which was to extend from Twelfth Street to Washington Avenue. The project was discussed with enthusiasm by the press, --but nothing came of the project.

In the year 1863 there was erected on the vacant plot on Twelfth Street between Olive and Locust a temporary structure in which was held the Mississippi Valley Sanitary Fair. It was one of the finest undertakings that was ever planned and carried out here for a benevolent purpose. The income from the project was intended for the care of wounded Union soldiers in field hospitals and other military hospitals. The sanitary commission for the Mississippi Valley was especially appointed by President Lincoln. At the head of it functioned our highly esteemed fellow citizen, James E. Yeatman, who in spite of his advanced years, is still president of the Merchants National Bank. The fair in question was the work of St. Louis women and the German element took a most active part in the undertaking. The chief direction was placed in the hands of Mrs. Henry T. Blow, the wife of the former American ambassador to Rio de Janeiro, and the mother of Susie Blow, the organizer of the local kindergarten.

On the south side of the street, between Twelfth and Thirteenth Streets the change from residences to business houses occurred much later than on the north side, where even at the beginning of the sixties large and little shops of the most varied kind could be found. In the present Merchant's Hotel, Spilker's confection shop was back of the drug store. Where today Westermann's Hotel Rozier stands, a couple of old maids had a little shop in which the neighborhood could procure its requirements of needles, thread, buttons, etc. Until in 1884 the exposition building was erected, and land was a park, which James H. Lucas had presented to the city. The

Missouri Park, therefore, extended from Olive to St. Charles Street, so that Locust Street ended at its eastern side and Lucas Place began on the west side. The park was well planted with trees, had a fountain in the middle and a great many bushes. From May to October it teemed with children of every age, their mothers, nurses and attendants. The latter two species wearing regulation white hoods and aprons.

In 1855 a building was erected on the northeast corner of Fifteenth and Olive in which since then the Central High School has been located. It has a front of 67 feet, a depth of 84 feet, and cost fifty-five thousand dollars. The building site at that time had a value of about twenty thousand dollars. At that time the structure and interior arrangement were no doubt adequate, but even two decades later the rooms did not suffice anymore and the nearby buildings of Foster Academy had to be taken over, chiefly for the work of the Normal School.

A few blocks west of Jefferson Avenue one could still see grain fields at the beginning of the sixties. From Olive to Chestnut Street, between Thirty-first Street and Grand Avenue was Lindell Grove, owned by Peter Lindell. Since 1861 this has been known as Camp Jackson.

When on that memorable afternoon of May 10, 1896[1], the first four Missouri Volunteer regiments under General Lyon marched to Camp Jackson there was not a trace of any houses to be seen on the low hills that extended several blocks beyond Twenty-eighth Street. (On this march the regiment under Frank P. Blair marched up Laclede Avenue. Boernstein's regiment marched on Pine, Schittner's on Market, and Sigel's on Olive Street.)

On the south side of the street were a few scattered houses. Only in the immediate vicinity of the camp the bankers Page and Bacon had built six three-story residences for speculation. When the bankers failed in 1859 these houses were bought by Captain James B. Eads.

Beyond Grand Avenue lay fields and meadows and uncultivated land. Here and there was the dwelling of a commercial gardener. Or one could see bits of forests to which St. Louisans walked on hot summer days after having reached the terminals of the Olive and Market Street street car lines. Three decades ago not even the most sanguine local patriot would have dreamed that the city should some day possess a Forest Park, with elegant residences around it, and that electric and cable lines would care for the traffic between Fourth and Fiftieth Street.

16. Pine Street

Like Olive and Locust, Pine Street was in former years a preferred residential street. West of Seventh Street only an occasional store or tavern could be seen. That has been changed later, and today four different street railways run through Pine Street east of Twelfth Street, and only the western half has become a really pretty street to which the asphalt paving and the absence of street car tracks have contributed much.

Older readers will recall that the banking business of Eugene Miltenberger & Co. was located on Pine and Main. The St. Louis Type Foundry was for a long time between Main and Second on the north side of Pine. Adjoining was the business place of Stifel & Plochmann, later Stifel & Benson, wholesale dealers in leaf tobacco. On the south side of the block there was, during the later fifties, Klymann, Meyers & Co., (Commission and shipping). When this firm was dissolved, one of the partners, J. Hellmann, together with his brother, Louis M. Hellmann, organized the still existing business for the manufacture of the well known bitters. Nearby was the F. W. Aufderheide Commission house, which was located there during the fifties and sixties, but later was transferred to Main Street.

At the southeast corner of Second and Pine was the restaurant of Frederick Buesching. The latter met death in a fall down the steps which led from the street into the gas office of that time. Habicht's printing shop was for nearly four decades under the Boatmen's Savings Bank, and was not moved to Fourth Street till 1891.

The office building of the old gas company was in the next block. Diagonally across from it was the tailor shop of Charles Bauer, who profited by the nearness of the gas office in that he acquired a large number of shares in the company while the stock was still very cheap. On the northwest corner of Third Street stood a building of which one feared that it might collapse. Nevertheless, there were all sorts of offices in it, among them those of several newspapers. In the rear part of the building was Joseph Waite's print shop. On the first floor on the Pine Street side, was Zimmermann's tavern, called The Genuine, a name which was justified by the excellent and unadulterated beverages that were served there. During the later fifties Zimmermann had a bartender by the name of Moritz Langeloth. He was the son of an official in Saxony, who had provided a good education for him. Before Langeloth came to St. Louis he had worked as attendant in the hydropathic institution of Dr. Munde in Florence, Massachusetts. In St. Louis he had the opportunity of applying the skill he had acquired in the bath-house in Kerzinger's care. (Dr. Munde came to America as a refugee after the May uprising in Dresden.) Presently Langeloth quit the water cure and devoted himself to preparation of hot whiskey punch, till Mr. Boernstein discovered the dormant talents of the young man and made him a local newspaper reporter. As such he occasionally caused his discoverer great vexation. It will suffice to give one illustration. One evening a frightful thunderstorm caused considerable damage in various parts of the city. Several persons were seriously injured and the whole community was in a state of excitement. While the other papers contained detailed accounts of the devastation and accidents on the next morning, the *Anzeiger* did not even mention it. When questioned about the matter, Langeloth replied that everybody already knew about what happened the evening before, so it was of no use putting it in the newspaper. It should be mentioned that this occurred at the beginning of his journalistic career, which concluded about twenty years later in Chicago as publisher of *Der Enlenspiegel*. For this paper his energetic wife "Diana" continually traveled in Illinois and neighboring states soliciting subscriptions.

In 1856 Ben de Bar leased the theater on the north side of Pine between Third and Fourth Streets, which till 1860 was known as the St. Louis Theater. This theater was opened as early as 1851. Until 1874, when Ben de Bar took over the opera house on Market Street, many great artists from both sides of the ocean appeared there. Among them Charlotte Cushman, the Italian actress Adelaide Ristori, Fanny Janauscheck (or Janauschek) (at that time only in the German language) moreover J. W. Booth, the comedian Bernard Canlin Florence, who made his first real hit in the West while playing in St. Louis. Then there was Ben de Bar himself, who played excellently in many most varied roles. Maggie Mitchell appeared on this stage, first as Fanchon, later as Lorle and the Waif of Lowood, and many other roles. Soon she was the favorite actress of St. Louis, and has remained such, in spite of the decades that have passed. Ben de Bar's niece, Blanche, made her debut here, and Adah Isaacs Menken made her last appearance here before her death in *Mazeppa*. Almost during every winter de Bar provided several weeks of opera. Christina Nilsson, Parepa

Rosa, Pauline Lucca, three of the most brilliant stars of the European opera, sang here. Among the Americans are to be mentioned Clara Louise Kellogg, Louise Cary, Mrs. Sequin. During the sixties the German opera under Leonard Grover of Philadelphia appeared here during two seasons. Among the cast were Karl (or Carl) Formes, Mrs. Johannsen, Miss Canissa, and Theodore Habelmann. Grau and Max Strakosch each year brought the Italian opera to this theater. In the spring of 1874 there were in Strakosch's company three prima donnas--Kellogg, Cary and Lucca. The successes of Lucca had aroused the envy and jealousy of Kellogg, even before the company came to St. Louis. Here, where the friends of the German opera crowded the theater, in order to hear Pauline Lucca, the Americans undertook to come to the aid of their troubled countrywoman. One evening, when both singers were scheduled to appear, they were tactless enough to present Miss Kellogg on the stage with a golden medallion. Good natured George Bain allowed himself to be persuaded to make a speech of presentation, which he later regretted often enough. The intention was to vex the German singer by this action. Reprisals on the part of the Germans were not lacking. From this evening on Mrs. Lucca was met with even more stormy ovations. These were led particularly by the Lucca Society, which was presided over by Mrs. Charles Stiesmeyer, and whose secretary was Miss Emily Wiedmann (now Mrs. F. Harrsen). Mrs. Lucca was honored with serenades and at each appearance was showered with flowers, particularly on the last evening, when Mozart's *Don Juan* was presented. On this occasion Lucca sang the role of Zerlina and Kellogg that of Donna Anna.

 Ben de Bar took over the opera house in 1874. In addition to financial difficulties it brought him annoyance of every sort. The formerly so robust man began to ail and in 1877 he passed away. In time we lost a great and enthusiastic actor and a most charming man. His funeral services were held in the large auditorium of the Masonic Hall, which proved to be much too small on this occasion. The theater on Pine Street passed into the hands of Director Mitchell, who converted it into a theater of the third class, and gave it the name, Theater Comique. At the end of the seventies it was completely destroyed by fire.

 On the south side of the block, on the corner of Third Street stood one large building, the Old Custom House. The rest of the block was occupied by old, low buildings in which were small restaurants, pawn shops and the like. The first office of the St. Louis *Times*, which Stilson Hutchins had brought here from Iowa during the middle of the sixties, occupied the second story of one of these houses. A rickety stairway led to the small rooms which served as editorial room, office and type setters room.

The building on the northeast corner of Fourth and Pine Streets, in which from 1863 on the office of the *Missouri Democrat* and later the *Globe Democrat* were housed, was erected on the site formerly occupied by Lippincott's lunch room. A part of the lower story was later occupied by the *Evening Post*, which, however, was soon fused with the *Dispatch*. In comparison to the rooms of the *Democrat* on Locust Street which were described in an earlier chapter, this building was a real paradise for the employees of the paper, particularly for the typesetters. In the summer of 1892 the *Globe Democrat* moved a bit farther west, but remained loyal to Pine Street. Its new building on the corner of Sixth Street is a real ornament. Between Sixth and Twelfth, Pine is in need of improvement by erection of new buildings. There are still many old structures that are poorly suited to business purposes.

17. Chestnut Street and Court House

For a number of years the offices of real estate agents were located on Chestnut, Pine and Eighth Street between Market and Olive Streets. In the fifties and sixties their number was relatively small. While a few were scattered here and there, the majority were located on Chestnut, which could justly be considered the center of the real estate business.

James H. Lucas could have been the most important real estate man of that time. The reason why he was not was due to the fact that he could not bear the idea of disposing of his possessions. It was quite an effort for him to sell any of them. In addition to several large buildings he owned a number of smaller buildings in different parts of the city, especially, however, between Walnut Street and Washington Avenue, moreover, whole blocks of building sites in the present west end. These latter he left unimproved for decades. It is true that the old building netted him good rents, but modern buildings were not erected on his land till after his demise in 1873. His action was generally considered an obstruction of progress, and since he was not alone in this conservative attitude, there was no lack of impious remarks, that all that St. Louis really needed was a number of magnificent funerals. In other words the overly conservative real estate owners would have to be buried if progress and free enterprise should have a free course. A "boom", of course, was something unknown at that time, and people of Lucas' type would have shaken their heads gravely. Everything proceeded at a well regulated and slow pace. To deviate from this pace would in Lucas' office have been synonymous with the upsetting of all existing things. This office was situated in the second story of the building on the southwest corner of Main and Chestnut. It consisted of two rooms, one of which served as a private office. The furnishings were extremely modest. According to present day concepts no one would suspect that several million dollars worth of real estate were managed there.

But even though the impious wish for "first class funerals" was not fulfilled for a long time, those who dealt in real estate had lucrative business. The best known firms in this line were located rather close together on Chestnut between Second and Third Streets. They were Belt & Priest, John Riggin, who was a member of the second metropolitan police board, Bailey & Co., Booth and Barada. Between Third and Fourth Streets were Dick Lancaster, who at that time was not yet known as a clever politician as later, Theodore Papin, who for a time had the lucrative office of county collector, Ephraim Obear, old man Leffingwell, who during President Grant's administration was a federal marshal for four years, and finally the brothers, Walsh. Opposite the court house, in the basement of the Planters House was the office of Hartmann & Roentgen. The latter belonged to the law firm of Wielandy & Roentgen. Between Fifth and Sixth Street Harper & Co., and Judge Lanham were located. The latter was known as an exceptionally fine auctioneer, so that his services were in great demand at public sales.

On the north side of the block between Main and Second Street was the building of the *Missouri Republican*. It was a sort of duplex building. The larger part of it was destroyed by fire on May 24, 1870. The fire had its origin in the bindery of the establishment. Even the richest daily newspaper of that time would not have thought of having its offices as elegantly furnished as papers now. In keeping with the former practice, the counting room of the *Republican* was simply equipped, and yet it was the handsomest in the city at that time. On the outside the building looked rather gloomy, and the interior was not much more inviting. Only in one part of the building there was elegance. This was in the first story, which faced Main, and it was a tavern. This was managed at the beginning of the sixties by Frederick Buesching, who sold out to Phillip and John Bamberger, who in turn were succeeded by Henry Schweickhardt.

For about two and a half years after the fire, the *Republican* occupied a temporary structure on the site of the conflagration. Then John Bamberger, who had been located on the north-east corner of Second Street, used the temporary building as a restaurant.

There are many things that clearly illustrate the growth of our city. Among them is the type of building that in the course of time has housed the offices of our municipal officials. Everybody knows that the city hall, which is now in the process of construction, should have been built a long time ago. There is no excuse for the repeated postponement of this undertaking. The four-cornered, barn-like, poorly built and not fireproof structure, which now for sixteen years has served as a city hall, was a disgrace for the city from the outset. But, at any rate, it at least contained enough space for all the bureaus of the city government. In this respect it was in marked contrast to the much smaller building on the south side of Chestnut, between Main and Second Streets, which for so long had served as a city hall. The latter was a three-story building which in 1864 was bought by the *Westliche Post* after some changes had been made in its interior. For several decades it had housed all the branches of the municipal government. On the ground floor was the health office with a very primitive dispensary, and the police station for the central part of the city, together with the office of the chief of police. On the second floor were the offices of the mayor, the comptroller, the treasurer, etc. On the third floor was a rather small and low room where the city council held its meetings. In the remaining rooms on this floor the other branches of the city authorities were crowded in narrow quarters. The city council at that time, and even later, held its sessions in the afternoon between five and seven o'clock. In the summer months the city fathers deliberated over the affairs of the city literally in the sweat of their brows.

The mayor of the city occupied a room that had two windows. The equipment of the room testified that in the household of the official family the greatest economy prevailed. Indeed the mayors of that time were men of the most simple and modest mode of life. They did not drive to their offices in their own equipages, nor did they attend horse races, nor did they reflect radiance from diamond studded breast pins. John M. Krumm, James G. Barry, Luther M. Kennett, John How and O. D. Filley never failed to be in their offices during office hours. They would rather leave their own businesses in the lurch than to be late at their post of duty. The announcement that his honor was unable to come to the city hall because of personal illness would have attracted general attention and aroused concern.

Another of these modest men was the elderly James S. Thomas, who assumed the office of mayor after the city hall had been transferred to the north wing of the court house. The excellence of his administration was attested by his reelection to office. He served as mayor from April 1864 to April 1868. This was the time when during two succeeding years our city was visited by cholera. The energy with which he administered the sanitary regulations that had been agreed upon, and the manner in which he personally attended to things, whenever possible, evoked unqualified praise even from his political opponents, so that many of his peculiarities, as for example, his wandering about the city at night, which earned for him the sobriquet of a modern Harun al Raschid, were gladly overlooked.

After the transfer of the offices of the city officials to a part of the courthouse, which had been leased from the county, the *Westliche Post* moved into the former city hall, and arranged it to meet the needs of the newspaper. The former office of the health department became the counting room. The power driven presses were installed in the old police station. The editor-in-chief occupied the mayor's room, and the third story was arranged for the type setters. In the yard stood a small building with uncommonly thick walls, in it the police had been accustomed to put obstreperous prisoners. This massive structure was particularly suitable for a boiler house and was so used. In this manner a complete metamorphosis of all the rooms took place. No one could guess that it formerly was the city hall. The *Westliche Post* remained here for nearly ten years. From here it moved into its own building on the corner of what was then Fifth Street, now Broadway and Market Street.

In former years most of the lodges and society halls were located in the center of the city, and with few exceptions, east of Seventh Street. On the northeast corner of Second and Chestnut, in the third story, above the banking house of Allen, Copp & Nisbet, a Harugari lodge held its meetings. At the opposite end of the block, likewise on the third floor, was

Erwin Lodge, one of the two German lodges of Free Masons. The first press club, that came into existence near the end of the sixties, had its quarters in a building on the north side of Chestnut, near Second Street. On the ground floor of this building the coal dealer, Donk, had his office. Later he moved to Olive Street. In a large, adjoining building Straszburger & Drack had for many years a stereotyping and electrotyping business. When the partners separated, Charles A. Drack found an electrotyping plant on the corner of Fourth and Pine Streets which for more than two decades has been the largest of its kind in St. Louis.

When the metropolitan police was organized, the police commissioner provided suitable headquarters for the department. For this purpose they leased the large building on the south side of Chestnut, between Second and Third Streets, in which up to that time, Jesse and Andrew Arnot had had one of their two livery stables. The lower story, in which the horses had been kept, was converted into cells for the prisoners. The livery barn office became the office of the police station. In the upper story were the commissioners, the chief of police, the detectives, and later also the police court with all its officials. The court room occupied the rear part of the second floor. The third floor was used as a gymnasium for the policemen. After the Four Courts had been completed, the city leased a part of it for the police department and the police court, as also space for a prison. But since a police station was absolutely necessary in the center of the city and near the Levee, a building on the corner of the alley, opposite Arnot's business place was provided for that purpose.

It is a singular fact that a certain type of law breakers keep themselves near those who are appointed to see that the law is obeyed. It may seem strange, but it is a fact, that directly opposite the police station on Chestnut Street for a long time there existed a "Ratpit," that is a place in which on certain evenings dog fights, cock fights and dog and rat fights were staged. These were regularly attended by the numerous followers of this sort of horrible sport. This occurred literally under they eyes of the authorities, and no interference with these sports was ever heard of. This may have been due to the fact that a former policeman was in charge of the place. In order that the shouts of the enthusiastic spectators could not be heard on the street, the windows and window shutters in the back room, where the fights took place, were not only tightly closed, but were hung with thick blankets. Only the initiated were allowed admission.

Five or six two-story houses stood between Arnot's building and Third Street. They belonged to James Archer, who in his time owned an extensive business in pig iron on the Levee. In one of these buildings was the office of Justice of the Peace Cunningham. Rarely a day passed without a trial. The proximity of the Levee was a rich source of income for the squire. Disputes between steamboat captains and roustabouts occurred only too frequently and were settled before the justice. Sometimes also a whole crew of a boat appeared which had not received their pay, and sought a legal restraining order to prevent the boat's departure. Then there occurred also bloody fights on the wharf or on board the boats and old man Cunningham had occasion to sit in judgement. On such occasions the constable often had great difficulty in getting a jury. The institution of permanent jurors, that is people who make it a business to render such service in the office of the justice of the peace, was not yet established, as later. Business men in the neighborhood were reluctant to sit for hours with the squire, and the constable often had to threaten with the severity of the law to get the necessary "six good and true citizens."

On the north side of the block were located the sign painters, Henkler & Krippen, the sign painter and artist, Henry Dollner. On the corner was located the St. Louis Mutual Building Association, whose founder and secretary was Rudolph Mackwitz. The latter had an office as notary there, and later he opened a Belgian Consulate. In the uppermost story of this building the Arion of the West had its quarters for a while, and in the small hall presented some of the most successful programs. In the matter of humor and wit it accomplished far more than was later accomplished with great pomp and at much greater cost in the halls of the Harmonic Club and the Germania Club.

Before the new Exchange Building was erected there stood on the north side of Chestnut Street, between Third and Fourth Streets, eight or nine buildings, none alike in architecture. The largest of these, on the corner of Third Street, was three stories high. On the first floor was O'Brien's office where tickets for steamship transportation to and from Europe were sold. Now this corner is occupied by the insurance agents, Roeslein & Robyn. One flight of stairs up was Kluender's printing shop, and above it was Josef Moser's pasteboard factory. Later the latter was transferred to Elm Street. The most elegant oyster saloon, the Capitol Oyster Saloon, occupied the lower part of the adjoining building. Hart & Scott were the proprietors, and the equipment had cost a nice piece of money in its day. The artistically carved wood was painted white and gold. The table tops were of white marble, and the ceiling was richly decorated with stucco. (Hart died many years ago and Scott was at one time Gregory's partner in the Wintergarden.)

Approximately in the middle of the block bordering on an alley which led to Pine Street, was located the second of the livery stables then operated by the Arnots. It was called the Planters Stable. Andrew Arnot was the older of the two brothers. During the forties he had swung his long whip over a span of six as he drove a mail coach over the road to California. He had given up this work a long time ago but still occasionally yearned to visit the regions of the West through which he traveled so often in former days. When the unforgettable Lincoln became the victim of a ruthless assassin in April 1865, the Arnots had just come into possession of a hearse, which had been built for them in the East for several thousand dollars. Jesse Arnot placed it and six of his pure black horses at the disposal of the committee that was in charge of the funeral at Springfield. The offer was accepted, and Arnot himself drove his span of six as they conveyed the casket with Lincoln's body to the burial place in the capitol of our neighboring state.

The Old Postoffice Saloon, a popular place for politicians and their friends, was situated on the other side of the alley. In the rear rooms of this place many a small private caucus was held. On the south side of this block there was not a single tavern until the time of the war. In this regard it differed markedly from the other side. During the war a beer cellar was opened under a small building on the southwest corner. However, it did not operate long, and a barber moved into place. On the other hand a very popular restaurant existed for several years in the basement of the Kennet Building, under a real estate office. In the just named building was also located the Accommodation Bank, which was organized by Erasmus Wells, Gustavus W. Dreyer and a few other capitalists, but it did not exist long. The brothers Fuhrmann, two old bachelors, had, in the early fifties, a watchmaker's shop in one of the two-story houses near Third Street, that were owned by the public school board. In another of these houses, owned by the school board, Boshold had his shoemaker's shop. In still another of these buildings three sisters had a coffee shop.

To the time of the transfer of the criminal court to the Four Courts the court room, now occupied by the city assessor, was in the south wing of the courthouse. On many occasions the courtroom proved to be much too small to accommodate the crowds that attended the trials. That was regularly the case at a murder trial. Since in those earlier years, the murders did not sit in the jail for a long time, and clever lawyers were not allowed to postpone trials, this sort of hearing was not infrequent. One of the most excellent men who ever sat on a judge's bench was Judge Wilson Primm, who presided over this difficult office for many years with unshakable honesty and impartiality. Before he was elected to this office the citizens had elected him repeatedly to the city council, of which he was the presiding officer for a long time, and had also sent him to the state legislature. Then, too, he had served on the public school board, where he had done much in the interest of education. He occupied the position of criminal judge for nearly fourteen years. He lived in Corondelet, and if court was in session, he came every morning on one of the first trains in order to avoid every delay, for he was punctuality itself in everything. On one occasion a heavy snowfall had delayed the arrival of the trains, and as a result he appeared in the courtroom fifteen minutes late. Because of this neglect he imposed on himself a fine of ten dollars, which he handed to the deputy sheriff who was on duty.

It was during Primm's term of office that Charles P. Johnson, circuit attorney first demonstrated his eloquence, which he later made use of so lucratively in the defense in the criminal court. When the-then-young circuit attorney addressed the jury in the closing speech of a murder trial, the number of listeners was so great that they filled the open windows of the courtroom, the corridors and even the entrance steps. He spoke loud enough so that one could understand him on the outside.

The clerk of the criminal court during the late fifties to the middle sixties was Frederick Kretschmar and his deputy was Michael K. McGrath. The latter subsequently served as secretary of state for twelve years, and played a prominent role in the Democratic party of Missouri.

The predecessor of Primm was Judge Henry A. Clover, who also was an honor to his office. At that time Charles G. Mauro, one of the ablest attorneys in St. Louis, was the prosecuting attorney.

While we now have five circuit courts, their functions were formerly performed by courts that had the following names: the Court of Common

Please, whose last judge was Judge Samuel Reber; the Law Commissioner's Court, over which Judge Dusenberry was the last presiding officer; the County Court, with Judge Lord; and a single Circuit Court, over which, prior to the change, Judge Sam H. Breckenridge presided.

As long as the state supreme court held two term sessions a year in St. Louis, it met in the small hall now used by the appellate court. The clerk of the supreme court had to use as his office a small enclosure, eight feet by eight feet, set up in the corridor.

The county board, formerly known as County Commissioners and then as County Judges, held two public sessions each week, on Monday and Thursday forenoon. They met in the room which is now the private office of city collector Ziegenheim. The county clerk occupied the present license office. The last county clerk was Charles F. Vogel, who is now a real estate agent. Frederick Schoenthaler was his predecessor. The county collector had his office in the basement, where later the city tavern tax collector could be found.

Extensive changes were made in the interior of the courthouse after the city had come to an agreement with the county, by which a part of the building was leased to the city authorities. The north wing, on Chestnut Street, was assigned entirely to the city, excepting only the office of the county treasurer. Where today, to the left of Chestnut Street entrance, the general taxes are paid, were from 1864 on, the offices of the mayor and the comptroller. To the right of the entrance were the offices of the auditor, the treasurer, and the registrar. In the basement toward Fourth Street was the collector of water dues. Toward Fifth Street was the inspector of weights and measures. As long as the city council consisted of only one body, the office of the city engineer, (whose duties are now performed by the street commissioner), was in the second story on the Fourth Street side. The hall of the city council was opposite it on the Fifth Street side. With the creation of an upper and lower chamber the engineer had to yield to the latter, and move under the roof, where also the fire alarm office was confined for many years until the council room of the circuit judge was assigned to it.

One of the best-known Germans who served in the engineer department of the county and city during the fifties and sixties may be mentioned Colonel Franz Hassendeubel, (who fell in the first year of the war),

Ferdinand Bischoff, E. Salomon, Julius Pitzmann, and first assistant engineer, Rauschbach, who served the city for many years.

The sale of Negroes and mulattoes to the highest bidder took place on the east side of the courthouse, on the steps which lead up from Fourth Street. It was in the year 1860 that such a repulsive spectacle was seen here for the last time. The new era which put an end to slavery was dawning on our national horizon, when this last sale of slaves took place, but another full year had to pass before one could say of Missouri that it had ceased being a slave state. In the same place where for decades Negroes were sold as chattels, later many public assemblies were addressed by dark-skinned speakers.

Even today the courthouse with various courts and many city offices is the center of much activity and lively traffic. The number of taverns near there testifies to this. To a still greater degree was this the case at the time when city and county officials were both in the same building. Henry Heuer was one of those who recognized the possibilities of this location. He opened a tavern on Chestnut Street, directly opposite the courthouse. Soon after doing so he discontinued his old tavern on Third Street. After his demise his brother-in-law, Emil Bessehl continued the business. In 1865 he transferred it to the northeast corner of Fifth Street, into the place until then operated by Phillip A. Bamberger.

The large corner building, known as the Times building, was really named Churchill Building after its owner. Originally all its upper stories were arranged as lawyers' offices and occupied by men of this profession.

Bamberger's place of business was at first in the basement. Then he moved to the first floor. He combined it with a restaurant which was famous for its fine kitchen. Philip was one of the first who installed large fans, that were suspended from the ceiling, and with them sought to make his customers comfortable during the summer months. The fans were kept in motion by a sufficiently large number of big dogs who worked in the basement. The dogs were relieved from work every half hour.

The upper stories of the building were arranged as a hotel during the sixties and Charles Leichsenring, the proprietor, did everything to make the place popular. His location was certainly excellent, but for some reason it did not pay, so Leichsenring gave the business up. Leichsenring was a good story-teller and a good entertainer. He never lacked material, and was endowed with so vivid an imagination that he could not always distinguish between fact and fiction.

Between the Times Building and the Planters House were for many years the storerooms of the Cherokee Brewery. Connected with it was a very popular restaurant, which was managed by Ferdinand Herold.

Just when the large building on the southwest corner of Fifth and Chestnut had been completed in 1863, it was leased by the Mississippi Valley Sanitary Commission, and used as a military hospital. It was the duty of this commission to care for the wounded and sick of the Union Army in this part of the country. This service was rendered by the equipping and managing of hospitals in cities to which the patients could be brought conveniently and quickly, as also by supplying field hospitals with the countless things which the Quartermaster Department could not furnish for the comfort and aid of the patients. The new building was excellently suited as a hospital, and the wounded recovered rapidly in the high and airy rooms, especially since in addition to the trained nurses, a number of big-hearted women and girls looked after their comfort. It was on this field of honor that the-then still very youthful Phoebe Couzins became known to the public, and under the direction of her father, who at that time was chief of police, made herself useful in the sick room.

Later this building passed into the hands of "Doctor" Rudolph Bircher, who made Hotel Bircher of it. It is the same building which today is known as Hurst's Hotel. The Laclede Hotel was built later on the site which had been occupied by city police prison and the county jail.

Where today the Hauser Building stands, on Fifth and Chestnut, there formerly stood a much less pretentious building. In its upper stories were the offices of the attorneys Taussig & Kellogg, and Rombauer & Finkelnburg. After Rombauer became a circuit judge, G. A. Finkelnburg was associated with Leo Rassieur. Until they moved to the Granite Building they had their joint offices on Chestnut near Fifth Street. Finkelnburg represented St. Louis in Congress at one time.

Between Sixth and Seventh Streets the watchmaker F. A. Buchroeder had his workshop during the sixties. Formerly he had been employed by Mermod, Jaccard & Co. Subsequently he moved to the Court House block, which is the fourth, and during the eighties to Walnut Street, the Temple Building.

The Hotel de l'Europe formerly stood on the southeast corner of Seventh Street where now several real estate offices are located. Also the abstractors August Gehner & Co. had their offices there before they moved to the Wainwright Building.

In the year 1865 the building of the Polytechnic Institute, on the southwest corner of Seventh Street, was begun. Until 1893 the school library, a part of the high school, as also the offices of the school board were housed in this building. In May 1867 it was dedicated to its original purpose, named O'Fallon Polytechnic Institute, and deeded to Washington University. Ample room was thus provided for a trade school and a library. To the latter Henry Ames contributed one hundred thousand dollars, while John O'Fallon gave two whole blocks of real estate and forty thousand dollars cash. (The Ameses and O'Fallons have become very scarce in St. Louis since that time.) In 1868 Washington University sold the Polytechnic Institute to the public school board for something more than two hundred thousand dollars. At that time, because of the location, this was considered a very high price, but the exodus of the real estate offices to this region had not yet taken place. Until the middle of the sixties this region was occupied by the elite. For example, Dings' residence, surrounded by a garden, stood on the northwest corner of Eighth Street. Later the offices of the city water department were moved into it. A few doors west lived Doctor Boisliniere, who in the early sixties served as coroner. Also a few other old French families did not leave this region till the end of the sixties. On the northeast corner of Fourth Street was an unoccupied place, on which a merry-go-round was operated for a long time, until the inhabitants of the surrounding property lodged complaint on account of the nightly noise, and secured its removal.

The erection of the "temporary" city hall (a temporary arrangement that has lasted much too long) brought no essential change in the appearance of this region. To the west of Twelfth Street to Twentieth Street, Chestnut still looks almost exactly as it did three decades ago. One must go farther west on this street to find beautiful, modern houses such as in the west end.

18. Market Street

Market Street was so named because the first market house was erected on the north half of the block which runs from the Levee to Market Street and from Walnut to Market. This old market house was still standing in 1846. Present Market Street now resembles but faintly what it once was. The fact is that it was at one time the busiest street in the business section of the city. It flourished most during the years between 1830 and 1854. After this quarter of a century of prosperity, traffic on this street decreased greatly. During the years of the war there was a revival of business here, but it relapsed again after peace was declared. Now a revival of interest seems to be in prospect since the main building of the central railway station will be built on it.

The firms which were located on Market Street in the early days, were almost exclusively in German hands. It is, therefore, natural that German taverns flourished here. One of the best known of these was that of Julius H. Hertter, who to the middle fifties managed the New Post Office House between Market and Chestnut.

The office of the Washington Fire Insurance Company and the German Mutual Life Insurance Company were for a long time on the south side of Market near Main Street. Charles W. Gottschalk was the first president of the Washington company and Charles W. Horn was the first president of the life insurance company. (Horn was for a time the owner of a cooperage.) Arthur Olshausen was the first secretary of the above fire and life insurance companies. Later he became the president of the two concerns, and Frederick S. Behrens of the commission firm of Behrens & Brandes became his successor as secretary. One of the most active directors of the life insurance company was, from the outset, Isidor Busch, who was considered an expert in this field.

The St. Louis Mutual Fire Insurance Co. was situated at the corner of Second and Market Streets, over the United States Savings Institution. About the middle of the seventies it moved to Seventh and Locust Streets. Its first president was the wainwright John Kern, the older brother of Jacob Kern, and its first secretary was T. Theummler. After the demise of Kern, John C. Vogel was chosen president, which office he held to the time of his death which occurred in the middle of the eighties. Thuemmler's successor in office was John J. Sutter, who served as secretary till his death in 1891.

The tavern which was operated by Gustav Wolf a few doors west of Hertter's was a popular gathering place for the employees of the *Westliche Post*, whose offices were in an adjoining building from 1857 to 1860.

In that neighborhood George C. Fabian had his window shade business. Later he gave this up to assume the position of treasurer of the bridge construction company.

Two doors from Fabian's place, Peter Ambs had his wine and liquor business.

One of the oldest shoe concerns of the city is that of George Dittmann. During the fifties and sixties it was located on the south side of Market Street, in the same block on the west end of which was the Gray Hat Store. In the latter Nick Guerdan was employed. He became Gray's partner, and subsequently the head of the Guerdan Hat Co.

On the southwest corner of Second Street was till 1862, Albert Fischer's hat store. In the third story of this building was the office of the *Tages Chronik* which in July, 1863, ceased to exist, after thirteen years of publication. In the second story of this building was a large hall. During the winter of 1860-61 it was the headquarters of a company of the national guard. Its commander was Thornton Grimsley, the owner of a harness store. Because of his sympathy with the secessionists this man was later banished to the South. The taking of Camp Jackson brought an end to this company. In the hall soon thereafter, the press militia company, consisting of the employees of the *Westliche Post*, and the *Tages Chronik*, held their drill exercises under Captain Daniel Hertle. This company never saw actual service. Hertle and Theodore Olshausen were at that time co-editors of the *Westliche Post*. At the beginning of the seventies the above drill hall served as office for *Puck*, published by Keppler and his brother-in-law Rubens, and edited by Louis Willich.

The lower story of the above building frequently changed occupants during the sixties. After Albert Fischer moved out, it was occupied by Franz Michenfelder's tavern, then by Mandelbaum's delicatessen business, and by the dealers in leather, Meyer & Braun.

The French weekly, *Revue de l'Ouest*, published by J. Wolf and edited by Louis Cortambert was in the adjoining building. Later the office of *Frank und Frei* edited and published by Henry Binder, was located here. In 1863 and 1864 J. Peyer published the *Staatszeitung* in this building. This last publication is not to be confused with daily by the same name that appeared at the end of the sixties. The print shops of Martin Seifert and of the brothers Rauth were likewise housed there. There was no lack of "black artists" in that region. In the basement of this building was George Schloszstein's wine store.

Adjoining was the concert Hall, a large building with accessory rooms, where balls and festivals of all sorts were given. This structure had been built by the dancing teacher, Xaupi. At the end of the sixties, Xaupi transferred his dance academy to another site. The place was then leased by the dancing teacher, Blemer, and after him by the dancing master, Fischer. In the winter of 1862-63 German theatrical performances were staged here under Alexander Pfeiffer's direction. In succeeding years the theater society, known as "Casino," presented plays on this stage.

In about the middle of the block was a candy shop and restaurant managed by Fritz Walter, who during the war sold out to Adolph Kleinecke. At noon a small company was accustomed to gather here regularly. It was presided over by Dr. Louis Beck. Other customers were Rudolph Finkelnburg, an older brother of G. A. Finkelnburg, the brothers Hermann and William Giesecke, the invalided Captain Max Goeden, A. O. Engelmann, Thomas Meiniger and others. Animated discussions often detained this company for hours.

In the adjoining house was Hermann Achenbach's toy shop. Achenbach was the brother of the Duesseldorf painter, and so the uncle of the singer Alvary. A few doors farther to the west was a similar business, managed by Bruening & Wehrkamp. Between these two toy shops was Ferdinand Singer's wallpaper business, and the wine shop of the Ochsner brothers. In one of the adjoining buildings, C. Theodore Uhlmann had his abstract of title office. Later he moved to a site between Fourth and Fifth Streets. His successor was his long time partner, Joseph Wachtel. Nearby were the printing shop of H. Ruppelt, and also the meeting place of the Orpheus. Lange & Sennewald's drug store occupied the southeast corner of Third and Market. This firm had for a long time the agency of the Hamburg Steamship Line. In 1865, Wm. C. Lange left the drug firm, to devote himself exclusively to the European passenger and packet transportation. In the course of time there developed a banking business from this business which later grew into an International Bank. The latter was for several years located next to the drug store. The drug business had been almost entirely in the hands of F. Sennewald from the beginning. Because of ill health the latter then turned the business over to his clerk, Hugo Krebs. From 1860 to 1864 the *Westliche Post* was located over the drug store. Three years after the founding of the paper, in the summer of 1860, Carl Daenzer sold the paper to Theodore Olshausen and Henry Lischer. (The latter has been publishing the *Davenport Democrat* for about thirty years.) After the latter left the firm, Olshausen had E. W. Hemann as a partner for a while. Then the *Post* passed into the possession of Arthur Olshausen and Theodore Plate, whom Emil Preetorius joined in 1864 as part owner and editor, after the *Neue Zeit*, which had been published by the latter, had been fused with the *Westliche Post*. Under Olshausen and Lischer, respectively Hemann, a single room housed the editorial department, the local department and the desk of the translator of dispatches. (In those days the translators did not have as much work as they have today.) For the business office a small room, with one window, sufficed for the one desk. In the third story the typesetters were at work. Night after night the forms with the type were taken on a wheelbarrow to Pine Street, next door to DeBar's Theater, where the printing shop of Joseph Waite was located and where the paper was printed. From the corner of Third to the corner of Fifth is a distance of only two short blocks, but how many miles of progress in every direction lie between the *Westliche Post* of 1864 and the same paper of today.

During the second half of the sixties, Dr. Hugo Kinner had his office over the already-mentioned drug store. He had participated as physician in the Scheswig-Holstein war. After his arrival in St. Louis he had at first an office in the southwestern part of the city.

On the north side of the Concert Hall block, opposite Kleinecke's confection shop, Charles P. Chouteau, in 1865, built a number of substantial houses between the house of the tobacco dealer Keyser and the alley.

In the corner building of this row of houses two daily newspapers were born, but they lived only for a short while. One of them was called *Die Neue Welt*. It turned out to be an expensive proposition for the owner, and after a few years was changed to the *Missouri Staatszeitung*. Early in the seventies it ceased publication. In the course of time these two papers had the following editors: Carl Roeser, H. Binder, C. Rotteck, E. Schierenberg, and Robert J. Rombauer.

During the first three years of the war there was, on the corner of Third and Market, a tavern that had all the characteristics of a low dive. The owner was Mike Sutter, Jr., the son of good parents, who brought neither pleasure nor honor to his parents. At the time establishments of that kind did good business. The regiments that passed through St. Louis brought much business to this place, which was often the scene of debauch and bloody fights. After Sutter moved out of the place, Florian Mueller opened a hotel, the Prescott House, there. Nearby this corner house, G. Helmrich had a tobacco business in the fifties. For a considerable time he also had a cigar store on Chestnut Street. Later this was managed by his brother.

The St. Clair Hotel on the corner diagonally across was originally called National Hotel, and was considered the finest in the city. But that was a long time ago, and in the meantime it has undergone many changes. During the fifties Henry Boernstein and S. Jacoby were the owners, and they changed the name to the Germania Hotel. It had the most elegant café which was frequented only by the best public. Later this place was called the Merchants Hotel, which during the later sixties was for a time managed by Valentine Gerber.

During the fifties and early sixties Alexander Frankenthal had a little corner store on Market Street. This store had only one door and one window. Here he sold men's furnishings at wholesale and retail. Then he moved to Main Street where he managed an exclusive wholesale store. By and by this business was expanded so that for some time now the firm of A. Frankenthal & Bros. has manufactured and sold its goods in its palatial store on Washington Avenue.

Another firm that started on a small scale and which today is one of the most important in its line is that of L. Baumann & Co. The founder of the business, the late Louis Baumann, had, in the early sixties, a store on the south side of Market between Third and Fourth Streets. This shop was just large enough for a short counter, a couple of show cases and an iron safe, in which Baumann locked his small stock of silver and gold watches for the night. At the only window of the shop sat young Kurzeborn and repaired and cleaned watches. Now Kurzeborn has for a long time been a member of the firm which stands at the head of the wholesale business in watches, gold and silver ware. Christian Wiszmann's book bindery occupied the site formerly used by Baumann, having moved from their earlier location on South Third Street, between Market and Walnut.

A few houses farther west was the porcelain and glass store of Joseph Arendes, a brother of our fellow citizen Fritz Arendes. The adjoining house has contained Leonhard's confection store for twenty-eight years.

This business was established in 1865 by Conrad A. Leonhard and his brother-in-law, Theodore Jahreisz, who was a clever confectioner. Leonhard was a printer by trade, and published a paper of which the present probate judge, Woerner, was the editor. Jahreisz died a few years after the beginning of the business, but by that time Leonhard had acquired sufficient information to carry the business on successfully.

During the fifties the following German businesses were already in this block: the watchmaker and jeweler, Anton Schubert; the lace makers Axt & Schacht (later the Schacht brothers); the maker of mathematical instruments, George Winzer; the bandage maker, Charles Schleiffarth; and after him, Phillip Werber in the same business; and over the drugstore on the southeast corner of Fourth street, the photographers Hoelke & Benecke; on the ground floor, Alexander's drug store; and the porcelain and glass store of Walter Bergner, who is now on Fourth Street, opposite the courthouse.

When General Fremont went to war from here in 1861 he was in need of a chef for himself and his officers. Such a one he found in old man Dahlmann. After his return he was for a while chef at the Rheinische Weinhalle. However, in the autumn of 1862, he opened a restaurant of his own on Market Street, between Third and Fourth. The front window displayed these words: "Hier wird auch Deutsch gesprochen." (Here German is also spoken.) One of the regular customers at this place was the hydropath, Theodore Kroschel, who had an hydropathic institute on Elm, near Third Street. Another regular guest was the notary Vermann, whose deep bass voice could be heard for half a block. In 1863 Dahlmann took the Swabian countryman, Sylvester Beck, who formerly had been a tailor, as partner. When Dahlmann passed away in 1865 Beck continued the business for some time, when he sold out and returned to Germany. Then Louis Haber managed the place for many years.

In addition to the two daily papers mentioned above another morning paper was started during the later sixties, which was also short-lived. This was the *Volks-Zeitung* published by Ernest W. Hemann. Its place of publication was at first the corner of Third and Pine Streets, and later on Market Street, near the Landesoberst restaurant. In later years this locality housed the office and composing room of the *Laterne*, which was edited and published by Louis Willich. A narrow room with only one window, situated on the ground floor served as the office of the *Volks-Zeitung*.

Persons who came to insert an ad, or even a notice of a death always treated the clerk, who took the item, to a glass of beer. Of course the number of ads was not very great in those days. However, it was nevertheless a bad habit that prevailed in certain circles, German as well as non-German, to invite newspaper men to take a drink as soon as one caught sight of them. Those who declined such an invitation were considered proud and haughty.

In the same block and on the same side, George Scharmann had his bookbindery and store of writing material. Until 1862 he had his store on Third Street, between Market and Chestnut. His main business consisted of reading material brought in from other parts. Above all it was the *New Yorker Criminalzeitung*, which later assumed the name, *Belletristisches Journal*. For a long time Scharmann was the sole agent for this journal, and the number of subscribers is said to have been more than eight hundred at one time. Most of the subscribers came to get their copy from his place of business. On the days when new issues arrived there was a tremendous crowd in his store. Today the *Belletristische Journal*, just as the *Leipziger Gartenlaube*, the *Daheim*, etc., has here and in other cities of the West only a few subscribers. The amount and richness of entertaining material which the Sunday editions of the German American newspapers offer their readers have replaced the other journals.

Under Fletcher's administration, Scharmann was the state bookbinder in Jefferson City. Influential St. Louisians had secured the appointment for him. However, he died long before the expiration of his term of office.

When, in 1850 and 1851, Jenny Lind, under Barnum's management, made her great concert tour through the United States, she sang here in Wymann's Hall, which was directly east of Freund's confection shop, opposite the courthouse. The price of admission to this concert was five dollars. That was too great a sum for the pockets of many friends of music, so that they had to forego the pleasure of hearing the Swedish nightingale. Some young fellows, however, heard the concert free of charge. Since it was summer and all the windows were open, they risked their necks in climbing to the flat roofs of adjoining buildings, and listened with devotion to songs of the great artist.

The grand reception of Ludwig Kossuth, the Hungarian revolutionary hero, also took place in Wymann's Hall. This reception was given during Kossuth's brief visit here in 1851.

The German Element in St. Louis

Edward Wyman, who died a few years ago in Alton, was the director of a private school for boys. This school had the rather pompous name of City University. Wyman was the owner of Wyman Hall. In this hall he established a museum in imitation of Mr. Barnum, the most varied assortment of natural curiosities, all sorts of living and stuffed birds, and as his greatest curiosity a skeleton of an antediluvian monster, the Zeuchlodons, which had been discovered by Dr. Koch. The museum was open to visitors day and night. After it had existed for a few years it lost its power of attraction for St. Louisians, and the visits by outsiders were so few that the expenses exceeded the income. The owner then sold all the things contained in the museum.

The new owner of the building, Thomas L. Price in Jefferson City–a good Union man, and not to be confused with his uncle, the Southern General, Stirling Price–had the interior rebuilt into a pretty theater. This was leased by William Koser, and in the autumn of 1864 was opened as the German municipal theater. As such it continued for two years. The local company had some fine artists who were supplemented by artists from New York, Milwaukee and from abroad. In April 1866 a fire destroyed the interior of the building, after which there were no more performances.

Jacob Blattner was the first optician who established himself in St. Louis. His office and workshop were for many years in the above building. In the next building to the west was the confection store of Christian Freund, and later that of Paul Adam. During the later sixties the two stories above the confection store were leased by the Harmonic Club. Later this organization moved into a building on Fourth, near Myrtle Street, which George Knapp had recently built. The rooms that had been used by the Harmonic Club on Market Street were changed into a hotel, the Loewenstein Hotel. The dry goods merchants, Donegan & Co., during the sixties, occupied the site where Jacob M. Gruen has now had his tavern for many years. Caffaretts's fruit store, which was fully described in the chapter that dealt with South Fifth Street, was moved and a four-story building was erected on the site. Into it moved the German Bank. The German Fire Insurance Co. occupied the second story. The president of the bank was A. Krieckhaus. The president of the insurance company was Dr. Frederick Hill, a member of the real estate firm of Hill & Hammel of Carondelet, and the secretary was Henry Hiemenz, which position has now

The German Element in St. Louis 117

been held for many years by Willam K. Walther. Subsequently the International Bank occupied the place which the German Bank had had.

The site which today is occupied by the Grand Opera House has been devoted to theatrical purposes since 1852. At first the building erected here was called the Varieties Theater. For a few years performances in the English language were given here. The income did not come up to expectation, and so the theater was closed. The Philodramatic Society, a theatrical organization, which Henry Boernstein brought into existence, and which his untiring zeal and great knowledge of the stage, as director and as actor, made successful, occasionally gave performances in the Varieties during the years 1856 to 1859. After deduction of the absolute expenses, the income from performances was, without exception, given to benevolent organizations. The actors contributed their work free of charge to the cause.

The income of the first performance was given to the German Immigration Society. The German Women's Club, the German Institute, the Samaritan Hospital, which was the fruit of Reverend Nollau's efforts, and Humbolt Institute, founded by Dr. Hammer, were the recipients of other performances.

The students of this medical school were naturally very much interested in the financial success of this performance. For propaganda purposes they drove through the streets, dressed like European students, in full dress, student caps, fraternity insignia, and boots with tops turned down. Thus attired they distributed handbills and sold tickets.

Among those who were particularly active in this cause was August Siegmund Boernstein, who shared his father's interest in medical science. He had laid aside his work as a printer, and had resolved to become a physician. The war stopped the lectures at Humboldt Institute. Upon his return from the service Siegmund Boernstein again devoted himself to his first love. Soon thereafter he obtained an appointment in the federal printing office in Washington. Later he accepted a call from the Khedive to come to Cairo to organize the Egyptian state printing bureau. Since then he has for a number of years occupied an important position in the bureau of labor in the United States.

In the autumn of 1859 Henry Boernstein leased the Varieties Theater with the firm intent of providing for our city a stable stage that should be worthy of the German element. Truly it was not his fault that this enterprise, which had such an auspicious beginning, should so soon come to an end.

During the later sixties George Diegle leased the Opera House, and for a few years met with great success. The beauty of the scenery and costumes exceeded anything that had been seen here. So it was possible that pieces, completely without content, such as "The Black Crook" and "The Green Huntsman" could play without interruption before capacity houses for eight and ten months.

Diegle's success, which, however, decreased in time, so that he became bankrupt, had encouraged Billy Carroll, the owner of an ordinary dance hall, to become Diegle's competitor. He opened Carroll's Varieties, directly east of Diegle's place. Carroll's Varieties may be regarded as the forerunner of the present realistic school, as the so-called actresses endeavored to do their utmost in naked reality.

The business of Klein & Friton was, during the middle sixties, already the *Westliche Post* building. A few doors farther west, where now Grimminger's cigar store is, was the dry goods store of the Gundlach Brothers. On the other side, in the same block, was Phillip Nuernberger's tavern, a favorite gathering place for elderly citizens. Later this place was called the Conrad House, after a later owner. On the north side of the next block was, at the end of the fifties, the Germania House. During the first year of the war it ceased to exist, and the new manager converted it into a place that had a bad reputation. On the opposite side was George Wiegand's stove and tin business. As early as the fifties the candy factory of the Blanke Brothers was also here. Of course, it was not yet the extensive business which it became in the later decades.

On the southeast corner of Seventh and Market Streets stood the Chouteau Mansion, which since that time has been made almost unrecognizable by additions and changes. Along Seventh Street extended the garden belonging to this property. It was surrounded by a seven-foot wall. On the garden side a broad porch extended the full length of the building along the second story. In the winter it was used as a sort of greenhouse. When Pierre Chouteau, Jr., the father of Charles P., had this house built for himself, it was regarded as a modern house that afforded every comfort. Mrs. Chouteau, a native Parisian, known for her hospitality, had equipped it with the most solid elegance. She died in 1863, and her husband, who for many years was completely blind, survived her by less than three years. After his demise the household was broken up. Among the various renters of the old house, and also another house which was built in the former garden were the baker, H. Block, and William Fischer, who for many years had a restaurant here.

On the south side between Seventh and Eighth Streets was the shop of the watchmaker and goldsmith, Julius Link, who was known far and wide for the fine hairwork that he made. Equally well known were his neighbors, the dyer Vallat, and the basket weaver Ernest Behne. On the north side the brothers Kreming had their lumberyard, during the fifties, at the corner of Eighth Street. Hazard and Wilson had their coal yard in the middle of the block. And where now the Masonic Hall stands there was from 1861 to 1865 John H. Andrew's lumber yard. On May 30, 1865 the cornerstone of the Masonic Hall was laid, and in the following year the building was dedicated. The great ceremonies were attended by members of the order who had come from all parts of the country.

The lower story of the Masonic Hall was occupied by the Jefferson Insurance Company. Earlier the Mechanics Savings Institution was located there.

In former years the large hall in the Masonic building was leased for all sorts of festivities. For example the charity ball, staged each year by the police department, was held here. A very mixed crowd was accustomed to attend this affair each year. This hall also brings up special memories to the German element. When in 1870 at the mass-meeting at the courthouse it was decided to raise a million dollars for the wounded of the German army and the families of those who had fallen in the French-German war, the German women of St. Louis also wanted to do their part. A committee was organized, and this committee arranged a fair which ran for a whole week. In Europe such an affair would be called a bazaar. Many thousands of dollars were taken in. From this it can be seen what a lively interest was taken in this affair. In the upper rooms the ladies had provided a restaurant where food and drink was sold to swell the contributions to this benevolent purpose. On the last evening of the fair, a ball was staged. Many of my readers will recall with pleasure the part they had in this extremely successful fair.

While on Market Street, between the Levee and Seventh Street many things have changed in the course of time, from there on west most things have remained as they were. A considerable part of the real estate belongs to old German citizens, who have always been inclined to be conservative, and so only a few new houses have been built here during the last decades. One of these was built by John Nies, on the south side, between Eighth and Ninth Street, in the same block where forty years ago he began to manipulate needle and shears as a tailor. Now he has been for many years the owner of an extensive merchant tailor establishment. A few doors to the west was Frederick Kaltmeyer's hosiery store. At the end of the block where Druid Hall now stands, John Simonds, the partner of James H. Lucas, lived at the beginning of the fifties. The house faced Walnut Street and was situated on an elevation. There was on the southeast corner of Ninth and Market a garden. During the later fifties the theater director converted it into a summer garden, which was well patronized by the students of Humboldt Institute. This medical college, by the way, was first situated on Ninth Street, separated from Druid Hall by an alley. Later it was transferred to Flora Garden on Geyer Avenue, and finally to the corner of Soulard Street, opposite the hospital, where it ceased to exist. In the middle of the fifties it had been organized, according to German model, by Dr. Hammer, Dr. George Bernays, Dr. Ernest Schmidt and a few other eminent physicians. Soon after the beginning of the war lectures ceased. During the middle sixties an attempt was made to reorganize the institute, but without success. Nevertheless, some of our ablest and best-known physicians had their training in Humboldt Institute.

During the first half of the fifties Lange & Sennewald had their drug store on the north side of this block. However, it was not the only drug store in this block, for what is now Moster's drug store at that time belonged to Dr. Baumgarten, and on the south side Dr. Hickey also had a drug store. The present Geyer House was, during the fifties, known as Timmermann's boarding house. The watchmaker Franz Wendl had his business in this block for many years before he moved into the next block. Wendl was in the habit of writing poems of occasions for his friends. Since the sixties, the stove and tin business of Otto Schmidt occupied the site where Wendl held forth. Wendl was one of the most enthusiastic members of Socialen Saengerchors.

Two other persons, well known in singing societies, were the saddle maker, Henry J. Alles, and the saddle maker, Julius fGroszenheider. Their workshops and stores were between Ninth and Tenth Streets. The former was one of the founders of the old St. Louis Saengerbund, and the latter an enthusiastic member of the Orpheus. Groszenheider's brother, Charles, who previously owned the business, lost his life, near the end of the fifties, as a result of a peculiar accident. He had put a new harness on the horse of a customer. In order to see if the harness was properly adjusted, he decided to ride along a piece of the way. A few blocks from the store the owner of the horse and buggy stopped to attend some purchases. Groszenheider remained in the buggy. A wagon, loaded with stones came by and collided with the buggy, lifting it off the ground. Groszenheider jumped, fell on the sidewalk and injured his foot in such a manner that tetanus set in, which took is life. A few doors west of Henry Alles' saddle shop, William Hirt had a furniture business during the fifties. After the war he opened a grocery store on Seventh and Elm Streets. When near the end of the seventies Druid Hall was built, he moved into it.

The old square box which is honored with the name of City Hall, between Market and Chestnut, stands on a site which was formerly a lumber yard. For the same business the site on the southeast corner of Twelfth was used, where now the public tobacco storehouse stands. The owner of this property is Christian Peper, one of the oldest and most respected businessmen of our city, who is also the owner of the well known tobacco factory on Main and Morgan Streets.

On Eleventh Street was the sodawater factory of John Cairns, a splendid Scot, who for many years was an able member of the city council. His successors in business were H. Grone & Co., who have greatly expanded the business. The square which was bordered by Market and Clark Streets, between Twelfth and Thirteenth Streets, where in the future the city hall will stand, was called Washington Square. It was intended to be a park, but as it was treated like a stepchild by the park commissioners, it became the loafing place of all sorts of idlers and tramps, which, perhaps, strange as it may seem, were attracted by the Four Courts and the jail. Instead of being an ornament it was very much neglected and a disgrace to the city that passengers coming from Union Depot should see this sort of thing, and that it should be called a city park. Opposite this park, on the north side of Market Street was the lumber yard of Jacob Luthy and William Druhe. Later on this business was continued by the latter alone and transferred to Clark Avenue.

The steam driven mill, which was operated for many years by the millionaire merchant Kaufmann, on the corner of Thirteen and Market, was in earlier times known as The Park Mills. At first it was owned by John F. Tolle, then by Buckland & Co., and later by Stanard & Kaufmann. On Fourteenth Street was for a long time Lindenschidt's grocery store, and near the southwest corner Steller's piano store. Since the fifties Joseph A. Bauer's great bakery has been in this block and opposite, on the south side, was formerly Caspar and Charles Soeding's hardware store. Between Seventeenth and Eighteenth there was, during the first half of the sixties, William Otto's piano factory. Otto was a bachelor who lived entirely for art. After years of contemplation and experimentation he had made a kind of upright grand piano, which in beauty and power of tone was not inferior to the best grand piano of that time. However, though the invention brought the maker praise it did not pay him in a material way.

The Union Brewery (better known as Winkelmeyer's) beginning on the southwest corner of Seventeenth and Market and extending almost to Eighteenth Street, was established in 1845 by Frederick Stifel and Julius Winkelmeyer. Frederick was the older brother of Charles G. and Christoph A. Stifel. The latter was an expert brewer. Winkelmeyer, who till then had been a clerk under Boeschenstein on Main Street, knew nothing about brewing, but he was a very popular person, and so looked after the business of the concern. Business was good, since the product continued to be excellent even after the demise of Stifel, which occurred during the middle fifties. Winkelmeyer married the sister of his partner. As a memorial to his former associate he caused a marble slab with a suitable inscription to be placed at the entrance to the ice cellar of the brewery. When in the middle sixties, Winkelmeyer passed away, a similar marble slab and inscription were placed beside that of Stifel. After the death of her husband, Mrs. Christiane Winkelmeyer continued the business, being assisted by her brother, C. A. Stifel, and her son-in-law, A. W. Straub, who for years has now been president of the International Bank.

The office as well as the stables and car barn of the Market Street Railway were in the immediate neighborhood. The president and chief owner of this line was Erastus Wells. For many years he was a member of the city council and twice its chairman, then he was elected to Congress. Naturally he had his strongest following in this part of the city, for he was at the same time part owner and president of the Olive Street Railway.

Prior to elections Winkelmeyer's tavern was a busy place. Alfred Henry, who was not only superintendent of Wells' street car line, but also his brother-in-law and campaign manager, was there almost every day. He was an extremely jolly fellow and a good mixer. Ward meetings and pre-primary meetings of various parties were held here, and occasionally conflicts between factions occurred.

In the early fifties Joseph Uhrig built the Camp Spring Brewery between Eighteenth and Nineteenth Street. He was not a brewer by profession but his partner Kraul was. Many years after Kraul's death the brewery came into the hands of the Excelsior Brewing Co. Caspar Koehler and Peter Saussenthaler, who substantially added to the physical plant. Later these buildings were removed to make room for the new Union depot. The brewery was united with that of the Winkelmeyers. Caspar Koehler retired, and his sons Charles and Julius and his son-in-law Rudolph Limberg founded the Columbia Brewery.

Widow Knecht was a well known personality, not only in St. Louis but beyond the city. She had an inn and stables between Twentieth and Twenty-first Streets. Here farmers and vegetable gardeners were accustomed to stop, who came via Manchester Road. Many of them were accustomed to arrive with their teams in the evening and spend the night there. But also from greater distances strangers were accustomed to stop here, as for instance from Washington and Hermann, who came on horseback or by wagon, for the Missouri Pacific had not yet been built.

Further on were the great stockyards, which contained at times more than a thousand head of live stock. At that time there were no stockyards in East St. Louis, and also few railroads that could haul stock from Texas in three days. Also great herds of mules were kept in the large enclosures. When these animals were driven on a run through the city, the pedestrian was in great danger of being run down. In like manner, beef cattle were driven through the streets. It is not so long ago that an end was put to this nuisance by a city ordinance.

19. Frenchtown

Not only in the last decades but even in the fifties, one was justified in calling that part of the city which is known as Frenchtown, Germantown, for the same reason that one accustomed to call a part of New York "Little Germany."

There was a time when the name Frenchtown was applicable not only to this part of the city. That was the time prior to the influx of the great German immigration at the close of the forties and the beginning of the fifties. Up to that time the French population of our city, which at the outset had only Frenchmen as settlers, extended almost exclusively from Walnut Street to the southern limits of the city of that time. Street names such as Lesperance, Duchouquette, Lafayette, Soulard, Gratiot, Labadie, LaSalle, Chouteau, etc., testify most clearly, that the French element at one time predominated in this region.

Where Frenchtown, geographically speaking, began, is hard to say. In general it was and is claimed that Park Avenue was the northern border. But with no less right Chouteau Avenue may be regarded as such. It must be assumed that the French Market, which is close to this street, was within the limits of so-called Frenchtown. In spite of the fact that for some years one of the streets has been officially called South Broadway, it will continue for a long time to be popularly known as Carondelet Avenue, which was its old name. In the same manner the road running south from it is still known as Carondelet Road. Who knows how many generations will pass before the people will cease to call this part of the city, Carondelet, though this little town was incorporated in the city of St. Louis in 1870. The old French settlers of St. Louis had a rather unneighborly nickname for this suburb. They called it Vide Poche, empty pocket, probably because the farmers and vegetable gardeners of this region often came with empty pockets when they wanted to make purchases in St. Louis.

Carondelet Avenue was the main street of the entire southern part of the city when the German immigrants took possession. It was a peaceful conquest, quite in harmony with the peaceful character of the Frenchtown Germans. They left everyone in peace who left them alone. This peace was interrupted only once in the course of half a century. That was in the storm and stress period of 1861, when the citizens took up arms for the protection of the city and state for the preservation of the Union.

The phrase: "Whoever can speak German can get along all right in Belleville," can be just as well applied to Frenchtown as to our friendly neighboring city in Illinois. This was still more the case in the fifties and sixties, for at that time one could wander from Chouteau Avenue as far as the Arsenal without hearing anything else than German. By and by this became different, of course. The growing German American youth brought English home from the school and the playground. Now for a long time young Americans of German ancestry, even in this the most German part of our city, prefer to speak the language of their adopted fatherland.

Customs and usages have, however, remained German. The traveler who but a few days before has disembarked from a Bremen or Hamburg steamer will find, even today, in Frenchtown much that reminds him of home. There no immoderate haste and hurry prevails. People do not hurry unless they have to. They go to work deliberately, but then demonstrate the proverbial German diligence and perseverance. They still find time to enjoy life. In the old days one took things even more easily than in our day. There existed no street cars at that time. If one was in a hurry, he made use of the omnibus. It required, a rather long time to get to Market Street. If one undertook to go on foot to the courthouse, he took leave of wife and child as if he started a real journey. Frequently he did not get back till afternoon or even till evening. Conventional formality was then disregarded even more than today. One went for blocks without his coat, and on hot summer days even without his vest, and without neckcloth and collar.

There was no lack of taverns in Frenchtown during the fifties. Because the streets were usually quiet one could hear at some distance when a new keg of beer was opened. (At that time the beer was not yet lifted from the cask by means of an air pump.) When the familiar sound of opening a keg was heard, work was dropped in order to get a fresh glass of the new tapping. Between ten and eleven o'clock in the forenoon the tavern-keeper would step outside of his place and ring a bell or strike a Chinese gong to announce that lunch was being served. If there was a particularly juicy piece of roast beef or a good veal roast, one also took a sandwich of these good things home to his wife.

In the matter sociability the inhabitants of Frenchtown set a good example. German club and society life in its midst took root early. On Sundays great crowds, young and old, were accustomed to wander to the parks and gardens, which in the good old times were the rendezvous for German families. Also a large number of lodges–Harugaris, Sons of Hermann, Red Men, Odd Fellows, etc., –at an early time fostered social life.

The southern part of the city has at this time only two rather large market houses. One of these, French Market, is properly called Convent Market. It does not belong to the city but it is the property of a private corporation, which was organized near the end of the thirties, in order to erect a market house north of Convent Street, on the open lot which results from the convergence of Fourth and Fifth Streets. The undertaking proved to be of great benefit for the surrounding region. The owners of the stores opposite the market house, and in the block between the convent and Rutger Street, as also between the latter and Hickory Street derived great advantage from the proximity of the market. Therefore, they were quite willing to put up with the inconvenience that accrued from the vegetable and other stands that in uninterrupted row lined both sides of the street. The lively traffic of the market naturally brought the stores many customers. And even the smallest stand on the street paid well the man, or more correctly, the woman that owned it.

The buildings of the aforesaid region, or at least the ground on which they stand, are for the greater part even now the property of the convent of the Sacred Heart, whose cloister buildings occupy the west side of Fifth as far as Sixth Street, and between Labadie and Hickory Streets. Since 1872 these buildings are practically unused. In 1827 Judge Mullanphy presented the real estate in question to this order of nuns, which many years before had come from France, and which in nearby Florissant had conducted a school for girls. The income from this property, which for many years was quite considerable, was expected to pay for the establishment of the educational institution and to cover its maintenance. The only condition imposed in this generous gift, was this, that the sisters must at all times give free instruction to twenty orphan girls. The buildings of the convent were increased from year to year, and served their intended purpose for more than forty years, till the transfer of the institution to one of the most beautiful parts of St. Louis with rural surroundings. From the old convent the street opposite it received its name (rue du convent), and also the market was named after it. For a long time the business in the latter was very lively. This was accelerated when the Soulard Market, which was a few blocks farther to the south, between Seventh and Eighth Streets, deteriorated to such an extent that not only many of the meat stands but also many of the vegetable stands were left in the lurch by the customers. Naturally this helped the Convent Market greatly until, thanks to the efforts of the businessmen in the region of Soulard Market, changes were made which directed a traffic in that direction and stimulated business in the entire region.

Frenchtown may boast to have had the first and only public bath house that St. Louis had. This pleasure, however, was of brief duration. Among the many fine services with which Mayor Thomas is credited –term of office, 1864 to 1868 – was the establishment of a public bath house. In it, adults could get a bath for ten cents, and children for five cents. At this price soap and towel were included. This public bath house was unfortunately kept open only for a few years. The lively patronage shows how necessary such an institution is. The one in question was located next to the southwest corner of Fifth Street and Chouteau Avenue. Since then a quarter of a century has passed, and the number of population has more than doubled, but all efforts to meet this urgent need have failed. All this in spite of the fact that the Americans glibly say that "cleanliness is Godliness."

On the corner itself there was, during the middle sixties, the workshop of the sculptor R. H. Follenius. Later he moved farther west on Chouteau Avenue. A few years later Gustav Cramer and Julius Grosz erected a photograph studio in the upper rooms of a house on Fourth Street near Rutger. Also Scholten's gallery was at one time in the same block, on the corner of Convent Street, over the business of the Lager Brothers, one of the oldest merchant tailor firms in the city. In the same block there were, also thirty years ago, the drygoods stores of Emanuel & Co., and Buddecke & Droege, also the stove and tinner business of Valentine Fath, William Sichers drygoods store, and the millinery store of Julia Adler (formerly Fuerth), Caroline Schwarz, L. Magnus and Josephine Fuerth. In the midst of these businesses was Brandtstetter's bakery, John Wamsganz's shoe store and Biedenstein's grocery. Some time later Otto Kerner's drygoods business and Phillip Burgh's grocery were added.

Further south, in the same block, was the porcelain dealer Moritz, who then moved to the block to the north, next to Metzger's drug store, which formerly, during the fifties, had been on Carondelet near Russell Avenue. Toward Rutger Street was Charles Beckmann's toy store, whose successor was Franz Scharwitz. There were also, at the beginning of the sixties, Schroth's wallpaper business and the hat store of Michael Goettler. At the corner, where now John Becker, the successor of Stoffregen, has his grocery store, was J. Koperlick and Loewenstein's haberdashery. On the opposite corner on Hickory Street, old and, one might add, stout Mr. Mentrup had a grocery store. A few doors farther was the dry goods store of Henry and John Neun (father and son), whom Jacob Stumpf later joined as partner. Out of this partnership subsequently two separate businesses developed, the John Neun & Co., dry goods, and J. Stumpf, carpets. On the corner of Short St. and Joseph Street, Emil Lange had his drug store during the sixties, which then for a number of years became the property of Dr. Charles Neubert and his brother Adolph. On the other side of this little street was Wibbermann's grocery store. The tavern of Francis P. Becker was at that time owned by John Neff, and near by was a branch business of The Monkeys, managed by J. S. Schandelmeyer. In this way famous monkey punch was also introduced in Frenchtown. Diagonally across the street was Stumpf's tavern. Its owner was a breeder of the finest breed of dogs, and as such known far and wide. Later this place was managed by Phillip Carl, who by profession was a musician, an excellent violin player. His place was much frequented by the older musicians and by the guild of newspaper writers. Then came George Fehl, the maker of the famous Blue Ribbon cigars, and Schnurmacher's merchant tailor shop.

Frenchtown has always had a large number of good taverns, and yet one rarely sees a drunk person in this region. Beer is not as intoxicating as whiskey or wine.

Between Rutger Street and Park Avenue few changes have occurred during many decades. There was the tinner Tirmenstein, the maker of instruments Boulanger, and Marie Boulanger, who dressed the hair of ladies for weddings, balls and other extraordinary occasions, and also sold patterns for embroidery and embroidery itself. Blank's drug store was established at the beginning of the seventies, but prior to that Dr. Charles Bank's office had occupied the same site in the late fifties. Bender's grocery store was there also at that time. A few doors farther was Brinkmann's livery stable, which was later transferred to Park Avenue, and subsequently taken over by Meyer and Stuessel.

The Underwriters Fire-engine House was one of the first that was established after the organization of paid fire companies. It housed the engine and the horses. It was a great day for Frenchtown when the crew entered its quarters. For many years no winter passed without at least one ball being arranged by the firemen in the upper story of the engine house.

Many of my lady readers will recall the time with pleasure when they danced at the Underwriters ball on Washington's birthday or at New Years.

The justifiable desire to have a bank in their own part of the city led to the organization of such an institution in 1856. It was financed by a number of German's in Frenchtown, who were joined by the capitalist, Thomas Allen. The latter had much real estate in the southern part of the city (Allen's addition). The First Ward Savings Institution was opened in the above named year. Over its door was also written in large letters; Erste Ward Sparkasse. The first president was Thomas Allen himself and Robert J. Rombauer, the former county assessor, was the cashier. The bank location was on the corner of Carondelet and Russell Avenue. The whole furnishings cost eighty-seven dollars and fifty-nine cents, therefore about as much as nowadays a chair of a higher bank official would cost. Even later, when the bank was transferred to the block between Park Avenue and Barry Street, the furnishings remained very modest. Only when the institution was transferred to the triangular building which now houses the Lafayette Bank, more attention was paid to the furnishings of the office.

In 1862 the First Ward Savings Institution was changed to the First National Bank of St. Louis. F. W. Cronenbold was its president and Peter Weisz the cashier. This bank flourished to a marked degree, for during the war much money was made by the purchase of vouchers on the federal treasury. The contractors who provided provisions, fodder, uniforms, boots, shoes, tinware, etc., for the army, horses for the cavalry, and mules for the pack trains continually needed money. Since the payment for the vouchers came slowly, they did not mind a very high discount. The strict regulations regarding loans governing the national banks, in the course of time proved burdensome, and for this reason the bank was changed and made to operate under the laws of the state of Missouri. It was now given the name of the Empire Bank.

An episode which caused the directors of the First national Bank much inconvenience and which will be recalled by all older readers, may be mentioned here. During the war it was certainly a justifiable practice to hoist the stars and stripes on flag poles that were set up at various places. On the open space at the north side of the Convent Market House, between the latter and the police station, then located there, such a flag pole was erected in 1864. Some time later the same thing was done at the place where Park and Carondelet Avenues converge. The erection of such a pole and the hoisting of the flag always brought the whole neighborhood out, for speeches were made and a bank played the Star Spangled Banner and other patriotic airs. In short it was a formal occasion.

The firemen of the nearby engine house punctually attended to the raising of the flag at daybreak, and the lowering of the same at the approach of darkness and during rainy weather. It was an enormous flag, and when it fluttered high in the breezes, young and old looked with pride and joy at the emblem of the Union. Only for the gentlemen of the First National Bank the great pole was a source of annoyance. It was set only a few feet from the narrow front of the building, and at the bottom was more than two feet thick, so that it certainly did not add to the beauty of the building. At the meetings of the directors the removal of the pole was sometimes discussed, but wisely enough no action was taken.

One morning, after a dark and stormy night, only a small part of the pole remained standing. Woodsmen had felled it. The indignation of the citizens, particularly in Carondelet Avenue, knew no bounds. And when it became known that Bernhard Heidacker, who at that time was the vice president of the bank, had something to do with the felling, public indignation concentrated entirely on him. The fact that he was a stout Democrat doubtless contributed much to this resentment. Thoughtful heads, who hoped to avoid worse action, succeeded in having the indignation of the crowd expressed in a noisy serenade and a few broken window panes in his residence. The part of the pole that had been cut down was on the next day wrapped in black crepe, and hauled through the main streets of South St. Louis. A band marched in front of it and alternately played funeral marches and patriotic airs.

During the later fifties the Peoples Savings Institution was organized. Its first president was Bartholomew Reis. Emil Ulrici was chosen cashier, but during the war gave up this position. This bank was located in its own building at the northwest corner of Carondelet and Park Avenue. The bank stopped its payments during the first half of the seventies. At the public sale by the assignee, John H. Fisse, the property was bought by William C. Lange, the president of the International Bank. Originally Lange had contemplated establishing a branch banking business there, but after mature consideration abandoned the plan, as at that time there was no lack of banking facilities in this region. In 1870 the Carondelet Avenue Bank had been created, with John Paul as president and Fritz Leser as cashier. A year

The German Element in St. Louis 131

later the Lafayette Bank was organized whose first president was Michael Helmbacher, and William Kossak the cashier. The last-named bank was at first on the southwest corner of Carroll Street and Carondelet Avenue, where it remained for four years, whereupon it combined with the Carondelet Avenue Bank. After this union the Lafayette Bank took possession of the building that had formerly been the property of the Empire Bank. After the consolidation, Frederick Arendes was chosen president, which position he held for many years, and P. J. Doerr was the cashier.

A branch office of the German Bank was for a short while in the Hiemenz Building, at the corner of Carroll Street. This branch owed its establishment mainly to the efforts of Peter Weisz. The Iron Mountain Bank, which after an existence of several years was absorbed by the International Bank, must also be considered as one of the banks of Frenchtown, although its building was a bit farther north, on the corner of Fourth Street and Chouteau Avenue. The last president of this bank was the lumberman, August Leisse and Oscar H. Guether was the cashier of the institution, which met all of its obligations to the last cent. From all this it is obvious that during a certain period Frenchtown had more banks than were needed.

In the short block on the east side of Carondelet Avenue, which forms the beginning of the latter, and opposite Park Avenue, Andrew Geisel, who later became city treasurer had a stove and tin business during the fifties. The present owner of the store, Emil Wachter, during the later part of the sixties, had a hardware store in this block. Prior to that he had a men's clothing store farther down the avenue. In the upper story of the building two doors farther, Max Saettele made photographs, thirty years ago. Since it was the custom at that time that bridal couples had themselves photographed on their wedding day, there was always an assembly of curious women, girls and children when a few carriages drove up, from which emerged the bride, dressed in white and with a long veil, and the bridesmaids with their escorts. In the corner house on Miller Street, Dr. Faber had his drug store. Continuing on the same side, a few doors south of Miller Street, the brothers Adolph and William Bang had a grocery store in the sixties. Five decades ago Gempp's drug store was already in the middle of the same block where it is today. After the death of old Dr. Gempp his widow continued the business, whereupon it was taken over by one of her sons, Henry C. Gempp. Unfortunately he died in his best years. Another old business in this block is that of the jeweler, John Heimbach, which now has, for a quarter of a century, been located on the he corner of Miller Street. Until his transfer to South Fifth Street, Louis C. Merkel, the piano manufacturer was also located here, as was Kortjohn's grocery store.

On the southwest corner of Park Avenue, Bush and Taussing had a wholesale grocery store during the late fifties and early sixties. After them F. W. Wotke's drygoods store occupied the site. This store was the largest of its kind in this part of the city at that time. Two doors from this place was the Commercial College of Mr. Bartram, who is still teaching bookkeeping etc., and who for many years has made himself useful in the locals department of the *American*. In the next buildings were A. Niemetz' confection store, and Carl Mehl's small tavern. Then came the office and residence of Dr. Gustav Fischer, who remained there till the second half of the sixties. In the adjoining house the Anheuser family lived for a while. In the same block was August Spilker's tavern and restaurant. He could be a charming companion, but at times he had a bad temper. On one occasion he chased away his wife and daughter, who worked in the kitchen from early till late. He declared that he did not need them at all and that he "would cook himself." But he did not "cook himself" but was heartily glad that his better half returned to her post at the kitchen range.

Between Barry and Marion Streets, on the east side of the avenue, was, during the fifties, a children's paradise. It was Noel's Missouri Bakery. It was by no means the only cake bakery in this region, but its products enjoyed, far and wide, a reputation of fine quality. There were at that time several rather large grocery stores in this part of the city, but most of them were small businesses. One of the latter belonged to an honest old Low German, who was simply called John by all his acquaintances, and whom every child for many squares knew. He was a substantial businessman, but was extremely cautious in his purchases. So, for example, he never kept a large supply of coffee on hand, but rather bought each day a dollar's worth from his friend, Steinmeyer, on the corner of Third and Rutger. Occasionally he had to send a helper in the afternoon or evening to Steinmeyer for more coffee. If friends asked him why he did that, he replied that the price of coffee may go down tomorrow, and then he would make no profit if he had a supply on hand. Nowadays such methods would not do, of course, but in the so-called good old times, the housewives and cooks went to the store themselves to make purchases, and if the weight of the articles was not too great, they carried their purchases home in their baskets.

One of the most pretentious grocery businesses was that of George Gehrke, who had his store on the northeast corner of Marion Street during the fifties. In the sixties the owner played a rather important role in politics. This may have been due to the fact that he was a close friend of F. W. Cronenbold. During the latter's term of office as chairman of the County Court, the Four Courts and other county buildings were being erected or planned. Cronenbold had an iron and steel plant on the west side, not far from Marion Street, and was also a partner in the Cronenbold plowshare factory, located on South Third Street. In spite of these activities he devoted a great deal of his time to other interests, as, for example, president of the First National Bank, later the Empire Bank, as member of the city council, and during the sixties its chairman, and as member and presiding officer of the County Court, etc.

The Philharmonic tavern of Jacob Vogel, which is now on the east side, between Barry and Marion, was during the seventies diagonally across the street. Vogel's place was always the gathering place of musicians. On some days one could find the entire guild, as far as Frenchtown was concerned, assembled there. It was a sort of musicians' "bourse," such as was for some time in Schiffmann's place on the corner of Elm and Fifth Street. From the early days the southern part of the city has had far more German musicians than all the rest of St. Louis. One of the oldest and best known among them was Jacob Kost, an excellent cornetist and a real virtuoso on the snare drum. He belonged to Frank Boehm's Silver Cornet Bank, which later became the Knights Templar Bank. Even in his advanced years, in spite of his gray hair and gray mustache, he marched straight as a candle as trumpeter or drummer.

One of the best known Germans of his time was Charles W. Gottschalk. In his younger years he was a watchmaker, and on Carondelet Avenue had a jewelry store between Barry and Marion Streets. In 1859 he was elected city registrar, and then represented the second ward for several years in the city council. He was a stern opponent of all limitations of personal freedom. When he passed away in the later sixties the German element suffered a great loss. Also, his older brother, Ferdinand, who is still living at an advanced age in Los Angeles, California, repeatedly held public offices. Toward the end of the fifties he was bailiff of the public schools, and later superintendent of the city poorhouse.

To sit in the city council was in these years an honor that was coveted by many. The same was true of the office of justice of the peace. In those days this office was usually held by persons who enjoyed universal confidence. F. A. H. Schneider was for many years a justice of the peace in the southern part of the city. His office was on the east side of Carondelet Avenue, between Soulard and Lafayette Streets. Due to his great popularity he had much work from the beginning to the end of the year. That does not mean that the people of Frenchtown sued each other in order that Squire Schneider should have much work, but if a matter had to be settled, complainant and accused were agreed to have it attended to in Schneider's court. During the middle sixties he was elected clerk of the circuit court, but died soon thereafter. In like manner Squire Charles Picker for many years served as justice of the peace. His office was located on the west side of Carondelet between Geyer and Allen Avenue. He has now withdrawn to private life.

In spite of his short residence in St. Louis, A. Kruer was elected justice of the peace in Frenchtown in 1865. He had published a newspaper in Madison, Wisconsin, and had also been librarian of the Wisconsin state library. Then he had edited a paper in Chicago, and on January 1, 1861 he became the successor of Adalbert Loehr as editor of the *Tageschronik,* which was owned by Franz Saler. A year later he gave up this position. He did not serve long as squire for he died in 1865. His eldest son, Mazzini Kruer, was very active in the Turner Society, and for many years superintendent of gymnastics of the Turners of St. Louis. For almost twenty-five years he was employed in Barr's drygoods store, and now has his own business. In later years the former municipal deputy marshal, Jacob Decker, and also the barber Louis A. Raum served as justices of the peace in this part of the city. In most instances the justices of the peace were also notaries. But there were many notaries who had no other office. Some of them had a fine income, as for example, Charles F. Blattau on Park Avenue near Seventh Street, and Captain Alexander Windmueller, who had his office diagonally across from the First National Bank and who at the same time was the bookkeeper and collector for Henry Soulard.

Many a hearing before a justice of the peace in those days constituted a real event for the whole region, particularly if well known persons were involved. It did not make any difference as to what might be the complaint, a fight, (and such even occurred at times in peaceful Frenchtown), or damages caused by chickens in a neighbor's garden, or if a poorly trained dog caused havoc to a flock of chickens. On such occasions the squires office usually proved to be much too small to hold the curious spectators. When then the verdict had been given, the dispute settled, and the embitterment between the contending parties was not too great, then all the participants, the judge, the jury, the witnesses, good acquaintances among the spectators, the constable and his deputy, and of course, the lawyers, if such were needed, betook themselves to a nearby tavern to drink a glass of reconciliation. If the disputants parted embittered, then also the adherents were divided in two camps and went to two different taverns. Sometimes the secondary meetings lasted longer than the trial.

A number of small, so-called halls, which served lodges for their meetings were also found on Carondelet Avenue in those days. One of these, located in the former bank-building on Park Avenue, was used by the Rheinische Frohsinn. Another, above Christian Niemann's tavern, at the southwest corner of Carroll Street, was used by several lodges, and farther south there were also several such halls.

During the war the dealer in stoves, Jacob D. Hiemez, erected a four-story building on the northeast corner of Carroll Street, its upper story was used by one of the lodges. The Sons of Hermann was the first lodge that moved in there. The dancing teacher, Mrs. Emily Carl, gave instruction there in the late sixties. Hammer's photograph gallery occupied one of the stories. The office of the American Central Fire Insurance Company was in this building till it moved to the business part of the city. Peter W. Berg moved his hat business into one of the stores immediately after completion of the building. In this same block Charles Bang had a drug store during the sixties. This he sold to Mattfeld and then moved to Franklin Avenue.

In the middle of the next block there was, during the later seventies, the dry goods store of John H. Fisse. He sold out to Paul & Cassel. When this firm dissolved partnership, Ferdinand Cassel continued the business alone. John Fisse was one of the most respected men in the city. He was particularly active as a member of the county court, whose chairman was Charles Speck.

Charles Hufnagel's inn was located in this block. Since he insisted upon good order, his place was frequented by the best citizens.

During the latter part of the sixties there was a temperance movement in our state. An organization, known as Reform Society, was formed. It consisted of the tavern keepers of the city, who did everything in their power to avert disaster to their business. Delegates of the society attended a national convention of tavern keepers in Cincinnati.

Hufnagel's neighbor, Lorenz Moskop, the saddle maker, had resided there for many years. There is also Frederick Arendes, who has had his merchant tailor business in that locality for over four decades, to be exact, in the second house north of Soulard Street. He was still a very young man when he established himself in Frenchtown, and where he has ever worked for the best interests of the community. In the southern part of our city he is a sort of advisor for everybody, and one of the most zealous representatives of the German element. In former times, city taxes were paid to collectors. There was one collector in each ward. During the sixties Arendes was the collector for the second ward. This was the only office that he ever accepted.

On the west side of the same block of Carondelet Avenue, George Weber for many years had his saddle factory. He was the father of Sergeant Weber who was assigned to the weather observation corps. On the northwest corner of Soulard Street was John Degenhardt's lumber yard. In spite of the enclosure this was one of the favored playgrounds for the school boys. At the southwest corner stood the Star Brewery, which belonged to George Rothweiler and Christoph Sutter, but which was discontinued during the later sixties. In 1866 the station house of the first police district, that stood near the French Market, was torn down, because it was necessary to support a police station farther south. For this purpose the city bought a building on the west side of Carondelet, between Soulard Street and Lafayette Avenue, and had it suitably reconstructed. Christian Kohlhund was for a long time Captain of this police district. He lived on Soulard Street, diagonally across from the Star Brewery. Next to Kohlhund resided the police judge C. D. Wolff. The transfer of the station house to the site, referred to above, was regarded as an important event, and was becomingly celebrated. At first, when the station was new, every person under arrest was followed by a numerous crowd of curious men and women, who remained in or around the station house until the object of their curiosity disappeared behind lock and bolt, or was let out on bail or was set free because of lack of evidence. In the early seventies the police moved into a new building which the city built on Soulard between Seventh and Eighth Streets.

Where now Ottenad's building stands, Adolph Fischer had his hat and cap store during the fifties. Fischer later leased the Flora Garden, and for several years he represented his ward in the city council. Till the corner building was put up, Ottenads furniture store was farther south in the same block, between Biedermann's hat store and Linck & Garrell's hardware store. The watchmaker and jeweler, Ferdinand Dauth, moved into this block during the later sixties. Prior to that he was on Soulard, between Seventh and Eighth Streets. Two doors north of Lafayette Street was the store and workshop of the tinsmith Frederick Nischwitz, the jovial singer, and on the corner was the tavern of Charley Strittmatter.

Strittmatter's tavern was not the only one in this block. In the middle of it was that of Charles Blind, who for many years was the bookkeeper in Theobald Eckerle & Co.'s brewery. This brewery was located in the same block toward Jackson Street, and was known as the Germania Brewery. When the brewery ceased to operate, Eckerle opened a wine cellar on the northwest corner of Fifth and Market Street. Near the brewery, Anton Schwartz had his bakery. Between the bakery and Ottenad's furniture store was Mrs. Marie Mueller's millinery store, which is now continued by the Zepp sisters. Mrs. Mueller operated her store for a full quarter of a century.

Christopher Rebenack, a German school master of the old school, had a private school on Jackson Street. He was eccentric, but straightforward and frank. He was beloved by his pupils. He spent his idle hours in writing poetry, and his products frequently appeared in the local papers.

Another German private school was that of William Glaeser. This school was also on Jackson Street, at first near Barry and later several blocks farther to the south. After the demise of Glaeser, his school was combined with that of Theodore Gerber, located on the he northwest corner of Tenth Street and Park Avenue. Also Gerber died young. In these private schools the children at least learned a better German than they learned later, allowing for a few exceptions, in our generally excellent public schools.

At one time a street car track lay on Soulard and Carroll Streets. This connected the southwest with the central part of the city. This was toward the end of the sixties. However, it did not pay. The route was a great convenience for the residents along the way and the neighborhood. The company lost money. The tracks were removed and put on Thirteenth Street which ran in the opposite direction toward Soulard as far as Columbus. Here John H. Amelung (or Ammelung) had his well known grocery store.

On the southeast corner of Carondelet Avenue and Lafayette Street was Mack's drug store. It was destroyed by fire during the later seventies. Then the furniture dealer, Louis Ottenad, built a three-story building on this corner. East of the drug store was, for many years, the office and dwelling of Doctor Fritz Hanck. He was one of the busiest doctors in the southern part of the city. His early death was mourned far and wide. Carondelet, from the beginning, has had a great number of German bakeries. One of these was that of Henry Vogel on the east side, between Lafayette and Geyer Avenue. On the corner of the latter was Peter Schardin's tavern, who, a member of the Democratic party, played a role in ward politics. Among the many taverns of this region, Eckerle's malt house was located on the northwest of Geyer Avenue. Later this came into the possession of Charles Hoppe. Eckerle first had Mathias Weisz and then Ferdinand Simon as his partners. Between Geyer and Allen Avenue was Schuh's drug store. The owner was one of the most respected German citizens, and known in all of Frenchtown. A few doors farther, Tony Faust had his tavern, in which one could also get meals, where "oysters in style" were served. Tony obtained his supply of oysters direct. It was a happy idea to combine the tavern with the oyster business, a business in which he practically held a monopoly in that part of the city. It was the only business of this kind south of Market Street.

Baer's clothing store, located between Geyer and Allen Avenue, is one of the oldest businesses in Frenchtown. The founder of the firm, Isaak Baer, from the beginning has enjoyed the reputation of a substantial businessman. Even in his advanced years, having turned his business over to his sons, he enjoys popularity far and wide.

The continuation from Geyer Avenue, from South Broadway as far as the wharf, formerly had the name Lesperance Street. Many other names of streets in this part of the city were derived from the French, or were chosen to honor old French families. The great Helmbacher iron rolling works, occupies almost one and a half blocks on Columbus and Barton Streets.

For years this business has been under the managership of Gustav L. Goetz. Originally this business was called the Iron Mountain Steam Forge. It was founded by Peter and Michael Helmbacher, Daniel Wolff, A. McDonald, and Carl Brummer (or Brunner) during the fifties.

The Pittsburgh Brewery, whose owners were Felix Coste and A. Leuszler, stood on the east side of Carondelet Avenue, near Victor Street. The tannery of John How was on Barton Street, east of Carondelet Avenue. On the latter street, in the same block, Franz Mols had his drug store during the sixties. Later this store passed into the hands of Dr. Schloszstein and C. V. Coelln. During the cholera year, 1866, there prevailed in this region a great embitterment against a stone quarry on the west side of Carondelet Avenue, which belonged to the contractor, Edward Augustin. The water, standing in the quarry polluted the air, but at the time of such an epidemic as this its effects on the neighborhood were much worse. The demand for removal was no doubt justified, but for a long time was unheeded. Druggist Mols and other citizens had repeatedly appealed to the bureau of health and the city council. They had demanded that the quarry be filled. But Augustin had many friends in the city hall, and so all effort was in vain. Thus things went on till this discontent and indignation brought about a demonstration which did not fail to bring results. Augustin himself was, however, not an unpopular person, and it aroused great indignation when several years later, in Jefferson City, during a quarrel, Joseph Pulitzer shot Augustin in the leg. The wound was not dangerous and healed soon. The reconciliation between the two was soon brought about. The late George Hillgaertner, who during the late fifties and early sixties was a co-editor of the *Anzeiger* and the publisher of *Die Neue Zeit* was accustomed to say that America was the land of reconciliation.

St. George, who in his time successfully fought with the dragon, must have had warm admirers in Frenchtown in former years, for not only the Market House, on the corner of Carondelet Avenue and Sidney Street were named after him, but also St. George mill on nearby Jackson Street. Henry Kalbfleisch was for a long time the owner of the mill. Originally he had Christian Lange as his partner. Kalbfleisch was always interested in the business development of Frenchtown, especially banking. The St. George Market was at no time not even remotely to be compared with the great public markets in the center of the city. It supplied only the immediate neighborhood, and did this chiefly with meat and on Fridays, with fish.

Between Lynch and Dorcas Streets there was a rather low hill on the east side of Carondelet Avenue. On it was situated George Schneider's small brewery. At the beginning of the fifties, Schneider operated the Washington Brewery on Third and Elm Streets. On the same side of the avenue, close to the arsenal, was a beer garden, called Arsenal Park, where there was also dancing on Sunday evenings.

Till 1871 the terrain belonging to the arsenal was considerably larger than it was later. The United States government gave that part of the property belonging to the arsenal that lay between the arsenal and Utah Street to the city of St. Louis. The gift was made on two conditions: first, that the ground be used for a public park and be kept up as such, and, second, that a monument be erected in it in honor of General Nathaniel Lyon who fell in the battle of Wilson's Creek on July 10, 1861. When the monument was unveiled in the autumn of 1874, Lyon Park was still in a very primitive condition. Colonel Charles G. Stifel acted as presiding officer at the unveiling ceremonies. Mayor Joseph Brown spoke for the city, whereupon Dr. Emil Preetorius delivered the festival address in the German language. The park was not put in good condition till the city park commissioner cared for it.

The arsenal as such had attracted the general interest of our city, and played a prominent role only once in the history of St. Louis, and that was immediately before the outbreak and at the beginning of the war of the rebellion. At that time the eyes and thoughts of our entire populations were directed to it. The citizens who were loyal to the Union,–and with a few notable exceptions they were chiefly the Germans, –knew only too well what danger threatened the city, if the guns, cannon, and the supply of munitions should fall into the hands of the secessionists, while those, who sided with the South, wished nothing more fervently than that the arsenal should fall into the hands of the rebels. Neither before nor after those stirring days was it ever so lively within the walls that enclose the arsenal, as during those times. Before and after it was very quiet there. During the forties and fifties this quiet was interrupted only when the officers staged a ball. The arsenal grounds were originally the property of the Rutger family which was one of the oldest French families in St. Louis. The federal government bought the land about the year 1830, but it was not until the early forties that the buildings were put up. At that time, and for a considerable time after, the arsenal was in a sparsely settled region.

When then this situation changed, and houses were built there, and the real estate rose in price, the Congress was stormed with petitions to have it removed. The petitioners argued that all its purposes would be met just as well by the Jefferson Barracks, which were situated near the city and could be reached quickly by railroad. After repeated, fruitless efforts, a measure was passed many years ago, which allowed the sale of the arsenal and all the buildings belonging to it, but, as yet, no use has been made of this permission.

A few blocks farther south was situated the United States Marine Hospital, which rendered good service, particularly during the years of the war. Dr. Hammer practiced there as chief surgeon after he returned from service in the field. For some time he lived in the neighborhood of the hospital, as did also Judge Woerner.

Not far from the hospital, on Carondelet Avenue, Niese and Knoblauch had a store during the fifties and sixties. Later Julius Niese was associated with Peter Thul in the commission business, and now he is the manager of the Niese Grocery Co.

In the course of time there have been many German taverns in Frenchtown. Few of them were as widely known as that of Louis Zepp on the west side of Carondelet Avenue, a little south of the place at which it unites with Seventh Street. Zepp was an eager politician and one of the main supports of the Republican party in South St. Louis. In the second story of his place was a large room for ward meetings.

20. South Seventh Street

South Seventh Street has undergone many changes during the last four decades between Market Street and Chouteau Avenue. It, too, was for a long time a residence street, and many of the oldest and best known French families lived on this street. The very large house on the southeast corner of Elm Street was erected during the early sixties for the Soldon private school, which had grown out of the school that developed out of the school which Theodore Plate had managed. Soldon's school had many pupils. At the beginning of the forties Dr. Charles A. Pope had, directly south of this school, a college of medicine, which was officially known as the St. Louis Medical College. Popularly it was known as Pope's Medical College. Only a few years ago it was transferred to another part of the city. Pope was the son-in-law of the millionaire Lucas. For about forty years, Henry Foerg managed the drug store on the northwest corner of Spruce Street. Because of advanced years he sold it to his long time clerk, Charles Gietner. At the northeast corner was for many years C. F. Meier's drug store. Indeed all the drugstores on this street were exclusively in German hands. Before the war, the hotel Zum Bremer Schluessel, in the middle of the next block, had Oswald Benkendorf as its owner. Previously Benkendorf had edited a German newspaper. At the southeast corner Gruens had a popular tavern. Later he transferred it to Fifth and Elm Street.

Central Market which ceased to exist during the middle eighties, occupied the square which is bordered by Seventh, Eighth, Spruce and Poplar Streets. In spite of the fact that the Market was inadequate to meet the demands, there was still considerable activity there. On the evening before Easter Sunday, 1872, this part of St. Louis was visited by such a storm as is but rarely seen. Between six and seven o'clock, therefore, at the time when the market teemed with buyers, particularly women and children, the storm broke suddenly with terrible fury. It was accompanied by a terrific downpour of rain. The storm ripped the metal roof off the Market House, actually rolled it up and hurled it over Market Street. Part of it fell into the street while another part lit on the roofs of the houses on the other side of the street. Many persons were seriously injured and property damage was, of course, very great. With the building of the Pacific depot the last remnant of Chouteau's pond disappeared, as did all the buildings between Cerre and Poplar Streets west of Seventh Street. On Cerre also many changes were made to facilitate the construction of the railroad. The buildings of the Academy of the Christian Bothers, and the adjoining McDowell's College disappeared to make room for more trackage. Likewise the Fritz & Wainwright Brewery was razed. Later Wainwright built a new brewery on Papin, between Tenth and Eleventh Streets. This became the Wainwright Brewery Co., whose president is Ellis Wainwright and whose secretary is William A. Haren.

Happy Hollow is not even known by name to the younger generation. Older inhabitants, especially those of the southern part of the city will surely recall it. The region so designated occupied the southern quarter of a block bordered by Sixth, Seventh, Gratiot and Papin Streets. As the name implies there was a depression, which was thirty feet lower than the street level. About half a dozen half-dilapidated frame shacks, occupied by whites and Negroes, were situated here. Between the two races often friction developed, requiring police intervention. It was wise for the pedestrian to avoid this place after darkness set in. The strange name, which seemed to be so ill-fitting, came into use when the cholera raged so terribly. Happy Hollow was completely spared, which was so much the more remarkable as untidiness prevailed and every shower made a swamp of the place, so that one should have expected the exact opposite. After filling the depression, and after the disappearance of the unwelcome neighborhood, the building sites on the west side of Seventh Street were occupied by houses, as for example, those of Franz Guerdan, the manufacturer of iron gratings, and that of Frank Feiner the mill owner. On the east side of the short block between Papin and Chouteau Avenue was the tavern of Jacob von Gerichten, whom his fellow citizens elected to the position of justice of the peace, which office he held for many years. The drug store on the southwest corner of Chouteau Avenue belonged originally to Adolph Godron, who is now practicing medicine. Now it belongs to Henry Braun who has done so much for the Turner Society.

Persons who passed along the southeast corner of Chouteau Avenue, between the months of December and February during the later sixties, must have admired the floral display in the broad bay window of a house that stood on Seventh Street, about twenty feet from the sidewalk, some ten steps up from the street level. The window was filled with blossoming hyacinths, as beautiful as could not been seen anywhere else in the city. This lover of flowers was Richard Unger, whom his friends called Champaign Unger, from the product which he handled in his commission house. Each winter he raised such flowers. Unger came from Breslau. His Silesian countryman, Emil Laszwitz, who came here and for some time was active as an actor and director, found in Champaign Unger a warm friend and patron.

The school standing on the northwest corner of Seventh and Hickory Streets, and which is now a school for Negro children, was originally the Madison school. Even near the end of the sixties it proved to be much too small. So the building on the corner of Labadie Street (now LaSalle), directly behind the Annunciation Church was erected. But after only a few years it also was too small for the large number of pupils. The board of education was compelled to build a second Madison school. For this the board bought the vacant plot on the east side of Labadie and Hickory. On this plot was located on the north side the residence of former Mayor Maguire, while on the south side stood the home of banker Tesson. (Maguire was the father-in-law of Charles W. Francis.) On the opposite west side of Seventh Street was a still larger, vacant plot, which at one end was a well-kept lawn, shaded by great, old trees. Through these one could see the huge Beckwith mansion, which faced on Eighth Street. During the later fifties and the first part of the sixties, it was occupied by Mrs. Tullia Beckwith. She was as eccentric a person as she was vivacious. She was a widow and played a prominent role in society, till the provost marshal banished her to the South for expressing secessionistic ideas too openly.

Hehrlein's Harmony Hall, on the west side of Seventh between Rutger Street and Park Avenue was, during the fifties and sixties, a meeting place. Over a tavern which was on the ground floor, was a large hall, in which concerts and dance music were frequently offered. The Pestalozzi school on the northeast corner of Seventh and Barry Streets was built in the late sixties on the place where previously was located the Phoenix Garden, popularly known as Flattich's Garden. There was a dance hall in which, in addition to dancing, there was often fighting. That was nothing unusual and in the earlier days the latter constituted a regular part of the program of entertainment. In Phoenix Garden things went on particularly bad, and the neighborhood, therefore, was glad when the garden came to an end. In the latter half of the sixties, Dr. Kinner lived on Barry Street, immediately next to the above mentioned garden, and probably nobody passed this house without admiring the splendid flowers and foliage plants that adorned all the windows. On the west side of Seventh Street, a few doors below Park Avenue, during the forties and early fifties, there was a private school conducted by nuns. This was the house which was later occupied by Mr. Taussig, and after him by Dr. Wichmann. The Saxon drug store located nearby, was established forty years ago by its present owner, F. W. Schuricht. Between Barry and Marion, on the west side, was Stephan Stock's brewery.

In the tavern, connected to the brewery, it was the practice of the keeper to turn out the gas lights at a certain time, in order that his customers should not get home too late. One of the best known and oldest bakeries in this part of the city was that of Dietrich, later owned by George Rueckert. It was located on the corner of Marion Street. On the east side, between Marion and Carroll was Fritz Becker's malt house, and on the lower corner of the block was one of the oldest steam driven mills in the city, the St. Louis Mills. During the fifties and sixties, Soulard Market was one of the busiest markets in the city. By and by the situation changed, so that only a few of the meat stands in the interior were leased and the sale of vegetables and field products decreased to such an extent that the space on the side of the market building was not used at all. (In recent times the situation has changed for the better and there is new life in the market.) In the small hall in the upper story of this building some stormy scenes were seen at times. So, for example, on the occasion of a meeting of depositors of the Peoples Savings Institution, and during ward meetings. In this room the politicians, such as Cronenbold, Charles W. Gottschalk, John H. Ammelung (or Amelung), Judge Louis Gottschalk and others spoke to their constituents. Here Edward C. Kehr, Chauncey J. Filley, E. O. Stanard and others made speeches at election times.

One of the oldest livery stables was that of Brockmann & Scheele, located on the corner of Soulard Street. The original owner is not alive anymore. After Bernhard Brockmann left the firm, he managed the livery stable of Thornton and Pierce on Walnut Street. Fritz Scheele was also a veterinarian, for which reason he was called "Doctor" in Frenchtown. Kohler's drug store, on the corner of Seventh and Lafayette was later owned by John Guerdan. Later he moved farther east in the block where formerly Mack's drug store had been, and who is now in the West End, corner of Garrison Avenue and Olive Street.

Dr. Schade built for himself one of the prettiest residences in this region, early in the sixties. It was situated on the east side of Seventh, between Soulard and Lafayette Streets. Dr. Schade was at that time a very busy physician. Later the building contractor, Uri, bought the place.

Gert Goebel (not to be confused with Missouri's pioneer, the long-time contributor to the *Westliche Post*, who at an advanced age is living near Washington, Mo.) built six residences on the west side of Seventh Street, between Lafayette Street and Geyer Avenue. This was known as Goebel's Row. These houses were erected at the beginning of the sixties. Goebel also owned the Flora Garden. This garden was situated at the corner of Geyer Avenue. It was one of the most popular places of amusement in South St. Louis. This was particularly true at the close of the fifties and the early sixties, while Adolph Fischer was the lessee. Concerts and theatrical performances were regularly offered on the fine stage which Fischer provided. Professor Marx often displayed his tricks of magic here. Unfortunately, Fischer did not make money and regretted that he ever took over the garden. His successor was a certain Guthart.

In a later chapter which will tell about the oldest German church organization we shall tell about St. Peter and Paul's church. On the northeast corner of Seventh Street and Allen Avenue, Thomas Allen had his office, from which he managed his considerable real estate holdings in this part of the city. Allen's addition was named after him.

The Green Tree Brewery was situated on Sidney not far from Seventh, during the early sixties, owned by Max Feuerbacher and Louis Schloszstein. After the death of the former, E. H. Vordtriede became a partner. Later the brewery of Schilling & Schneider was combined with that of the Green Tree.

A few doors south of Sidney Street, on the east side of Seventh was the Evangelical Lutheran Hospital, popularly known as the Saxon Hospital. It was located in a two-story house. It remained there for several decades, until a new, large building, suited as a hospital, was erected in the southwest part of the city. On the next corner of Lynch Street was a small house in a large, rather neglected garden. Here Henry C. Lynch, the maker of Lynch's "Entericon," a patent medicine, lived. The Excelsior Brewery on the east side of Seventh, between Lynch and Lancaster Streets was owned by C. Hoelzle, during the fifties. He was no brewer by profession. Older readers will remember him as a notary and as a third-rate lawyer. He was also interested in real estate deals and land speculations. In 1860, Caspar Koehler bought this brewery and operated it himself for some years. Then he was associated with his brother, Henry.

One of the oldest breweries in St. Louis was the Bavarian Brewery. At that time it was owned by Dr. Hammer, who sold it in the early sixties to Eberhard Anheuser, who until that time had been in partnership with Schaeffer, manufacturer of soap. The firm name was Schaeffer, Anheuser & Co. No one would have believed that the small Bavarian Brewery, near Pestalozzi Street, in the course of time should assume the proportion of a giant establishment which, as the Anheuser-Busch Brewery, sends its product to all the zones, and for a long time has been known as one of the best known breweries of the world.

II. German-American Life

21. Public Gardens

In the early decades St. Louis had many public parks and gardens. They had their origin and their support chiefly from the German element of the city. It was the philosophy of the Germans to enjoy life in their own way, that led to the creation of the summer gardens. With the German mass immigration at the close of the forties and early fifties the German concept of entertainment and amusement was transplanted here. To the American element all this was extremely strange, and it required a long time before this sort of social entertainment ceased to astound them. Most of them had no correct understanding for the joys of sociability according to German model. The transfer of the German idea of observing Sunday to American soil was the cause, not only of great displeasure on the part of so-called natives, but gave occasion for much bitterness, indeed even of brutal attacks and bloody fights. Many years passed before one saw an American in our summer gardens, no matter whether on Sundays or week days. Only just before election times, and then only on special occasions were Americans seen here.

In the course of time the situation changed. The Civil War did much to bring about this change. The Germans of St. Louis won a prestige from their behavior during these stirring times , which nothing else could have given them. Common dangers, victories won, the fruits of the conflict and mutual sacrifices brought the various nationalities closer together. Certain classes of the people now had respect for the Germans, a respect which was absent before. This was manifested even during the war not only in the political realm but also in daily life. The events of 1870 and 1871 on the other side of the ocean, the triumph of German arms over the French army, and the unification of the German nation increased the prestige still more. So the Germans had every reason to be proud of the achievement of those days.

It was Christian Nunz who made the most effective propaganda for the summer gardens among American circles, when, during the sixties he leased Uhrig's Cave and introduced regular garden concerts. He engaged a fine orchestra which provided good music, and the owner saw to it that good order was maintained. The location of his establishment was favorable to such an undertaking. The region around the garden was inhabited almost exclusively by Americans. By and by they overcame their prejudice against German gardens, and also got to like German beer. The summer theater came many years later and constituted at once an important factor in the Germanization of our Anglo-American fellow citizens.

Camp Spring Garden on the corner of Twentieth and Market Streets was a favorite place of entertainment for young and old. On Sundays the place teemed with people. Not only beverages but also the famous Camp Spring sausages were served. The latter were a specialty of this garden. The newspapers carried ads announcing when these sausages were served and when dances were scheduled here. But what was not announced in the papers were the fights that occurred almost every Sunday evening. The region at which Market Street and Laclede Avenue converge was at that time called Vinegar Hill. If a real fight occurred at Camp Spring Garden one could be sure that the rowdies of Vinegar Hill had provoked it. Kunz, the owner, was a peace-loving man who did everything to prevent them, without avail. No one blamed Kunz for these unpleasant incidents. Mrs. Kunz was a very busy person on Sundays as she labored in the kitchen. After the death of her husband she carried on the business for a while, when she married the well-known wine dealer, Peter Ambs.

In South St. Louis, Union Park was superior to all gardens, when it came to concert gardens, during the sixties. Originally this was a part of a farm, which belonged to the United States Land Register, Russell, the father-in-law of Thomas Allen. The Russells, after whom the avenue south of Union Park was named, inhabited a massive house in the middle of the park. From 1860 to 1868 the family of Hermann Bachmann, who during this period had leased this park, lived here. During the last six years of this period he was associated with the brewer Frederick Stumpf as a co-lessee. Stumpf and Bachmann made the park a splendid place of recreation. Even on hot afternoons the many old trees gave ample shade. Beautiful flower beds were placed in various places and the terraced, nicely sodded slope dipped toward Ninth Street. From May to October there were concerts here on every Sunday and also during the week. These orchestras and bands played here –Sauter's, Kellermann's, Waldauer's and Vogel's. Union Park was always preferred by lodges and societies. Many of them held their festivals in this park. At Pentecost and on the Fourth of July the place was congested during the afternoon and evening. After a spacious hall had been built, there were also dances scheduled, and well attended concerts on Sunday afternoons in the winter. The largest festival of veterans was held in Union Park on the Fourth of July 1868, being sponsored by the Grand Army of the Republic. After Stumpf retired, Bachmann continued the management alone till 1869. Then Oscar Roessel took over. From then on the popularity of the park decreased more and more till finally there was little left of interest.

Jaeger's Garden, on Sidney Street, was in a summer, due to its high location, a favorite goal for pedestrians. After a tavern and a large dance hall were built, many societies held not only their summer festivals there, but also their balls in the winter. After Jaeger's death, the tavern and the garden passed into the hands of Anthony & Kuhn.

The Concordia Park was originally called Scholten's Park. The lessee was John Scholten, the father of the photographer, John A. Scholten. The elder Scholten managed the Frederick House on Second and Pine Street. His partner in the park business was Moritz Schilling. After Scholten's death his widow and her son continued to manage the park till Charley Leichsenring took over. From that time on, the park was named Concordia Park. Leichsenring took as his business partner, the popular Fritz Heitkamp. The latter was the owner of the hotel that bore his name. He was a rich man, and invested a good piece of money in beautifying the park. The building with the dance hall was erected at that time. Lorenz Schlenker was the next manager. About six years ago Hermann Bachmann, who, during the immediately preceding seven years had managed the Concordia Turner Hall, took over the park, which William J. Lemp had thoroughly renovated.

In the course of time many great festivals of the most varied kind were held in Concordia Park. But none was so largely attended nor so important as the one celebrating the unification of Germany, and the victory of Germany over France. All the German element of St. Louis took part in it. The parade opening the festival took place in the forenoon. To this day one has seen no greater parade here. All the singing societies, Turner societies, church organizations, without consideration of their faith, all German lodges, and other societies participated with complete unity of purpose. One can gain an idea of the attendance at this festival, when it is known that the amount of money collected for the wounded of the German army netted twenty-thousand dollars. The beer that was consumed on this occasion was donated gratis by the brewers. The restaurant and kitchen were supervised by a committee of women. Everyone who entered the park on this day had to pay a quarter of a dollar admission fee. In this manner such a large net profit was made possible.

One of the oldest breweries was that of McHose & English. On Arsenal Street, east of what is now Benton Park, this firm had a cellar which was known as English Cave, (for many years now the property of E. H. Vordtriede). In former years artificial refrigeration and artificial ice were unknown. Therefore the use of the "cave" was resorted to. The above-named brewers owned a large tract of land over and around the "cave." A part of it was forest and on another part the beginnings of a garden were made. So there was plenty of space for picnics. It was a favorite place for outings of our French populations.

Among the public gardens that have existed a long time is the Cherokee Garden. For many years it was made famous by the excellent kitchen of Mrs. Besch. This garden was in no direct connection with the Cherokee Brewery, which at first belonged to Herold & Loebs, and then for many years to F. Herold alone, the present owner of the Cherokee steamboat line. The Clara Hill Garden, situated nearby, was established later. Staehlin's Garden on Carondelet, between Lafayette and Geyer Avenue had its name from Christian Staehlin, the owner, who also owned the Phoenix Brewery. Christian Staehlin's first partner was Joseph Halm and later Henry Breidenbach. For a considerable time the garden was managed by the owner of the brewery himself. Since the time when Anton Griesedick bought the latter, the garden was called Koerner's Garden, after its lessee. Even in the sixties, Sunday afternoon and evening concerts were given here. Schnerr's Garden was located near Constantine Schnerr's brewery, at the corner of Park Avenue and Rosatti Street, but ceased to function during the sixties. This garden also had a dance hall, in which the conduct was at times improper, so that the police had to interfere. Compton Hill Park was made a favorite place of recreation by Tony Niederwieser during 1868 and 1869. It occupied the southeast corner of Lafayette and Grand Avenue, therefore, close to the reservoir. It was on city property which the waterworks commissioners leased to Niederwieser, who made it a rendezvous for the best society during the years above indicated. The property of Peter Weizenecker on Grand Avenue, near Michel's greenhouses, and Tower Grove Park was, even during the fifties, numerously attended, especially on Sundays. Weizenecker had his own vineyards. Later his son-in-law, Andrew Auer, became the owner. The

The German Element in St. Louis 153

latter at one time served as a member of the city council. Schnaider's Garden was the creation of Joseph Schnaider. During the early sixties he had a brewery, the Chouteau Avenue Brewery, to which he added the garden. He made it an attractive place. In the late sixties the New Orleans Orchestra, under the capable direction of Mr. Starke from Dresden, played in this garden for a long time. The Grand Orchestra and Vogel's Band for many years gave concerts on Thursday evenings and Sunday afternoons and evenings, which were very popular. The Saxon Military Band which toured America for several months soon after the German-French war, gave several concerts here before capacity audiences. During the festival of the singing societies in 1872, the concourse of people exceeded the capacity of the garden. For many years Joseph Schneider managed the garden himself, later leased it to Charles F. Schneider, and then to Tony Niederwieser. But neither of the two were very successful in spite of their experience and business acumen. Tony's losses were particularly heavy because of many rainy Sundays during three summers. Kerzinger's Cave, between Easton Avenue and the Fair Grounds, belonged to Franz Kerzinger, the owner of the Mound City Brewery. Till 1862 it was a much frequented place of amusement in this part of the city. Toward the end of the fifties a bath house was established in the garden which belonged to the Cave. Small societies were accustomed to hold their festival in Kerzinger's Cave. A part of the large place was planted with grape vines and an arbor, over one hundred feet long, was formed by the grape vines strung over lattice work. Lindell Park in the early days played a great role. Lodges and societies preferred to patronize it. The gatherings of the Sons of Hermann, Harugaris, and the Redmen, and others attended by the thousands.

Only my older readers will remember that there was at one time a restaurant in Lafayette Park. Meals, but no beer, were served here. Though the park was the property of the city, its management was from the outset in the hands of a citizen's committee whose members lived in the immediate neighborhood of the park. Edward Bredell, Stephen D. Barlow and John C. Rust, a brother-in-law and business partner of Adolphus Meier, were the first commissioners. They allowed the Superintendent of Parks, Krausnick, to sell refreshments in a glass-covered building that had been used as a greenhouse, and which stood in the middle of the park. In the winters of 1859-60 and 1860-61 Sunday afternoon concerts were given there by Waldauer and also by Vogel's band. It was a family resort for the best of society. It is to be regretted that these winter concerts were not continued after 1861. Edward C. Krausnick was the son of the celebrated court gardener of the same name, who created the splendid plantings in the gardens of Sanssouci near Potsdam. His son, one of the most able landscape gardeners, now resident in America, laid out Lafayette Park, which today is one of the most beautiful of our parks.

22. Instrumental Music and Song

There was a time when Americans, who could play a tune on a fiddle, even if it was out of tune, or a few songs which the Negroes sang on the plantation, were stared at in admiration, and if they could play a piece for a dance, they were considered artists. The demands in the field of music were at that time extremely modest. The simplest achievements of a quartet or octet evoked boundless admiration. If the young folks wished to dance, one violin, one flute, and one bass fiddle were regarded a full orchestra, not only in the country but also in the city. Forty years ago Kinsalla's Quadrille Band, consisting of six, or at the most, eight men, furnished the music for even the greatest balls. It was not till the middle fifties that an incisive change set in, when the teacher of dancing, Albert Mahler brought together an orchestra made up of twelve and more musicians, which number was doubled on special occasions.

Nowadays the piano is played much in America–some people say, too much. That was not always so, and the general introduction of piano playing in American circles must unquestionably be ascribed to the Germans. This was due not only to the numerous music teachers, men as well as women, but also the example which German families set in that regard. Many a German family brought an old piano with the rest of their household belongings, sometimes only a spinet. Mother and daughters then attracted the attention of their American neighbors by their playing. This awakened in them the desire to emulate their new neighbors. Many a modest instrument, weak with age, that caused amazement in the customs offices of New York, Baltimore, Philadelphia or New Orleans, became the carrier of culture to the remotest parts of this expansive country, for from the far north on Lake Superior, where formerly only the ax of the woodsman disturbed the silence of the forest, to the smallest village in the

The German Element in St. Louis 155

deep south, where formerly the mockingbird had no competition people are now playing the piano.

St. Louis may boast to have developed an active musical life relatively early, and to have supported its development to the best of its ability. In the old French families, which at that time and during the entire first half of this century were the leaders in local society, music was fostered, and also in the homes of some Americans there was much singing and playing. In the middle of the thirties the musical circles of St. Louis received a valuable addition in Henry Weber. It is true that he did not settle here permanently till 1839, but prior to that date he often came to the city from his farm near St. Charles. He was usually accompanied by his highly gifted daughter, Theresa, who has been so intimately connected with our musical life for decades, and still takes such a lively interest in it. In 1840 Theresa Weber became Mrs. Charles Balmer. She and her husband did so much for music in St. Louis that their names will for all time be identified with the contribution which they made to this fine art. Mr. Weber and his daughter, as also Theresa's brother, Henry Weber, Jr., were regularly invited to musical evening entertainments. Miss Weber was considered the best pianist of St. Louis at that time.

In the spring of 1839, Madam Caradori-Allen, a celebrated singer of that time, came here to give a few concerts. In New Orleans she had engaged for the concert tour, a young man as pianist and violinist, who was so pleased with St. Louis during his short stay that he returned after the tour was completed and made this his home. This young man was Charles Balmer, who remained here till his death, which occurred in 1892. He had no more than settled here, when in the fall of 1839, he proceeded to organize an orchestra, which consisted in part of professional musicians, in part of amateurs. That same year, 1839, the Weber family moved to St. Louis. Soon thereafter Henry Weber, Sr. organized a singing school, which was at once supported by the ladies of the best families.

A very good orchestra had existed here prior to this time, but it played only in the old St. Louis Theater. William Robyn, who came here in 1837 joined this orchestra the following year. He was a cellist. There was no brass band at that time in the city. When, on one occasion, the Old Grays, a militia company, which is perhaps still remembered by my older readers, moved out, there marched at its head four musicians with one violin, one clarinet, one cornet and one trumpet, certainly a strange military band, but the Old Grays nevertheless marched proudly and no doubt were glad to have some music to march to. One can imagine that there was real rejoicing when the German Brass Band was organized in 1838. Robyn was the director, and he, as well as all the members, contributed their service practically gratis.

So now St. Louis had an orchestra, a brass band and there was no lack of good voices. But above all the necessary enthusiasm had been aroused, without which there is neither good singing nor good playing.

The German Protestant congregation, which had its first church on the corner of Seventh Street and Clark Avenue, dedicated its building in 1840. The musical portion of the services had particular merit. Henry Weber, Sr. and Charles Balmer, who in this year became Weber's son-in law, undertook to furnish the vocal and instrumental music. Whoever, among the Germans, could sing, reported for the choir, so that all four parts were well taken care of. For the services, the hymn by Schulz was selected which was certainly not an easy work to learn. All the singers worked hard under the direction of Mr. Weber. The same was true of the orchestra under Balmer's direction. This was the first time that this orchestra accompanied a choir. The solo parts were sung by the four Angelrodt sisters and by Mrs. Kretzer and Mrs. Balmer. (The Angelrodt sisters later became Mesdames Felix Coste, William Hunicke, Henry Robyn, and Robert Barth.)

Ben de Bar had a very good orchestra in his theater early in the forties. A German by the name of Mueller conducted it and young August Waldauer played the first violin. The latter came from a musical family. His father was a member of the regimental band in Landau, and was an excellent trumpeter. Young Waldauer played in the orchestra of the St. Charles Theater in New Orleans, where he attracted the attention of Ben de Bar, who induced him to come here, and who introduced him to musical circles.

Two of the greatest violinists of this century came to St. Louis in 1843, while they were on tour through America. First came Ole Bull, the serious-looking Norwegian, and later the Frenchman, Henri Vieuxtemps. Both were, as may be imagined, enthusiastically received.

In 1845, W. Robyn founded a large orchestra to which he gave the name, Polyhymnia. To it belonged, among others, the following: the lawyer, Christian Kribben; the machine builder, William Palm; the banker,

Eugene Miltenberger; the merchant, Louis C. Hischberg; William Heinrichshofen; Statius Kehrmann; the later French Consul, Emil Kurst, an excellent violinist; also the Baron von Wangelin; Franz Obert; the musician, Louis Schnell; Philipp and Henry Burg; Ernest Neuer, the owner of a bone mill and others. The instrumentation of this orchestra was very good, particularly was the violin section strong. It also had a bassoon player. It may be remarked that that was really remarkable for twenty and thirty years later, it was necessary to import such an artist from Cincinnati, if such a man was needed.

Prior to 1838 to 1852, Robyn gave music instruction at the St. Louis University, popularly known as the Jesuit College. After this time he taught for a long time at the Convent of the Sacred Heart, until advanced age compelled him to retire. His son, Alfred Robyn, is a talented musician, and a composer, and an excellent organist –a worthy successor to his father. Henry Robyn, a brother of William Robyn, was likewise a clever musician. In the fifties and sixties he was an instructor in music at the Institute for the Blind, and the high school. He lost his life when the steamer *Pommeronia* sank.

In 1845, through the effort of Charles Balmer, the Oratorio Society was organized. The first work presented by this body was Hayden's *Creation*. Later followed *The Four Seasons, The Messiah,* and similar works.

The year 1846 brought a great event to musical interests. Lepold de Meyer, the celebrated piano virtuoso, was scheduled for two concerts which were to be given in the hall of Planters House. The friends of music decided to prepare a worthy reception for the artist. The hall was festively decorated, and the Erard grand piano, which the virtuoso brought from Paris, was surrounded with garlands. At the second concert, August W. Hauer played the then-so-popular variation of Mayseder, and the applause which the violinist received for his excellent playing almost exceeded the stormy ovation which the pianist received. In the following year a concert was given to procure an organ for a church located on Seventh Street and Clark Avenue. At this, the Oratorio Society also participated.

About this time the construction of Wyman's Hall on Market Street, opposite the courthouse, was completed. The first concerts in it were given by Katharine Hayes, the Swan of Erin. From that time on, most touring artists gave their performances in this hall, since larger concert halls were not available at that time.

In the winter of 1847-48, great excitement prevailed among the friends of music. This was the year when Henry Hers, the originator of virtuosoism, the composer who was celebrated by the whole world, appeared here. His compositions were played everywhere and made use of in all concerts, with or without orchestra accompaniment. At the last concert given here the overture of Rossini's *William Tell* was played by sixteen pianos. For this purpose, Herz had invited the best men and women piano teachers and also some amateurs, all of whom considered it a great honor to be permitted to play with the great artist, and to be seen with him.

Musical interests received some valuable additions in the later forties. These were the two violinists, P. G. Anton and Dr. Fellerer, the cello player Dr. Hammer, and the music teacher Reinhard Fuchs. The latter soon organized the Cecilia Singing Society. It was a mixed chorus and rendered good service. Now chamber music could be introduced. Quartet evenings were now arranged, at which Franz Obert played the first violin, Balmer, the second violin, Anton or Fuchs, the viola, and William Robyn or Dr. Hammer, the cello.

In 1851, appeared two women singers in St. Louis. One of them was on the lowest round of the ladder of fame, which she climbed later, while the other had already made many triumphal tours through Europe, and now had come across the ocean to take the New World by storm. The former was the twelve year old Adelina Patti, who came with her brother-in-law Maurice Strakosch, who had discovered her phenomenal voice. A few months later, Barnum brought the Swedish nightingale, Jenny Lind, who was at the height of her world fame. The seats for the Lind concert, which took place in Wyman's Hall were sold at public auction. The hatmaker Keevil, bought the first ticket for three hundred and fifty dollars. It was a bit of expensive business advertising. However, it paid well for his name was on everyone's lips, and the curious wanted to see the man, who had paid such a sum for a concert ticket, and so brought many customers to his shop.

The first men's singing society, organized according to German pattern, which was formed west of the Mississippi, had the name of St. Louis Saengerbund. It was organized in 1846 and would now be the oldest singing society, if, after thirty years of existence, it had not fused with the

Orpheus group. A few Germans who brought the love for singing with them across the ocean, one day held a meeting. The place was the bedroom of George Schneider's Washington Brewery on Third and Elm Streets. From this meeting came the above named society. The musician Fuchs was the first director. After him, Charles W. Gottschalk, a zealous friend of music assumed the post. Rehearsals were held in the tavern on the corner of Main and Walnut (Our House). Occasionally the group also went for rehearsal at Philipp Dauernheim's place, who was a member of the organization. His place was on the corner of Second and Elm. The German folk songs were mainly rehearsed, and at all German festivals the singers were most welcome guests. A union with Cecilia Society, founded and directed by Charles Balmer was striven for, but was not realized. Balmer's group sang regularly in Picker's church, and participated chiefly in church concerts and on similar occasions. The union of the two groups of singers could not be consummated because the Cecilia club objected to the drinking of the Saengerbund during rehearsals.

The Social Choir traces its existence back to 1850. At first it was called Choir of the Cultural Society of Workers, a name which was soon abandoned. The first president was Joseph Holzman, and during the first years, Frederick Kretschmar, the clerk of the Circuit Court, was the director. This organization first met in the Kossuth House, on South Second Street, then on Third between Locust and Vine, and in the third year of its existence in the Rhenish Wine Hall. In 1853 a song festival, great for the time and under the circumstances, was held, at which the Choir played an outstanding role. When two years later a song contest was held in nearby and pleasant Highland, the Social Choir won the first prize, a beautiful banner. (Incidentally the Swiss settlers of Highland were very fond of music and offered stiff competition in a contest.) One of the most enthusiastic members of the Social Choir was Robert Feustel, who during the twenty-five years was repeatedly chosen president. Other enthusiasts were Carl Hergesell, who was named an honorary member, Jacob Christmann, A. Reinder, Otto Schmidt, who held the presidency during the middle seventies.

In the first half of the fifties St. Louis had many musical treats which it owed to men and women artists who came from Europe. During this period came, in addition to Jenny Lind and the youthful Adelina Patti, the latter's older sister, Amelia, a fine alto singer, the wife of Maurice

Strakosch, moreover, Signora Parodi, who came to St. Louis again a few years later at the head of an opera company that bore her name. In 1853 Miska Hauser, the Hungarian violin king, gave two concerts. In the same year appeared the Germania Orchestra of New York, which was conducted by Carl Bermann. With this organization appeared as soloists, the violin virtuosa Camilla Urso and the pianist Alfred Jael.

In 1853 Severin Robert Sauter came here. He is a musician, thoroughly educated in Germany, an excellent violinist, who even today is one of the most sought-after teachers, who has educated many hundred violinists. It was he who conducted a twenty-six piece orchestra that gave a festival performance in 1856 on the occasion of the opening of the local German Institute for Art and Science. In the same year the one hundredth anniversary of Mozart's birth was appropriately celebrated. All the musicians that St. Louis had, vocalist and instrumentalists, participated in the program, which of course, consisted of compositions of the unforgettable master.

The first Italian opera company that ever set foot on the soil of St. Louis appeared in 1854 at the Varieties Theater, now the Grand Opera House. Its musical director was Arditi, whose Il Baccio could be found on every piano, and which was sung by great as also by non-great women singers. The chief numbers of this opera company gave a concert in October, 1854, on the occasion of the dedication of the just-completed hall over the Mercantile Library, where from then on almost all great concerts were given.

In 1857, the piano virtuoso, Thalberg together with the lyric tenor, Brignoli, gave concerts. They were followed by the pianist, Gottschalk.

The winter season of 1859 to 1850 offered an abundance of concerts and opera performances. Boernstein transformed the Opera House into a German Theater. In the fall of 1859 the latter was opened with twenty-eight performances of an Italian opera company, whose prima donna was Theresa Parodi. Then a French opera company performed for a week. In the course of the season the concerts of the Colson Concert Company and the Anna Bishop Concert Company alternated with German theatrical performances.

The musical event of 1859, however, was the founding of the Philharmonic Society. It came into existence through the efforts of a number of musicians and lovers of music, such as Waldauer, Balmer, and

Dr. William Tausig. With pleasing readiness the members of the older organization assembled under the banner of the younger sister organization, and devoted themselves with enthusiasm to the task. As director, Edward Sobolewski was appointed and brought from Milwaukee, where he had been active in a similar capacity, since 1856. Sobolewski was already advanced in years, but his enthusiasm for music was still the same as at the time when he was the director of the opera in Koenigsberg and later in Bremen. He was a musician from the crown of his head to the soles of his feet, and brought a fresh impetus into our musical life. The society first gave its concerts in the Mercantile Library and later in Veranda Hall, corner of Fourth Street and Washington Avenue. From the outset it enjoyed a lively interest on the part of amateurs as well as of professional musicians, so that Sobolewski had a large and able mixed chorus as well as a suitably large orchestra at his disposal. The ablest talent of our city participated. The programs included works of the older as well as the modern composers, thus offering the necessary variety. While old Sobolewski by no means catered to popular taste, he was nevertheless wise enough not to have the professional musician alone in mind when he prepared his programs. There was no general sale of tickets. The tickets were exclusively in the hands of subscribers. The number of these was so great that one very rarely could find a vacant seat in the concert hall.

To show how excellent the orchestra of the society was, a few names shall be mentioned. Among the violinists were such excellent players as Waldauer, Dr. Fellerer, Karst, Sauter, Valentine Schopp, Anton, Bollmann, Schnell, Vogel, cello players Robyn and Gustav von Deutsch, at the double bass stood Jacob Amann, and John Richter, as well as Frank Gecks, Sr., (who came to us from New Orleans, and who for three decades has been instructor in music at the Academy of the Christian Brothers), among the flutists were Kieselhorst, Schillinger (or Schilliger) and Loewe, clarinet players Henry and Philipp Burg, French horn players, the brothers Keller.

The soprano solos of the society were mainly in the hands of Mrs. Edwina Dean-Lowe, who, in addition to her excellent and well-trained voice, presented a most pleasing appearance. Both of these qualities served to good advantage when in 1864, Flotow's *Martha* was presented by home talent under the direction of Charles Balmer. The performances, two of them, were given for the benefit of wounded and sick soldiers, for whom the Mississippi Valley Sanitation Commission was caring. This commission had its headquarters in St. Louis, and our aged fellow-citizen, James E. Yeatman, who was appointed chairman of this body by President Lincoln, presided over its sessions. A considerable sum of money was taken in. The old de Bar Theater on Pine Street was occupied to the remotest corner during the evening performance as well as at the matinee. Never again has an opera been presented in this city with as large a chorus, but also in quality it has not had a rival since. The title role was sung by Mrs. Dean-Lowe, Mrs. Tomlinson, a superb alto, was the maid Nancy, a young merchant, Anderson, a native Scotsman, sang the role of Lionel, Max Ballmann was Plunkett, the druggist Harless had the comic role of Martha's cousin, and Frederick Kluender was the sheriff. (Subsequently Max Ballmann studied music in Vienna and Berlin. Since then he is a popular voice teacher in our city.)

We have already noted that the old St. Louis Saengerbund and the Social Choir joined their memberships. In the second half of the fifties and the Rheinische Frohsinn and the Germania Saengerbund also joined up with these. The former organization was formed in 1855. Among its founders were August Lenz (now in Lenzburg, Ill.), Gustav Meisenbach, Carl Hage, Carl Becker, Thiebes, Hammerstein, Haeusgen, Herkenroth, Adrian L. Steinhauer and others in the matter of a director the Rheinische Frohsinn was perhaps the most conservative of all local singing societies. First it had Franz Boehmen, who held the post for seventeen years, then Louis Dahmen (or Damen) and after him Carl Richter. The office of president was in turn held by most of the founders and later by Leopold Dingert, Carl Eckhardt, Robert Stoecker, Carl Schweickhardt, John W. Krone, Joseph Keller and since 1882 by our old fellow-citizen, Julius Hertz, one of the most enthusiastic singers and one of the best known Germans in Frenchtown. The place of meeting was, during the first years, on Market Street between Tenth and Eleventh Streets, later between Sixteenth and Seventeenth. Then the club moved to Carondelet, in the later sixties, near Soulard Street, into the police station situated there, from there to the Harmonie Hall on Seventh Street, then into the Tyroler House, and since 1870 at the corner of Park and Carondelet in the building in which at one time was the People's Savings Institution. Like most of the other societies, so also the Frohsinn, in the course of time, has made honorary members of those who have belonged for twenty-five years. It has also made Hertz, who has always done so much for the society, an honorary president.

The Germania Saengerbund was organized in 1857 by William and Anton Reisse, Julius Rapp, F. Siedler, W. Gottschalk, F. Nischwitz, C. Hauck and others. The following functioned as directors: Gottschalk, F. Glaeser, F. Boehmen, Sabatzki, E. Froehlich, Th. Abbath, A. Grauer, and F. Koch. As meeting place the following places were used: Jaeger's Garden, Flora Garden, Lafayette Hall, the old Tyroler House, Harmonie Hall, the third story over the Lafayette Bank, and finally the Concordia Turner Hall. Among its most zealous members are, in addition to the founders, Charles Reichelt, Hermann Elsner, R. A. Karguth, G. J. Berne, Frederich Bonnet and F. Ibermeyer.

The first brass band whose members were professional musicians was organized in the early fifties by Frank Boehm, who later became the manager of Washington Hall. For a long time it was called the Frank Boehm Band. Later it took the name Knight-Templar Band, because the local commanderies of this order were accustomed to engage this band for its parades and festivals. The Knight Templars took this band to Baltimore to a national conclave. On this occasion forty brass bands competed for a prize, at which the St. Louis band won the first prize. Frank Boehm was a better businessman than he was a musician. The arranging and instrumenting of marches he left to others. The trumpeter and violinist, Jacob Stueck, perhaps rendered him the greatest service in this regard. But Boehm knew how to gather good musicians around him and to procure as well paying employment as possible for them. For though that was the heyday of militia companies that often marched to music, though processions of lodges and societies were numerous, concerts were playing in the public gardens, at least on Sundays, and from autumn to spring there was a good deal of dance music to be played, this did not suffice to support the increasing number of musicians that flocked to St. Louis from everywhere.

For this reason local musicians at times went to one or the other cities in this state and the neighboring state of Illinois in pursuit of their profession. Sometimes small wandering theatrical troops took a few St. Louis musicians with them on the road. Among such itinerant musicians was one Frederick Koenigsberg, who had come from the other side of the sea. On the other side he had been musician director in the employment of

Prince Wittgenstein. He did not like American ways at all. He was therefore horrified when an honest butcher, one of the most prominent Germans in Peoria, engaged Koenigsberg and his colleagues for half a day, to drive through the streets, and with their music call attention to a fat ox that was led in front of the wagon and which was to be slaughtered on the next day. In the course of time Koenigsberg became accustomed to such things, but at that time it was too new and surprising for him. He refused to mount the butcher's wagon, but the others persuaded him, and the prospect of four dollars, promised each musician, was too alluring under the circumstances, he yielded with repugnance, and as he saw the ox, decorated with gay ribbons leading the parade, he uttered these words: "Koenigsberg, how low you have fallen." And who could blame the one time princely orchestra director.

Good old Koenigsberg! He was a good music teacher. He has been dead for a long time, but his laconic: "How low you have fallen" is still heard among the musicians on suitable occasions. The old fellows who were young then, such as Frank Gecks, Henry Foelsing, Keller Schnell, Porberg and others still recall with pleasure the times that once were.

Frank Boehm's brother, Christoph, also had a brass band and the two brothers were in competition with one another. This was particularly true when they competed for the contract to play at the fairgrounds during fair week, which engagement was considered particularly lucrative. Later Herwig's Band also became a competitor. This organization played marches particularly well. The largest military band that St. Louis ever had was the one that was organized by Waldauer upon the order of General Fremont in 1861, and which was attached to Fremont's headquarters. To this band belonged all musicians available here. When they played in front of the headquarters, on Eighth and Chouteau Avenue, one could imagine himself transfixed to Berlin or Frankford and witnessing the change of the guard.

In addition to the above named organizations the North St. Louis Chorus was organized in 1856. Among the founders were: F. Peters, F. Geszner, A. Horskotter, H. Obermoeller, H. Fricke and William Horskotter. Some of the early presidents were: F. Peters, August Horskotter. J. H. Knepper held that office for twenty-five years, and Theodore Pluesz was elected several times to this honor. Henry Saeger was its first director, and after him came Henry Herzog. Professor Berg, L. Haar, and then L. Damen (or Dahmen), who served in this capacity for seventeen years. It must be said in praise of this organization that after the middle sixties it participated in all the festivals of the North American Saengerbund, and also willingly cooperated with all the older societies in the great German festivals that were held here.

The war, of course, had an effect on these societies. Mars and the Muses have never been compatible. The more singers entered the ranks of the defenders of the Union, so much wider became the gaps in the tenor and bass sections. The depressing mood which prevailed at least during the first few years, also acted disturbingly in this direction. Rehearsals were poorly attended and so at times entirely postponed. The number of German families from whose midst fathers, sons or other members had gone into the field was so great that in German circles they could not think of gay festivals. And yet the Social Choir arranged a program in July, 1863, the proceeds of which were intended for wounded soldiers. During the last two years of the war great activity was again noted in the field of song. In 1863 there was organized the chorus of Free Men in the northern part of the city. It is one of the most active of our singing societies. It uses the hall of the Free Congregation as its meeting place. Of its original number, the following still belong: Karl Nohl, Henry Clarner, and Theodore Sessinghaus. The first president of this chorus was Henry Schwarner. Among his successors were Karl Nohl, Karl Salomon, Robert Nagel, Albert Bornmueller, Louis Essig, Ernest Sostmann and August Hoffmann, who also served as secretary for some time. In this capacity the following have also served their organization: H. Clarner, A. Kurtzeborn, A. W. Koehler, H. W. Kaltwasser, C. Wallstab, L. Essig, L. Stiefel and B. Brunschweiler. These men served as directors: Moritz Wurpel, and after him, L. Damen (or Dahmen), F. Partenheimer, Oscar Schmoll, A. Scheufler, and F. Schillinger (or Schilliger). The Chorus of Free Men took a lively interest in all the national music festivals, and also in appropriate manner contributed to all festive occasions of the Free Congregation.

A large German opera company with strong solo parts, a good chorus and suitable orchestra was unknown in America till the winter of 1863-64. It was the service of an American to bring such an organization to American soil. It was Leonard Grover, at that time the director of a theater in Philadelphia who undertook the risk, and it was indeed a risk in more respects than one. The Italian opera had become so firmly established in the large cities of the east during the fifties, and had such great drawing power in New York, that the Academy of Music, especially built for its special use could each year schedule an uninterrupted season, running from October to April. After the close of the season the company was accustomed to make a tour of two or three months. The Italian opera had become a matter of fashion. To plan a German rival in the field was, therefore, a difficult matter, and the condition of the times, in the midst of a war did not seem to favor the cause. But Grover was not the man to be deterred. He presented his troupe first in the east and then in the west. In both regions he was successful. De Bar's theater on Pine Street proved almost too small during the two weeks in February, 1864 when the opera played here. Although our German countrymen made up the bulk of the audience, the non-German friends of the opera and music in general also took an enthusiastic part in the enterprise.

That was the time when Theodore Habelmann made so many friends here and Carl (or Karl) Formes was welcomed anew by his old acquaintances. The latter had appeared here a few years before in concerts in which Theodore Thomas was also heard as violin soloist. The director of the opera was Carl Anschuetz, a small man, who always pulled his shoulders high.

The Apollo Singing Society was an outgrowth of the North St. Louis Liedertafel. It was formed at the end of the fifties. A part of the members had previously left the Liedertafel to join the Chorus of Free Men. The meeting place of the Liedertafel was on Eleventh and Salisbury Street. The founders were C. Lappe, G. Becker, S. Bergg, E. Kreuter, W. Grumme, F. Ellerbeck, B. Kankemeier, M. Hoffmann, L. Johler, Ernest Scroka (or Stroka), Frederick Beinert and L. Meiszner. The latter served as the first president. J. Klein was the director. In 1864 rehearsals were interrupted till the end of the war. Not until the spring of 1866 were steps taken toward reorganization. The meeting called for this purpose met in the upper story of the Magwire Market Hall. Among those present were: Henry Deubach, Frederick Beinert, P. A. Bender, H. Wertz, S. Oblicke, Frederick Detmerin, E. Lenze, E. Kreuter, H. Kreuter, Ernest Scroka (or Stroka), and G. Becker. They organized with Deubach as president and they chose F. Partenheimer musical director. The rehearsals were held in Magwire Market, and two dollars per month were paid for the use of the room. The honorarium of the director was also very economical. In the list of members the best German names of New Bremen were represented, and the number of participants grew rapidly. In order to avoid confusion with other societies, it was decided at an early date to change the name to the Apollo Singing Society. Partenheimer served a long time as conductor, and during the last seven years, this position has been held by Frederick Schilliger (or Schillinger), the son of the flutist, and himself a clever musician. Since 1872 the Apollo Singing Society, with the exception of two years, has had the same president, namely, the well-known cigar manufacturer, A. F. Baerens, who is just as eager a singer as he is an experienced presiding officer. It is mainly due to his energy, that the Apollo owns its own home, having bought the Magwire Mansion on Bremen Avenue and Ninth Street, and made it suitable for its purpose by reconstruction. This society also participates regularly in the festivals of the North American Saengerbund, being represented by a handsome group of active members. This Society is also noted for the praiseworthy variety that it puts into its programs for evening entertainment. A similar endeavor was shown by the older societies, the Social Choir of Singers, the Rheinische Frohsinn, the old St. Louis Saengerbund, and the Germania Saengerbund, when the war was over. When the swords had been put in the scabbard again, and peace returned, our singing societies again took up their activity with new zeal. Song and sociability were fostered and yielded the most pleasing results, proclaiming the fame of the German element far and wide.

The Arion of the West owes its origin to a secession of the friendliest kind. It was in January 1866, when a small number of active members of the St. Louis Saengerbund resolved to form a new society. The Saengerbund at that time was holding its rehearsals in the building of the First National Bank, on Carondelet and Park Avenue. It was the wish for a meeting place farther to the south which was the cause for leaving the old society. The conductor of the latter was attorney Gustav von Deutsch, a passionate lover of music, a good cello player and a charming companion. He became one of the founders of the new society, to which belonged, among others, Rudolph Schlulenburg, H. Spannagel, August Doerner, and H. C. Upmeyer. During the first period of its existence the Arion held its rehearsals, with Mr. von Deutsch conducting, over the office of the patent medicine manufacturer, McLean, on Chestnut Street. Immediately in the first year the young society took part in the Saengerfest in Louisville. On its return, Dr. Gericke, the president, had the misfortune to break a leg on leaving the ferryboat.

The hall over Rudolf Mackwitz' office at the northeast corner of Third and Chestnut Streets, formerly used by the Erwin Lodge, served the society for several years as a meeting place. Here the number of members, particularly the inactive members now singing members, became larger from year to year. This was mainly due to the fact that this society, more than any other, cared for entertainment and variety, and gave to sociability the widest scope.

At the beginning of 1866-67, Sobolewski resigned as conductor of the Philharmonic Society. The season, however, was continued with Balmer and Waldauer conducting during the interim. Dr. William Taussig, who from the outset had been one of the most zealous promoters of the society, spent the following summer in Germany. He was requested to secure another conductor as successor to Sobolewski. He engaged Egmont Froelich, who came here in the autumn of 1867 from Stuttgart. He conducted the Philharmonic society concerts for two years, at which time the society was dissolved. The reason for this discontinuance of the organization was that its expenses exceeded its income. In part this condition was brought about by the practice of bringing a couple of out of town artists for every concert, who, as a rule, charged a high honorarium. Though some of the members were ready to make further pecuniary sacrifices, it was decided upon mature deliberation to disorganize. This step was greatly regretted by the friends of music, as the organization had been so eminently successful in its musical offerings.

The Orpheus Society was formed in 1867 by William Homann, Otto Dickmann, Henry Frey, G. Kunsemueller, William Lahrmann, Frederick Schwanecke, and Ernest and Herman Keisker. The Keisker brothers and Emil Cheric were particularly enthusiastic singers. In general the activity of the various societies was good during the next following years. Most of them participated in the Saengerfest, which was held in Indianapolis in 1867, Chicago in 1868, and Cincinnati in 1870. For many years William Homann was president of the Orpheus Society, which in 1878 merged with the St. Louis Saengerbund. Of the later presidents the following deserve especially to be mentioned: Adolph Kleinecke, H. Spakler, and Charles Schweikard. The Ladies Chorus which was organized in 1872, chiefly through the effort of Mrs. Doctor Jenks, was closely affiliated with the

Orpheus Society, and ably assisted the group on many occasions. Its most successful conductors were Oscar Schmoll and F. W. Norsch.

The Arion Society had a ladies chorus as an auxiliary, but it was soon discontinued because of the cost involved. The Germania Club also had mixed chorus for a while. Emil Feigenbutz was its able conductor. In 1871 the, earlier mentioned Lucca Society originated. Only ladies sang in this organization which existed for about three years. At the beginning of the sixties the number of piano students, boys as well as girls, increased greatly, and, of course, the number of piano teachers increased correspondingly. One of the best known piano teachers of this time was Karl Bode, who is no doubt remembered by the older lovers of music.

One of Bode's most gifted students was Mrs. Carl Conrad, the daughter of the also very musical Mrs. Vogelsang. Moreover, he instructed for a few years a talented girl pupil, who ten years later, as pianist, won the plaudits of experts in the concerts in the Singakadmie of Berlin. This student was Anna Spaeter, who later became Mrs. Bausemer. She received her first musical instruction in her native city of Breslau. Here, as a girl of ten years she first had Bode and then Egmont Froehlich as instructor, and from her sixteenth year on she had Franz Bausemer, who later became her husband, as teacher. She was so proficient in music that she was for some years employed as teacher of piano in the Kullak Academy of Music in Berlin.

During the second half of the sixties, as also later, during the winter seasons the Italian opera came here. The impresarios, which headed these touring companies, were glad to come to St. Louis because they had a good income here. As long as de Bar had his playhouse on Pine Street the companies showed there, and also remained loyal to him for a while when he moved to the Opera House on Market Street. Max Strakosch came most frequently. Jacob Grau came several times, and Max Maretzek came twice as director and once as conductor. Later appeared "Colonel" Mapleson with Her Majesty's Opera, first in the Opera House, and then always in the Olympic, which was preferred as being more fashionable by the elite, who attended the opera mainly to be seen.

In those years the Italian opera completely domineered this side of the ocean. The repertoire offered but little variety. Again and again it was: Norma, Lucia, Lucretia Borgia, La Sonnambula, La Favorita, Il Trovatore, Barbier di Siviglia, La Traviata, etc. Only in later years did Faust, Rigoletto, L'Africana, Aida, etc. appear as novelties. There were also opera failures in the course of times, as for example that of Henry Grau (primadonna–Eugenia Pappenheim) a nephew of old "Giacomo."

In the later sixties Flotow's Alessandro Stradella was presented at the Olympic Theater under the direction of G. von Deutsch, the director of the Arion Society. Ferdinand Diehm, the tenor soloist of the Arion, sang the title role and Miss Sobolewski, the daughter of the conductor Sobolewski sang the soprano part. In Diehm the musical world of St. Louis had a valuable addition he had a high tenor voice of wide range.

When in 1869 the Philharmonic Society ceased to exist, S. R. Sauter organized the Haydn Orchestra. In contrast to the orchestra which he had conducted so successfully in Buena Vista Garden, in Union Park, and in the Tivoli, the Haydn Orchestra consisted of amateurs, and only when great concerts were scheduled were professional musicians added to the group. Among the members of the Haydn Orchestra were Otto Eisenhardt, W. Pommer, Kieselhorst, (the fine flutist), Schuler, Laser, Sellers, and others. At one of the great concerts the youthful pianist Lina Anton played for the first time in public, and was enthusiastically received. It was so difficult to hold together an amateur orchestra whose members had so many varied interests, that the group, which had won much approbation for its accomplishments, was discontinued.

The Arion of the West, in 1869, elected Egmont Froehlich as its director. When, in the following year, at the Saengerfest in Cincinnati, our city was chosen as the next place of meeting, the local societies chose Froehlich as musical director of the eighteenth North American Saengerbundfest, which was held here from the twelfth to the sixteenth of June, 1872. At a cost of sixty thousand dollars a special building was erected between Eleventh and Twelfth Streets, St. Charles Street and Washington Avenue. This building had a seating capacity of twelve thousand, and on its stage was room for two thousand singers. Franz Abt had come across the ocean as guest of honor. When, at the concert of reception, he stepped to the podium in order to wield the baton during the performance of his own composition –*Abendlied*, the singers and the audience gave him a most rousing ovation.

The festival orchestra, which was also conducted by Froehlich consisted for the most part of local musicians who had received reenforcement from Milwaukee, Chicago, and Cincinnati. The playing of this orchestra was excellent, as indeed the whole festival was a distinct success. It brought honor to all participants and to the citizenry in general, the Germans as well as the non-Germans, for they had all furthered this event with enthusiasm.

At the beginning of the seventies a musician by the name of Williams came to St. Louis. After he had been here for a while he was convinced that St. Louis was a good field for a conservatory of music. He therefore proceeded to establish such a school. For this purpose he joined up with Waldauer and with the pianist Hermann Lawitzky who had recently come from Mobile. The former became head of the violin department and the latter of the piano department. After less than a year Williams withdrew. Waldauer and Lawitzky paid him a certain indemnification and bought the instruments and music, and continued the institution till the time of the death of Lawitzky. The Beethoven Conservatory was then for many years under Waldauer's own management, and he was in such an advantageous position that he could meet all competition. Later the piano teacher Marcus Epstein became co-owner of the school, from which came many hundreds of young musicians in the course of the years.

In the winter of 1872 the Chouteau Valley Men's Chorus was created. The founders were Joseph Schnaider, Fritz Wahl, Julius Foerstel, Frederick Nedderhuth, Christian Starck and Dr. Edward Borch, who did most for the organization's origin. Joseph Schnaider accepted the presidency on condition that the vice president would have to look after business matters, but if it was a matter of money, he would see to it this was forthcoming. Dr. Borch was elected vice president. A private residence on Chouteau Avenue was leased as a meeting place. Carl Froehlich, a younger brother of Egmont, whom the latter brought from Stuttgart, was made director. For the first all twelve active members attended, but by and by their number increased, and the inactive members still more, for the society offered its members as much entertainment as possible, moreover the organization was exclusive, non-members were not admitted to the regular evening entertainment.

Among those who first belonged to the Men's Chorus were the jovial Conrad Rose, the Justice of the Peace Anton Michel, the druggist Charles Starck, the brewer Fritz Wahl, moreover B. Thalmann, H. Chapman, John Bohlen, H. Lerch, D. Lager, William Ohm, C. Behrens, R. Niebert, which latter did so much for the organization for he built a pretty hall for it. In the summer of 1873, the Chouteau Valley Men's Chorus gave its first public concert in Schnaider's Garden at which twenty-four active members and a quartet of soloists participated. By special permission of Mayor Brown, and under the command of Major Fuchs, a cannon was fired every five minutes, therefore, a la Gilmore at the peace jubilee in Boston. The concert was so well attended that every nook of the garden was occupied. Dr. Borch, who, during the first few years, so to say, had been the soul of the organization, then moved from Chouteau Avenue to the northern part of the city, and so could not devote himself to the interests of the club. But there were always some who could step in his footsteps.

Even at the 1872 Saengerfest there were, in addition to the societies which were already mentioned, several other singing societies, among them the Druid Men's Chorus, the Harugari Saengerbund, the Swiss Men's Chorus, the Jaeger Saengerbund, the Saengerbund of the Sons of Hermann. The old St. Louis Turner Society had had a section for vocal music, whose best supporter was Emil Mueller. Thus St. Louis, even at that time, had a goodly number of German singing societies. And their number is still growing, as is a generally known fact. Incidentally, it may be remarked, at the Saengerfest of 1888 no less than twenty-nine local societies participated.

As at an earlier date the Arion of the West sprang from the St. Louis Saengerbund, so from the Arion of the West there came in 1870 the Liederkranz. About twenty active members had become tired of the nagging of the combative Dr. Hammer. They made an effort to have Hammer expelled from the organization, but since inactive members had a vote in this society, the effort failed. He remained in the club, and the best and most enthusiastic singers resigned. Among the founders of the Liederkranz were the following: Ferdinand Diehm, J. Schoenthaler, E. Boehl, A. Mueller, Oscar Steins, and A. Krieckhaus. After a short time Egmont Froehlich resigned as director of the Arion, to assume a similar position in the Liederkranz, which has been his hands since. The Arion was the first of local singing societies to provide for itself suitable quarters. Its members leased the two upper stories of a duplex house on the southeast corner of Fourth and Elm Streets, and arranged a large ball room, with a stage, a game and billiard room, a dining hall, kitchen, etc., in a word, complete club rooms.

The Arion, from the outset, made the entertainment of its members its principal problem. It had sociable elements, such as could not be found in any other St. Louis society, either then or now, who in addition to the will, and the readiness to make sacrifices, had the ability and skill to offer entertainment of great variety. In these matters the following, for example, have shown themselves ever ready to render service: the druggist Harless, Dr. Otto Greiner, Dr. Herrmann, Dr. Gericke, Emil Donk, Dr. Spiegelhalter, Stiesmeyer, Buechel, Keppler, Armin Zott, Herminghaus, Raacke, Paust, the newspaper writers J. Rittig, Udo Brachvogel, and the author of this book. the carnival festivals of Arion are unsurpassed and unequaled. It is true that the motto of this society was: Money is no object.

There was no lack of banquets, toasts and speeches, and although the game of skat was not yet played with such restless zeal as later, the club rooms were well filled on every evening. Until the very last period of its existence there was also much singing. Under the direction of P. G. Anton, who repeatedly served as director, the society did excellent work. Carl Schramm and A. Willhartitz also served as directors during the early seventies. In the summer of 1876 Hans Balatka was called to this position. During the preceding the twenty-five years he had founded and conducted similar musical organizations in Milwaukee and Chicago. During his stay in St. Louis, which was limited to one and a half years, the Arion presented, among others, Hoffman's *Schoene Melusine* and Max Bruch's *Odysee*.

The permanent organization for chamber music, the Philharmonic Quintet Club, was organized in the winter of 1876. It came into being mainly through the efforts of P. G. Anton and Carl Ludwig Bernays. The latter made propoganda for the undertaking in American circles. Bermays was a great friend of music, a Beethoven enthusiast of the highest caliber. His son-in-law, Ernest Spiering, who came here in the middle sixties, was a fine violinist. In the Quintet he played the first violin, John Boehme, the second violin, Anton, the viola, and at first Palmer from Belleville, and then Balatka, the cello. That took care of the string instruments in good fashion. The pianist was Lina Anton, who for many years had received instruction from her father, and then from Miss von Hoya, a very fine teacher. After Balatka's departure Louis Meyer, the conductor of the Grand Orchestra, played the cello, and after him young Gottlieb Anton, who played this instrument masterfully. After Lina Anton secured a position in New York pianist Louis Hammerstein took her position in the Quintet.

Spiering had played first violin in Albert Mahler's orchestra, whose dance music was considered the best in the whole west. After Mahler's death Spiering headed this orchestra. In the winter months it played almost every evening till far into the night, and as Spiering also gave violin lessons from morning to night, he overworked himself to such an extent, that he died relatively young.

John Boehme came here in 1860. His main instrument was the viola. However, he was also a clever violinist. As such he first appeared in the Flora Garden. (Corner of south Eighth and Geyer Avenue). Boehme also belonged to Mahler's orchestra, and later to Spiering's, which he continued to conduct till it merged with Felix Saenger's orchestra, which for thirteen years furnished music for the Germania club, and also for many years for the Liederkranz.

In P. G. Anton, who has lived here since the end of the fifties, St. Louis has undoubtedly one of the best informed theoretic musicians and classically educated composers. His father was conductor of the concert theater at Darmstadt and one of the best violinists of his time. The son received instruction not only from his father but also from such famous teachers as Rink and Snyder von Wartenburg. This was a music education of rare thoroughness. Here he was, for many years, the organist in Pastor Elliot's church (Church of the Messiah), and also conducted the choir, whose soprano was Mrs. Dean-Lowe). In the course of many years he conducted, even though only as an accommodation and intermittently, now this and that singing society, but his main activity was that of a composer, and it is to be regretted that most of his work is still locked up in his desk.

The West St. Louis Liederkranz was brought into life in 1870. It was organized at a meeting, which was held at Christ Comrades' Threemilehouse. The founders were J. H. Meyer, F. Wiese, William Heil, Frederick Haberstroh, A. Huber, J. Oberreider, H. Bohlmann, G. Gruenwald, L. Wiesler. In the course of time the following were the presidents of the group: H. Bohlmann, W. Schilling, W. Heil, G. Kramer, G. Gruenwald, Theodore Hoel, Philipp Dueber, Otto Keil and Louis Schaefer. The latter was elected honorary president. At the beginning Trimbe was the director. After him F. Partenheimer held the post for sixteen years. His successor was Norsch. For a number of years the West St. Louis Liederkranz has participated in the national Saengerfests, and at one of these contests, held in Highland, won the second prize.

The German Element in St. Louis

While most of the European artists that toured America had come to St. Louis, the seventies brought us in truth embarras de richesses of them. These famous violinists came: Sauret, Winiawski, Karl Rosa, Remenyi, Wilhelmy; these pianists: Rubinstein, Anna Essiposs, Hans von Buelow, Julia Rive-King, Anna Mehling, Clara Careno, Gustav Satter; and the violinist Winiawski. On this occasion the brothers Charles and Jacob Kunkel met with great distinction. The Kunkels came from New York to St. Louis in 1869. By their performances as pianists they quickly attracted attention, so that few great concerts were given at which they did not contribute at least one number on the program. Their specialty was duets played on two pianos. It was such a performance that won for them the praise of Rubinstein. Upon his various visits to the conservatory, which was managed by the Kunkels, he expressed himself in the most flattering terms in the newspapers regarding the two brothers.

Waldemar Malmene followed his profession as voice and piano teacher here from 1869 on. Since 1890 he has been teaching music in the local Institute for the Blind. In his native city, Berlin, he received theoretical and practical instruction from A. W. Bach on the organ, and from Julius Schneider, Grell (the director of the Sing Akademie), Loeschhorn and others, in other branches of music. Upon the intervention of Meyerbeer, Malmene, at age 19, was accepted as a pupil by the imperial conservatory in Paris, where he was educated as a teacher of music by the celebrated singer, Bordogni. After considerable activity in England as organist and conductor of church choirs, he came to America, and together with the organist Creswold, organized an oratorio company, which after three years disbanded because of lack of finances. For two years he conducted the Druid Men's Chorus, and an equal length of time he gave singing instruction, in the public schools. However, his main activity was that of music teacher at Washington University, which position he held for ten years. Of his many song compositions, the one based on Freiligrath's poem, "Oh love, as long as you can love," is perhaps the most popular. He is extremely productive. More than sixty of his songs have appeared in print. However, his larger works still slumber in the depth of his desk.

The Liederkranz, whose first president was Eugene Haas, at first, like most singing societies, led a nomadic life, till it secured for itself a home of its own in 1880. Under the direction of its director, Egmont Froehlich, who held this position for more than twenty years, this organization presented, among the larger works, during the first ten years, the following: Gades's Earl King's Daughter, Mendelssohn's First Walpurgis Night, Schumann's the Rose Pilgrimage, Erdmannsdoerfer's Princess Ilse, Verdi's Requiem, Vierling's The Rape of the Sabien Women, Brueh's Odysseus, Hoffmann's Beautiful Melusine. The concerts of the Liederkranz were characterized by carefully selected programs and diligent study of the single numbers. The society has a strong Women's chorus, which participated in almost all the concerts. Also in the field of sociability the Liederkranz did a great deal, especially after it united with the Arion in 1879. The possession of a home of their own with plenty of room, a garden, a billiard room, bowling alley, etc. facilitated this task very much.

The Mendelssohn Quintet Club was organized by Carl Froehlich. He played the cello, George Heerich, a very able violinist, played the first violin, Victor Ehling, a St. Louisan, who got his musical education in Vienna, was the pianist of the club. Victor Ehling is the song of the flutist Ehling who was active here in his profession during the sixties.

In former times Germany furnished the music teachers for this country even more than now. In St. Louis they constitute even today a solid phalanx, to which music and musical interests owe much. Among the older teachers of music in our city should be mentioned, in addition to those already noted in this chapter, Edward Nennstil, who, however, has sold pianos for the last twenty-five years, also the brothers Kluever, Franz Boehmen, who was also a clever maker of violins, Theodore Abbath, Rudolph Bondi, Gustav Pommer, and Mrs. Doctor Strothotto. Most of the directors were accustomed also to give instruction in music, and some of them rendered great service in this field.

In 1879 the Musical Union came into existence, thanks to the efforts of our fellow-citizen, A. Naldauer. For eleven years the musical direction of this organization was in his hands. Then the Union merged with the choral Society with Joseph Otten as director. The Musical Union gave each year five, and sometimes six concerts. It brought in well-known soloists to almost every performance, and also presented local soloists as, for example, the violinists Heerich and Frank Gecks, Jr., and the pianists Ehling and Epstein. It is to be regretted that St. Louis does not have such programs any more. This sort of program offered something for the taste of everyone.

The German Element in St. Louis

The twenty-fifth song festival of the North American Saengerbund was held in St. Louis in 1888. Leopold Methudi (or Methudy), a most enthusiastic friend of music was chosen president of the Saengerbund and at the same time presiding officer of the festival. The director of the festival was Egmont Froehlich, who had served in a similar position at the festival of 1872. The 1888 festival was not so much a song festival based on folk songs and male choruses, as it was a festival of artists. The virtuosos predominated at the concerts. Such male singers as Alvari, Fisher, Steger, Kalisch, and women singers as Lillie Lehman and Emma Juch, and the pianist Adele aus der Ohe participated.

The account of the musical life of our city is finished. It embraces a period of more than fifty years. With the abundance of material, an undesired brevity was necessary, and it is, therefore, possible that many a more or less deserving name is omitted. If this is the case, it hardly requires the special assurance that it was unintentional.

23. The German Theater

It is now more than fifty years ago that the first tribute was paid the German dramatic muse in the far west, on the banks of the Mississippi. Schiller's *Robbers* was chosen for the first German performance which took place in 1842. *The Robbers* was Schiller's first play. It was first staged in Mannheim in 1782. At the performance in St. Louis, sixty years later, the enthusiasm was scarcely less than at Mannheim. The income from the St. Louis performance was for the aid of an actor, named Riese, who had arrived sans any means. On a very primitive stage, in the dining room of a hotel, the play was given. Riese played the role of Karl Moor, while the remaining roles were taken by amateurs, but no woman could be found for the role of Amalie. Before the last act Riese positively refused to continue without an Amalie, who up to that point had been only talked about in the play, but who was very essential in the last act, as she is expected to be stabbed before the final curtain. The cook of the house was therefore hastily attired in a white dress and pushed on the stage. Since she did not sink to the floor at the right time, as directed, Riese gave her a mighty blow that did not fail to have the desired effect.

This performance of *The Robbers* may, therefore, be regarded as the beginning of the German theatrical performances that were to come in the following years. The number of amateurs that were able and willing to study the roles and participate in the performances was not very large. Moreover, they had their own daily work to do. Nevertheless there were among the young German men of that time, enough who were sufficiently able to meet the undertaking. In this manner it was possible for the actors and directors who came to St. Louis to practice their profession. In this way Mr. and Mrs. Thielemann, who later managed a theater in Chicago, were enabled to play here during the winter of 1844 to 45. The principal participants were: Attorney Christian Kribben, his younger brother William, who was a pilot on a Mississippi steamboat, the newspaperman Benkendorf, Herman (or Hermann) Achenbach, Julius Buechel, A. U. Ross, Henry Lischer, William Mackwitz, George Reichard and Mrs. Hippo Krug. From 1846 to 1849 there was a Thalia Society which staged performances at regular intervals. The above-named Kribben brothers were leaders in it. The building in which this society showed was at the corner of Main and Pine Streets. It was destroyed by the conflagration in 1849.

In the spring of 1851 director Strasser, his wife and two daughters, all actors came here. He was willingly assisted by local amateurs. After a few performances in the Tontine, Second Street near Elm, Strasser built a large, dark frame building, with only a few openings for ventilation in the Arsenal Park of that time, and opened a summer theater in it. On the very first evening the play could not go on since the musicians did not arrive. The public was very much dissatisfied, and after a stormy scene it obtained its admission price refunded. In less than three months the undertaking failed, and the Strasser family turned their backs on St. Louis.

The oldest local singing society, the St. Louis Saengerbund, gave, from February to May 1852, a performance once in two weeks. These programs were given in the old Washington Hall. (The present, much larger hall was built much later.) For the first performance *Heirothsantrag auf Helgoland*, (Marriage proposal on Helgoland), was chosen. A prologue, composed by Adalbert Loehr, preceded the performance. After the singer and actor Benrodt and his wife, assisted by local talent, gave a few performances in late summer of that year, the dramatic section of the Saengerbund played several times from December 1852 till the spring of 1853. These performances were given in the Varieties Theater, the present Opera House, also in the Peoples (later Woods) and Bates Theater, which later was owned by de Bar on Pine Street.

The German Element in St. Louis

The Philodramatic Society was organized in 1853 by Henry Boernstein, the publisher and editor of the *Anzeiger des Westens*. With it was aroused a general and lively interest, so that almost all endeavors and accomplishments of German art, during the immediately following years, could be traced back to it. The society, whose activity extended over a period of four years, played during the first year in the above mentioned theater on Pine Street, later in the Varieties. Among the itinerant directors who came here during this period, were Bonnet and Wolf. The performances of the Philodramatic Society were staged for benevolent purposes. For those times the income was very ample. The German Immigration Society, the Free Congregation, and the ladies societies of those days, and such bodies were the beneficiaries. One of the most interested members was Frederick Kluender. He had talent and devotion for the stage. So that he could serve as director for a while in 1857, when Boernstein decided to give up the task of directing the amateur society which for various reasons had become distasteful to him. The latter and his wife had participated in almost every performance. He directed the actors and also provided the scenery. The success of the organization was mainly due to him. By his efforts there had been sown a seed which was to bear rich fruit for the German element in our city, for from this seed grew Boernstein's great as well as difficult undertaking, namely the attempt to assure a German stage for St. Louis.

It was a difficult task which he set for himself in this enterprise. However, since he was firmly convinced that nothing furthered culture and refinement more than a good theater, and that this was in truth the school for adults, no sacrifice of time, work and money was too great for him in carrying out his plans. And so he created a theater of which the Germans in St. Louis could be proud. Under the name of St. Louis Opera House he opened the theater on Market Street, between Fifth and Sixth Streets on October 1, 1859. For the first performance he chose Goethe's *Egmont*. The company of players was excellent and could have held its own with any of the larger stages of Germany. Besides the director, Mr. Boernstein, there were Alexander Pfeiffer, who was also manager, Roepenak, Julius Grossman, Stierlin, Frederick Schwan, the very youthful A. Foellger, Ostermann, H. Dietz, and the women actors Mrs. Marie Boernstein, Alwine Dremmel, Caroline Lindemann, Rohardine Otto, the youthful Lina Boernstein and many others. The musical director was the very able

Adolph Willhartitz. Under this direction were staged *Undine*, *Zauberschleier* and other works. These performances were very good and had to be repeated several times. A fair-sized orchestra supported the cast ably. Later this man taught music for several years in the local school for the blind.

The hundredth birthday of Friedrich Schiller, November 10, 1859, was commemorated by a whole Schiller week. The following works were performed: *Intrigue and Love, The Robbers, Mary Stuart, Wallenstein's Death, William Tell* and *Fiesco*.

The company played every evening, and the summer months of 1860 brought no interruption in the performances. The first year brought the most satisfying returns. Under the most favorable auspices the second year was begun in the fall of 1860. The company of actors had not changed materially and the performances were given with the accustomed care. On week days the attendance might have been better, but on Sundays the income was good. In this manner pleasing progress was made during the winter months till Sunday, March 14, 1861. On that day the performance was prevented by the caprice of the police. This violent action was taken by police authorities that had taken office lately. These authorities, who sided with the south, wished to let the Germans, who were loyal to the Union, feel their power by prohibiting Sunday theatrical performances. Their attempt was only too successful. With the Sunday evening performance prohibited the theater could not meets its expenses. But even if this had been possible, the Civil War, which flared up soon, would have put an end to the undertaking, for it affected every kind of business. The curtain of the great theater of war suddenly rolled up. The theater director, Boernstein, became Colonel Boernstein, who went into the field at the head of his regiment. The first permanent German stage in St. Louis ceased to exist.

Alexander Pfeiffer gathered the remaining members of Boernstein's theater about him in the winter of 1861 to 1862, and gave a number of very good performances in the Concert Hall. In the same hall a year later the amateurs of the Family Circle, which later became the Casino, presented plays during two or three winters. There was no lack of amateur theaters during the sixties than during the last three decades.

If some time a detailed history of the German theater of St. Louis is to be written, then a comprehensive chapter will have to be devoted to the

Apollo Theater, for during a quarter of a century, allowing for frequent interruptions, the German muse has found a shelter there. In its room, in addition to much that was mediocre and some that was poor, also a great deal that was good, and not infrequently even excellent, was presented. It is true that perhaps no other theater in this country, in an equal period of time, underwent so many changes as this one, –changes with regard to directors, actors and the public.

With a company that was good in almost every department, Director William Koser held his entrance in the Apollo in 1863. Ludwig Knorr, an outstanding artist and for a long time stage manager of the New York Municipal Theater, played here during this season on eighteen evenings. The management was in the hands of Ignatz Wolf (or Ignaz Wolff), a good portrayer of hero and character roles, and Julius Koch, also a clever actor. However, in the middle of the season these two resigned, whereupon Leopold Mader, who was a journalist by profession, assumed the vacated position. In November of 1864 Koser moved to the National Theater on Market Street, between Fourth and Fifth Streets. Here Antonie Becker-Grahn played a long while as guest artist. In this theater Koser played during three winters. During this period he had among others as guest artists Johanna Claussen, who at that time was a youthful soubrette, Otto von Hoym, who had resigned from the management of the New York Municipal Theater, and had participated in the war, Edward Haerting, Hedwig Hesse, who had been engaged in Milwaukee, and Ottilie Genee from Berlin, who later became the directress of the German Theater in San Francisco. During the summer of 1865 Hannes Lewens managed the Apollo Theater. In the fall Anton Foellger became his successor. The financial management was in the hands of his wife. Mr. and Mrs. Pelosi and the comedian Julius Ascher appeared as guest artist, also Roepenack and Ludwig Knorr. This made possible a performance of *Faust*, during which the title role in the first two acts was taken by Knorr, and in the last three acts by Foellger, the Mephisto role by Roepenach, Gretchen by Ludovika Pfeiffer, and Martha Schmertlein by Mrs. Lindemann.

After the National Theater, which Koser had renamed the Municipal Theater, was destroyed by fire in April of 1866, Tony Niederwiesser had a stage built in the Walhalla, Fourth Street, between Market and Walnut, on which Koser's company played for a while. In the summer this company then gave very good performances in Washington Garden. In the following winter Emil and Louise von der Osten, Louise Haase, and Conrad Mueller appeared, under Koser's management, in the former Opera House, which had assumed its former name of Varieties again. In the summer of 1867 Louis Kurth and Emil Laszwitz managed the Apollo Theater. (Laszwitz' best roles were Tell, Hamlet, Franz Mohr, and Secretary Wurm.) As guest artists appeared the soubrette Antoinette Fehringer and Gustav Ostermann. During the winter they played on week days in the Apollo Theater and on Sundays in the Varieties. The company consisted of the Messrs. Franzmueller, Ignaz Wolff (or Ignatz Wolf), Steidel, Alexander Kost and Weidmann, and the ladies Lindemann, Haase, Ludovika, Franzmueller, Pfeiffer, Hofstetten, Kost and others. Laszwitz and Lewens functioned as managers.

The later sixties brought three celebrated guests from Germany to American, and also to St. Louis. Two of these had their own companies –Fanny Janauschek (or Janauscheck) and Marie Seebach. The former was famous for her presentation of the roles Deborah and Mary Stuart. The latter triumphed as Princess Eboli in *Don Carlos*, Louise in *Intrigue and Love*, and Jane Eyre in *The Waif of Lowood*. The third of these guests artists were Theodore L'Arronge, in his time the best comedian on the Berlin stage. In company with his wife, the singer, Hedwig Surry, he toured America. This pair of artists played here for three weeks and presented sold-out houses *Die Schoene Galathee* eight times, *Orpheus in the Underworld* four times, and *Pechschulze* three times. The latter play was presented in January 1868. At New Years, Kurth took over the management alone, and during the following month there were guest artists without number. Among these was Joseph Keppler and a trio of German-Hungarian dwarfs, which were just as great artists they were small physically. In May Alfons von Zerboni took over the management. His wife was a good soubrette singer. *Der Postillon von Muencheberg* was given eleven times without diminishing success, more over *Leichte Cavalterie,* and *Zehn Maedchen und kein Mann*. At the end of July Kurth retired. Zerboni became ill and died, and a few weeks later his young widow, because of grief over the loss of her husband took her own life. Krueger and Schiller, the lessees of the tavern took over, and Lewens and Koch, the husband of Johanna Claussen, became the managers. Early in 1869 the management was in the hands of Louise Haase. Mrs. von Baerndorf came for a rather long visit as guest artist, and appeared successfully on various occasions as *Adrienne Lecouvreux, Mary Stuart* and *Maid of Orleans*. She was followed by the soubrette Auguste Hoefl, the character actor Dombrowski, the comedian Heinsdorf and others. Hardly had the summer season begun when Miss Haase laid down the scepter. Mrs. Hoefl had the courage to take it up, but here career as a manager lasted only a few weeks. Then her husband, the chemist and wine adulterer, with the Bluffton Wine Co., Frings, took up the task. Before the end of the year, he too, resigned as manager. In January Kurth once more took the rudder in hand, and now Otto and Elise von Hoym, Laszwitz, Mrs. Velguth (or Vellguth), and Ignaz Wolff (or Ignatz Wolf) appeared as guest artists.

The summer season under Krueger and Schiller, and under the management of Laszwitz and Lewens brought Mrs. Wagner-Maertens as guest artist. She appeared in *Von Stufe and Stufe* nine times. They also brought an operetta season to the Apollo Theater. The able conductor Schramm, who unfortunately died too young, accomplished much good with rather limited means during this summer. He presented *Blaubarth, Flotte Burschen,* and *Schoene Helena*. In the following winter with more singers participating (Anna Jaeger, Mrs. Schramm-Rolff, Humbser, Kost, Ahlfeld and Conrad Mueller) under the management of Laszwitz still more operettas and light operas were given. The winter season of 1870 to 1871, with the singer Julius Hermann as director, was devoted to the opera. Then Krueger and Schiller stepped into the breach, which gave occasion for another opening performance. In regard to the number of "opening performances" the Apollo Theater achieved astonishing things.

Late in October, 1871, Louis Pelosi took over the management. He, as well as his wife, were pleasantly remembered from their earlier appearance as guests artists, and their coming was greeted with delight by the theater-going public. They had played for five years on the other side of the ocean, and had now returned to make their home here. The season brought very many good performances, among them Raupach's *Schule des Lebens, Narcisz, Die Raeuber, Die Sternenjugfrau,* and on Schiller's birthday *William Tell*. At the close of the season Dr. John Hartmann's *Die deutsche Landwehr, oder die Belagerung von Strassburg* was presented. This had the support of Simpson's battery and the Guard Uhlans. This performance drew a packed house. During the winter of 1872-1873 the Pelosi company only played on Sundays. All their performances were in the Olympic. To this company belonged, among others, Mrs. Lindemann, Miss Magius, Mrs. Neidmann, and the Messrs. Lewens, Kroener, Rolf, Meuschke. Max and Josephine Lube appeared as guest artists.

In June 1872 the opera held its entrance in the Apollo Theater. The business manager was the local merchant Waldstein, and the director was Julius Hermann. The personnel consisted of Theodore Habelmann, Otto Schueler, Beets, Franosch, (and later also Fritz Lafontaine), Bertha Roemer, Mrs. Schueler-Jaeger, Sophie Dziuba and Miss von Frankenberg. The above took the principal roles and were supported by minor performers. From February 1873 on, Habelmann was director, and St. Louis had for a year and a half a permanent German opera, whose excellent performances are vividly remembered by German as also by non-German friends of music.

In the winter of 1873 to 74 the Pelosi management presented a season of performances in the Olympic that was in every way successful. To the company belonged, among others, the fine artists, Mr. and Mrs. Lube, Clara Solia, Mr. and Mrs. Carl Helmer. In 1874 J. G. Woerner's *Sklavin* was staged with a strong cast in the Apollo Theater, and was repeated several times. The main roles were taken by Mrs. Koppe, who later became Mrs. Stephanie, Johanna Claussen, Lewens, Duprez, Koch, and Koppe. The author of the splendid piece was called to the footlights by the insistent audience, every time that he appeared at a performance of his play.

During the winter of 1874-75 the Sunday performances in the Olympic were continued under Pelosi's direction. The same was true of the following winter, in which also two weekly programs were offered at the Apollo Theater. In the summer of 1875 the Apollo again had operas, among others *Tannhaeuser* and *Die Juedin*, under Habelmann's direction and with Carl (or Karl) Formes as guest artist. The winter season dragged along its weary way. Krueger and Schiller, from necessity, not from their own choice, had to come to the financial aid of the thespians. In the winter of 1876 to 77 things were not much better, so that the performances were discontinued in February. Then under the direction of Schreiber-Soli-Silberberg a number of performances were given in the Opera House in which the excellent actress, Methua-Scheller participated. (Unfortunately, this lady succumbed to the yellow fever soon thereafter in Memphis.) *Diebeiden Waiseu* was performed eleven times. During the same winter the company which Alexander Wurster brought here, and which played only on Sundays, in the Olympic, did such fine work that the management fared well financially. To this troupe belonged Marie Wolf, Emily Brambilla, the soubrette Nofstetter, Mrs. Otto and Herr von der Osten.

The winter season of 1877 to 79 was enlivened by the fact that after a year's sojourn in Germany, Mr. and Mrs. Pelosi returned to St. Louis, to head a company that played regularly at the Opera House. At the Olympic it was lively also. Wurster was the manager and Gustav Donald was the director. Donald was a clever actor. Later he became the editor of the Davenport *Democrat*. The competition, thus created, enlivened things very much. The rivalry became keen. In the musical farce the utmost was accomplished, for Wurster had the soubrette Cottrelly (or Cotrelly), and Pelosi had the comedian Lube. The public was actually divided into two camps.

In the spring of 1877 the Apollo Theater had no more theatrical performances. Krueger had died and his long-time business partner gave up his tavern. For almost two years the stage was unused. Only a few sporadic performances were presented there during the interim. Such an interruption was the appearance of Helene von Racowitza, Emil von der Osten and Franz Kirschner in April of 1878. Until the end of the season they had been guest artists with the Pelosis. In the customary manner the Pelosi management also continued in the following winter, that of 1878-79, to give Sunday performances in the Olympic Theater. The same in the following season, during which, on November 23, 1879, Mr. and Mrs. Pelosi celebrated their twenty-fifth anniversary as artists.

Here the chronicle of our German stage in former years might come to a close, for the last fifteen years do not by rights belong in the realm of our report. For the sake of completeness, to obtain a complete picture regarding the development of German art in our midst, also the history of a later time may be added.

In the summer of 1879 the German muse again moved into the Apollo Theater. With Director Rieckhoff a new spirit held its entrance in the old place. It was an ensemble which made the performances of the Rieckhoff company during the next winter as also during the following two seasons the best that were offered theater-goers for a long time. Toward the end of the season, plays were also given on Sundays in Pope's Theater. During the two winters of 1880-81 and 1881-82 Director Rieckhoff confined himself entirely to Sunday evening performances in the just named theater. To his personnel belonged in the course of three seasons, the Messrs. Otto, Carlmueller, Axtmann, Klotz, Puls, Tentsch, and the Mesdames Kuhse, Vellguth (or Velguth), Gaertner, Spahn, and Stephanie. During the last two winters also Mr. and Mrs. Pelosi assisted. As guest artists appeared during this time Marie Wolf, Magda Irrsehick, Ida von Trautmann, Katie Schratt, Mathilde Cotrelly (or Cottrelly), and Franz Rainau. In the winter of 1881-82, Wurster took possession of the Apollo Theater. He, too, had a good company, and for many weeks Karl Sonntag, the court actor of Hannover, appeared in his brilliant roles.

This competition affected Rieckhoff's undertaking noticeably. But the appearance of the Geistinger Operetta Troupe, which showed for several weeks, did this still more. Then also the eight performances by Friedrich Haase in the first days of 1882, which finally compelled the Rieckhoff company to go on a tour through the state, which cost much and netted but little profit. But also Wurster ailed to make a profit during the guest performances of Sonntag, in spite of the fact that the able soubrette singer Anna Wagner was a guest artist during the greater part of the season.

In May of 1882 the Apollo was made a people's theater with Victor Sarner as manager. Admission prices were reduced, and dances were scheduled to follow the performances. But even after a few months Sarner gave up the management. Then a certain Gené (no relative of Ottilie Genee) announced with great pomp, an operetta season. In the person of Marie Koenig he had an excellent operetta singer. But after a few weeks there came a disgraceful failure, and Sarner made his get-away. The soubrette Alwine Heynold was mad enough to take over the management. This came to an even more rapid close. In the fall of the same year Collmer and Isenstein gave Sunday performances in Pope's Theater. This also came to an early end, in spite of the fact that the company was very good, and in the able soubrette Malwine Friedhold had a valuable contributor to farces and comedies. In December the brothers Victor and Hugo Sarner formed a partnership to present popular pieces and farces in the Apollo Theater. After a short time the partnership was dissolved whereupon Hugo Sarner carried on alone. During the winter of 1883-84 the Pelosi company played in the Olympic. Mrs. Marie Pelosi died in 1884, which was a great loss to the local German stage. After this her husband took over a management only one more time, this time in partnership with Hugo Sarner. The veteran preferred to yield the field to younger talent.

The last of a long list of directors who performed in the Apollo Theater was Edward Schmitz, the son of the old actor Johann Friedrich Schmitz, who for a long time was the director of the municipal theater in Basel, and who came to America in the fifties, where he was first engaged in New York and later here. "Eddie" Schmitz was engaged as a comedian by various directors, among others for a whole season by Wurster, until he himself took over the Apollo Theater. For several years he made a popular stage of it, but failed to make it a financial success.

With great perseverance Hugo Sarner collected troupes around him, and after 1886 gave Sunday evening performances during five or six winter seasons. He showed now in this and then in that theater, usually in the Olympic. The performances were sometimes very good, but more often mediocre. He enjoyed the favor of the public and the press, however, and so he succeeded, with the aid of frequent guest artists, to hush the wish for something better. The friends of a really good theater were therefore greatly pleased when Hermann Riotte promised, in the spring of 1890, performances for the following winter, which should be equal to those of the larger stages of Germany. The undertaking was well supported before and after the beginning of the season, but Riotte's complete ignorance of local conditions, his total lack of business sense, and mistakes of every sort necessarily brought failure to the undertaking. His worst mistake was his bringing of an opera company which was very bad and which cost much money. While the men in his dramatic personnel were very good, –Otto, Grube, Zimmermann and Waldemar, the women, with the exception of Mrs. A. Weckes and Johann Botz, left much to be desired. The repertoire did not suit the taste of the public. When guest artists appeared, the subscription tickets were not honored. The small hall of the exposition building proved to be wholly inadequate, because of poor acoustics, a stage that was much too small, and a lack of good seats. Moreover, the company was truly nomadic, for in the six months it played in nine different houses. With such a state of affairs it was entirely natural that discontent and indifference prevailed in the public, so that one was generally delighted when Riotte's regime came to an end.

The decade from 1881 to 1891, which closed with this failure, had nevertheless been extraordinarily rich in artistic events. After Friedrich

Haase, the great artist, who was unsurpassed in his roles, had made the beginning, he was followed by Ludwig Barney, then by Mitterwurzer, and a few years later by Ernest Possart, and then the women artists Marie Geistinger, who like Mrs. von Racowitza was here three times, Elizabeth von Stammwitz and Josephine Gallmeyer, Ottilie Genee's small troupe, the Münchner company, the Meininger, the Amberg and Conried companies and not to forget the Lilliputians, although with regard to the artistry of the latter, opinion is divided.

The Riotte company, among other works, presented two plays composed by local authors: the American social play *Sibyl* by Charles Gildehaus, and Woerner's *Sklavin*. The number of St. Louis authors of plays is not great, for that reason it may be but just to name them here: Henry Boernstein, Dr. John Hartmann, E. A. Zuendt, J. G. Woerner, Louis Gottschalk, F. Harrsen, E. Buhlert, Carl Winter, and C. Gildehaus.

The foregoing embraces the fifty years, which began with 1842 and closed with 1891. It was a varied life which German art lived during this period, a rough road that it traveled, abounding in hindrances and difficulties of every sort. Often it collapsed on the way, and yet it always arose again. Often the flame went out, but each time it was kindled anew. But never before was this done so vigorously, so methodically, circumspectly and practically as in 1891 when it was a question of creating a permanent German theater for St. Louis.

A stock company was formed for the purpose of building a suitable, large and beautiful theater. As directors for this enterprise were chosen Charles F. Orthwein, William J. Lemp, Anton Griesediek, Gustav Cramer, Dr. E. Preetorius, William Schreiber, J. H. Conrades, George Fritz, Charles G. Stifel, and S. H. Leathe. On September 4, 1892 the Germania Theater; on the corner of Fourteenth and Locust Street (Lucas Place) was opened, the most beautiful theater, that St. Louis has at this time. Under the direction of Carl Waldemar and Edward C. Buechel it closed its first season in the spring of 1893.

24. German Physicians

The number of German physicians who have died here since the fifties is very large. Most of them attained an advanced age, but many died

The German Element in St. Louis

relatively young. To the best known among the above these reminiscences are dedicated.

In 1851 Dr. Henry Gempp, who also owned a drug store on Carondelet Avenue, and who was already mentioned in the chapter dealing with Frenchtown, passed away. Eight years later a railroad accident took away Dr. Klier in the flower of manhood. He was at that time a member of the Board of Health. He was on his way to the quarantine station (the present small pox hospital) when Iron Mountain train was derailed. The other passengers received light contusions while he was injured fatally. He was very popular. He was the husband of Eberhard Anheuser's eldest daughter. His immediate successor in office was Dr. Stelzleni. After the latter resigned from the Bureau of Health he opened a successful practice in the northern part of our city. He was active in his profession till his death which occurred a few years ago. In 1861 Dr. Baer passed away. In addition to his practice he had a drug store on the west side of South Second Street near Elm. In the passing of Dr. Baer we lost not only a good physician but also a delightful companion.

Dr. Carl Roesch died at the beginning of the sixties at an advanced age. He was of a reserved nature but he was very kind to his patients. St. Louis was at that time not large. West of Fourteenth Street only a few German families lived. Even physicians with an extensive practice could get along without horse and buggy. So one could see Dr. Roesch, like his colleagues, hasten along the streets in any kind of weather. In the later sixties Dr. John Lebrecht, while still a young man, succumbed to the hardships of his calling. He was the assistant to Dr. Pope, the founder of St. Louis Medical College. In Pope's clinic he had acquired valuable experience. After his release from army service, he became a very busy physician in the city. Unfortunately the hardships of the war had impaired his health so much that he succumbed while still young. No hour in the night was too late, and no road too long, if he could bring aid, even if no pay could be expected for his services. Dr. Baumgarten, who passed away several years ago, had an equally extensive practice. Until the middle fifties he owned a drug store on market Street, between Eighth and Ninth Streets. He was highly esteemed as a physician as well as a man. In the southern part of the city three well-known physicians passed away in the second half of the sixties. One was the very busy, and very skillful Dr. Fritz Hauck. He looked like a picture of health but died in his best years, mourned by many friends. He was a younger brother of Dr. Carl Hauck, who died ten years ago. Their colleague, Dr. Dorn, was somewhat older. He was the brother-in-law of Attorney Fritz and of Judge Louis Gottschalk.

Dr. Beck, who came here in 1862, may quite justly be called one of the most charming doctors, who is still in our midst. As a young physician he had participated in the Crimean War on the side of the Russians. He received a bullet wound in his right leg, which rendered the limb stiff. The Czar decorated him with a medallion which he displayed in his buttonhole on special occasions. Aesthetic as he was, he was particularly enthusiastic about the theater and music. To the German stage he devoted such a lively interest that he not only attended the performances regularly, but also wrote very detailed reports for the *Volks-Zeitung* which was at that time published here. The disciples of Thalia had in him a warm and sympathetic friend. Without pay he served as theater physician. As a great friend of music he rarely missed a good concert. Dr. Beck was politeness itself toward everybody. Toward ladies he showed the greatest gallantry. He was a good conversationalist and with it all of such a modest nature that all who became acquainted with him could not help but like him. In his exterior appearance he was immaculate, and in his bachelor quarters, which at the same time served as his office, a somewhat pedantic order obtained. This splendid man, however, had one peculiar quirk. Now and then he dropped a remark which made it appear that he was on this side of the ocean on an important mission, as a secret emissary for the restoration of the Kingdom of Poland. Evil tongues even maintained that he had persuaded himself that he should some day be chosen as the King of Poland. This was a wicked invention which none of his friends believed. He was at the most forty years old when a certain type of typhoid took him away on a hot summer night in 1867. In the burial grounds of the family of the former theater director Kurth, where also Alfons and Rosine von Zerboni have their last resting places, in Pickert's cemetery, a grave was made for him. The hands of friends still decorate it with fresh flowers.

Another enthusiastic friend of the theater was Dr. John Hartmann, who, during Boernstein's theater period, often wrote criticisms. Later he at one time headed a group that considered founding a permanent German theater, which was to contain under one roof, rooms for clubs, societies and concerts. It was not the doctor's fault that this beautiful plan was not realized. Until 1870 he remained a bachelor. In this year he married the

The German Element in St. Louis

seventeen-year-old Sarah Valentin, who later became Sarah Hutzler-Kainz. But the difference in age and still more in the philosophy of life was too great. The marriage was not a happy one, and the doctor was glad that a separation with mutual understanding was effected.

Another old homeopathic doctor, who, like the just-named, had an excellent practice was Dr. Dietrich Luyties, whom many of our oldest German families for many years had as their family physician. A third homeopath was Dr. John Conzelmann who passed away a few years ago after practicing medicine for thirty years. During all this time he lived on Fourteenth and Carr Streets, and repeatedly represented his district on the school board.

During the fifties old Dr. Koch lived here. He differed from his famous Berlin namesake in everything. Particularly, however, in the fact, that while the Berlin professor devoted himself to the conceivably smallest organisms, observable only with the microscope, his St. Louis namesake made chase upon the remains of antediluvian mammoths, and really found the skeletons of two mastodons. For this reason he was popularly known as Mastodon Koch. But later he was called Golconda Koch, because he moved from here to Golconda, Illinois, where he died at an advanced age. One of the exhumed skeletons was for years exhibited in Wymann's Museum, on Market Street, opposite the courthouse. The other one Koch sold to London, and is said to have received a nice piece of money for it. His search for megatheres and that sort of monsters, or rather their remains, was not so much in the interest of science as for dollars and cents. In this respect he differed from his son-in-law, Dr. Theodore Hilgard, who passed away some years ago. The latter was content, if his limited practice permitted it, to collect all sorts of vermin and examine them under the microscope. His hobby was an aquarium before which he could sit for hours and observe animal life in it.

Dr. George Bang resided for a long time in the southern part of the city. About the middle of the sixties he moved to the northern part, where he died some years ago. Near the end of the sixties the well-known Dr. Petri also passed away.

In Dr. Rimberger, St. Louis had an able physician, even though he was known to only a rather small circle. There was also Dr. Hillegeist, whose practice was most extensive. Also Dr. Hausmann, who gave up his practice because of old age, some time before his death. On the other hand Dr.

Boesewetter, the old charming gentleman, remained active in his practice till shortly before his death. He also was numbered among those who were friends of the theater. Dr. Spinzig, who died relatively young was a well-known physician in the southern part of the city. He did not appear much in public, but he took an active interest in all German undertakings. Once he represented his ward on the school board. Old Dr. John Castelhuhn, who had long ago given up his practice, died in 1874 in San Francisco.

Dr. Hammer returned to Germany after twenty-seven years of residence in St. Louis. He was one of the best-known German doctors, and could have been one of the most popular, if his eccentric, domineering nature and combativeness had not been in his way. He seemed, indeed not to feel comfortable if he did not have a feud with somebody, and he did not care if this somebody happened to be a colleague or not. The doctor was a passionate nimrod, a great friend of music, a connoisseur of music, a good cellist, and a still better skat player. But he often could not find anyone to play with, for whoever could not trump his rudeness, and there were only few who could, simply could not play with him. However, incredible as it may sound, he could a times be very affable, if he was in the proper humor, but this did not happen very often. In his profession he did excellent work, particularly in surgery. His practice was so extensive for a long time that he would settle in Wiesbaden in comfortable circumstances. This the doctor did when Tilden failed to become president, and his prospect of a consul's post went to pieces. Two years after leaving here, he died.

Two other old physicians were the Doctors Engelmann and Wislizenus, who came here about the same time, and remained inseparable friends till the former died at the beginning of the eighties. For four decades their residences and their offices were only three blocks from each other, and so they saw each other almost daily. Frequently there were differences of opinion during these visits, which led to violent disputes, and which not infrequently ended by one of them rushing away with the declaration never again to enter the house of the other. But on the next day, or at the most, two days later, they were together again, in perfect accord, and the dispute was completely forgotten. Engelmann devoted himself preferably to botanical study, while Wislizenus had weather observation as his hobby. His careful recordings of weather conditions extend over more than forty years. If collected in book form, they would certainly be of great value to the experts. While Engelmann made extensive journeys, particularly in his younger years, Wislizenus found his best recreation in spending a day now and then on his farm along the Iron Mountain Railroad. He was altogether a German doctor of the old school. By this we do not mean to say that he was not accessible to new things in science, but being conservative by nature he remained faithful to that which had been proven of old. At an advanced age he followed his friend into the grave.

When Dr. Gebser passed away thirteen years ago, ophthalmology lost one of its most prominent representatives, and the world lost a most charming man. By his unpretentious, friendly nature he won the respect and veneration of all who came in contact with him. He died much too soon for science as also his friends. Another oculist was Dr. Edward Hasse. Generally, and probably not unjustly, he was regarded as an odd fellow. However, those who knew him more intimately discovered his good points, which were in marked contract with his gruff exterior.

At the beginning of the eighties Dr. Louis Bosse passed away after having had a very extensive practice. Dr. Carl Kauck, who died very suddenly, was for three decades one of the busiest physicians. In spite of his somewhat reserved nature he was a very popular family physician in many old German families. He had one great passion –a love for flowers, and his splendid garden on the corner of Ninth Street and Morrison Avenue gave testimony of the tender care with which he attended his favorites. He was particularly fond of cacti, of which he had many of the rarest varieties. At his casket his friend and colleague, Dr. Gustav Fischer, made an address. In January 1884, a year later, this excellent physician also passed away. A year before he had celebrated his seventieth birthday, and at the time of his death, his German colleagues were making preparations to celebratehis fiftieth anniversary as a doctor. He had fine bedside manners, and was a most charming companion. He was a friend of literature and art and music. His going was sincerely mourned by all the German element. Dr. Ferdinand W. Haeuszler died in 1884 at an advanced age. He had participated in the war. On his return from the service he served as secretary of the Bureau of Health. About this time Dr. Edward Rose also died at an advanced age.

In November, 1888, Dr. George J. Bernays died of blood poisoning which he contracted during an operation, and which had caused him unspeakable pain. With him passed one of the most excellent physicians from our midst, after he had practiced here for nearly thirty-five years. On one occasion he interrupted his practice for a residence of several years in Heidelberg. This was near the end of the sixties. Zeal for and devotion to his profession characterized this very active man, who, in spite of his years, went wherever duty called him, whether by day or night, and in any kind of weather. Another old St. Louis doctor, particularly well-known in South St. Louis was Dr. E. Seemann, who passed away near the end of the eighties.

Dr. Otto Greiner, who was the festival speaker of the Liederkranz, and in former years also of the Arion, and of the organization of former students of German universities, passed away in his prime. He had been a Heidelberg student. As the result of a student duel he had a long and deep scar in his face. Dr. Auler, who for several terms was a member of the Board of Education, and who was at all times a strong defender of the German element, also did not live to a ripe age. The same is true of delightful Dr. Bierwirth, who was a victim of the grippe in May 1891. Dr. Oscar Blank, who was known far and wide by his "black medicine," as also the aged Dr. Philipp Ewald, passed away at this time. Dr. Nagel was called to the beyond some three years ago. He was widely known. During the last years of his life he practiced only in a few families of very good friends. He was widely read, never missed a good concert and was greatly interested in the theater. The last one in the list that includes the period of forty years, is Dr. John Hermann, who was not only a popular German physician for a quarter of a century, but a loyal friend, and charming colleague. Six years before his death, he gave up his practice because of eye trouble. He died in New York in 1892.

If, in the reading of the foregoing, there have been brought recollections of a physician and friend, a helper and comforter in hours of danger, who has passed on, then the purpose of this chapter is more than amply fulfilled.

25. The Independent Protestant Congregations

The first German church organization can be traced to the year 1834. The congregation was evangelical and the minister was Mr. Korndoerffer, as can be seen from meticulously kept records of weddings and baptisms. At that time the Methodist meeting house was on the corner of Fourth

The German Element in St. Louis

Street and Washington Avenue. In this the little German congregation held its services till the year 1839. Whereupon it found refuge in the Presbyterian church on Fourth, near St. Charles Street. Korndoerffer was succeeded in 1836 by Reverend Wall, who four years later paved the way for the building of a church of their own. This was erected on the northwest corner of Seventh Street and Clark Avenue. It was dedicated to its purpose in the summer of 1840, and was given the name: Evangelische Heilige Geist Kirche, (Evangelical Church of the Holy Ghost). At the dedication the Cecilian Society, a chorus of mixed voices, recently organized by Charles Balmer, and also an amateur orchestra assisted in the services. Later the musicians gave a concert, the income of which was applied on the purchase of an organ.

Differences of opinion between a part of the congregation and the Reverend Wall caused the withdrawal of a part of the members. The result was that two evangelical congregations were organized. The one in South St. Louis was named St. Marks and the one in North St. Louis, St. Peters.

Frederick Picker was chosen to take the place of Reverend Wall. In keeping with the principles, advocated then and adhered to now, the name was changed to the Independent Protestant Church of the Holy Ghost. Picker was an extremely active man of great energy, conscientious, and mindful of his duties for the best interests of the congregation. But he assumed too many obligations which took too much of his time and effort. People accused him of having too many irons in the fire. Noticeable discontent arose in the congregation. The result was that in 1855 an assistant pastor, Dr. Hugo Krebs was appointed. The old and the young pastor could not agree. What Pope Leo and Chancellor Bismarck were able to find thirty years later, namely a modus vivendi, Picker and Krebs could not agree upon. The result was the former resigned his position and left the field to the younger man.

The founding of the independent congregation in 1843 was inaugurated by the adoption of a constitution. Among other things an annual pastor's salary of three hundred dollars was provided for. It is to be assumed that this salary was increased in the course of time. But even if that was not the case, Pastor Picker would have gotten along very well, for almost no day passed without weddings and baptisms. And it was not only in the city, which did its utmost to increase his salary, no, bridal couples and infants together with their godparents came from afar, bringing him a rich harvest of fees.

It will certainly not be uninteresting, if here a few of these are named who fifty years ago became the founders of the first Independent Protestant Congregation by signing their names to the above-mentioned constitution. Among the thirty-two names appear the following: Adam Conrad, Henry Laumeier, O. Oeters (or Oerters), R. Ewald, Frederick Dings, J. F. Bergesch, John C. Vogel, J. C. H. D. Block, Henry Kaiser, Henry Marquard, Jacob Kurzeborn, Ferdinand Gottschalk, Jacob Blattner, Robert Barth, William D'Oench, C. Ulrici, John Wolff (or Wolf), H. Lohmeyer, K. Buschmann, and Adam Petersen.

Dr. Hugo Krebs assumed the pastorate in 1855. When, after the outbreak of the war in 1861, thousands of St. Louis Germans hastened to the flag for the preservation of the Union, he joined them and went into the field as a chaplain. In 1866 he fell a victim of the cholera. A few hours after returning from a cemetery where his duty had called him, he was seized by the terrible disease, and snatched away in the best years of manhood. How terribly the dread disease raged here is attested by the fact that in the cemetery of this congregation thirty-four burials took place in one day.

It was during Rev. Krebs' pastorate that the building of a church was decided upon and begun. A committee, consisting of Adolph Kehr, J. H. Fisse, Bergesch, Hetlage, Benz, Pellitz, and Boll, decided in favor of the southwest corner of Eighth and Walnut Streets, bought the site for eight thousand dollars, and later sold the old church on Seventh Street, after it had served its purpose for nearly nineteen years. The building committee consisted of Krenning, Hetlage, and Distelhorst. In the fall of 1859 the new church was dedicated with suitable exercises. The Rev. Krell and the Rev. Eisenlohr were invited as festival speakers, and music and song added their part to make it a festive occasion.

In 1869 J. G. Eberhard was chosen pastor of the congregation. A rich field was opened for him. With energy and perseverance he attended to his duties. Soon after assuming his position, he organized a Women's Society, which since then has been a valuable auxiliary organization, that has worked in the interest of the congregation, and repeatedly has contributed to the beautifying of the interior of the church. At all times these women have done their part. One of their services was the establishment of a soup kitchen. A fair which this society arranged netted four thousand dollars. In addition to the wife of the pastor, the following ladies were particularly active in this project: The Mesdames –Adams, Mueller, Beschestobil, Kraft, Stark, Herche, Hafkemeir, Waldecker, Winkelmeyer, Schmidt, Schloehaum, Torlina, Strattmann, Pfeil, Oerters (or Oeters), Wiszmann, Lahmann, Krenning, Haumeier, Schroeder, Boehmer, and Kerksiek. The soul of the whole undertaking and its main director was the Rev. Eberhard himself. The twenty-fifth anniversary (1892) offered the congregation a welcome opportunity to show this man the most varied tokens of appreciation, and gave his fellow clergymen far and wide the occasion to come and participate in the festivities. The congregation commemorated the fiftieth anniversary of its existence in worthy manner. This was in 1884. It was a day of particular gratification for Franz H. Krending, who for twenty-five years had held the office of president. At the time of this celebration the congregation numbered considerably more than two hundred families, with at least three times that many communicants.

The second independent Protestant congregation was organized in 1856 in the northern part of the city. The first impetus for such an organization came from Rev. Picker, after he had given up his position at the old congregation. The founders of this second congregation were: Charles Meyer, John Gutberlet, A. Meinhold, W. Hoegemann, Frank Vogt, C. Picker, C. Heitmann, and W. Hagemann. Meyer became the president of the first board of trustees. Later Meinhold held this office. Then came Frederick Angelbeck who served with untiring zeal till his demise a few years ago.

In the beginning the services were held in the hall of the Mound Markethouse. Then the congregation bought the Presbyterian church on Seventh and Mound Street, for forty-five thousand dollars. In the very first month after organization, the Northwest Singing Society was formed, which added to the services so much. In 1865 this society disbanded. It left its beautiful silk banner for the congregation and it is still borne at the head of the procession of the school children on festive occasions.

After three years Rev. Picker gave up his position because of advanced age. He was followed by Rev. Polster who resigned in 1862 to enter the army as chaplain. The next pastor, Rev. Lepique remained only a short while, being followed by Rev. Lorentzen, who was replaced by Rev. T. G. Gerber in 1865. This frequent change of pastors was most harmful to the growth and development of the congregation and discouraging for those who entertained high expectations. Then came the war with its direct and bad consequences. Nevertheless the young organization did not lose courage, but did everything in its power to overcome all great and small obstacles, in order to assure for the free Protestant tendency in North St. Louis a permanent place of worship. It was particularly W. Lehmann who, being elected president in 1863, devoted himself with unshakable confidence to the task, and to the fulfillment of his duties. Lehmann passed away a few years ago.

The limited space in the church on Seventh Street matured the resolve in 1867 to build a new church with suitable accommodations. This plan was soon consummated. A suitable building site on the northeast corner of Thirteenth and Tyler was bought, and in June 1868 the cornerstone for the new church was laid. In a years' time the structure was completed, so that it could be dedicated to its use in August 1869. The old church was sold. The new one, including the lot, cost thirty-eight thousand dollars, half of which sum was provided by a loan. This obligation, considerable as it was, was in the course of time liquidated, chiefly through the incessant efforts of Mr. Bloebaum. Later the tower was finished, new bells were purchased, and the interior beautified by the fresco paintings by the artist Krueger. Since then a new organ has been purchased.

Rev. Roeder, who succeeded Gerber in 1873 had to give up the position after a few months because of poor health. He was followed by Rev. M. Thomas. In 1877 Rev. J. F. Jonas was chosen, and he has since then performed the duties of his office with energy and a due sense of duty. At the time of his appointment the congregation had only sixty-nine members. Now more than two hundred families belong. While all this increase is not the result of his own effort, the greater part of the credit must be ascribed to Pastor Jonas.

The following in turn served as chairmen of the board of trustees: F. W. Angelbeck, C. W. Bramsch, W. Lehmann (from 1863 to 1882) F. H. W. Krenning, and H. Bloebaum. These served as secretaries: J. Gutberlet, C. W. Bramsch, H. Bloebaum, W. Milfeil, H. Pins, G. H. Hengelsberg, F. Krenning and J. D. Stegemann.

As an essential factor in the course of the development of the congregation must be mentioned the Women's Society, which was organized in 1864. Aside from the regular contributions of the members, the society raised considerable sums of money with which the work of the congregation was furthered again in a material way. The most enthusiastic women, particularly during the storm and stress period of the church, were the Mesdames Charles Stuermann, Catherine Milges, Catherine Lehmann, and Loise Hilkes. Of these the last named is the only one still living. The first president was Mrs. Henriette Stoppelwerth, who was succeeded by Mrs. F. Vollmann. For five years, from 1868 to 1873, Mrs. Gerber, the pastor's wife, was the presiding officer. Mrs. C. Schroeder succeeded her, and since 1879 Mrs. Jonas has headed the group.

A desire to have the German language preserved in the growing generation was doubtless the main reason why the independent congregations desired to have their own schools. Secondarily the wish prevailed to see the young people educated according to the German model which was not the case in the public schools. The congregation of the Church of the Holy Ghost, on Seventh and Clark Avenue, opened a school of its own as far back as the thirties. In 1845 the church opened a second school on Eleventh and Biddle Streets. The building site was bought from John O'Fallon. To these two schools was presently added a third in the southern part of the city. It was built on Ninth Street and Geyer Avenue under the supervision of Bruns, Kortjohn, Brinkmann, Cordes, and Buddecke. With the building of the new church on Eighth and Walnut Street the school of the middle district naturally was transferred to the church where suitable rooms were provided in the building plan. We do not mean to imply that the congregation did not assume quite a burden and some embarrassment when they started the schools. There were differences between the school committee and the teachers. After the German language was included in the curriculum of the public schools the congregation discontinued two of its schools −one in the northern and one in the southern part of the city. It only retained the one on Eighth and Walnut Street. Of the teachers, who came and went like doves in a dovecote, the following may be mentioned: Hardt, Buehrle, Bartels, Remnitz, Bauchholz, Werz, Mettlemann, Seidel, Rebenak, Luecken, Schoenfeld, Wolf, Gruner, Trexler, Obenhaus, and Braeutigam.

The congregation in North St. Louis supported a school in its first church building. This school was attended by a hundred and fifty children. Of the teachers which worked there successfully for a course of time should be mentioned here: Werz, Wetteroth, Herzog, Jaeschke, Knickmeyer,

Wettle and Damen (or Dahmen). For some years now only two classes are kept up in this school.

One of the founders of these two congregations only few are now alive, but their names are not only to be read on the headstones of their graves in the two cemeteries on Gravois Road, but they remain in permanent recollection of the generation which succeeds them, and tradition will surely transmit their names to later generations.

26. The Oldest German Church Organizations

The oldest German Evangelical settlement was the one at the now so little-known Gravois community. This settlement was not directly on the present Gravois Road but more to the east and about ten miles south of the courthouse, not far from the Jefferson Barracks.

Gravois Settlement originated at the beginning of the thirties. The Germans, who had immigrated to this place very soon organized a church congregation. Its first pastor was E. L. Nollau, a man who later became one of the best known German clergymen in St. Louis.

It is now exactly fifty years ago when two Evangelical congregations were brought into existence at the time when a number of members left the Congregation of the Holy Ghost. This division took place in 1843 and the seceders presently organized one church in South St. Louis and one in North St. Louis. The former, St. Marcus, was erected on the site where now a large church stands, at the northwest corner of Jackson and Soulard Streets. The St. Peters congregation had its first church on the corner of Sixth Street and Franklin Avenue. Originally the property of the two congregations was held in common, and for a number of years the pastors Wall, Nollau, Cavizel, Ries and Baltzer preached alternately in both churches.

The new, spacious St. Peters church, on the corner of Fourteenth and Carr was built as early as 1850. During the many years of work at this church, Rev. E. L. Nollau founded two benevolent institutions, which will preserve his name in permanently revered memory. The Samaritan Hospital now situated on Jefferson Avenue and O'Fallon Street, was founded in 1850. It was at first a very modest undertaking in a few rooms near St. Peters church. Among the large number of immigrants that came at that time there were many unmarried persons who in case of sickness had no place to stay and be cared for except at their boarding houses. Therefore a German hospital, in which patients without consideration of creed, could be received, was a real necessity. After only a few years the founder received so much help that the present building could be erected, which in the course of time was enlarged and improved suitably. In addition to patients of both sexes there are a present a number of invalids and aged persons cared for, so that the institution is one of manifold blessings.

The other benevolent institution that was founded by Rev. Nollau is the widely known German Protestant Orphan Home on St. Charles Rock Road, in which thousands of children have been brought up, and in which, at this time, some three hundred orphans and half orphans are cared for and educated. To these two institutions the founder devoted his restless energy to the end of his life, and their well-being was always close to his heart.

The end of Rev. Nollau's life came earlier than was expected, on February 20, 1869, in his sixtieth year. It may be mentioned here, that Rev. Nollau's sons, first John and after him Louis Nollau, in recent years were called as pastors to St. Marks church. The latter occupies that pulpit now. His immediate successors at St. Peters were the Rev. Roeder and Rev. Roos.

In the same year in which Rev. Wall died (1867), after many years of service at St. Marks, the new church of that congregation was completed and dedicated. It is not an imposing building, but it contains ample room for the large congregation, and in the basement are rooms for a school of several classes. After Rev. Wall's demise Rev. Braschler had this pulpit for eight years. Then he resigned to accept the pastorate of St. Matthews church located at South Seventh Street and Cave Avenue.

The third oldest church belonging to the Evangelical Synod of North America is the St. Paul church, which was built in 1848 on the east side of South Ninth Street between Lafayette and Geyer Avenue. The first pastor was the Rev. Baltzer (later in St. Charles) who for a long time edited the official paper of the Synod here. He was followed by Rev. Will who held the pastorate for ten years, and is still living in good health in Mehlville, below Carondelet. Then came Rev. Seybold, and after him Dr. John, who was called to Edwardsville, Illinois after fifteen years of service here. The St. Johns church on Fourteenth and Madison Street was built in 1855. It is a very spacious church in which the conferences of the Synod have repeatedly been held. The school building situated behind it can house over five hundred pupils. The Friedens (Peace) congregation was organized in 1855 by Rev. J. M. Kopf, who since then has uninterruptedly served this pulpit. At the outset this congregation had no church of its own but held their services in a Presbyterian church in the northern part of the city. But after two years this congregation moved into a beautiful church built by it on Thirteenth Street and Newhouse Avenue.

The oppression which the adherents to the Augsburgian confession suffered, and the hindrances they had to endure in the exercise of their worship became so great in the second half of the thirties in Saxony, that many of the Lutheran living there decided to emigrate. The United States offered them a new home, in which they needed to fear no restrictions in the exercise of their religious belief. So they emigrated to Missouri where they arrived in the winter of 1838-39. Some of them remained in St. Louis while others settled in Perry county where they founded the little town of Altenburg. Soon after their arrival they made an agreement with the church officials of the Episcopal Christ Church, corner of Fifth and Chestnut. The lower rooms of this church were placed at their disposal, and for three years they held their services here. In 1842 they decided on the erection of a church of their own, which plan they carried out the same year. This was Trinity church on the north side of Lombard, (now Papin) Street, between Third and Fourth Streets. This very plain building served its purpose for twenty-three years, whereupon the congregation moved into the church, erected at great expense, on the southwest corner of Eighth Street and Lafayette Avenue. In the old church preached the following: Rev. Hermann Walther, then his brother, Rev. C. F. W. Walther, who later became the head of the Synod of Missouri, Ohio and other states, and who at the same time undertook the direction of Concordia College. After him came Rev. Frederick Wyneke and finally Rev. G. Schaller. The latter moved into the new church where he continued till he was called to a professorship. He was followed by Rev. Brauer, and now Rev. Otto Hanser is the pastor there.

The long distance from the northern part of the city to Lombard Street, the absence of street cars and some other reasons resulted in the construction of a more conveniently situated church in the northern part of the city in 1848. It was erected on the southeast corner of Eleventh Street and Franklin Avenue. It was a very plain building, but served its purpose amply. In the conflagration of 1865 it was destroyed. It was found that the walls were well enough preserved to warrant the replacement of a roof. Services were held here for three more years. In the meantime a building site for a new Immanuel Church was purchased on the southwest corner of Sixteenth and Market. Here the new church and also a large schoolhouse were erected. The dedication occurred in 1868. It may be worth mentioning that the church has an organ which was built, according to specifications, in Merseburg, Prussian Saxony. Its builder came here to supervise the installation personally.

The first pastor of this congregation was Rev. Ringhoff and his successor was Rev. Buenger, a brother-in-law of Professor Walther. He occupied this alter from 1869 till his death in 1882.

A third congregation was organized in 1858 in the southwestern part of the city. During the first nine years it did not have a church of its own, but made use of rooms in Concordia College, which had been transferred here from Altenburg in Perry county. The new college buildings were located on Jefferson Avenue and Winnebago Street. The congregation which named its edifice the Church of the Holy Cross, built its place of worship in 1867 on Texas and Ohio Avenue. This structure as also Concordia College are an ornament to this part of the city.

The first German Methodist congregation dates back to 1841. Its founder was L. S. Jacoby, who, during the first two years, and later again for a while, functioned as pastor. Its church was on Wash Street, between Tenth and Eleventh Streets and remained there for thirty years. Then the spacious new church on Sixteenth and Wash Street took its place. the German theologian, Dr. William Nast, whose main field of activity was the Ohio district, and especially in Cincinnati, came repeatedly to Missouri and Illinois in the interest of Methodism. In both states he and Rev. Jacoby were active and very successful among the German population.

A second church was opened in 1854 at the corner of Thirteen and Benton Street. At the beginning of the sixties a German Methodist congregation was formed in the southern part of the city. The church was located on the southwest corner of Eighth and Soulard Streets. With each of these churches was connected from the outset, a Sunday School, which was attended by a large number of pupils.

In 1857 the first German congregation of the Cumberland Presbyterian church was organized. It was only a very small group which assembled on

Sundays and holidays in the upper story of Biddle Market House, where Rev. Frederick Lack conducted the services. The latter subsequently became known extensively from the fact that for nearly three decades till the time of his death, Mr. Lack managed the distribution of contributions for the Provident Society. The congregation built a church of its own, at the end of the fifties, at Fourteenth and Chamber Streets. This church was used for twenty years, when the congregation moved to Twentieth and Sullivan Avenue. A second such church originated in 1862 when the Rev. Landel was compelled to flee before the guerillas in the interior of the state and seek refuge in St. Louis. He became the organizer of a congregation which consisted of only a small number of members. Their church was at first on Eighteenth and Montgomery Street. The German Presbyterian congregation, which was served by Rev. van der Lippe, and had its church at the corner of Tenth and Rutger Street, held its services during the first eight years in the basement of the church on Fifth and Walnut Street, at which place the Temple Building now stands.

It was in 1840 that the first German Catholic congregation was organized. During the first years the Jesuit fathers placed their chapel on Washington Avenue, between Ninth and Tenth Streets, at their disposal. In 1844 the cornerstone for St. Joseph church was laid, at the corner of Eleventh and Biddle Streets. The dedication took place in 1846. The clergymen of this church, from the first belonged to the order of Jesuits. It took only a few years till it surpassed in scope and influence most, if not all, the Catholic congregations in the city. By the process of rebuilding, and by new additions, there was developed a completely new church of enormous dimensions. More than three thousand persons can find room in it. Its interior decoration is so rich, so that, like St. Peters and Pauls, it belongs to the sights worth seeing in St. Louis. The site on which the church and parsonage stand was donated to the congregation by Mrs. Anna Biddle. The clergyman was Father Cotting, who was followed by the Fathers Hofbauer, Seisl, Weber, Tschieder, Hagemann, Etten and Braun. (Father Seisl died in Washington, Missouri.)

In 1844 the building of St. Mary's church was completed. After only a few years this proved to be too small for the rapidly growing congregation so that at the end of the fifties an annex was added which increased it considerably. Father Fischer was followed by the Vicar General Melcher, who in 1868 was called as bishop to Green Bay,

Wisconsin. Thereupon Vicar General Muehlsiepen took his place. However, the duties of the vicariat became so heavy that he gave up the pastorate. In this capacity he was followed by Father Faerber, who is still serving the church. The church, the school, the parsonage, together with the home of the sisters who teach in Notre Dame, and a branch building for nurses of the St. Mary's hospital occupy almost the entire western half of the block on Third Street, between Cedar and Gratiot Street.

German and non-German members belonged to St. Vincent church which was built in 1845 at Ninth Street and Park Avenue. The services are held in German as well as the English language. The clergymen who serve this church belong to the Order of Lazarists. Father Uhland who served this church for nearly thirty years was a most tolerant man, who is still fondly remembered by Catholics and non-Catholics. The Christian Brothers instruct in the boys' school and the sisters of St. Joseph teach in the girls' school.

The church, together with the parsonage and school of the Saints Peter and Paul congregation occupy nearly the entire south half of the block between Seventh and Eighth Street and Geyer and Allen Avenue. It is one of the largest Catholic churches in the city. It was organized in 1848. At first a very modest structure on Seventh Street and Allen Avenue sufficed. In 1854 a larger church took its place. In the course of time this proved to be entirely inadequate for the constantly increasing congregation, so that, at an expenditure of two hundred thousand dollars, a building was erected which may justly be considered one of the most beautiful church buildings in our city. The glass painting and sculpturing in this church comes, in part from artists in Munich. Till 1858, Father Siegrist was at the head of the congregation. Since then Father Franz Goller together with his long-time assistants Ruesse and Groll have served this church. In the large parochial school the sisters of Notre Dame impart instruction.

As early as 1839 a Jewish congregation was organized here. Til 1848 it had services in a house on Carondelet Avenue, and from then till 1851 on Fifth Street, a few doors north of Washington Avenue. In the last-named year the United Hebrew Congregation moved into the temple on the east side of Sixth Street, between Locust and St. Charles. Here it remained till in 1880 it moved into its synagogue which was erected on the southeast corner of Twenty-first and Olive Street. In the sixties the Rabbis Vidaver and Kuttner, and since the middle of the seventies Rabbi Messing have been in charge. In 1840 the Bnai El congregation was organized. Its members live exclusively in the southern part of the city. The members are mainly from Bohemia, for which reason it is known as the Bohemian congregation. It built its own Temple in the first half of the fifties on South Sixth Street near Gerre Street. In 1875 it bought the Presbyterian church on Chouteau and Eleventh Street. During the middle sixties H. Kuttner was the rabbi. Rabbi Wolfenstein succeeded him, and since 1878 Rabbi Spitz is serving these people.

Members of both these congregations founded a third congregation in 1867 on the basis of various reforms. The temple built by this body –Share Emmeth Portals of Truth– was dedicated the following year on Seventeenth and Pine Street. At first Dr. Sonneschein served this congregation. Now Dr. Sale is in charge.

The above-named are the oldest German religious organizations of our city. Their number has since then quadrupled, and the number of churches has increased in like proportion. There are now two hundred and seventy of these. Brooklyn is called the city of churches, but it is very much a question whether the city of St. Louis cannot now, with even greater right, lay claim to this designation.

27. The German Immigration Society of St. Louis

The above society existed under the indicated corporate name for twenty-five years, from 1859 to 1884. At the latter date its name was changed to German Society of St. Louis. It is the third oldest organization of this kind in the United States.

The feeling of consciousness of kind on the part of the German Americans manifested itself in the organization of singing societies, Turner societies, clubs, and social groups, professional societies of various kinds. The earliest of this sort of bodies was, of course, the church organizations. Then those who had come earlier wished to do something for the immigrants that came form Germany. The first society having such an objective was organized in Philadelphia. Then followed New York City with a similar organization. In 1847 the St. Louis German Immigrant Society was formed. Its object was the same as that of the metropolises in the east.

It is easily understandable that among the immigrants which landed in the ports of New York or Philadelphia there was, at all times, a greater or lesser number who needed material assistance in one form or another. Not a few of them stepped upon American soil nearly or entirely without means. Erroneously they seemed to think fried pigeons flew around in the air and into one's very mouth. Others who did not come with entirely empty pockets, did not know what to do in the strange land, so that they could at least be helped with sound advice.

St. Louis, it is true, was not a port city in the literal sense of the word. But from the middle of the thirties Missouri was the goal of at least a small part of the German immigrants. When, at the end of the forties, the mass immigration set in from every part of Germany, St. Louis also had its full share of newcomers. Those whose goal was farther to the west in any event passed through our city, since the great majority of the arrivals, which sought the west, came up the Mississippi via New Orleans, or if they arrived at one of the eastern ports they were accustomed to come by water from Pittsburgh or Louisville.

It was, therefore, a wise step, when a few of the most respected and best known local Germans made the idea a reality to create an organization to take care of the immigrants. The purpose was to secure employment, to provide the means for the continuation of the journey, should such means be needed, to care for the sick, to protect them from overcharges, and to secure justice for them.

After the society had been in existence for three years, the legislative assembly of Missouri passed an act in February 1851, by which the German Society of St. Louis was recognized as a legal corporation. The following were the incorporators: John Wolf (or Wolff), Adolph Abeles, Thomas J. Meiers, Edward Eggers, Henry W. Gempp, Andrew Krug, Charles Muegge, Louis Speck and John C. Meyer. The above law was revoked in 1859 and another was passed in its place which changed the name to German Immigrant Aid Society of St. Louis. In this new act the following were designated as incorporators: Robert Hennig, Frederick Bergesch, Julius Schrick, Gustav Mueller, Arthur Olshausen, William Stumpf, Gerhard Strechmann, George Bremermann, Franz Wagner, Ferdinand Overstolz, Hermann Panse, Hermann H. Meier, Henry W. Dreckmann, John H. Niermeyer, and U. F. W. Bentzen. The means required to carry out the purpose of the organization were raised by contributions of the members. For a long time dues were four dollars a year. Some members paid more. During the first years money was raised by theater performances, concerts and festivals. The first president was Jacob Tamm. During the first ten years George Reichard held the post of agent. It was his duty to collect the contributions, pay out the sums that were allowed for expenditure, provide shelter, secure employment, etc. When a boat with immigrants arrived from New Orleans, he had a great deal to do, for most of the newcomers did not understand a word of English. So he often had to act as interpreter. As a matter of fact his successors had to continue to do so during later decades.

During the first years of the war, when trade and commerce was paralyzed more or less, a few members advocated the dissolution of the society. However, a statement from the executive committee stopped the movement. The committee had the satisfaction of seeing their prophecy fulfilled, namely, that immigration would increase again. Even at the end of the war, and later still more, there was a marked increase of immigrants from Germany. In 1866 nearly six thousand immigrants arrived. The demands upon the society increased greatly, because the task of finding work for the unemployed was enormous. The office, which was at that time on Elm Street in the basement of the Tivoli, was surrounded from morning to night by men who sought work.

During the years 1866 to 1869 Isidor Bush was chairman of the executive committee. Since he was at the same time the secretary of the state immigration board, he rendered the most valuable services in the dual capacity. In 1867 the number of immigrants increased still more, and in the winter of 1868, as a result of poor business conditions which prevailed here as everywhere else, the distress was very great in our city. Under these circumstances the number of those seeking help increased to such an extent that in 1868 more than fourteen hundred persons received relief. It was, therefore, a good thing that in the preceding year the annual dues were increased to six dollars per member. Even so the income was not enough to meet the needs. At that time, as also later, all efforts to increase the membership were unfortunately unavailing. In every annual report the executive committee complained about the indifference and lack of interest which made itself felt in benevolent German circles. Nevertheless the society did a great deal of good with the small means at its disposal. All appeals for more support availed nothing.

At the end of 1871 the demands upon the society increased, due to the severe winter and the large number of immigrants that had arrived the preceding fall. The directors instructed chairman Bush, to direct an appeal to the German inhabitants and make a plea for help to alleviate the prevailing distress. Because of the lateness of the season the call could not be issued that year. In its report for the year 1872 the executive committee took occasion to point out, in clear words, the annually increasing number of immigrants, and in bitter terms the decreasing number of members of the society. In 1869 there were three hundred and twelve members, in 1873 only two hundred and sixty-eight, in 1875 two hundred and eighty, and in 1883 the number had dwindled to two hundred and sixteen.

From 1874 the immigration from Germany decreased visibly. On the other hand so many more Germans came from other states of the Union to make Missouri or other parts farther west, but principally Texas, their new home. Hereby the work of the local society, particularly of its agent, was greatly increased. Now it was not so much a matter of securing support but of forwarding the travelers to their destination at the cost of the society, or of securing reduced rates on the railroad. Much was accomplished by the agent in this matter.

On February 26 the society secured a charter under the laws of the state in which its name was changed to German Society of St. Louis. As incorporators and directors the following are named in the document: Edward Breitenstein, Isidor Bush, Albert Fischer, C. R. Fritsch, L. Gottschalk, E. E. Kargau, Dr. H. Kinner, Arthur Olshausen, C. G. Rathmann, Christian A. Stifel, A. W. Straub, Charles H. Teichmann, and H. T. Wilde. Under the new charter the purpose of the society continued to be limited exclusively to the support of immigrants. As the German immigration for some years had been declining, and so its field of activity was reduced, the executive committee decided to reduce the annual contribution to a nominal fee of one dollar. The property of the society, which through an economical and practical administration has, in the course of time, risen to more than eight thousand dollars, is invested in safe, interest-bearing papers. This fund has never been touched to meet running expenses. All aid as also the cost of administration have been met by current income. Great recognition is due to those who with small means have accomplished relatively much.

Obviously all cannot be named who have assisted, but many have done so much by their eager activity in the interest of the society and of immigration that special mention must be made of them. There was first of all Isidor Bush, who for nearly forty years was a member of the board of directors, and with brief interruptions served as chairman. Arthur Olshausen was likewise for some years either chairman or treasurer, and for three decades a director. F. S. Behrens was for some time treasurer of the society, and C. R. Fritsch held this office for nearly twenty years. The following served as secretaries: J. H. Herter, Julius Conrad, W. C. Lange (who also was chairman o several occasions), Dr. H. Kinner, C. G. Rathmann, and H. T. Wilde, who served in this capacity for a longer period than anyone else, and who also was chosen treasurer several times. C. A. Stifel was one of the most active members. He repeatedly served as chairman and vice chairman. Hermann Eisenhardt also has held the chairmanship for a few years. Among the directors who have done much for the society during the years should be mentioned: Adolph Kehr, Albert Fischer, C. H. Teichmann, A. W. Straub, R. Boesewetter, Frederick Laumann, C. Th. Uhlmann, L. J. Holthaus, M. Goettler, H. H. Biermann. As agents the following served after the already mentioned George Reichard, –Frederick Jaentsch, F. M. Schinkowsky, Robert Leuszler, William Holz and William Vogel.

For some time a few of the members of the executive committee had striven for a sensible expansion of the sphere of activity of the society. Finally this idea was consummated. On June 16, 1891 the charter was amended so that not only immigrants, but also any needy persons worthy of support in the realm of our activities be included. Provision was made that such persons be taken to an old people's home or a hospital, or that they be provided with medicine, medical treatment and other care, and in case of their death that they be decently buried or cremated. Moreover, in so far as possible, protect the poor in court. Furthermore it was agreed to work not only for benevolences but also to advance science and education. Therefore, an originally very limited field of activity was very much expanded.

The present executive committee consists of Chairman Hermann Eisenhardt, Vice Chairman Dr. H. Kinner, Secretary-Treasurer August Klassing and other members: G. R. Fritsch, C. A. Stifel, William Heinrichshofen and E. D. Kargau.

As the third oldest German Society in the country our organization will be entitled to celebrate its fiftieth anniversary in 1897. It is hoped that all who participate may derive much satisfaction from it.

28. The Free Congregation of North St. Louis

None of the many German organizations of St. Louis are so well known on the other side of the ocean, and not merely in Germany, as the Free Congregation of North St. Louis. This is mainly due to the fact that Carl Luedeking who, in 1869, was sent by this congregation to the Congress of Free thinkers that met in Naples, was one of the most outstanding members of this world convention, and that the resolutions which he submitted found general acceptance. In this way the attention of the free thinkers of Europe was directed to the Free Congregation on the Mississippi. But even before this, those in the old fatherland, who fostered this sort of thinking, had known of this organization in far-off America. For were they not our own countrymen, who had brought free thought across the sea and prepared for it a place of safety, something that it was not to enjoy for a long time over there, and then only after a hard struggle.

It was a small group of free-thinking men who, in the late forties, came to North St. Louis, or as it was then called, Bremen, and founded the Society of Free Men. It is this society from which the Free Congregation grew. The above-named society lived only for a very short time. Almost immediately after its dissolution a new body was formed. Its name was The German School Society and Free Congregation of St. Louis and Bremen. This was due to the fact that the part of the city which was called Bremen, was an independent incorporation, just like Carondelet up to its union with St. Louis. With the founding of the above-named society in 1850, there came into existence the first free congregation in the United States. The names who brought it into life surely deserve to be named here. They were: F. Schulenburg, F. A. Gottschalk, F. Kerzinger, U. F. W. Bentzen, Edward Eggers, C. Kleemann, Zurstraszen, Spannagel, Kurtzekorn, Tebbe, Rosebaum, and Kurlbaum. The first suggestion for the founding of a school society came from Franz Schmidt, who came from Loewenberg in Silesia. He had sat as one of the Silesian delegates to the parliament in St. Paul's Church in Frankfort in 1849. With the rump parliament he had gone to Stuttgart, and had then come to America in order to escape penal persecution, which the Prussian government, when it had again become reactionary, sought to inflict with great severity on all members of the rump parliament. Schmidt had come directly to St. Louis, had opened a school here, in which he worked with great success, till an incurable pulmonary ailment took him from his useful work in 1853.

The first president of the above society was F. A. Gottschalk, and U. F. W. Bentzen was the secretary. In the following year the congregation built its own, very modest, home, which, however, met all requirements for the time being. It was located on North Fourteenth between Herbert and Palm Streets. It was a one-story house, that contained two school rooms. A two-story annex served as residence for the speaker, who at the same time gave instruction in the upper class of the school. For a third class, space was later provided by the addition of another room. At the beginning there were sixty-five members.

The purpose of the newly-created society was primarily the education of youth by suitable school instruction from which was to be excluded all religious teaching. In the place of the latter, pure moral and ethical teaching was to be substituted. The further purpose was the instruction of the members and the dissemination of the basic principles which were set up and adhered to by the Free Congregation. This was to be accomplished by lectures and addresses at regularly held meetings, to which non-members should be allowed admittance. Rid of all dogma, its great main goal is –to develop men on the basis of free thought and philosophic atheism.

A formal, one might say, official establishment of the principles took place in 1852 after the arrival of Carl Luedeking who was called here as speaker. As a former Evangelical student of theology, he had come in conflict with the church and state authorities in his native Hessia. He came to New York in 1851, where he developed his news in a number of addresses, the same views that cost him his position abroad and compelled his emigration to America. These addresses were printed in the New York newspapers in whole or abstract. In this way they had also become known here. The Free Congregation communicated with him, and his transfer to St. Louis resulted. How welcome the local field of service was to him is best shown by a few words which he wove into the address which he delivered at the dedication of the new assembly hall of the congregation in 1867. He said: "The year and a half which I at that time spent in this environment belong to the most beautiful, because they were the most fruitful and intellectually stimulating of my life." (For a better understanding of this utterance it must be observed that Luedeking gave up the office of speaker in 1853, in order to devote himself to the continuance of the educational institution which Franz Schmidt had begun. This school he headed till 1856.) He was received here in a very friendly manner. In the congregation his addresses had from the outset aroused great enthusiasm. His love for free thought was transferred to his hearers, and the impulses emanating from him were of lasting effect.

During the time that he spent in Dresden, in the late fifties, Dr. Rudolph Doehn was the speaker of the congregation. After the outbreak of the war, Dr. Doehn entered the army as chaplain. He was not able to take Luedeking's place adequately, for to date that required a great deal more than he had to give. Above all he lacked the fire of enthusiasm which burned so brightly in the apparently and outwardly cold Luedeking, a fire that burned to him till his end.

The Free Congregation received its first charter from the Secretary of State in Jefferson City in 1857. In this document most of the six founders already mentioned are named as incorporators. A new charter was granted in 1884. In this the following are mentioned as the executive committee: Rudolph W. Rammekamp, B. Hoffmann, August Hoffmann, G. Sessinghaus, W. Petersen, C. L. Salomon, H. Clarner, F. Forthmann, and J. Teuteberg. In 1859 this congregation joined the Union of Free Congregations of North America with eighty members, and thereby confirmed its identity with others and solidarity of common endeavor.

When, in 1861, Luedeking again assumed the office of speaker, he stipulated that he would not accept the speakership in official form and with pay. He did not wish to be bound and obligated to do certain things. Nevertheless he was no less active in furthering, in spoken and in written form, everything that was in harmony with the aims of the Free Congregation. The constant growth of the number of members is the best proof of the effectiveness of his addresses.

The building on Fourteenth Street had for some time proven to be inadequate. Therefore, it was decided, in the later sixties, to build a suitably large structure, and this resolve was carried out immediately. To this end a site was bought on Dodier and Twentieth Street, at St. Louis Place. For the time being only the north half of the building known as The

Hall of the Free Congregation was erected. This part of the building was completed in 1867 and on September 29 was dedicated to its purpose. As might be expected, Luedeking delivered the festival address on this occasion. In concluding his address he described the philosophy of free thinkers and of Free Congregations as the bulwark of consistency on which all attempts of reconciliation would come to shame, as an unfailing beacon of truth, to which all could turn who still drifted on the sea of doubt, as a strong rock on which all obscurantism must go to pieces, as a sanctuary of reason and justice.

The call for an ecumenical council, which was to convene in Rome in December of 1869, induced the free thinkers on both sides of the ocean to call a convention for the same time as a vigorous protest against ecclesiastical government and all that goes with it. The place where the delegates were to meet was Naples. The local Free Congregation saw to it that America was worthily, as also vigorously, represented at the congress of free thinkers. Hardly had the invitation to participate in this meeting arrived when the necessary steps were taken to send a delegate. A public meeting in its hall was arranged which was attended not only by its own members but also by a large number of free thinking citizens, Germans and others. After Luedeking had made an address, Dr. Preetorius also spoke. He presented to the assembly some resolutions, drawn up by himself, which motivated the sending of a delegate to Naples, and which nominated Mr. Luedeking as the person best suited for this purpose. The resolutions were unanimously and enthusiastically accepted. Mr. Luedeking was immediately named as delegate. The Free Congregations of New York, Philadelphia, Chicago, Sauk City and several other North American cities immediately sent him their mandates, and so he appeared at that congress as the fully endorsed representative of the free thinkers of the United States, a position, which in itself, assured him respect and influence. However, the suggestions and resolutions which he presented and which he defended by speeches won him still more respect and influence, so that the St. Louis delegate was regarded as one of the most prominent participants at the convention, and his attitude was followed with special attention by the press. His detailed correspondence he supplemented upon his return in the form of a lengthy address, which he delivered in May of 1870 before his constituency.

In the just-named year occurred an essential change in regard to the schools of the Free Congregations. In that year, as is generally known, instruction in the German language was generally introduced in the public schools. With this act the main reason for the school of the congregation was removed. The public schools did not maintain instruction in religion like the church schools. Any school that avoided instruction in religion was in complete harmony with the ideas of the free thinkers. Therefore, it was decided to discontinue the school of the Free Congregation, since instruction in the German language had been included in the program of the public schools. The school of the Free Congregation had existed for nearly twenty years and some very able teachers had taught in it during that time. The Board of Education of the public schools leased the school and arranged in it the Dodier School, which name was later changed to the Blair Branch School.

Obviously the Free Congregation is no church organization. Indeed it differs in every respect from such. Therefore the expression *mulier taceat in ecclesia* (Let woman be silent in the church) has no application here. It should be expressly stated here that the feminine members expressly had a voice and vote. The women's society, working independently for mutual aims, developed great activity in the interest of the Congregation and in the cause of humanity. For a number of years the women maintained a school of handicraft for girls. Attendance was not limited by any means to children of members. Many girls attended this school. In addition there was also a drawing school which was also attended by a large number of pupils.

The south half of the building was not completed till seventeen years after the north half was dedicated. On the occasion of the dedication of the new structure the Messrs. Luedeking and Preetorius delivered the festival addresses. On all festive occasions the Chorus of Free Men, which was affiliated with the Congregation, contributed to the programs. This chorus was one of the most active in the city. The regular concerts of the chorus as well as other entertainments were all given in the hall on Dodier Street. Also other societies and organizations used the hall. From these there accrued a regular income for the Free Congregation, which at all times watched its finances with meticulous care. As proof of the good management it may be added that its property is valued at thirty thousand dollars. It also owns a library of twenty-one hundred volumes.

In the course of time the following have served as presidents: F. A. Gottschalk, U. F. W. Bentzen, F. H. Evers, K. Salomon, Charles Temme, R. Rammelkamp, W. Petersen, and August Hoffmann. The secretaries were: U. F. W. Bentzen, George Hoffmann, B. Hoffmann, and H. Clarner. For many years August Hoffmann was the treasurer. Upon his election to the presidency the present incumbent became treasurer.

The official speakers, in addition to Luedeking and Doehn, were Moritz Wurpel, J. Mettelmann, and Engelmann. Next to Luedeking, Dr. Emil Preetorius delivered more addresses before the Free Congregation than any one else. He was also the main speaker at the celebration commemorating the twenty-fifth anniversary of the building of the hall. Schuenemann-Pott, Frederick Schuetz, Robert Reitzel, Mrs. Hedwig Henrich-Wilhelme, Dr. Bork, Max Hempel, who now serves as speaker, and others delivered addresses before this audience in the course of the years.

The Free Congregation may justly be called the center of intellectual life in that part of the city where most of its members reside. For more than four decades it has worked incessantly on the fulfillment of the task which it set for itself in the service of freedom of thought, of enlightenment, of humanity and the preservation of the rights of man. Of its founders only few still dwell among us. Carl Luedeking also has passed away. He died on March 22, 1885, after protracted illness, and much too soon for the cause for which he had fought all his life. At his casket his long-time friend and companion, Preetorius, spoke in the name of the Free Congregation. The services were simple and therefore so much the more impressive. The body was cremated in Lancaster. The last will of the departed expressly stated that his remains should be disposed of by cremation. (At that time the crematorium in St. Louis was not yet completed.)

29. The Turner Societies

The fact that St. Louis was again and again, for many years, chosen as the home of the highest authorities (Vorort) of the North American Turner Bund, speaks more eloquently than anything else, that our city was considered the chief fostering place of Turner activity on this side of the ocean. This distinction was as much justified as it was deserved in consideration of the number of local Turner societies, as also their accomplishment. When the first Turner society was brought into existence here there were already a few organizations of this kind in the eastern states (in New York, Boston, Philadelphia, Newark, etc.). Cincinnati had the first Turner society that was organized in the United States. This organization was formed in November 1848. The St. Louis Turner Society, on the other hand, has the right to claim the distinction of being the oldest in the west, and to have set a good example in this part of the country.

As early as the second half of the forties Charles Speck, the highly respected and energetic chairman of the County Board and head of the oldest business firms, had endeavored to bring together a number of young men, and organize them in a group that assumed the name Bestrebung, (Endeavor). The young fellows met on Sundays to harden their bodies by playing ball, exercising and swimming. They began to do this on May 12 of the above-named year. On the following June 17, this small body of men formed the St. Louis Turner Society. The founders were C. Speck, Frederick Roever, C. B. Dieckriede, W. Moll, George Meyer, Theodore Hildebrandt, John Bolland, William Grahl, L. A. Bennet, Louis Barthels, and William Myer. Roever was chosen chairman, Dieckriede-secretary, J. Bolland-treasurer, and Speck, superintendent of gymnastics. At first the group met in the Rhenisch Wine Hall, and the number of members increased quickly. But there was a lack of suitable place to exercise, and for more than four years the society led a nomadic life. During this time it first went to Degenau, the dry goods dealer, on Second and Plum, then to Poplar, between Second and Third, from there to the fourth story of a house owned by Frank P. Blair, on Second and Morgan, and finally on Collins Street. On the 18th of May, 1851 it celebrated its first anniversary. On this occasion the German girls presented the organization a beautifully embroidered white silk banner. In December of the same year the society joined the Turner Bund. A short time after that it had as guests Professor Gottfried Kinkel, who had escaped from a Prussian prison, and his liberator Carl Schurz. In March 1852, it opened a Turner school under the direction of A. Stickels. And in May it held a great festival to which societies in Belleville, Evansville, Quincy, Peoria, Louisville and Cincinnati sent representatives.

The incorporation of the society took place in the winter of 1852-53. It was the first Turner society in the United States that acquired corporate rights, and it was the work of Attorney D. M. Frost who brought this about.

In gratitude for his services the Turner tendered him a serenade in front of his home on Seventh Street near St. Charles Street. It was a bitterly cold evening in January, and the instruments of the musicians literally froze up during the playing. Frost invited his guests to come in after the first number, where the trumpets and valve cornets were thawed out with old bourbon. On that evening, while they were happily together in Frost's home, surely neither host nor guests suspected that some time they would face each other as bitter rivals. It was this same D. M. Frost, who on May 10, 1861, had supreme command in Camp Jackson, at the taking of which the Turners, as everybody knows, played such an important role.

The Incorporators who are named in the act adopted by the legislature were: Christian A. Stifel, Theodore Reif, Robert Feustel, Albert Juengst, William Hirt, Otto Stickel, Henry Schwedel and Frederick Beck.

In November 1854 the society decided to build a Turner Hall. For this purpose it leased a plot on Tenth Street, between Market and Walnut on which to erect the building, for the time being only one story, which would suffice the needs of that time. But even this was not an easy matter since all the members were young people who were by no means blessed with worldly goods. However they possessed, at least some of them possessed, what the Americans call "spunk." They went to work undismayed to raise the necessary money for the building by selling shares, which cost only two and a half dollars. A few of the most enthusiastic, to whom our city owes the first Turner Hall were: Charles Speck and Christian A. Stifel, the art dyer Carl Vallat and William Hirt. Not until many years later was the Turner Society, thanks to the efforts of one of its members, Leo Rassieur, able to purchase the lot also. The old schoolmaster Elihu Shepard, to whom almost all of the block belonged, and later also his heiress, Mrs. Barclay, persistently opposed the sale.

The hall was dedicated on January 13, 1855. That same year a beginning was made to obtain a library. In the course of time this has grown to more than three thousand volumes. At the same time the singing society was organized. The most ardent proponent of this undertaking was Emil Mueller. In the same year it resolved to purchase a burial plot for Turners in Picker's cemetery.

The one-story building soon proved to be too small. On November 12, 1855 the cornerstone was laid for the building which, after its enlargement, in 1858, has remained as it is today. It was called Central Turner Hall, and

The German Element in St. Louis

is, in many ways, most intimately connected with the activities of the German element of St. Louis. In the above-named year the society had more than five hundred members, among them ninety non-Germans, and still more members came. In the matter of gymnastics, as also in intellectual endeavors, the greatest activity obtained. This healthy condition prevailed during the next few years. In 1860 St. Louis was the host of Turner festival of the Turner Bund. In the winter of 1860-61 the black clouds of war appeared on the horizon. From the beginning of 1861 the Turners took a definite stand in regard to the great question. Vaulting horse and parallel bars were pushed aside. Instead of gymnastic exercises, military drill was practiced. When it became known that, except for the Germans, the majority of the population of the state sided with the South, and a large part of the non-German citizens of St. Louis likewise favored the secessionists, the St. Louis Turner Society, with stormy enthusiasm, adopted a set of resolutions which Chairman G. A. Finkelnburg had prepared, which declared that the members of the Turner Society would stand loyally by the Union, that it would fight for the existing government and the indivisibility of the United States, pledging their lives and their property to attain this end. The grave mounds on many a cemetery attest that they kept their word.

Long before the regiments that were formed here moved into the field, Turner Hall seemed changed into barracks. This appearance it retained also during the first years of the war. During the entire duration of the war gymnastic work was suspended. A board of trustees was charged with the duty of protecting its interests.

After 1866 the regular routine was resumed, even though the membership was considerably smaller. In time the membership rose again. The organization of other Turner Societies took some members away from the old society, nevertheless it had in 1880 more than three hundred and fifty members, a very well attended Turner School for boys and girls, and a very active singing division.

In 1889 the society moved into its new building on Chouteau Avenue. The structure together with building site and equipment cost fifty-four thousand dollars. The old Turner Hall on Tenth Street, however, as long as a piece continues to exist, will be a milestone in the history of American Turner work in St. Louis and in the state of Missouri. In equal measure it forms a landmark in the history of the Republican party.

The speakers of the society were, among others; C. A. Stifel, Hugo Gollmer, Leo Rassieur, G. A. Finkelnburg, Valentine Grimm, Arthur Dreigus and Henry Braun. The latter served for a whole decade, from 1883 to 1893, being chosen again and again, which is perhaps the best proof of the fact that he performed the duties of his office excellently. In September of 1892 he was elected chairman of the executive committee of the North American Turner Bund, and at the last convention in Milwaukee he was reelected to the same position.

The following functioned as teachers of gymnastics: Albert Neusche, Hermann Schacht, William Gehrmann, W. A. Stecher, and it is Hermann W. Ritter, who is at the same time teacher of gymnastics at Toensfeldt's Boy's Institute.

Among the many who have rendered outstanding service for the society and the work of Turners in general, none have done more than Hugo Gollmer. He served the society as speaker, as secretary, and with special zeal for many years as librarian. His name will be forever inseparably bound up with German-American Turner interests.

Inspired by the same zeal was and is the present first superintendent of gymnastics, Mazzini Kruer, who has held this post, except for a brief interruption, since 1867. From 1882 till 1889 he was also district superintendent of gymnastics, and from 1867 to 1870 teacher of gymnastics in the society.

After moving to the new Turner Hall, which is arranged most suitably, and complies with the most modern requirements, the number of members increased very much. At this time it amounts to 965. The Turner school is attended by 320 boys and 268 girls. Twenty-eight members belong to the singing section, and there is a ladies' chorus of forty-five.

The present officers are: Carl Adelmann, first speaker; William A. Stecher, second speaker; J. E. Cremer, first secretary; Carl Retzer, second secretary; M. Krueer, first superintendent of gymnastics; George Kahle, second superintendent of gymnastics; Julius Friton, treasurer; Hugo Herting, cashier; William Soest, overseer of gymnastic apparatus; F. J. Wippold, librarian; F. Rohlke, chairman of the committee of the intellectual program.

The St. Louis Turner Society was well represented to all festivals of the Bund. In all matters it was a good model for the other societies that organized here. Even this should justify the special attention devoted to its history. It is after all the stem from which they sprang.

The South St. Louis Turner Society is the second oldest of the local societies, and the history of its origin is the following. The St. Louis Turner Society in 1865 decided to establish a Turner school in the southern part of the city, in order that the German youth of this section might have the benefit of practical gymnastics. The distance from the Central Turner Hall, on Tenth near Market Street, was too far for the boys and girls in Frenchtown to attend the instruction regularly. August Krieckhaus, Charles Speck and C. A. Stifel undertook the task of procuring the required means for the building and equipment of a Turner school. They were successful so that in the fall of that same year it was possible to erect a building, which was not large but adequate, on Ninth and Julia Street. In the course of time the members of the old Turner Society, who lived south of Chouteau Avenue, conceived the idea that a second society would not only be a convenience to them but also an advantage to Turnerism. Formerly there had been a difference of opinion on this point. Some held that one society would compete against the other and do harm. The experiences of later years have amply shown that this assumption was incorrect. St. Louis with its ten Turner Societies is the most eloquent proof that with the increase of their number the accomplishments and results also increased. So there was created a new society in that on September 12, 1869 a number of members of the old society organized the south St. Louis Turner Society, which has become one of the most flourishing. The first officers were: Francis P. Becker, first speaker; Jacob von Gerichten, second speaker; John H. Kassing, first superintendent of gymnastics; C. Gattung, second superintendent of gymnastics; F. C. P. Tiedemann, recording secretary; J. C. Mohrstadt, corresponding secretary; Frank H. Dietz, first cashier; Henry E. Vortriede, second cashier, Philipp Kaiser, custodian of apparatus. The origin of the society can be mainly ascribed to the efforts of Francis P. Becker. He was its first speaker, was repeatedly reelected to this office, and incessantly had the best interests of the Society in mind. At the founding there were only fifty-two members, but their number increased rapidly, so that more room was required. Yet the building of a new Turner Hall was not undertaken till 1881. The site for this structure had been purchased some time earlier. It was located on the northwest corner of Tenth and Carroll Street. It was not easy to raise the necessary money.

Therefore, it is worth while to name those who were particularly active in this work: F. P. Becker, F. C. P. Tiedemann, William Mehrkens, George Loebs, and Frederick Pfisterer. On May 15, 1881 the cornerstone was laid, and a year later, on May 6, 1882 the building was dedicated. It contains two stories toward the front and four stories to the rear, measures one hundred and twenty by eighty-five feet, and contains in addition to the room designed for gymnastics, a thirty-foot high hall, which contains a stage, various side rooms, a billiard room and a bowling alley. This building formed the central meeting place of the German element in this part of the city. The property of the society represents a total value of over thirty-eight thousand dollars.

The South St. Louis Turner Society distinguished itself in its accomplishments. In general it strove to live up to the principles and teachings enunciated by Father Jahn, and to make its benefit available as widely as possible. Like the other Turner Halls it also had bathing facilities, and indeed it was the first one to provide for warm baths. This arrangement, without doubt, will be adopted by the other halls. Theodore Klipstein, of the West St. Louis Turner Society, had for years made propaganda for its introduction.

The South St. Louis Turner Society at this time has 648 members, a fine class for the older folk and a ladies' class, and supports an extraordinarily well-attended Turner School. George Wittich is the instructor of gymnastics; he is also the superintendent of gymnastics in the local public schools.

The following were the speakers of the society since its founding: Francis P. Becker, twelve years; F. C. P. Tiedemann, one year; Dr. Emil Seemann, one year; Jacob von Gerichten, one year; William Koken, one year; Henry Lange, eight years. Former teachers of gymnastics were: Kassing, Muegge, Neusche (or Naeusche), Toensfeldt, Bissing, Rieken, and Feldmann. The present officers are: Henry Lang, first speaker; Charles Becker, second speaker; Henry J. G. Meyer, first secretary; Philipp Steller, second secretary; F. W. Heuer, first cashier; A. H. Brueggemann, second cashier. Chairman of the committee on entertainment was Jacob von Gerichten; of the Turnrath, Louis Becker; of finance, Henry Ploehn; of administration, Henry Troll.

The North St. Louis Turner Society started with the North St. Louis Turner School which was established in connection with the kindergarten

The German Element in St. Louis

in 1868 by a few well-meaning German heads of families. The Turner Society that stemmed from this school was organized on October 15, 1870. The names of the founders are: L. Edward Witte, Adam Schmid, John Schmid, Hermann Schmidt, Louis Ulrich, Frank Birkmann, Charles E. Kircher, Julius Vogt, Tobias Spengler, William Schreiber, Anthony Nacke, Charles J. Doerr, Louis Hammer, Charles Kohlberg, August Allerhausen, Mathias Hermann, and H. Schwartze. The gymnastic exercises were first held in the Magwire Market House, then in the hall on Broadway and Bremen Avenue, (which was destroyed by fire in 1878), the temporarily in a warehouse, and after that in Kreienbaum's bowling establishment.

In 1879 the society decided to build a hall of its own. The building committee that consummated this resolution consisted on: F. H. Brinkmann, L. E. Witte, L. W. Teuteberg, A. Haeseler, W. H. Indermark, H. Unrath, L. K. Hammer, A. Nacke, and Hugo Meunch. The Turner Hall, which was built on the corner of Fourteenth and Salisbury Street, and the site cost a bit more than eighteen thousand dollars. Later an annex was added that cost eleven thousand dollars more, then a total of nearly thirty thousand dollars, to which should be added the cost of the interior equipment.

At the time of its founding the society had a membership of an even hundred, of whom half the members were active. At this time there are seventy active, and two hundred and sixty inactive members. The section for the aged includes twenty-four and the ladies' section, thirty members. The Turner School is attended by three hundred and ten boys and one hundred and thirty girls. The society owns, on Twentieth Street, between Farrar and Bremen Avenue, a nicely arranged and electric-lighted summer gymnasium, which is used by Turners young and old. Its library contains some six hundred volumes. This society also owns two bowling alleys in the basement of their hall.

The following have served as speakers: L. Edward Witte, Charles E. Kircher, L. W. Teuteberg, Albert H. Haeseler, William Indermark, F. Brinkmann, L. K. Hammer, Anthony Nacke, Julius F. Vogt, J. J. Link, Charles J. Trebus, Charles Haeseler, Louis L. Kohlberg. The present incumbent is Charles W. Steiner. The following served as gymnastic teachers: William Hembold, Albert Naeusche, (or Neusche), George Muegge, Adam Riedel, Carl Bruck, and at present F. W. Froehlich. The North St. Louis Turner Society brought back various prizes from the festivals of the Turner Bund, and in general, manifested the greatest interest and activity. Among its present officers we note: Charles W. Steiner, first speaker; Charles O. Weber, second speaker; Charles Gescheid, first superintendent of gymnastics; Arthur Weig, second superintendent of gymnastics; A. J. Clabes, corresponding secretary; George W. Freuger, recording secretary; Frederick L. Steiner, Henry Borgmann, and Frank Brinkmann, Jr., managers of finance; Walther Gaffron, keeper of equipment; Erwin Harchert, first librarian; Edwin Zettlage, second librarian.

Turner interests were further increased in North St. Louis by organization of the Social Turner Society. On October 1, 1872 Charles, William and Louis Wedig, Henry Rau, F. Meszmer and J. Wiemann were the organizers. The number of members was at first quite small, only nine, and resources available very limited. The first exercises were held in the parlor of Charles Wedig, Nineteenth and Montgomery Street. The only piece of apparatus was a horizontal bar which two Turners held on their shoulders while the third one exercised. Then Turner Wiemann made a horizontal bar. In the next year the parlor and the scant apparatus burned. Then the members practiced in the open on Fifteenth and Chambers Street. That was quite satisfactory in the autumn and summer. In the winter a room was rented on Fourteenth and Benton, where the stay was only for a short time. After several more moves the young society landed at the Sturgeon Market House. Here the first gymnastics teacher was employed. The membership grew and it was decided to build a Turner Hall on the corner of Thirteenth and Market. It cost thirty-six thousand dollars, the greater part of which was secured by the sale of shares. The Turner Society itself, now an incorporated body, owns shares to the amount of sixteen thousand dollars. With the entrance in a home of its own (1878) the nomadic life of the society ended. Regarding the growth and development of this group, the following figures speak most eloquently. As we have said, it began with nine members and today it has four hundred and eleven, of which number sixty are active and three hundred and fifty-one are inactive. The Turner school has three hundred and ninety pupils, two hundred and sixty-two boys and one hundred and twenty-eight girls. The ladies' class numbers twenty-four, and there are sixteen old Turners. The song section has twenty singers, and there are four hundred and eighty-five volumes in the library. Caesar Spiegelthal is the present director of music.

At all Turner festivals in which this society participated actively, it has given a good account of itself. As early as 1878 at the festival of the Bund in Philadelphia it brought home the first prize. In speaking of further distinction it should be mentioned that at the District Turner festival, held a few years ago in Hermann, this group won ten prizes, more than any other society, and at the latest festival of the Bund held in Milwaukee in 1893, with forty-eight actives present, it won the seventeenth prize.

But also in the intellectual realm the Social Turner Society did its full duty. Among those who were particularly active in this direction should be mentioned the well-known German physician, Dr. William Drechsler, R. Boesewetter, William Ahrens, G. Monschein, William Sessinghaus. The speakers office was held in turn by C. Wedig, William Wedig, A. Dietz, Henry Lange, Edward Wagner, C. Lange, H. Oberschelp, R. Boesewetter, A. Bornmueller, E. Eschmann, Henry Pins, F. Lammersick, A. Kallmeier, H. Petersen, A. Monschein. The present incumbent is William Ahrens. Teachers of gymnastics were Henry Lange, George Muegge, Theodore Bissing, E. Guenther, F. Stuesser, D. Osterheld, and at this time, O. Ruther.

The present officers are: William Ahrens, first speaker; Edward Peters, second speaker; C. Fritsche, treasurer; O. Kallmeier, cashier; Otto Schaefer, corresponding secretary; Christian Bloecher, recording secretary; Albert Heidenreich, chairman of the Turner council; Frederick Lammersick, chairman of the executive committee; William Sessinghaus, chairman of the entertainment committee; and C. Simone, head of the song section.

During the first years the hall was ample for all purposes, but with the increase of members it has long ago become too small, particularly at the festivals which are at all times attended in large numbers.

The Concordia Turner Society had its beginning on December 27, 1874. The direct reason for its founding was probably the fact that many members of the St. Louis Central Turner Society, who lived in the southern and western part of the city wished to have a place for their gymnastics closer home. The founders were C. H. L. Graffmann, C. C. Goedde, Charles Reinhard, C. Lohrum, Richard Fisher, Louis Wagner, M. Leopold, E. F. Schreiner, H. W. Ocker, Nicholaus Berg, Charles Vogt, John Breitinger, Jack Jochim, William J. Lemp, Carl Petzold. The first officers were: President, E. F. Schreiner; vice president, Nicholaus Berg; secretaries J. R. Bollinger and C. F. Groffmann; and treasurer C. Goedde.

For nearly four years the society used the rooms in Concordia Park. On November 18, 1877 it moved into its own quarters, Concordia Turners Hall which a corporation, created for that purpose, had built on the northwest corner of Thirteenth and Arsenal Street. The original cost amounted to nearly eighteen thousand dollars. The present buildings have a value of forty-five thousand dollars. Those who deserve particular mention for providing such a splendid Turner Hall are: William J. Lemp, Hermann Stamm, Charles F. Vogel, Oscar Hoefer, William Hahn, and C. C. Goedde.

Ownership brought new enthusiasm. It was not only the younger generation which manifested this, but mainly the older well-established men, who devoted themselves with zeal to the interest of the society and worked for its progress. The Concordia Turner Society indeed gave a new impetus to German life in that part of St. Louis. Many fine things that were accomplished there, in the last three decades, could be traced back to this source. Particular importance was attached to the Turner School, loyal to the principle that a sound mind is found only in a sound body. At this time there are four hundred and fifty-seven students in the class for boys, girls and ladies. The number of members was forty-seven at the outset, and now four hundred and eighty-five, –eight-one active and four hundred and four inactive. The division for older men has twenty-five members. The society has a song section and a swimming pool.

Of the speakers, the following are especially to be mentioned: E. J. Schreiner, H. W. Ocker, C. C. Goedde, H. Stamm, Nicholaus Berg, Oscar Hoefer, Kuno Werner, Jak Walther, Karl Ungar. The present incumbent is Dr. Hugo Toeppen. During the years these have served as teachers of gymnastics: Gustav Hansen, Jack Schmidt, Hermann Ritter, and since March, 1893, Louis Kittlaus.

The present officers are: Dr. H. Toeppen, first speaker; Frederick Eszmueller, second speaker; Max Meyer, recording secretary; John Braun, corresponding secretary; Karl Hofmann, first custodian; Franz Klickermann, second custodian; Albert Mauch, treasurer; K. Schraubenbach, first cashier; Albert Rist, second cashier; Julius Weinbrecht, chairman of the academic committee; W. Koch, chairman of the school council.

At the Turner festivals of the Bund, the Concordia Turner Society was always worthily represented and its active members brought many a prize home.

The German Element in St. Louis

The Germania Turner Society of Carondelet was founded in that part of the city in April 1875. Immediately it was decided to build a Turner hall and the plan was so quickly set in operation that the cornerstone could be laid on September 4 of that same year. All the St. Louis societies participated in this event. The building was erected on Fourth and Taylor Street and, together with the site, cost nineteen thousand dollars. On March 11, 1876 the dedication exercises took place. Directly a Turner school was provided and a society library started.

Among those who have rendered especially laudable service for the society are: H. Hinsmann and Christian Koeln, who were repeatedly chosen speakers, moreover, Charles Bruno, Rudolph Giebermann, E. G. Hofmann, John Wette, Thomas, Martin Stein, and above all Dr. H. H. Starkloff, who for many years, was chairman of the academic section, and till the time of his appointment as consul in Bremen was the first speaker of the Bundesvorort. In F. Boetger the society had a very capable teacher of gymnastics.

The West St. Louis Turner Society grew directly out of the Schiller Club, an organization which flourished during the second half of the seventies. It was primarily a social group but also pursued more serious purposes, particularly did it foster art by regular presentations of dramatic works by its members. This work was under the management of E. A. Zuendt in the Sheridan House on Franklin and Leffinwell, which at that time was in charge of Mathias Spoeri, who did everything to further the organization. The evening entertainments were about the best that were presented at the time. The impetus to create the club came from the journalist and poet, E. A. Zuendt (now in Jefferson City) and August Schuermann. In addition to these two, the following should receive mention: Christian, Gustav and Philipp Hertwig, J. J. Conrad, J. J. Sutter, S. Goldstein, George Paul, Louis Wagemann, L. Benig, Fritz Block, D. Kreling, John Dierberger and M. Spoeri. Christian Hertwig was also an active member of the club, and he was one who advocated the creation of a Turner Society. The agitation for a new society emanated from the Turner district. H. Ruppelt, H. Ocker, and Kuhlmey, particularly the first named, did most of the agitating.

The founders of the West St. Louis Turner Society, which was organized in the autumn of 1879, had all belonged to the Schiller club. So the society had a membership of one hundred and twenty members from the outset. At first they had their exercises in Uhrig's Cave, but as early as the winter of 1880 to 1881 they acquired a hall of their own. This was made possible by the rebuilding of the Baptist church on Beaumont and Morgan Street, which had cost them a little more than five thousand dollars. The new structure, which was soon undertaken, and the suitable annex buildings cost three times as much.

The building committee consisted of: J. J. Sutter, A. W. Straub, John Dierberger, J. F. Conrad, L. J. Holthaus, J. H. Trorlicht, John Nies, J. L. Bernecker, F. W. Henze, John Schoenle, and Julius Hirschfeld.

The Turner Society has for a long time owned the buildings together with all the equipment, gymnastic apparatus, and two bowling alleys –representing a total value of twenty-six thousand dollars.

The following members have functioned as speakers in the course of time: J. J. Sutter, A. W. Straub, Christian Hertwig, Louis Schaefer, J. F. Conrad, J. P. Heinrich, H. Dauernheim, Emil A. Becker. The present incumbent is J. R. Bollinger. Most of these men served for two terms.

But others also rendered valuable service to the society, as for example the chairman of the academic section, the previously often-mentioned Theodore Klipstein, and the chairman of the entertainment committee, August Schuermann. Both worked untiringly in their respective capacities.

With regard to the teacher of gymnastics the West St. Louis Turner Society has certainly been the most conservative of all; from the first day on, August Muegge has held this post. (He also teaches gymnastics at Washington University.) Of the present members, which number four hundred and fifty, there are about fifty between 15 and 35 years old, and of men beyond this age, about forty active members. There is also a ladies' class of forty members. The Turner school is attended by an average of three hundred boys and two hundred girls. The drawing school of the society is conducted by the able artist, A. Schenk, and the library has more than five hundred volumes of German and English work. Of late, a women's chorus has been organized, to which some forty ladies belong. In addition to fostering the art of singing, they assist much in the entertainment of the society and many other things helpful to the society.

It is a well-known fact that in all phases of work of the Turner societies this particular society has developed the greatest activity. Among other things the idea of giving the older members something definite and appropriate to do at the festivals of the Turner Bund originated here. This

The German Element in St. Louis

has aroused a keen interest in the older Turners. At the festivals of the Bund this society has participated repeatedly and with distinction. Lately again at Milwaukee, where the older members of West St. Louis gave cause for their associates to be proud of their achievement.

For some years this society has had a publication of its own. First it was called: *Bahn Frei* (Clear the Track) and now: *Anzeiger des West St. Louis Turnvereins*. Zuendt, Dr. Castelhuhn, Christian Hertwig, Henry Lange and the late Carl Luedeking were and are valuable contributors. Ruppelt is the able editor.

The present officers are: J. R. Bollinger, first speaker; Hermann Ruppelt, second speaker; Frederick Wieden and E. Weidner, secretaries; M. Koch, treasurer; Otto Keil, cashier and collector; H. Schwaerzel and William Straszacker, gymnastic teachers; Adam Lilliger, custodian; Theodore Klipstein, chairman of the academic committee; H. Hoster, chairman of the entertainment committee; C. Hertwig, chairman of the council; Mrs. Otto Keil, chairman of the women's section; L. Entzeroth, chairman of the executive committee.

In addition to the above-named, St. Louis had three other Turner societies. One of these was the Swiss National Turner Society. In addition to regular gymnastic exercises it fostered wrestling, in keeping with their native practice. It has in George Pfaff an able teacher of gymnastics. Then there is a Bohemian Turner Society, which, however, does not appear much in public. Finally, there is the Northwest Turner Society, which was organized in 1892 under propitious auspices. From the outset it had over three hundred members. In a short time it plans to erect its own home in conjunction with the West St. Louis Liederkranz, which will meet all the demands of both organizations, that of gymnastics and that of the singers.

If St. Louis is at times called the City of Turners it would seem that the content of the preceding chapter would justify that appellation.

III. Business and Industry

30. The Levee and River Traffic

As long as there was no bridge between St. Louis and East St. Louis the ferry boats were most important factors in our entire communication. The heavily loaded freight wagons, which in pre-railroad times brought goods of every sort from the east, were put across the river by the ferry boats. And after the railroad yards in Illinoistown and practically disposed of the teamster, the large transfer cars were likewise conveyed on the ferry-boats to and from the freight depots on either side of the river.

When the Wiggins Ferry Company began its operations, more than sixty years ago, their boats made two trips a day. They traveled from the foot of Market Street to Morgan Street, which was their second landing place, and then to the opposite bank. For a long time these two trips a day were enough. By and by more became necessary so that in the sixties eight boats had to be on duty from morning till evening. In 1865, between forty and fifty railroad cars a day were ferried to and from East St. Louis, and probably between a thousand and fifteen hundred persons were so daily transferred across the river. The number of transfer trucks amounted to five and six hundred per day, and the farm wagons, which brought the products of the soil to the market here, number, on the average, two hundred a day. It needs hardly to be mentioned that under such circumstances the income of the company was enormous, and the dividends attractive. As the traffic, due to increased business and industry, rose, the income became enormous till the completion of the bridge and the tunnel brought incisive changes that affected the ferry company severely.

The era of the railroads gave river traffic a painful blow. This became more and more apparent as the railroad lines increased from year to year and curtailed communication by boat. It is true that there is considerable activity at the local wharf even today, but it isn't what it was formerly. In the fifties and to the outbreak of the war, and again at its close, there was day after day a forest of smokestacks along the bank, extending from the foot of Biddle Street to Chouteau Avenue. Crowded together lay the boats, often in double rows, and only too frequently one boat would have to await the departure of the other before it could lay by. Thousands of workers attended to the loading and unloading. The levee was so covered with barrels, boxes and bales of ware that only narrow passageways were left for the trams and wagons to get through, and even the pedestrian had to zig-zag his way among them.

The floating palaces, as the Mississippi steamboats were justly called, offered the passengers every comfort, and the number of travelers, except in the hottest months, was always very great. While now a half dozen cabs and coaches drive to the levee when one of the few boats arrives from the south, formerly all the carriages that stopped at the courthouse would hasten to the levee as soon as a steamboat announced its arrival. The large hotels regularly sent their own carriages to the landing place to receive the travelers.

From the middle of the forties the traveling time between here and New Orleans, which till then had always been a few weeks, was reduced to six to eight days. And even though now and then a boiler flew into the air and some passengers flew into the water, during a boat race, or a whole boat burned up, and so and so many people lost their lives, these things acted no more as determent than nowadays a collision of trains or the collapse of a railroad bridge. In addition to the passenger boats, which, of course also carried freight, a few freight lines, that is barges hauled by tug boats, were established in the sixties. These suffered less from competition with the railroads than the passenger boats.

One of the first steamboat connections with St. Louis was that on the Illinois River between Maples and Peoria, 1848. Soon thereafter came regular trips to the Minnesota River, 1851. The Quincy boats began operation in 1857, and a line to Vicksburg and Memphis started operation in 1859. Later followed lines to Dubuque and St. Paul, 1860. In the same year to Omaha, and in 1863 the Missouri River Packet Line and Red River Line. Passenger transportation to New Orleans and intermediate points is handled, since 1878, mainly by the Anchor Line, which, like the other steamboats, also carry freight.

The St. Louis and Mississippi Valley Transportation Company, on the other hand is devoted only to the freight business, and only to the terminals of its route without stopping at any of the places between here and New Orleans. The company is identical with the Mississippi Valley Transportation Company which was organized in 1866. It was created for the purpose of hauling bulk loads of grain and other products by means of barges which were conveyed by a steamboat that had them in tow.

The first president of this company was Captain Barton Able, who was succeeded the following year by George H. Rea. From the same year on, 1867, Henry C. Haarstick was vice president and superintendent, in which positions he continued till 1881. In this year the St. Louis and New Orleans Transportation Company, organized the year before, was merged with the older company which than resumed the name of St. Louis and Mississippi Valley Transportation Company, at the head of which Captain Haarstick served as president. In 1879 the company had six towboats and forty-three barges in operation. Today the number of its steamboats is ten and of its barges eighty.

Each of these barges can hold fifty to sixty thousand bushels of grain, in bulk, and the steamboats by which they are towed are of the greatest efficiency and especially built for this service. Moreover, the company has a grain elevator at Belmont, Missouri for the storage of grain, and another such elevator for the same purpose in New Orleans, where it also has three floating elevators which care for the reloading from the barges into the ships for overseas transportation. Then, too, the company owns shipbuilding yards and docks with excellent equipment in Mound City, Illinois, where not only its own boats are repaired and reconditioned, but also those of other concerns.

Ordinarily six to seven barges and an additional barge for the fuel supply are hauled in tow by one steamboat. If the water is sufficiently high the load of a single transportation amounts to seven to ten thousand tons. The number of loadings depends on the demands of the trade, and therefore varies, so that per month between four and ten, sometimes even twelve such shipments are dispatched. The journey down the river requires on an average six days and from New Orleans here, twelve days. The company is by no means limited to the hauling of grain, but also flour, lard, and other products of the most varied kind, which are intended for consumption down south or are intended for export. One barge in almost every transport is loaded with this sort of freight, which usually has a weight of two hundred tons. The return freight from New Orleans usually consists of imported articles of trade, such as cement, salt, building material, shingles, earthenware, chemicals, rice, dye woods, sugar, etc.

As was already mentioned the boats of the company do not stop anywhere. From the departure till the arrival at the destination, therefore, there are no delays, and consequently the time of arrival in New Orleans can be calculated with fair accuracy. From this accrues a considerable saving of time and expense for all parties concerned, for the freight intended for export does not arrive any sooner than the time when it should be put on board the ocean-going ship, and the latter loses no time in waiting for the cargo to arrive.

The following figures show better than anything else the enormous amount of freight which this company handles. It carried:

Year	Tons down Stream	Tons up Stream	Bushels of Grain
1882	328.411	64,949	8,189,425
1883	412,884	41,055	11,178,303
1884	313,029	25,295	7,088,899
1885	339,677	17,843	8,811,487
1886	334,596	47,651	9,215,361
1887	417,191	78,453	11,563,979
1888	310,137	47,118	8,119,881
1889	575,211	34,253	14,999,685
1890	405,298	45,384	11,081,797
1891	361,009	52,770	10,281,083
1892	413,088	42,993	12,716,735

The present officials are: President, Henry C. Haarstick; vice president, William T. Haarstick; treasurer, Austin R. Moore; secretary, Henry P. Wymann; general freight agent, James P. Burdeau. Like the president so also the other officials have been connected with the company for a long time. The great success of the company can primarily be ascribed to its president, for it, without question, owes its extent of operation to the zeal, and the energy and business acumen of this man. For more than a quarter of a century –(fifteen as general manager and the rest in his present position) –he has devoted himself to the interests of the St. Louis and Mississippi Valley Transportation Company. At the same time St. Louis owes him thanks, for during this entire period he has unceasingly tried to expand the grain export of the west. It was he who, twenty-five years ago, paved the way for the grain trade with Europe. He effected the first contact for this enterprise personally, and since then has worked incessantly to

The German Element in St. Louis

make St. Louis a center for the export of bread stuffs, a primary market for this sort of grain business. He has every right to look upon his accomplishment with satisfaction.

The directors of the company at this time are: H.C., William T. Haarstick, A. R. Moore, S. H. H. Clark, R. S. Hayes, D. S. H. Smith, Samuel D. Capen, F. W. Meister, and E. Dickinson. The "barge line," as it is called in brief, is the largest transportation company of this kind in the world. The extent of its operation is not even approached by other concerns. The trade of the Mississippi Valley and the grain-producing states of the west has been furthered more than by dozens of conventions and other endeavors.

31. The Omnibus Period   The First Street-railways

Iron rails, on which the cars of the electric and cable lines run every two or three minutes, extend along the streets of St. Louis in all directions. There is probably no region of the city to which one can not go with such a line. It is only a few years ago that the cable and electricity replaced teams of horses and mules, and the power-house took the place of horse stables. But also the horse-drawn line had its predecessor and that was the omnibus.

The first St. Louis omnibus was at the same time the first vehicle of this type west of the Mississippi. The local builder of coaches, Theodore Salorgne had built it, and indeed upon the order of Erastus Wells. At that time, 1844, Wells was still a very young man. Later he became the founder of our street railway system, as he was the originator of the omnibus transportation.

At first this one omnibus sufficed for the transportation of passengers on Olive Street. From seven o'clock in the morning till evening after the close of the theater, it drove to and fro at regular intervals. The owner, Wells, drove the omnibus himself and also collected the fares.

The establishment of two further lines followed the first shortly. One of these started from the corner of Market and Third Street, ran through the latter and up Broadway to North Market Street. The other went up Market Street to Camp Spring, therefore, approximately to the present Jefferson Avenue.

For the purpose of expansion of operation Erastus Wells had looked around for business partners, and had found them in Robert O'Blennis and the two brothers Case. Bob O'Blennis, who later ran a gambling establishment, was a terrible ruffian, who in time killed several persons, drove the bus for New Bremen. Mike Sutter, Sr., who kept a tavern on Main and Spruce Street in the forties, ran an omnibus from Second and Market to the arsenal, from where another line connected Carondelet with St. Louis. John C. Vogel, (later member of the city council and in the second half of the sixties was the sheriff of the St. Louis county of that time), had an omnibus run on Franklin Avenue, and another undertaker had a bus run from Third and Green to Seventh Street and Geyer Avenue to Flora Garden. With this line the young ladies of Frenchtown traveled to and from the high school, which was situated at that time in the old Benton school house on Sixth Street.

Missouri Railroad Company

For fifteen years the omnibus was good enough for St. Louis. In 1859 the street-car took its place. Again it was Erastus Wells who also introduced this innovation. On the fourth of July, 1859, he drove the team that pulled the first local streetcar over the recently-laid tracks on Olive Street, between Fourth an Twelfth Street. The line, therefore, extended only about eight blocks. The corporation whose property it was, opened in the same year the operation of the Market Street line, which at first ran only to Thirteenth Street. At the head of these two lines was Wells, then twenty-two years old. He must not only be regarded as the founder of the St. Louis street railway system, but he must also receive recognition for the fact that the service on his lines is better and more punctual than on other lines.

The incorporators of the company which started the two lines on Olive and Market were: Erastus Wells, William van Zandt, M. M. Hodgman, Charles Hathaway, Henry B. Leach, William M. McPherson, Marshall Brotherton, and George Trask. These names have a good sound, and their bearers are among the most enterprising and at the same time most benevolent citizens of our city.

The line on Olive was very soon extended from Twelfth Street on. For a number of years Jefferson Avenue constituted the western terminal, then

Garrison Avenue was the end of the line for some time until the extension to Grand Avenue followed.

The Market Street line, during the first year only, reached Thirteenth, then Nineteenth and later was extended to Twenty-ninth, which was called Summit Avenue (now Ewing Avenue).

The Olive Street line was a double track affair from the outset, while on Market Street was a single track. On Chestnut Street there was a double track from Sixth to the Twentieth Street. On this stretch the cars ran to the west and then east on Market Street, but from Twentieth Street they ran in a westerly direction along Market and then east on Clark Avenue. In the course of time this line was extended to Grand Avenue. At the beginning of the eighties the Laclede Avenue line was added. This ran direct to Forest Park, and was the first line which established connection between the park and downtown. The fact that Fourth Street formed the eastern terminal of this line was of especial value for the line itself and for the public, for it led into the real business center of that time. We know that traffic about the courthouse is very lively at this time because of the increased population. It was particularly lively at the time when all the city offices and the county offices were under one roof. People who lived some distance west of the courthouse were glad to use the time-saving streetcar. It was especially welcome to the people who lived at the West End of that time. The greatest benefit from these means of transportation accrued to the real estate agents on Fourth and Fifth Streets, and the real estate owners and house owners in those parts of the city that were touched by the outrunners of the streetcar lines. The cost of operation was very great, and during the years of the war the property was not profitable, but it became so later, and particularly so when the exodus to the west end assumed considerable proportions, and a new part of the city west of Grand Avenue was developed.

In November 1881, the three lines went into other hands. Erastus and Rolla Wells, father and son, retired. The new owners, who at once doubled the operating capital of $300,000, organized and chose the following officers: P. C. Maffitt, president; John R. Lionberger, vice president; William D. Henry, secretary-treasurer. The directors were: P. C. Maffitt, John R. Lionberger, Charles Parsons, Daniel Catlin and James Clark. For six years the Olive Street horse-drawn line was kept, but then the company changed it to a cable line. The cable, woven of wire, ran under the street.

The cable and the electric wire relieved the quadrupeds of their duty. The old horse-drawn car was not fast enough for our feverish time. For many years the omnibus was quite sufficient. The telephone had not yet been invented. The retailer could not send his orders over the electric wire to the wholesaler or manufacturer, nor could he in the same way inquire the price of goods. He had to go himself or send a messenger or write a letter. The era of rapid transit came and on Olive Street the power house, which was built in the spring of 1888, replaced the horse barn.

On the other two lines, on Market Street and Laclede Avenue, electricity has now been used as motive power for nearly four years.

The total length of the three lines amounts to twenty-seven and seven-tenths miles. The rolling stock consists at this time of three hundred and eight cars –grip cars, motor cars and passenger cars. The number of daily trips is twenty-five hundred, from which it may be seen, that the intervals between trains is extremely small, so that the traffic justifies the term "rapid." In order to show to what degree the demands of the public are complied with by the Missouri Railroad System the following figures are added. In 1883, 6,984,102 passengers were conveyed. Five years later, in 1888, 10,272,196, and after four more years, in 1892, 14,708,156. Therefore it was more than doubled in ten years. In consideration of so extensive operation it is not surprising that it requires the services of 508 employees, and that the capital of the company amounts to $2,300,000.

Aside from the fact that these three lines lead directly to the most beautiful residential parts of the city, the west and the southwest parts, they take their passengers in uninterrupted journey to the two largest parks of the city, namely with the Olive Street and the Laclede line, to the Forest Park and via the Market Street line to Tower Grove Park. Thus these splendid places of recreation are also made available to those who have no conveyances of their own or can not afford to hire such conveyances.

The cars of the company are of the best workmanship. Their summer cars are especially comfortable. If a passenger wishes to get off, he needs only to press a button, which is near his seat, to give the conductor the sign to stop. On the two electric lines the cars are also illumined by electricity.

The present officers of the company are: P. C. Maffitt, president; John R. Lionberger, vice president; Frank R. Henry, secretary; James F. Davidson, superintendent. The directors are: P. C. Maffitt, John R. Lionberger, John A. Scudder, Charles Parsons, and Daniel Catlin.

The People's Railway Company

The People's Railway Company, which is known as the Fourth Street or Chouteau Avenue line, was also organized in 1859. In the charter which it obtained from the state the following are named as incorporators: R. M. Renick, B. Able, H. Lightner, P. L. Foy, H. Crittenden, J. B. Sickels and John S. Cavender.

The line ran only during the first five years from its eastern terminal on Fourth and Morgan Street to St. Ange Avenue (Fourteenth Street). In 1864 it was extended to Lafayette, corner of Mississippi Avenue (Twentieth Street). From here it was built to Grand Avenue (Thirty-sixth Street) in 1882, on which it now runs to the main entrance of Tower Grove Park, and in this manner established the most convenient connection between the main business part of the city and the southwest. The length of the line amounts to nine and a half miles. The operation of capital was at first $300,000. Like all others it also was at first a horse-drawn line. In 1889 it was changed to a cable line. As presidents of the concern the following served from 1859 till 1884: R. M. Renick, Gustavus W. Dryer, John H. Lightner, James H. Britton, J. R. Lionberger, D. E. Walsh and Julius S. Walsh. The first superintendent of the line was Stephen Brock. At that time neither speed nor comfort were demanded as at present. The requirements of the public were kept in modest boundaries. But it must be said regarding this line that from the outset it had only good cars and good horses, and always endeavored to please its passengers.

The cable line was constructed in 1889. It was mainly due to the energy of Charles Green that the work was begun. He became president of the company in 1884, and so directed its business. In the removal of the earth which preceded the laying of the cable, and in the preparation of the roadbed, the greatest of care was taken. The pains applied and the considerable expenditure made brought the result that after more than three years the roadbed and track are still in good condition. The cars pass smoothly over the tracks and the passengers do not feel the discomfort which a poor and uneven under structure and defective rails can cause.

The powerhouse, which stands on the northwest corner of Second Carondelet and Park Avenue, occupies, on the former, half a block and on the latter a third of a block. The structure cost over thirty thousand dollars. It may well be designated as the most beautiful powerhouse in all America and its inner equipment, especially of the office, is in full harmony with it. In the machine room are two steam engines, each of five hundred horsepower. One of these is being used and the other is held in reserve for emergencies. There are, moreover, the two drums over which the cables of the two circuits pass, which run to the east and west, so that one cable furnished the motive power from Second Carondelet Avenue to Morgan Street, and the other for the part of the line from the first named street to Tower Grove Park. At the first the cable was obtained from a factory in Trenton, New Jersey. The one that is used now is a local manufacture, coming from the works of Broderick and Bascom Rope Company.

The company now owns forty grip cars and can put forty trains in service at any time. In the morning, from six to nine, thirty cars run at intervals of two and a half minutes; from three till five-thirty in the afternoon, at intervals of two and a half or two and a fourth minutes. Later, at intervals of three and a half, four and six minutes. After midnight the "owlcar," horse-drawn, ran now and again till five a.m. The car barn is situated on the south side of Park Avenue, diagonally across from the powerhouse and covers an area of about three blocks. The number of employees approaches one hundred sixty-five, and the capital of the company amounts to one million dollars.

The change of the line to a cable line evoked not only extensive recognition on the part of the inhabitants of the parts of the city concerned, but contributed also to the occupation of countless vacant building sites with splendid buildings, new streets were laid out and whole regions were beautified. There is no doubt that the continued rise of real estate in parts touched by the lines where traffic has become in the last years is shown by the following figures. In 1892 the line made 231,024 trips and carried 4,731,379 passengers, and in April, May, June of 1893, 115,154 trips were made and the number of passengers reached the extraordinary number of 2,361,775.

The directors of the People's Railway Company at present are: Charles Green, John Mahoney, A. B. Ewing, James Campbell, W. W. Whitnell, John Mullally and Charles J. Maguire. The management rests in the hands of President Green, and Vice President and General Manager, John Mahoney, who at this time also holds the position of secretary-treasurer. The latter entered the service of the company as secretary-treasurer as early as 1876. The charter of the company was, a few years ago, extended for twenty years, so that it will not expire till 1932.

The Fourth Street and Arsenal Railway Company, whose officers and directors are exactly the same as those of the People's Company, was organized in 1866. Originally it was called Tower Grove and Lafayette Railroad company. During the first years the company ran a branch line through Carroll and Soulard to Thirteenth Street, and then south. However its tracks were removed after some time. The line runs from Fourth and Morgan Street to the Arsenal, and is one of the few lines which have not yet been transformed into cable lines or electric lines.

Citizens Railroad Company

Under this name a company began operation in 1859, whose president was B. Gratz Brown, who later became the governor of Missouri. It began at the corner of Fourth and Morgan Street and ran down Franklin Avenue to Garrison. From 1865 on it extended its service to Prairie Avenue and north to the Fairgrounds, and later to St. Charles Road to Rinkelville, etc. In an easterly direction its tracks entered from Garrison Avenue to Morgan Street. In 1874 the company was reorganized with Julius S. Walsh as president, and increased its capital from three thousand to six thousand dollars. As early as 1883 the line had a length of thirteen miles, and since then has made further extension. A few years ago this line passed into the hands of a Chicago syndicate, in which, for the most part, Chicago capital is involved. The president of the line is D. G. Hamilton of Chicago.

St. Louis Railway Company

The line of this company also began in 1859 and ran, during the first years, from North St. Louis to the Arsenal. The extension in a northerly direction to Baden, and in a southerly direction to the Wild Huntsman was made in the second half of the sixties. From the northern terminal as far as Elm Street lay a double track from the beginning of operation. Beginning with Elm Street a single track ran down Seventh Street to the south, and likewise from the southern terminal along Carondelet and Fifth Street to Elm Street.

For some time the company changed its president often. Among these were: D. H. Armstrong, Hudson E. Bridge, General W. T. Sherman, John F. Madison, Robert A. Barnes, and Christian Peper. Under the administration of the latter the cable line was built in 1888. Until the great extensions of the different streetcar lines were built, the Bremen-Arsenal line, commonly known as the Fifth Street line, was the longest of all of them. For this reason it was far less profitable than its owners had a right to expect. By its connection in the northern and southern part of the city it rendered real service and met a real need. However, the cost of operation was too high and the stretch too long to fulfill the hopes of the stockholders. This has changed in time. In 1892 the line carried 12,301,596 passengers on 818,354 trips. In April, May and June of 1893, 6,195,153 persons were hauled on 409,860 trips. Since the installation of the cable line, track on Seventh Street is not used. A double track serves the operation from one terminal to the other. The president of the company is D. G. Hamilton of Chicago, and our fellow citizen, Christian Peper, is the vice president.

The above-named five lines constitute the beginning of the local street railway system, which as early as the second half of the sixties, had a considerable extension, and in the course of time has undergone an increase that forms a real net of tracks in all directions of the city. Fifteen years after opening the first line there were fourteen lines in operation with a length of one hundred and twenty miles, which were traveled by six hundred cars, and required twenty-three hundred horses and about seven hundred mules to haul. It was no favor to the public when on some of the ones so-called "bobtail-cars" were installed, in which the driver is at the same time the conductor. The principle enunciated by the railroad king, Vanderbilt, regarding the public seems to hold here, too. The companies cared little for the wishes and rights of the passengers.

Today the number of miles of the St. Louis street railway network amounts to 51½ miles of cable lines, 218 miles of electric line and about three miles of horse-drawn line (Jefferson Avenue). During 1892, 5,361,973 trips were made by all the lines and carried 91,685,555 passengers. In the first six months of this year, from January 1 to June 30, 1893 there were made 3,085,312 trips carrying 47,671,799 passengers. That is what rapid transit accomplished.

Railroads

At the Union Station in St. Louis one hundred and seventy passenger trains, coming over twenty-five different lines, arrive every twenty-four hours, and an equal number departs. This does not include the so-called accommodation or local trains which connect the city with its suburbs and the surrounding localities to a distance of fifty miles. Whoever wants to go from here to St. Paul, or New York, or Chicago, or Philadelphia, Boston or Cincinnati boards the train at the Union Station, and, in most cases, reaches his destination without change of cars. The tunnel and the bridge take the traveler to the other side of the Mississippi to East St. Louis, from where the different trains take their way in all directions of the railway net, which serves the communication of the country east of the Father of Waters. In like manner the travelers who arrive on the other side of the river come here. The enormous bridge which connects the neighboring states of Illinois and Missouri and the east with the west, and then the tunnel under the streets brings the trains to Twelfth Street, and in a short time will bring them to Eighteenth Street, therefore, still closer to the center of the city.

The convenience is ours, however, only since the completion of the bridge and the tunnel, connected with it, which were planned and completed by the engineer Eads, that is since 1874. Prior to that time there were three different stations in St. Louis. But there were also only three railroads here. All other lines, that connected our city with the other parts of the United States, terminated at East S. Louis, or more correctly, Illinoistown, as our neighboring city was called in the sixties. Not only all the freight yards, but also all the passenger stations of the lines east of the Mississippi were there, and the connection of the two river banks was by means of the ferryboats, owned by the Wiggins Ferry Company. In some winters, however, there was occasionally a complete stoppage of traffic, when, for example, the river was in the act of freezing over, and the ice prevented the boats from crossing, or later when the ice began to break up and the floating ice was even a greater danger. As long as the river was frozen solid, the ice cover furnished a sufficiently safe bridge for even the heavily loaded coal wagons, and naturally also for the passenger traffic. In such times many passengers preferred to leave the railroad omnibuses, which were usually drawn by four horses, and walk over the icy surface on foot.

The roads that terminated on the east bank of the Mississippi during the fifties were the St. Louis, Alton and Chicago, which at first ran only from Alton to Springfield (1852), but soon was built farther from Alton to Illinoistown (1856), then the St. Louis, Alton and Terre Haute (1856), which was later called the Indianapolis and St. Louis Railroad; and finally the Ohio and Mississippi line (1857) which connected Cincinnati with St. Louis.

On our side of the river there were during this period three railroads: The Pacific Road, the construction of which began in 1851; the North Missouri (now the Wabash) Railroad, started in 1855; and the Iron Mountain Railroad, which began in 1855. Before the establishment of the Union Depot, the trains of the Pacific Road started from the corner of Seventh and Poplar Street, but also stopped in going and coming at Fourteenth Street at a branch depot. The old North Missouri Road had its depot at the foot of North Market Street, where it remained until the Wabash acquired the right-of-way in the extreme north and west of the city, and thus secured an entrance to the Union Station. The Iron Mountain had its terminal at the corner of Plum and Main Street, from where its accommodation trains were dispatched to Carondelet and Jefferson Barracks till its branch station was built at Chouteau Avenue and Fourth Street. Its through trains were routed over the tracks on Poplar Street in and out of the Union Station.

The three named roads are, therefore, the oldest roads which ran to the west and south respectively. Their history is so closely connected with the growth of St. Louis, and its development of trade and industry to be entitled to a place in this book.

The Missouri Pacific Railway –St. Louis, Iron Mountain and Southern Railroad

When Thomas Allen, on January 31, 1850, outlined his plan of building a railroad from here to Kansas City, before a meeting of business men and capitalists, most of his hearers were visibly astonished. Allen's scheme was received by shaking of the heads and with doubts of every sort. Only a short while ago, at one of the meetings, a suggestion to connect St. Louis and Jefferson City by a railroad had been discarded as too risky an undertaking. Nevertheless, in spite of all doubts, the first practical step to build the first railroad west of the Mississippi, and the origin and beginning of the magnificent railway system, known as the Missouri Pacific Railway, date back to that meeting. It was decided to build a line that for the time being should reach Jefferson City, and also serve the localities between St. Louis and that point.

On July 4, 1851 Mayor Kennett, who intentionally chose the national holiday for the occasion, dug the first shovelful of earth of this project, which dirt he threw in Chouteau pond. This pond was in time completely filled in order to gain terrain for the eastern terminal of the road, for the necessary depot building. Herewith disappeared the remaining part of a large swamp which originally extended between Sixth and Seventh Streets on the east side to Thirteenth Street on the west side, with Papin as its southern and Spruce Street as its northern border. A portion of it extended also between Ninth and Eleventh Street, reaching as far as Clark Avenue. In former years the pond had clear, pure water. With the increase of the population and the growing spread of the city, the creeks and springs (Mill Creek) carried more or less impurities into it, so that the pond, in which at one time young and old were accustomed to bathe and to fish, became a giant puddle and the receptacle of dirt and filth. The building of the Mill Creek drainage canal helped to improve this bad condition to a great extent but not completely. The complete removal of the pond was an imperative necessity for sanitary reasons. The filling of the pond was made gradually, but too slowly for the inhabitants of the region. They therefore, rejoiced when the Pacific Railroad bought the strip of land between Cerre and Poplar Street and had the pond filled. Where now the countless strands of steel form a real network, and where at night hundreds of white, green and red signal lights seem to spring out of the ground, fish once sported and frogs set up their horrid concert, there now the sounds of bells and whistles of locomotives are heard. Chouteau Pond is a thing of the past.

The train yard of the Pacific Road was laid out in the simplest manner, as it was customary at that time, on the west side of Seventh, corner of Poplar Street. Old and young were highly pleased when the frame structure, intended for the depot was completed. Even greater was the rejoicing when the first division of the road, thirty-nine miles, were opened for operation on July 19, 1852.

The following year Thomas Allen, who from the outset had been president of the company, resigned the office, and Hudson A. Bridge became his successor. In 1855 the line was extended to Washington, (Mo.), then to Hermann, and in November to Jefferson City. In 1861, Sedalia had been reached, but then came the war, and for the time made a temporary end to construction. Strangely enough, the road suffered its real serious losses only in the last two years of the war through the destruction of two large bridges over the Gasconade and the Osage, the burning of depots, the tearing up of tracks and the damage to every type of property. The damage amounted to more than a million dollars, and the operation of the road was almost completely interrupted by the work of destruction of the rebels. The reconstruction of the road and the extension of the line then took place under the protection of the U.S. government, and in the fall of 1865 the road reached Kansas City.

The first meeting of businessmen, previously mentioned, was attended, among others, by: J. H. Lucas, John O'Fallon, Daniel D. Page, Edward Walsh, George Collier, Adolphus Meier, Ernest Angelrodt, Henry Shaw and Pierre Chouteau. The decision which they arrived at appeared like a fantastic undertaking. But now it had been accomplished. In about twelve hours one could travel from St. Louis to Kansas City.

Shortly afterwards C. K. Garrison assumed the management of the road. Under his administration, on a Sunday in July 1869, within sixteen hours, and without interrupting the running of trains, a piece of work was accomplished, that was described in all the newspapers, on both sides of the ocean, as a miracle of speed. On that day the change from a wide gauge track to a standard gauge was completed on the entire length of the road as far as Kansas City, a distance of 283 miles. An army of workers was necessary for this project, which had been planned and prepared to the smallest detail, so that the taking up and moving together of the rails proceeded as by magic –an achievement that aroused the wonder of specialists in railroading, and which was not imitated by any other road till seventeen years later. The enormous advantage that accrued to the road by the introduction of standard gauge track in the handling of freight is so obvious that it requires no further explanation.

Upon the instance of the holders of the third mortgage the Pacific Railroad was sold at Auction in 1876. A new organization was undertaken under the name of Missouri Pacific Railway. In 1880 Jay Gould and other stockholders obtained control over the road, and with it began a new era for the later. Its motto was: Improvement and consolidation. Up to this time the length of the main line amounted only to three hundred miles. Under the new management, extensions and connections with other roads put thousands and thousands of miles under the control of the Missouri Pacific. By the end of 1882 the length of the consolidated lines amounted to 5877 miles. In 1886 these roads also added the connecting lines to the principal places in southwest Kansas. In the midst of this business activity there came in the spring of 1886 a strike that lasted for six weeks. It put a complete stop to the freight business, and caused a loss in income of approximately twenty million dollars, and injured the business world in an inestimable manner.

By means of purchase and consolidation the mileage was increased as follows: In 1887 by 389 miles, in 1888 by 100 miles, in 1890 by 37, in 1891 by 164, in 1892 by 90 miles. The main roads which belong to the Missouri Pacific and Iron Mountain Southern system, are: Missouri Pacific itself; St. Louis, Iron Mountain and Southern and their branch lines; Missouri, Kansas and Texas; International and Great Northern; Galveston, Houston and Henderson; Central Branch Union Pacific; Little Rock and Fort Smith. These roads alone, without the numerous others, which the system includes at this time, had a 1888 in the matter of operating material 750 locomotives, 372 Passenger Coaches, 169 baggage and mail cars, to which are to be added corresponding number of sleeping cars and reclining chair cars. And for the freight service there were available at the same time 22,737 cars of most varied type. Since then, of course, this operating material has considerably increased from year to year.

The St. Louis, Iron Mountain and Southern is, next to the Missouri Pacific, the most important link in the chain of roads, of the system in question. Its main line runs from St. Louis to Texarkana on the order of Arkansas and Texas, while from Bismarck a branch line runs to Belmont on the Mississippi, opposite to Columbus, Kentucky, at which point the connection with the network east of the Mississippi begins. The charter of the St. Louis and Iron Mountain Railroad Co. was issued by the state on January 6, 1851. The main purpose of the road was to connect St. Louis with the mineral region of Iron Mountain and Pilot Knot. The first directors of the company that were chosen were: John O'Fallon, Henry Kayser, who previously was city engineer, and later city comptroller, Francis Kellermann, William H. Belcher, L. V. Bogy, Frederick Schulenburg, and J. S. Cavender, and the second board of directors was:

John How, Adolph Abeles, Frederick Schulenburg, L. M. Kennett, Edward Haren, William M. MacPherson and James Harrison. the first presidents were: L. M. Kennett, Madison Miller, L. V. Bogy, S. D. Barlow, who held that office from 1859 to 1866, in which year the state brought the road under the hammer, because the company, like so many others, was not in a position to pay the interest on its bonds, which bonds were secured by mortgages. The state was the main creditor and bought the road, but sold it again at auction the same year. In 1867 it came into the possession of Thomas Allen, in whose hands and under whose management it remained until 1881 it was bought by the Missouri Pacific and so became the property of Jay Gould and other eastern capitalists.

The construction of the road as far as Iron Mountain was completed in 1856 but the war and the various difficulties and hindrances, especially financial, particularly those which the state imposed on Thomas Allen, delayed the extension of the road to Belmont till 1869. By the end of 1872 the branch line to the Arkansas border was completed, and in April 1873 was put in regular operation. Also the Iron Mountain system changed its track in 1879 to agree with the gauge of the lines east of the Mississippi. The system includes more than a thousand miles and brings St. Louis, respectively Kansas City in direct connection with New Orleans, and all southern states, particularly with Texas and Florida. It takes the traveler via Texarkana to the gulf of Mexico, the Rio Grande, to Old Mexico, and the places on the Pacific Ocean. The main line runs via Poplar Bluffs to Hot Springs, the much-sought watering-place in Arkansas. It presents uninterrupted connection with Little Rock and Fort Smith, Arkansas, with Memphis and other points in Tennessee. It, together with the Missouri Pacific System, furnishes the Missouri River Country and the Arkansas River country with a network of rails that criss-cross this great territory in every direction.

These two roads have rendered pioneer service for agriculture and trade, have made vast stretches of land tillable, covered these acres with fields of grain and orchards, created flourishing cities. Culture and civilization followed the iron rails mile upon mile. On these rails the products of the farms of the west, of the cotton-fields of the south, and the fruit of the California orchards find their way to the best markets of the world. It goes without saying that the passenger service of these lines meets the requirements of the present with regard to speed and comfort.

In 1874 the company was reorganized with Julius S. Walsh as president, and increased its capital from three thousand to six thousand dollars. As early as 1883 the line had a length of thirteen miles, and since then has made further extension. A few years ago this line passed into the hands of a Chicago syndicate, in which, for the most part, Chicago capital is involved. The president of the line is D. G. Hamilton of Chicago.

St. Louis Railway Company

The line of this company also began in 1859 and ran, during the first years, from North St. Louis to the Arsenal. The extension in a northerly direction to Baden, and in a southerly direction to the Wild Huntsman was made in the second half of the sixties. From the northern terminal as far as Elm Street lay a double track from the beginning of operation. Beginning with Elm Street a single track ran down Seventh Street to the south, and likewise from the southern terminal along Carondelet and Fifth Street to Elm Street.

For some time the company changed its president often. Among these were: D. H. Armstrong, Hudson E. Bridge, General W. T. Sherman, John F. Madison, Robert A. Barnes, and Christian Peper. Under the administration of the latter the cable line was built in 1888. Until the great extensions of the different streetcar lines were built, the Bremen-Arsenal line, commonly known as the Fifth Street line, was the longest of all of them. For this reason it was far less profitable than its owners had a right to expect. By its connection in the northern and southern part of the city it rendered real service and met a real need. However, the cost of operation was too high and the stretch too long to fulfill the hopes of the stock-holders. This has changed in time. In 1892 the line carried 12,301,596 passengers on 818,354 trips. In April, May and June of 1893, 6,195,153 persons were hauled on 409,860 trips. Since the installation of the cable line, track on Seventh Street is not used. A double track serves the operation from one terminal to the other. The president of the company is D. G. Hamilton of Chicago, and our fellow citizen, Christian Peper, is the vice president.

The above-named five lines constitute the beginning of the local street railway system, which as early as the second half of the sixties, had a considerable extension, and in the course of time has undergone an increase that forms a real net of tracks in all directions of the city. Fifteen years after opening the first line there were fourteen lines in operation with a length of one hundred and twenty miles, which were traveled by six hundred cars, and required twenty-three hundred horses and about seven hundred mules to haul. It was no favor to the public when on some of the ones so-called "bobtail-cars" were installed, in which the driver is at the same time the conductor. The principle enunciated by the railroad king, Vanderbilt, regarding the public seems to hold here, too. The companies cared little for the wishes and rights of the passengers.

Today the number of miles of the St. Louis street railway network amounts to 51½ miles of cable lines, 218 miles of electric line and about three miles of horse-drawn line (Jefferson Avenue). During 1892, 5,361,973 trips were made by all the lines and carried 91,685,555 passengers. In the first six months of this year, from January 1 to June 30, 1893 there were made 3,085,312 trips carrying 47,671,799 passengers. That is what rapid transit accomplished.

Railroads

At the Union Station in St. Louis one hundred and seventy passenger trains, coming over twenty-five different lines, arrive every twenty-four hours, and an equal number departs. This does not include the so-called accommodation or local trains which connect the city with its suburbs and the surrounding localities to a distance of fifty miles. Whoever wants to go from here to St. Paul, or New York, or Chicago, or Philadelphia, Boston or Cincinnati boards the train at the Union Station, and, in most cases, reaches his destination without change of cars. The tunnel and the bridge take the traveler to the other side of the Mississippi to East St. Louis, from where the different trains take their way in all directions of the railway net, which serves the communication of the country east of the Father of Waters. In like manner the travelers who arrive on the other side of the river come here. The enormous bridge which connects the neighboring states of Illinois and Missouri and the east with the west, and then the tunnel under the streets transferred to the Planters House. All the rooms which were used then would now not accommodate a single branch of the administration.

The Great Western Railroad of Illinois, which first took the name of Toledo, Wabash and Western, and later Wabash, St. Louis, and Pacific has been called the Wabash since 1880. It runs through the richest and most fertile regions of Illinois, Indiana and Ohio, and soon became the most popular passenger route between the east and west of the United States. By a system of consolidation, such as the American railroads previously had not yet shown, and which is unique in its kind, the Wabash Road has by and by obtained a gigantic expansion, which assures to it the predominant rank that it occupies in the railroad system in this country. It forms the fastest connection from New York, Boston, Philadelphia, Baltimore, Cincinnati, Louisville and other points in the east and south with St. Louis, Kansas City, St. Joseph, Denver, Omaha, Salt Lake, San Francisco and the whole remaining west. A glance at the map teaches that this road system includes in its operation not only the best farming region of the middle states but also has more connections and important terminals for passenger and freight traffic than any other road.

The single lines which belong to the system can be divided as follows:

St. Louis to Chicago	286 miles.
St. Louis to Kansas City	277 miles.
Toledo to Moberly	533 miles.
Moberly to Des Moines	212 miles.
Chicago to Detroit	273 miles.
Peru to Montpelier	98 miles.
West Logansport to Chili	21 miles.
Clayton to Keokuk	42 miles.
Bluffs to Quincy	105 miles.
Streator to Forrest	37 miles.
Attica to Covington	15 miles.
Champaign to Sidney	12 miles.
Edwardsville to Edwardsville Crossing	9 miles.
Brement to Altamont and Effingham	63 miles.
Brunswick to Omaha	225 miles.
Salisbury to Glasgow	15 miles.
Centralia to Columbia	12 miles.
Total:	2,235 miles

From the above it became obvious that the main places of trade and industry, as also the most important market for the products of the soil of an exceedingly great territory either lie within the limits of the Wabash system or are connected most directly with it. As proof thereof it may be pointed out that Omaha, Kansas City, Des Moines, Keokuk, Quincy, St. Louis, Chicago, Toledo and Detroit are brought together by an uninterrupted network of rails. It is, therefore, only natural that enormous quantities of agricultural products, livestock of every kind, and products of industry of the west should be conveyed over this line to the other parts of the country, while the manufactured articles of eastern states reach the line to the west. The facilities of the Wabash line are unsurpassed for the transportation of the enormously numerous products of the slaughter houses and packing establishments of Kansas City, St. Louis to Detroit, Toledo, and the markets of the east. The same is true in like manner for the rapid transportation of grain from Kansas, Nebraska, Iowa, Missouri, Illinois and Indiana to the east. In regard to the freight tariffs the management of this railroad system has always held to a liberal policy, and has always accommodated shippers, being mindful of the fact that the settlement and improvement of the lands along the road depends in part on the facilities which the farmers, manufacturers and merchants may receive from the railroad company.

As far as the passenger traffic is concerned, the Wabash road has, from the beginning, done everything to make this service as complete as possible. The first requirement to this end, naturally, is the condition of the roadbed, and for this reason this is solidly built. On a massive road embankment is the well-laid track of all steel rails. The bridges are substantial structures. The greatest attention is given to safety and punctuality of the service. The coaches are of the best construction and afford the travelers every wished-for comfort. On the main line, dining cars and sleeping cars are operated. At the head of the passenger department, F. Chandler has for years presided as General Passenger and Ticket Agent. He has a suitable number of able assistants, and a corps of agents at all important points, and a number of traveling agents. The publicity department is managed by H. Durand.

The principal officials of the Wabash system at this time are: O. D. Ashley, president; Edgar T. Welles, vice president in New York; in St.

Louis the vice president is James F. How, who, for more than two decades, was at the head of the Main Office; Charles M. Mays, general manager; H. A. Loyd and F. L. O'Leary, treasurer. The executive offices occupy two stories in the Commercial Building on Sixth and Olive Street, and the main ticket offices are situated on the corner of Fifth and Olive (southeast corner) and at the Union Depot.

The passenger trains of the Wabash West reach the Union Depot via the tracks from the northwest and west of the city. In the future the passenger trains of the Wabash East will not come though the tunnel, but over the river via the Merchants Bridge and so reach the depot.

The buildings which will constitute the new Union Depot are calculated to meet the demands of a modern station, in which twenty-five different railroad lines converge. The practical and the modern will be combined. The contrast between the old and the new will be very marked.

32. The Mail Service

St. Louis got its first post office in October, 1804. The first post office was at the northwest corner of Third and Elm Street. The first postmaster, Judge Baston, lived with his family in the house, and one room was sufficient for the mail service. During the first four years after the establishment of the post office there was no newspaper here, and every three months the postmaster tacked a list of unclaimed letters on his door. The last of such lists, for the quarter ending on June 30, 1808 contained thirty-nine names, among them two German names. From then on the list of names was printed at regular intervals of three months in the *Missouri Gazette*, the first local paper, from which the *Missouri Republican* developed. Eaton held the position of postmaster for ten years. His successor was Attorney Robert Simpson, who was the father-in-law of General A. J. Smith, who, after the war, became postmaster, and under Mayor Francis was city auditor. From that time on the post office was located now here and then there.

First it was housed in a house on the east side of Main St, between Elm and Myrtle, then later on the northwest corner of Main and Elm, where letters were deposited and received from the street through a small window, out of which the postmaster temporarily removed a window pane. In the thirties a larger space for the post office was provided in the houses belonging to James H. Lucus, located on the northwest corner of Main and Chestnut Street. During the forties the house was built, which still stands at the southeast corner of Second and Chestnut Street, where the post office occupied the lower story. After a few years this locality seems not to have been ample, for in 1852 postmaster Archibald Gamble made the suggestion to the county authorities to arrange a wing in the courthouse which was then under construction, for a post office and lease it to the federal government.

The above suggestion was not accepted, on the other hand the Congress appropriated money for the construction of a suitable federal building which should house the post office as well as the customs office, the federal court and the sub-treasury. The customs office had, up to that time, occupied a four-story building at the southwest corner of Third and Pine Street. Later this building was popularly called the Old Customs Building, and which was not removed until the present Exchange Building was built. For the new federal building the southeast corner of Third and Olive Street was chosen. The St. Louis Theater located there was torn down, and in 1853 the building was begun under the direction of architect Barnett. After its completion it was considered one of the most beautiful buildings in the city. This, in spite of various defects that it had. Not the least of which was the fact that in the main workroom of the post office the gas flames had to burn throughout the day because the interior of the building was so dark.

Compared with the early days the local postal traffic was quite considerable even in the fifties. Of course, when compared with the later incoming and outgoing mail, it was relatively small. A large part of the mail was conveyed by water, even in the decade following the fifties. The mail clerks on the steamboats had a rather easy time compared with those who worked on the railroad. With Memphis, New Orleans, Hannibal, Quincy, Keokuk, Peoria, Naples and the town on the Missouri the postal service was exclusively by steamboat. Gradually the railroads also brought a complete change in this service. As nowadays, the well-known mail trucks carry the mail pouches between the post office and the depot and return, so at that time they drove to the various landing places on the levee upon the arrival and departure of mail steamers, on which appeared in huge letters these words: United States Mail.

In winter, when the rivers froze, the postal service suffered some bad interruptions or at least delays. This was also true in the spring when the ice went out. Delays were also frequent at those times in the service with East St. Louis. This condition was remedied only when the bridge was built. When the ferryboats had to stop their operations and the ice blanket was not strong enough to carry a team and wagon the mail sometimes remained for days at the stations on the east side or in the post office on the west side. If this occurred there was great embarrassment, particularly in the editorial rooms of the newspapers, for they lacked the indispensable foreign papers, especially the German papers. It was different then than now, when columns of cable dispatches have actually annulled the distance between continents, as far as news is concerned. If the ice was too weak to allow crossing it, even on foot, the mail pouches were pulled across the ice one by one, by long ropes. This was a toilsome and tedious task, but one that always attracted a crowd of onlookers to the levee.

Before 1863 there were no letter boxes on the streets of St. Louis, and there were also no postmen. Mail had to be gotten from the post office and letters had to be posted there. The traffic in the post office building was, therefore, prior to the above date, and even some time later, just as lively as now. And all this in spite of the smaller population and smaller volume of business. Now the city has two branch post offices, which handle a considerable part of the work and the delivery and the collection of mail throughout the whole city save the public and also a large part of the business world the trouble to go to the post office at all.

Before the introduction of the just-mentioned arrangement, every letter and every newspaper had to be carried to the post office to be posted and all mail had to be received there. The transfer of the office to the corner of Third and Olive Street immediately made that region the center of lively traffic, which continued almost uninterruptedly from morning till evening. Although there were between three and four thousand mail boxes that were rented by business firms and other parties, the space in front of the general delivery window teemed with people during some hours of the day. During the sixties the list of letters was published every day, except on Sundays, in the newspapers. For every such advertised letter the addressee had to pay an extra cent, since the post office paid for the printing of the list of letters. A few years after the introduction of free delivery the post office department eliminated the advertising of lists of letters from its budget.

Since then the newspapers publish them free of charge in the interest of the public.

From 1848 on, the enormous German immigration increased the correspondence from abroad greatly. Since, during the fifties and sixties, only four or at the most five mail steamers arrived per month, one can easily see that each of them brought a number of letters for St. Louis. After the arrival of the European mail the crowd in the post office was greater than ordinary. Now letters and newspapers from Germany arrive, on an average, in eleven or twelve days, yes, even at times in ten days. In those days it required in most cases three full weeks. Now an ordinary letter to any country belonging to the postal union costs five cents. Postage for letters in this country was much higher. Now it has gradually come down from twelve to two cents.

When the first postmen were appointed in St. Louis there were seven of them and their activity was confined to the business part of the city, where they made two deliveries a day. That was thirty years ago. Now there are two hundred and sixty-seven postmen and forty substitutes in this service. In the business part of town there are five deliveries, and in the rest of the city three. In case Postmaster Harlow's plan to use the street cars for the delivery of mail is carried out, four or five times a day letters will be delivered even to the remotest parts of the city. The first mail boxes were installed thirty years ago. At this time there are nine hundred and eighty of them, and the system of collecting the mail is always being improved. Twenty years ago the number of postal employees here numbered one hundred and fifty. At present there are exactly six hundred and fifty. Moreover, there are now needed two hundred and forty-nine railroad postal clerks for the mail cars leaving this point. These data we owe to Mr. Isaac H. Sturgeon who was formerly assistant postmaster here, and who now holds the position of city comptroller.

To get the right idea of the extend of the local postal service one need only to cast a glance, between five and six o'clock in the evening, into the spacious room where the letters are sorted and prepared for sending on the various railroads. The place resembles a giant bee hive. No less interesting is the sight when, between five and six in the morning, the postmen make ready for their first round, and scatter to all parts of the city.

From the post office, which was in the one-story house on the corner of Elm and Mail street at the beginning of the twenties, to the splendid structure, sixty years later, which covers an entire block, is an enormous difference. Three generations have passed in review. Of the St. Louis of that time but little is left. It is a far cry from the postrider who came once or twice a week with the mail pouch thrown over the neck of his horse, to the activity of the post office on Eighth and Olive Street.

33. German-American Industries of St. Louis

In keeping with the title: "St. Louis in Former Years," the preceding part of this book is devoted, almost exclusively, to the past, and in the following pages will also be so devoted, but at the same time the account will extend into the present in order to show what German-American industries have accomplished here in the course of time, what successes it has attained and how much it has contributed to the development of St. Louis in the most varied industrial branches, and thereby has added to the well-being and growth of our city.

With this in mind we shall, in the following, speak of the most important branches of local industry, in which the German-Americans have achieved outstanding success. This can, probably, be accomplished best and most suitably by a discussion of those firms which properly may be regarded as representative of the various industrial branches. The establishments chosen for this purpose, barring a few exceptions, have been in operation for many decades. Almost all arose from small beginnings, and only gradually grew great. They have, therefore, kept even pace with the uninterrupted growth of the city which owes its present importance in the matter of trade and industry above all to the spirit of daring and activity of those who, in addition to the peculiar qualities of manufacturers and producers, must be considered expanders of fields of labor, and therefore, important factors in the economic life of our people.

Helmbacher Forge and Rolling Mills Company

During the forties and fifties Missouri was next to Pennsylvania the most important state in the iron industry. Its ore deposits were very extensive and of good quality. Its foundries and iron works were ample and its fleet of steamboats and barges facilitated traffic in every direction. The iron deposits were in Iron Mountains and Pilot Knob, both situated on the Iron Mountain Railroad, from where the greater part of the ore was transported to Pittsburgh, and to the iron works along the Ohio. A considerable part of the ore was worked over at Iron Mountain into pig iron and blooms for the smelters and rolling mills. Later also the rich deposits in the southwest of the state came into consideration –the St. James Iron Works, whose product was valued highly.

Iron Mountain has to date produced three million tons of iron ore, Pilot Knob over one million.

Since the rich ores of Minnesota, Wisconsin and Michigan (Lake Superior) have come into use, the shipments of local ores to Pittsburgh have almost stopped, and our mines have ceased operation almost completely. During the war the iron industry in St. Louis flourished. Then gunboats were built here. After the war the industry in Carondelet took a sharp turn upward, by the establishment of foundries and rolling mills for the manufacture of railroad rails. Unfortunately this industry could not cope in the competition with eastern works. Because of higher cost of production there resulted great losses which forced the works to cease operation.

Formerly charcoal was used in the fabrication of pig iron. Because of the abundance of timber charcoal could be made anywhere. In the last ten or fifteen years coke is used, which is cheaper, but since Missouri has no coal suitable for coke production, the industry has suffered considerable setbacks.

Under these circumstances the Helmbacher Forge and Rolling Mills Company deserves recognition and praise for developing an iron industry in St. Louis, which in spite of hindrances and difficulty has contributed much to the city and the state. This firm started in a modest way. When Michael and Peter Helmbacher established it in 1857 a couple of workers were sufficient to handle the job. In 1859 the Helmbachers became associated with the Daniel Wolff, Alexander McDonald and Carl Brunner (or Brummer) under the firm name of Iron Mountain Forge and Iron Works. When after 1860 Peter Helmbacher died, and the other partners left the firm, Michael Helmbacher became associated with his brother, Alois, and with J. C. Fink. The latter quit early in 1866, whereupon the firm name was changed to Helmbacher Brothers. Ten years after the original firm had started the business, that is in 1867, the name of Helmbacher Forge and

Rolling Mills Company was adopted, and has continued to bear that name for the past twenty-six years.

To the one original trip hammer several more had been added in the meantime. In 1869 also rolling works were added, after the operating capital had been increased by the sale of stock. Among the new stockholders were John C. Degenhardt, Nicolaus Schaeffer, Conrad Stauff, Thomas Ferrenbach, Bernhard Hauschulte, and Adolphus Meier. The expansion of operation of this time, however, was small in comparison with the development which later years brought to the establishment which today belongs to the most extensive in its line. To mention just one article –the company produces more coupling pins and links for railroads than any other firm in the world. In 1892 this company produced eighteen thousand tons of finished articles. Some of the articles produced are rods and bars for bridges, axes for railroad cars and other heavy articles used in the railroad business and steam boating. Special attention is paid to cotton presses and sugar mills. A few years ago the old charter expired and a new incorporation was undertaken. The capital amounts to three hundred thousand dollars. The officers are: President, James J. Green; Vice President, George A. Clark; Secretary, J. L. Goetz; Superintendent, John N. Lauth. These four and Henry Miller constituted the board of directors. Secretary Goetz has occupied this important post for twenty-seven years. Therefore he has lived through the periods of storm and stress which this concern experienced. He may look with special satisfaction at the healthy and extensive business of which he is a part. The technical part of the business is under the direction of Superintendent Lauth, who grew up in the Pennsylvania iron district, and come from a family which for generations has devoted itself to the iron industry, first in Alsace and then in America, and who knows it in every detail. He is the inventor and owner of a patent of a heating and puddling oven of entirely new and practical construction. The general use and adoption of this oven is only a matter of time.

The works of the Helmbacher Forge and Rolling Mills Company is located in South St. Louis. They occupy the whole block which is bordered by Lami, Barton, DeKalb, and Second Streets, and also half a block north of this location. They are, therefore, near the Mississippi River and are connected by their own tracks of the Iron Mountain railroad. So that they can easily obtain their raw material, and have the facilities to ship their finished products to Chicago, St. Paul, the entire south, the entire west, and to Mexico. The reader can gain an idea of the extent of this plant when he knows that two hundred and eighty workers are required, to whom, in 1892 the sum of $170,000 was paid in wages, and that the cost of coal and coke for this same year amounted to $60,000. Not only those who head such an establishment may feel pride, but also all who are interested in the industrial development and growth of St. Louis.

John J. Ganahl Lumber Company

One should think that Missouri, which is so rich in woodland, should at least be able to supply its own need of wood. However, that is not the case. Certain types of wood never existed here, or the senseless destruction of the forests has done away with it. The trees were felled without any thought of after growth. The destruction of the American forests, no matter whether it was done earlier or is done now, seems to be based on the premise: *After us the deluge.* We are now reaping the results of that sort of thinking. There was a time when all the lumber and the firewood that was used here and much that was sold from here came from our own state. During the twenties and thirties it was brought here from that part of the state which is now Gasconade county, from the Big Piney on the Gasconade River and the Missouri. This was exclusively pine limber. From the region around St. Genevieve and Cape Girardeau poplar wood was brought. But even in the middle of the thirties a great quantity of wood was shipped from Pittsburgh, Pennsylvania to St. Louis.

The first steamdriven planing mill (now there are a quarter of a hundred of them) was put in operation in 1836, and it was regarded as an astonishing achievement when it furnished six hundred boards a day.

The location of our city was a most favorable one for the importation of wood from the remotest parts of the northwest, as also from the wooded regions of the southwest. The Mississippi brings the forest products directly to our levee, respectively to our yards. For shipments of finished products we have the use of water and the continually expanding railroad net. We have ample and convenient means of transportation. With the increasing growth of the city also grew the necessity of having sufficient supplies of various kinds of lumber on hand. This led to the establishment of lumber yards, which increased with the greater demand. In the forties the beginning was made to import timber from evergreen forests of

Wisconsin and Minnesota, which since then has assumed gigantic proportions. The major portion of lumber is now derived from there.

The John J. Ganahl Lumber Co. Drives its white pine from the northern woods. This lumber is shipped in enormous rafts which float down the Mississippi in twenty-five to thirty days. From the beginning the company has made a specialty of importing yellow pine from the south. Since it has always insisted on having the best quality of lumber, it has won the favor of architects, builders and workmen. Of the other types of lumber which the firm handles, the following are in greatest demand, cedar, poplar, and the different lines of hardwood. The fact that in 1892 the firm handled twenty million feet of lumber will give an idea of the scope of its business. Because it had advantageous connections in the timber country of the north as also in the south, it was always assured regular service and good quality. In addition to unfinished lumber, the John J. Ganahl Lumber Co. Had an extensive business in finished frames for doors and windows, as well as doors, windows, shutters, laths, shingles, flooring, etc. The plan is situated on the South Seventh and Barton Street and the planing mill is on Lesperance and Kosciusko Street, therefore, like the two yards of the firm, near the river. The yard on Second Street and Park Avenue, where the main office was also located, proved insufficient after some years, and a second yard was established farther to the south. It occupies a whole block between South Broadway and Seventh Street and Allen and Russell Avenue.

The founding of the business occurred in the summer of 1863, at which time John P. Fleitz and John J. Ganahl became associates. The former moved to Saginaw, Michigan after a few years, and in the heart of the lumber country there worked for the interest of the firm, leaving the management of the business on the shoulders of Ganahl. This the latter handled with brilliant success. The business increased from year to year, and when Fleitz withdrew in 1879 the firm was incorporated as the John J. Ganahl Lumber Co. At the head of the business is President J. J. Ganahl, vice president, John A. Reheis, the secretary Louis J. Ganahl, the son of the president. The paid-in operating capital amounts to $100,000. As the firm is one of the most substantial, its president is one of the most respected businessmen in St. Louis. Proof of this is the fact that he has for four years served with distinction in the city council. He comes from Tyrol and the proverbial honesty and uprightness of his people is exemplified in him.

Regina Flour Mill

There was a time, and it isn't so far ago, when St. Louis, in the fullest sense of the word, dominated the flour business of the United States. It actually formed the center of the flour production of the world. The wheat flour put on the market here, enjoyed the reputation of being the best in America. This well-deserved reputation it still has. The regions near St. Louis, which form the main source of the wheat that is milled here, is particularly adapted for wheat production because of soil and climate. This gives the product the quality of the highest rank, and assures the locally-produced flour its prestige.

The fact that the milling industry plays a prominent role in the business life of the city is shown, among other things, by the creation of the local grain exchange which, incidentally, was the first of its kind in the United States. This exchange was organized by the local millers. As early as 1847 St. Louis had fourteen mills; in 1850 there were twenty-two. From that time on the number increased, till there were twenty-seven at one time. At this time there are eighteen, but the capacity of the present mills exceeds by far the older mills. Now a single mill, for example the Regina has a daily capacity of twelve hundred barrels a day, while formerly a fourth of the amount was considered a great achievement. Until 1880 St. Louis supplied more flour on the other side of the ocean, particularly in England, Scotland and Ireland. Bain was at that time the owner of the Atlantic Mill, which is now called the Regina. Since that time St. Louis has had a successful flour export to Europe.

At the world's fairs in Paris and Vienna, St. Louis flour won a number of prizes, and the same is true of the exposition in Philadelphia in 1876.

One of the largest local mills, the Atlantic, was destroyed by fire near the end of the seventies. In 1882 it was rebuilt and equipped with the most modern machinery. The latter was still more improved when the present owner bought the Mill in 1885. The buyers were Louis Fusz and Mathias Backer, two of the best known and most experienced millers of our city, who since 1873 had been in partnership. The name of the mill was changed to Regina, and its product enjoyed a reputation that was known far and wide, particularly its brand "Ultimate" and "Regina." These have wide distribution in the United States, South America and Great Britain, while the less choice varieties go to Holland and Belgium. The good quality of the wheat produced in the vicinity of St. Louis, which the Regina Mill uses exclusively for milling, assures a uniform product, whose value is increased by careful processing.

The buildings occupy the entire west side of Main, between Poplar and Plum Street, so that they stand close to the tracks of the Iron Mountain road, as well as other roads, and just as conveniently near the wharf. The incorporation of the Regina Flour Mills Company took place in 1885, with Louis Fusz as president, and George H. Backer as secretary. The latter became his father's successor, when, in the above-named year, he retired from business because of advanced years.

Mathias Backer had come to St. Louis from his home in Hannover as early as 1837. Then he had lived for a while in Chicago, but soon returned here. First he worked in the old Smith Mill on the Levee. Then he entered the service of the grocery firm of Mauntel, Bulte and Co., which, on the basis of his knowledge of the flour business added this article to their stock, and thus opened the local commission business in flour. He remained with the firm of Mauntel, Borgess and Co. till, in 1873, he joined Louis Fusz in the operation of a flour commission business.

In 1853 Louis Fusz, as a fourteen-year-old boy was brought here from France. Soon after that he was employed as the lowest clerk in the office of Chouteau, Harrison and Valle, owners of the iron smelters at Iron Mountain, and the rolling mills of St. Louis. He was advanced to the most responsible position of trust in the firm, but in 1866 he resigned to become associated with the commission firm of Imbs and Meyer, which from then on was called Imbs, Meyer and Fusz. At the request of Mathias Backer he left this firm in 1873. As one of the most prominent members of the grain exchange he served as vice president and repeatedly as director of the same, also on important committees. He, at all times, furthered the commercial interests of St. Louis, and on various occasions represented the interest outside the city. By his personal endeavor he created a market for St. Louis flour in the New England states. He also made valuable connections for the local flour business in the south. He was highly respected by the business world because of his honesty and other fine qualities.

His business associate, George H. Backer, was born in St. Louis. He also learned the business from the ground up, and also holds a prominent position among the business men of St. Louis.

William J. Lemp Brewing Company

As the first and oldest lager beer brewery of St. Louis and of the west, the Lemp Brewery is surely entitled to represent the brewing industry among our local businesses.

It was in 1838 that Adam Lemp, a trained brewer, came from Hessen-Darmstadt to America. Here in St. Louis he began his business in a very modest way. It is no legend, but the actual fact, that he brewed his first lager beer here in a large copper wash boiler. He certainly did not suspect that with that mast he laid the foundation fro one of the greatest breweries in the world. In his father's small brewery, which, of course soon assumed greater proportions, William J. Lemp, from early youth, learned the trade in every detail, and then served as foreman in his father's brewery which, in 1840, had been erected on South Second Street between Walnut and Elm Street.

Adam Lemp died in 1862, sixty-five years of age. Two years later the beginning was made in the construction of the new brewerym, which in the course of time should assume such great dimensions that its buildings occupy three whole city blocks, and a terrain of six more blocks are necessary for the shipment of its product. These six blocks adjoin the tracks of the St. Louis, Iron Mountain and Southern. They are also hard by the banks of the Mississippi. The brewery buildings are connected with one another by means of a cable line, whose tracks run through the yards and the storehouses of the brewery, to the landing on the river as also to the sidetracks of the Iron Mountain road, and over its tracks to the freight yards of the other railroad lines.

The operation of the new brewery was begun in 1866. During the decades that have passed since then there has been continuous expansion, one bulding was added to another till the establishment is one of the sights worth seeing.

The buildings are between Lemp Avenue, South Broadway, Thirteenth and Cherokee Street. Some of these are seven stories high, while others are eight stories high: These include brewing houses, malt houses, lager houses and office buildings. There are large rooms for the filling and packing of bottle beer. The capacity of the brewery is half a million barrels per year. Its annual production amounts to three hundred thousand barrels, and its annual sales more than three million dollars. The equipment of the bottling department is calculated to fill ine hundred bottles a day. In 1892 the brewery shipped ten thousand refrigerator cars loaded with its product. By means of this type of car the beer can be kept at the required temperature during a transportation of any length. For this purpose the company has had over five hundred refrigerator cars built, for which the ice is made in one of the buildings there daily one hundred and fifty tons are produced. Five cold air machines of the most modern construction produce the necessary low temperature -31 to 32 degrees of Fahrenheit $-$for the cellars and other lager rooms. These machines reduce the temperature as much as could be produced by seven hundred tons of ice.

Here in St. Louis the various branches of the establishment employ over seven hundred persons. To these must be added a large number in branches and agencies of which the firm maintains nearly two hundred and fifty. They are distributed over thirty states of the Union $-$of these there are fifty-eight in cities in Texas, forty-three in cities in Missouri, nineteen in Nebraska, eighteen in Iowa, ten in Montana, nine each in Illinois and Arkansas, eight each in California, Colorado, New Mexico. There are also depots of the company in most of the southern states, in Utah, Wyoming and Washington. Then, too, the Lemp product is exported to Canada, British Columbia, Old Mexico, Central America, South Amerca, Australia and England. For the distribution of the beer in the city itself, a hundred horses and forty wagons are used the year round.

A visit to the brewery, which one can make under the guidance of an accomodating employee, who takes one through all the various parts of the plant, will show even the layman who sees a brewery for the first time, how much work and what great care is taken in the preparation of this beer, from the first preparatory steps to that moment when the finished product leaves the brewery. After one has climbed the various stories of one of the malt houses, or by means of the elevator arrives under the roof of the lager house, seven stories high, where one is met by an icy atmosphere, even though it may be a hundred degrees outside in the shade, he can, after a few minutes stroll in one of the three lager cellars, sixty feet under the ground, which cellars are illuminated by countless electric lights. The company supplies all its buildings with light produced by its own dynamos. In the further course of his journey the visitor will be amazed by the giant brewing kettles, each having a capacity of five hundred barrels. With special interest will he see how artificial ice and cold air are produced. He will also be surprised to see the bottling department, where before his eyes thousands of bottles are filled in a few minutes and closed with a wire, while in another room the packing in boxes is attended to. The Lemp Brewery represents an expenditure of more than four million dollars.

The best of malt and hops are used by the Lemp company. At the Centennial Exposition in Philadelphia, and at the World Exposition in Paris, in 1878, it was awarded the first prize, not to speak of many other honors which it received in various parts of the country.

Till the first of November, 1892, William J. Lemp was the sole owner. From this day on his two eldest sons, William J. Lemp, Jr., and Louis F. Lemp, received shares in the business. From that date on the firm was incorporated as the William J. Lemp Brewing Co. At its head is William J. Lemp. William J. Lemp, Jr. is the vice president, Louis F. Lemp, the superintendent, and Henry Vahlkamp, the secretary. Like their father, the two sons have learned the brewing business from the ground up; moreover, they attended and graduated form the New York Brewers Academy.

Nedderhuth Packing and Provision Company

Because of its geographical position, St. Louis was destined to become the center for the distribution of provisions for an extensive territory, particularly the entire south and southwest of the United States. The Mississippi valley, most, if not all, southern states, as also many states of the west, were and are tributary to our city in a double sense. They buy from us and sell to us. For this reason trade in provisions occupies a prominent position in our local trade. As one of the most important branches, if not the most important, must be considered the preparation and the trade in pickled and smoked meat. For decades more than thirty firms have been engaged in this business, and employ several thousand workers. Before the field was opened to this extensive business, small slaughter houses and packing houses sufficed the domestic needs of the thirties. Somewhat large plants became necessary when, in addition to the local requirements, inquiries from the outside arrived, where before was ... the pork, (hams, shoulders and bacon), acquired a reputation. The result was that from 1843 to 1844 sixteen thousand, and from 1845 to 1846 thirty-one thousand hogs were slaughtered. During the years of the war this business took an enormous swing upward, for St. Louis was the point from which the great army of the southwest was supplied with provisions, and meat and bacon constitute an important part of these provisions. In this matter three of the firms, then existing here, rendered the government a real service by making uninterrupted and large deliveries on long time credit, indeed even for uncertain periods of time, to supply the regiments in the field. To this fact may be ascribed a large share of the reason why from then on the provision business assumed such great dimensions. The extensive river connections, which St. Louis enjoys, contributed extensively to the development of this business, and later also the increasing number of railroad lines which converge here. At the beginning of the eighties the capital invested in this branch of business amounted to twelve million dollars. In 1882 the sales amounted to approximately the same sum. In 1892, on the other hand, the sales were double this amount.

The Nedderhuth Packing and Provision Company has been in operation for nearly three decades, for in 1865, August Nedderhuth gave up the commission business which he had on Commercial Street, and established the extensive business which he has since then operated on the west side of South Main, between Myrtle (now Clark Avenue) and Spruce Street. It required extensive remodeling to prepare it for the purposes of a slaughter, smoke and packing house, for previously it had been used as a foundry. The packing operation began with the 1866-1867 season. At the time and for a long time thereafter work was done only between autumn and spring, during the cold season. The production of cold air and artificial ice was still far in the future. The "Packing Season" was limited to the winter season. Now this work can be continued throughout the whole year without consideration of the season, which is due to the fact that the rooms are cooled artificially. The invention of refrigerator cars made the transportation of meat possible even in summer, which without regard to distance arrives in the best, namely in a frozen, condition, at its destination. The articles, namely hams, shoulders, bacon and lard, which the firm puts on the market are sent exclusively to the south, where they have established a reputation for quality and are in great demand.

The firm name of August Nedderhuth was changed, years ago, to Nedderhuth Packing and Provision Company,. The president is the founder of the concern, August Nedderhuth. His oldest son, Charles O. Nedderhuth, is the treasurer, Bernard J. McSorley is the secretary, and a younger son, Emil A. Nedderhuth is the bookkeeper. All are partners in the business. In addition to this main business the firm also has a warehouse for all(? Page 326) sorts of goods, which is located on the corner of Main and Plum Street. This building has a front of two hundred and thirty-five feet and a depth of one hundred ninety feet to the alley. The Nedderhuth Warehouse Company is under a separate management.

August Nedderhuth came here in 1838 as a boy. He is one of the most respected business men in St. Louis, and his sons are emulating the example set by their father.

Mallinckrodt Chemical Works

In no field of science has there been made such great progress, such important discoveries, such valuable contributions during the recent decades as in chemistry. Its twin sister, Physics, which in many respects goes hand in hand with chemistry, can also show for the same period, numerous and astonishing achievements. But with reference to practical value, particularly in the realm of medicine and drugs, industry and the arts, agriculture and commerce it can scarcely equal chemistry. From the time of the English naturalist, Boyle, and the German scholar, Stahl, who in the second half of the seventeenth century were the forerunners of those men, that in the nineteenth century have accomplished such great things in the field of chemistry, the science has seen an ever-increasing development. Its practical application kept pace with the new theories. The world owes sincere thanks to such men as Justus von Liebig, Bunsen, Kolbe and others, their contemporaries and successors, who in the lecture rooms, in laboratories, in books and in journals, by research and experimentation have contributed so much to the general welfare.

Naturally the factories that undertook the manufacture of chemicals contributed much to the progress of this science. St. Louis has such a plant whose products have for a long time earned a brilliant reputation on both sides of the ocean. It is the Mallinckrodt factory which was founded in 1867, and is one of the greatest of this kind in America and Europe. From a small beginning the firm soon attracted attention among experts for the quality as well as the great variety of its preparations. The rapidly increasing demand of its products, after a short time made an enlargement of its plant necessary. In a relatively short time the Mallinckrodt Chemical Works occupied a terrain of five acres, situated in the northern part of the city, next to the Mississippi, and bordered by Hall, Main, Salisbury and Mallinckrodt Streets. The buildings erected on this land are suitably large, of massive construction, and the machines and apparatus in them are of the newest and most thoroughly tested construction. The whole plant meets the demands of science in a most practical manner.

In addition to the local plant the firm has a second factory in Jersey City, New Jersey. The latter occupies twelve acres of land, and also possesses all the necessary facilities for procuring the raw material and for shipping the finished product, either by steam boat or by railroad. In these works are manufactured mainly those articles for use in the east, whose transportation from St. Louis would be too expensive, and also those that can be produced more cheaply in the east than here.

The company manufactures all chemicals for the drug business, for analytical purposes, for the use in photography, and a great number of articles which are used in the most varied industries, as, for example, ammonium water and ammonium gas for the production of cold air in breweries and artificial ice. Moreover, this company has the exclusive agency for the sale of the products of several European firms, among others of the celebrated preparations from the Braunschweig quinine factory, which product enjoys a world-wide reputation.

If it is considered that many of the articles manufactured by the company have a value of many dollars per ounce, and that they are produced in enormous quantities, that hundreds of workers are employed by the organization from one end of the year to the other, and that the sale of goods increases from year to year, then one can get some approximate idea of the scope of this business enterprise. The products of the two establishments go to all parts of the United States, and are also exported in large amounts to foreign lands. The eastern states are supplied by the branch offices and storage which is at No. 90 William Street, New York City. The millions of large and small flasks and boxes, filled with the various products of the company, are put on the market in the course of the year, which carry not only the name of the Mallinckrodt Chemical Works into all the world, but at the time also the name of our city. St. Louis has every right to be proud to have such a prominent representative of such an important branch of modern industry. At the head of this company is Edward Mallinckrodt. The post of secretary is held by Oscar L. Biebinger.

William Waltke and Company – Soap and Sal Soda

The assumption that one can measure the stage of civilization of a people by the amount of soap it uses, turns out to be a well-deserved compliment for our country, for the use of soap in the United States has assumed enormous proportions during the second half of the nineteenth century, and is still on the increase. Ever-progressing since has created new methods in this field also and has brought improvement. The Waltke Soap factory has always been on the alert for such changes, has given them a trial, and if found worthy, has adopted them.

It was in 1858 when William Waltke, the senior partner, began the soap business on a small scale. He employed only three workmen, and on some days they did not have enough to do. Now fifty employees are at work throughout the year. If it is remembered that the perfected machinery has replaced many manual workers, it can easily be seen what a great establishment has grown from the small beginning.

The factory had its beginning at the same place where it is today. Of course, in the course of time, more and more room was needed. Particularly during the last ten years, repeated expansion had to be made. Two years ago a large annex was added, so that now the factory buildings, situated between North Second, Benedict, John Street and Grand Avenue, cover an area of 155,000 square feet.

In the Waltke factory all sorts of soaps are made. Here in St. Louis its brand called "Extra Family," which, introduced twenty-five years ago, is in great demand and most popular. Special care is applied to its manufacture. Another brand that is popular in family use is the "Pandora." The same is true of the Waltke castile and toilet soaps. Laundries prefer the product of this factory because of its purity and good workmanship.

In the early seventies the beginning was made with the manufacture of sal soda, which since then has been in great demand. Up to that time sal soda was manufactured only in Pittsburgh. The Waltke factory was one of the first that added this article to its various products. In Texas, Mississippi, Arkansas, Tennessee and other states in the south the sales are made by agencies. In Louisville, Kentucky are branch offices, and in Missouri, Illinois, Iowa, Kansas, etc. the firm has its own traveling salesmen. Moreover, professional journals, price lists, and circulars serve to make the goods known.

William Waltke, a native of Westphalia, came to St. Louis at the beginning of the fifties. He is now nearly seventy years old. And though he, because of habit, still visits the factory every day, he has for some years withdrawn almost completely from business activity, leaving the management in younger hands.

Since 1877 Charles H. Steinkamp has been a partner of the firm. In 1882 Louis H. Waltke is also a partner, who since that date has successfully managed the business. Both of the men have learned the soap business from the ground up. Because of his thorough knowledge of chemistry L. H. Waltke devotes himself to the technical operation of the plant, while Charles H. Steinkamp heads the business administration, where his energy and diligence have contributed much to the success of William Waltke and Co.

Lungstras Dyeing and Cleaning Company

In the field of art dyeing and cleaning of material in a chemical way science and technology have brought about a real transformation during the last decades. The Lungstras company has at all times made extensive use of innovations and improvements in its field.

The Lungstras Dyeing and Cleaning plant was established twenty years ago on the same site that it now occupies. At that time one small house was sufficient. Today a large number of buildings is required for the operation, which each year is on the increase. The buildings occupy an entire block which is bounded by Park Avenue between Thirteenth and Linn Street. All these structures are fireproof. All are designed and built with consideration of the purpose which they serve. All machines and apparatus are of the most modern construction.

The founder of this extensive business is Eugene Lungstras, whose name is known far and wide. He came from the Rhineland. His home was near Cologne. His father was a postmaster. He came here at the beginning of the fifties. First he worked in a wholesale dry goods house to become acquainted with American business methods. After a few years he moved to Sedalia, where he established his own business. In 1871 he had the happy idea to go to Berlin, in order to acquire the expert knowledge which he needed for the art dyeing plant which he contemplated establishing. Berlin, for a long time, had had several plants of this kind, such as the

Spindler plant, which was known all over Germany. With the machinery which he bought there he then began operation in St. Louis in 1872.

Eleven years ago the firm was incorporated. Eugene Lungstras heads it as president. In his hands is the management of the entire plant and the financial part of the concern. The secretary is Lungstras' brother-in-law, Charles Springer. The business is divided into a dyeing department, a cleaning department (both wet and dry), a repair department and a department for cleaning, renovating and disinfecting carpets. By excellent work and prompt service the firm has been able to defeat its rivals. That it has done this so successfully is shown by the fact that in 1872 its earnings amounted to a million dollars.

With the exception of New York City no other metropolis has an equally large establishment in this line of business as that of Lungstras in St. Louis. The feminine world, which constitutes most of its customers, has long recognized its merits. Patronage does not come from St. Louis alone but from an extensive territory. From places thousands of miles removed come orders. A special department sees to it that these outside orders receive prompt attention. Dry goods stores, fashion stores, wholesale and retail stores, have their wares re-dyed which, due to long lying on shelves, or due to exposure to sunlight in the show windows or otherwise have faded, or due to moisture or some other cause have become spotted. Material thus redyed was velvet, silk, wool, cotton, silk ribbons, etc. These things are made to appear as new. This part of the business alone occupies an amazing amount of space. One can convince himself of the quality of the work of this concern by a visit to the works on Park Avenue, as also in the center of the city, where the firm occupies, on North Sixth, near Chestnut Street (Number 105 and 107) a part of two five-story buildings. These serve chiefly for the convenience of the public. These rooms are elegantly equipped. There are separate rooms for ladies and gentlemen. A further branch office has for years been maintained at 2326 Franklin Avenue for the convenience of the residents in the northwestern part of the city.

In addition to the numerous business personnel there are in the works more than a hundred workmen who are continually employed. There is also a steam engine of a hundred horsepower which drives the various machines in the different divisions of the extensive establishment.

Ringen Stove Company – Quick Meal Stove Company

Where today the approach to the Eads Bridge is located on the east side of North Third, between Green Street of that day, and Washington Avenue, John Ringen had a modest tin shop in the late fifties. He did not need any outside help to do his work. From this small beginning grew two of the largest businesses in St. Louis. Their course of development will be recited briefly in the following.

Ringen remained in the little tin shop till the house in which it was, was razed to make room for the building of the bridge. This was in the year 1868. A short time before, a young man had sought and obtained employment with Ringen. Neither he nor Ringen suspected at that time of what importance for the future of the business the coming of George Kahle was. From the beginning he devoted himself with zeal to the business. It is due to his enterprise, in the main, that the concern gradually grew to its present proportions.

The move to Fourth and Morgan was of the greatest benefit. The business improved visibly. The result was that in 1870 Kahle became a partner in the firm. Soon the place did not afford enough room, so another move was made to No. 708 on Fourth Street. With increased sales the business increased from year to year. Here it was where John Ringen and Co. Took over the entire sale of the gasoline ranges, which were manufactured by the Stockstrom Brothers, and which were the forerunners of the now famous Quick Meal Stoves.

On September 15, 1881 Louis Stockstrom, who had just come from Europe, together with his brother, Charles A. Stockstrom, began to manufacture the gasoline stoves. In a room, 25 x 40 feet in size, situated in the third story of No. 708 North Fifth Street, opposite the Union Market, they worked all alone for a while. Before long the value of the stoves made by them was recognized. Sales increased to such an extent that it became necessary to employ a number of workmen, and also to take over the second story of the house. On August 10, 1882 the Quick Meal Stove Company was organized, and was incorporated with a capital of six thousand dollars. George Kahle was its president and Charles A. Stockstrom its secretary. (On the next day followed the incorporation of the Ringen Stove Company with a capital of twenty thousand dollars, with John Ringen as president and Kahle as secretary.) In the following year the

Quick Meal Stove Co. Factory required more room and was moved to Ninth Street and Cass Avenue. Within six months the space had to be doubled, and after a year's time it was necessary to look for still larger quarters. The new site was on the corner of Third and Spruce Street, where in 1886 additions to the building had to be provided.

In 1886 the Ringen Stove Company also found it necessary to move into larger quarters. It took possession of the three-story building, No. 508 on Fourth Street between St. Charles Street and Washington Avenue. Here it remained till 1891, since when it occupies the six-story building at Nos. 415 and 416 North Broadway, between Locust and St. Charles. On the ground floor is the sales department while the upper stories are used as store rooms and for the manufacture of cooking dishes for the Quick Meal stoves. Seventy-five workers are employed.

In the autumn of 1887 the old Sol Smith mansion on Chouteau Avenue, between Eighth and Ninth Street, together with the plot of land belonging to it, measuring one hundred by three hundred eighteen feet, was purchased by the Quick Meal Stove Company. The main building of the factory, erected here, is three stories high and measures seventy-five feet in the front and two hundred feet in depth. The two-story building in back of the main building measures fifty-five by one hundred feet. The boiler house is forty by fifty feet in size. For the enlargement of the factory, a building adjoining the plant on the west side has recently been bought, and the construction of the annex has already begun. The number of employees is at present five hundred. Twelve years ago the two Stockstrom Brothers made their first stoves without any help.

Since the sale of stoves is very much reduced in mid-summer, the fiscal year of the factory closes on August 10. From 1891 to 1892 the company sold 54,751 stoves. (The next largest factory of this kind in the United States sold during the same period of time only 45,000 stoves.) From 1892 to the end of July 1893 the company sold nearly 70,000 stoves. The manufacture of gas ranges was begun in 1889. In 1892 more than two thousand of them were sold in St. Louis alone. The Quick Meal stoves are sold by the company's own traveling salesmen. Their sales territory extends from Maine to California, from Florida to Minnesota, though the major part of patronage comes from the middle states.

In 1888 John Ringen retired to private life, whereupon George Kahle assumed the place of the president of the Ringen Stove Co. In 1892 he also retired from active business, and only retained his place in the directorship of both corporations. On August 10, 1892 the operating capital was increased, that of the Ringen Stove Company to $100,000 and the Quick Meal Stove Company to $200,000. The officers of the former company are: President, George Kahle; secretary, Charles Stockstrom; treasurer, E. H. Stockstrom; of the latter company –Charles A. Stockstrom, president; George Kahle, vice president; Louis Stockstrom, secretary; who is at the same time technical manager of the factory, for which post he is especially qualified.

The astonishing success of the two so-closely related businesses is, next to the other contributing factors, above all to be ascribed to the principles to which George Kahle adhered from the beginning which run like this: Use only the best material and sell only good wares.

The St. Louis WoodenWare Works

St. Louis has for a long time been the place from which the country west of the Mississippi has obtained all those things which come under the heading of woodenware. For decades it has been the principal article of trade of some of the largest local business houses. Prior to the middle fifties these goods were not produced here, but had to be procured elsewhere, mainly from Marietta, Ohio, which place at that time supplied the central states and the west with these articles. It signified the introduction of a new branch of industry in St. Louis when, at the time mentioned above, Tamm Meyer, Jacob Tamm and Henry Meyer began the manufacture of woodenware, for which at that time cedar and cypress wood was mainly used.

After Meyer left the firm, it was called Jacob Tamm and Company. Theodore Tamm, a nephew and son-in-law of the senior partner, became a partner in the firm in 1864. Prior to that time he had already taken over the management of the factory. In the following year Charles Everts, likewise a son-in-law of Jacob Tamm, became an associate, and at the same time business manager in the office. For a quarter of a century the office was from 1863 on the west side of Main, between Market and Walnut Streets. Then it was moved to its present location on the southeast corner of Main and Chestnut. This building at the same time serves as the downtown warehouse of the firm. Till 1872 it had its factory on the north side of Chouteau Avenue near Twenty-third Street. Then it was transferred to the southern part of the city, to the foot of Anna Street, in the immediate vicinity of the river and the tracks of the Iron Mountain and Southern railroad, which provided the desired facilities for the obtaining of raw material and the shipping of the finished products.

The factory on Chouteau was for the most part destroyed by fire, causing the owners great loss. However, the later-built factory has much more space for its operation, and because of its location the already-mentioned advantages. It is equipped with machinery of the newest and best construction, and the whole arrangement is calculated to provide wares of the best workmanship, made of the best material. These qualities have won for the product of the St. Louis WoodenWare Works an enviable reputation.

In 1873, a year after the opening of the new factory, came the incorporation of the St. Louis Wooden Ware Works with Jacob Tamm as president, Theodore Tamm as vice president and Charles Everts as secretary-treasurer. The direct management of the factory is in the hands of William B. Tamm.

Twenty years ago the old firm began to compete with factories in Ohio, and indeed with increasing success. At this time it is increasing its operations and expanding its sales. Its business has for some time extended itself over all states on this side of the Mississippi. Since the products are to be found in daily use in the households and kitchens, on the farms and in the dairies, as also in the vineyards and orchards of California, one can have an idea of the extent of the firm's business connections. In the city and in the country the housewife knows the advantages of the Tamm washtubs and washboards, just as the people on the farm know how to value the churns, buckets and other wooden vessels from this factory because of their durability and other good qualities. More than three hundred workers are occupied the year around in the manufacture of these articles.

Because of advanced age Jacob Tamm withdrew some years ago from active work in the business which he founded. In 1836 he came to St. Louis from Cuxhaven near Hamburg. He has lived here, therefore, for nearly sixty years and is counted among the most respected businessmen of the city.

Charles Everts died five years ago. The management of the establishment is now exclusively in the hands of Theodore Tamm, who has thirty years of experience, and to whom must be credited, in the main, the expansion of operation. The German American business world of St. Louis has in him one of its best representatives. At the head of the St. Louis WoodenWare Works, in addition to President Theodore Tamm, are Vice President William B. Tamm and Secretary-Treasurer Frank Everts.

Keller and Tamm Manufacturing Company

This business, like the preceding ones, belongs to the older industrial establishments of the city. It was founded more than twenty-five years ago, and at first had the name of Chester and Harris Manufacturing Company. Its owners were E. L. Chester, George Keller, and Lloyd G. Harris. After the latter left the concern it became the Chester and Keller Manufacturing Company. Its successor is the present firm with Theodore Tamm as president and George Keller as secretary-treasurer. The factory is also situated in the southern part of the city, at the northeast corner of Victor and Main Street, close to the tracks of the Iron Mountain railroad, and with the latter also connected with the other railroads. It is only one block from the wharf and the boat landing. The local plant is the main factory. There are two branch factories, in Rives, Tennessee and Knobel, Arkansas. The number of employees is two hundred and fifty, and at times even more.

The product of this factory consists in the main of handles, made of hickory wood, for axes of every kind, hatchets, hose, etc. Also spokes and other parts of wood for wagon makers and wheelwrights. There is no state in the Union in which a certain number of factories do not obtain their need of the above-named articles from the Keller and Tamm Manufacturing Company. This company is noted for its conscientious and prompt attention to orders and honest treatment of its customers. The hickory handles, made of the hardest hickory wood, constitute indeed a specialty of this firm. They are in use everywhere in the United States, and are also sold to Europe and Australia. Thus they contribute in full measure to make the products of St. Louis industries known far beyond the limits of our own country.

Busch's Vinery in Bushberg

"Israel lived happily, each under his own grape vine and fig tree. They were at peace, each under his own arbor and his fig tree."

This is the picture of earthly bliss, the ideal of the Jews, whose first reading text is the Bible. Centuries of oppression and persecution, when they could call not a clod of earth their own –except the grave –could not erase from their souls this ideal, the hope and yearning for its realization.

Isidor Busch was only one of the thousands who strove to realize this dream, and to exchange the precarious position of a tradesman for peaceful and contented agriculture pursuits, to trade the pen which he had used as book dealer and publisher and author for the plow. However, he knew very well that this is not easy, that one must be trained for this sort of work. When he emigrated for America in 1848, it was his firm resolve to have his only receive this sort of training. He apprenticed his boy to George Husman, the celebrated wine grower in Hermann, Missouri. In February, 1865, as soon as the southern rebellion was happily concluded, he bought two hundred and forty acres of hilly land, especially suited to viniculture. This land was situated on the banks of the Mississippi, less than twenty miles from St. Louis, and has since then been given the name of Buschberg.

Busch by no means shared Husman's sanguine hope of rich pecuniary gain from viniculture. He rather hoped that he might secure for himself and for his son a peaceful and agreeable employment. In this hope he was confirmed by his good and loyal friend, Frederick Muench, one of the pioneers of American viniculture, and a real philosopher. Not young enough to do the practical field work, and compelled to earn with his pen a subsistence for himself and family, Busch endeavored, by diligent study and observation to acquire some knowledge of the grape vine, its culture and its botanical characteristics.

When in 1870 the first news came from France concerning the devastation of the vineyards by the grape gall-louse (phylloxera), and Professor C. V. Riley proved its identity with the American aphis, Busch was the first one, who, on the basis of Darwin's theory, recommended the resistant American grape as a means of saving the French vineyards, and, for experimental purposes, sent, as a present, several thousand of his grape roots to Montpellier, France. The result proved the correctness of his idea. In spite of much prejudice against the wild grape, which were indeed wild things compared with the highly cultivated French grapes, and in spite of hindrances and difficulties which ignorant law makers at first interposed to the importation, American grapes, roots and cuttings, proved to be the only practical and effective means fro the restoration of vineyards which had been devastated by the philloxera. From year to year came larger and larger orders to the famous Busch vinery for hundreds of thousands of roots and millions of American grape vine cuttings, which are now planted and grafted far and wide in the French vineyards.

At the same time grape culture in the United States was greatly expanded. With it also grew the popularity of the Buschberg grapes, under the clever management of the younger Busch, Raphael Busch and of Gustav E. Meiszner (Firm of Busch, Son and Meiszner). This is especially shown in a book, entitled *Amerikanische Weintraube* (American Grape), published by A. Freiherr von Babo, director of the Royal Oenological Institute at Klosterneuburg near Vienna, and Theodore Ruempler, General Secretary of the Garden Society. There we read: "The firm of Busch, Son and Meiszner near St. Louis (Missouri), owners of numerous vineyards and one of the largest vineries in existence, which carries on its business not only from the practical but also from the scientific point of view, issued some years ago a grape catalog, which enumerates not only several hundred American species and varieties, but with each discusses the experience gained in America and France regarding the value of the grapes and their resistance. A botanically scientific part precedes this descriptive catalog, which gives us information concerning the various species of grapes which are found in America in a wild condition. Finally it contains a description of grape culture in America, and makes known Mr. Busch's experience in the improvement of grapes. As proof of the excellence of the book the fact may be mentioned that it has been translated into the French and Italian languages."

And so our friend, Isidor Busch, in his seventy-second year enjoys the fulfillment of his long-cherished hope. He lives in the circle of his family on his beautiful vine-clad Buschberg, which is only an hour's ride from St. Louis. He is known, respected and esteemed by everyone.

G. Cramer Dry Plate Works

Photography is an achievement of the second half of this century. It was not until 1851 that the Daguerre process, which was the process of making pictures on silver-coated metal plates by exposure to light, was replaced by photography. This art has been perfected from decade to decade till it has reached a degree of perfection, which the original inventors hardly expected could be attained. With the continued development of the art of photography any number of pictures could be made from a negative on a glass plate. This process became the most dangerous competitor of the portrait painter. But it was a great boon to the world when the camera became available to everybody, for the brush of the artist was, after all, available only to the favorably situated minority. Then there came the invaluable service to science, the arts and industry, which the photograph apparatus brought us. The small instrument which the investigator carries with him to the heights of the Himalayas, to the pyramids, to the icy regions of the north pole, or in the dazzling heat of the desert, has made us acquainted with the remotest parts of the earth. It brings the stars closer to us; it perpetuates the single phases of every eclipse of the sun for posterity. It multiplies the creations of the fine arts, so that they are available not only to the specially privileged. It serves industrialists in the most varied branches of activity.

The results of photography do not depend only on the greater or lesser ability of the picture taker, though obviously a great artist can get better results than a dabbler. There are certain factors upon which the quality of the pictures depend. Of these factors the most important is the plate on which the exposure is made. The improvement of the plates was therefore the problem that was of the greatest importance. It is therefore gratifying that the most perfect product in the field was made in a St. Louis establishment. The dry plates which come from Cramer's Dry Plate Works are recognized as the best not only in this country but throughout all the civilized world.

Gustav Cramer, the founder and owner of the Works, came to the United States in 1859. That same year he came to St. Louis. While still in his home country –he came from Eschwege– he had manifested a preference for the study of chemistry and physics. He was twenty-one years old when he arrived here. Soon after his arrival he became acquainted with John A. Scholten, who at that time was the most prominent photographer in St. Louis. From Scholten he received instruction in the art of photography. Presently he had sufficient theoretical knowledge and ample practical experience to take Scholten's place as operator in the gallery. After some time he established himself and became associated with Julius Grosz. Their gallery was at first on Fourth near Rutger Street. In 1872 it was transferred to the corner of Fifth and Chouteau Avenue, where Cramer and Grosz had a building erected which still serves its original purpose. There they established the best gallery in the city. In the summer of 1879 Cramer decided to devote himself to the manufacture of dry plates. In the execution of this plan he became associated with H. Norden. The beginning was on a very small scale, and the prospects were at first not too promising. But in spite of every difficulty which came their way, Cramer and Norden pursued their course. So they became the first on this side of the ocean to introduce dry plates. When they exhibited the plates at the convention of photographers in Chicago in 1880, such plates were new to most of them. For many years now the "Cramer Plates" have been in use everywhere.

At the beginning the basement of a house was used for the manufacture of the plates. But soon a handsome factory was erected on Chouteau Avenue near Ninth Street. After a few years, however, this proved to be too small for the operation. Then Cramer (Norden had in the meantime left the concern) had a factory built on Shenandoah, corner of Buena Vista Street. This afforded ample room. Moreover, it was in a region in which the air was as free of dust as possible, which is one prerequisite for the making of dry plates. The building occupies almost an entire block. It has two stories above ground and also two underground. The extensive space under the ground serves for the entire process which the plates have to pass through, till they are ready to be packed, because the coating, prepared in a chemical way, is so sensitive that the whole process must be completed with the total exclusion of daylight. The small electric lights over the tables of the workers are therefore surrounded by dark-red glass. The glass chosen for this purpose must be made with the greatest care, that is, it must not contain the slightest unevenness. The connection with these subterranean rooms and the upper stories in which the packing takes place is by means of a number of elevators. Steam boilers and dynamo are in a separate building.

Large as the factory is, it still does not contain enough room for the operation which increases from year to year. For that reason the owner, sometime ago, bought the old Miller Brewery, which is nearby, from a London syndicate. On this site a second factory will presently be built, which will make this the largest industry of this kind in the world.

Because of their excellence Cramer's dry plates enjoy world fame. How justified this is is shown from the fact that the pictures which, during the last years, have won the first prizes at photograph exhibits have without exception been made with these plates. That is certainly the best recognition of the ceaseless striving of Cramer to raise his product to the highest stage of perfection, which science and technology can attain. The fact that Cramer had years of experience in a gallery put him in a position to test every new discovery and improvement in this field and if it proved to be of merit, apply it. Moreover, he had surrounded himself with the most able and most capable assistants. At the head of these he had his former partner, Norden; the photographer, Robert Bennecke; his son, Ernest Cramer; and others. Of the various distinctions that have come his way from the colleagues of the profession may be mentioned that he was the chairman of the national convention of photographers held in Chicago in 1887. During his stay in Europe in 1888 he received the most honorable reception in professional circles in Berlin, Munich and other places, which was intended as a compliment to him as also to the product of the Cramer Dry Plate Works.

Dr. Enno Sander's Mineral Water Factory

The assumption that mineral water is efficacious only when drunk at the source or from bottles that were filled at the spring has been disproved long ago. The experience of many decades has taught that the wholesome effect of the various mineral waters can be gotten just as well through the use of artificially produced waters, if, in their preparation, scientific principles are in harmony with the constituents of the natural mineral waters are observed. It was the celebrated Professor Doctor Frederick Struve in Dresden, who, after repeated use of the water cure at Karlsbad and Marienbad came to the conclusion to let chemistry take the place of natural processes. In other words, he produced the various types of mineral waters after the content of the different springs had been determined by careful analysis. Thus he became the discoverer and founder of the process of producing artificial mineral water, and thus became the benefactor of suffering humanity.

He established the first institution for the utilization of his discovery in Dresden near the end of the twenties. A second plant was established in Leipzig. After his death in 1840 his son, Dr. Gustav Adolf Struve took over the management and established a third plant in Berlin. Since then this sort of institution has been extended beyond the borders of Germany, and during the last decades have also been established on this side of the ocean.

Dr. Enno Sander's factory for making artificial mineral water is one of the oldest in the west. Its products are recognized and recommended by the most eminent physicians in all of America, and hundreds of them have considered it their duty to acknowledge their merit in writing. The list of mineral waters produced by Dr. Sander is very extensive and includes, among others, (to mention only the most commonly used), the following: Apollinaris, Carlsbader, Emser, Kissinger, Ragoczi, Kreuznacher, Marienbader, Ober-Salzbrunnen, Selters, Vichy. Moreover the purging waters: Friedrichshaller, Puellnaer, Hunyadi, Gieszhuebler and others. In addition to these there are some mineral waters that are produced exclusively by him, which are no imitations of natural springs, but because of their sanitary value are highly valued by the medical world. The use of his various kinds of waters containing lithia, iron and carbon, as also his benz\oic and bromic waters, are frequently recommended. There is also to be had Dr. Nega's effervescent pyrophosphorous iron water and Garrod spa or lithia sodium water, which can be had effervescent or non-effervescent, and which has been expressly recommended by more than four hundred physicians. Moreover, the establishment furnishes and extremely pleasing aromatic ginger ale, which is used to good effect for stomach and digestive disorders.

One specialty by which Dr. Sander has made a real contribution is the Carlsbad water which he has prepared. This he furnishes in its normal strength or in double or tenfold strength of the natural water. By the addition of some hot water one obtains the qualities which are the same as those gotten at the spring. Dr. George J. Bernays, one of the best physicians of this country, who passed away in 1888, in his time wrote an article in a medical journal, in which he declared that the Carlsbader with ten percent concentration was to be preferred to the imported water as also to the Carlsbader salt which was obtained by evaporation at the source. In connection with this it may be of interest to know that the authorities in Carlsbad brought suit in an American court against Dr. Enno Sander to prevent him from manufacturing the artificial Carlsbad mineral water, because the sale of his product greatly affected the sale of the natural water. After a long legal process the courts decided in favor of Dr. Sander.

At the centennial exposition in Ohio in 1888 a number of the mineral waters from Sander's factory won the first prize from a committee that subjected the products to chemical analyses.

The work in the laboratories as also the business management is under the direct and personal supervision of the owner. The water is shipped in ordinary bottles and in larger containers. All drug stores have it for sale. Of course, it can also be obtained directly at the factory, Nos. 125-129 South Eleventh Street. There are branch establishments in New York, Washington, D.C., Cincinnati, Chicago, Milwaukee, Kansas City, Omaha, and Hot Springs, the well-known watering place in Arkansas.

Dr. Enno Sander is a native of the capital of the duchy of Anhalt-Koetheu, however, he spent the years of his young manhood in Berlin. He participated in the uprising of 1849 in Bavaria, and during this period temporarily occupied the position of minister of war. On January 8, 1852 he came to St. Louis. It happened that on the evening of that day there was a meeting in the interest of the revolutionary movement in Germany. This was held in the old state tobacco warehouse. The speaker was Gottfried Kinkel and his secretary, Dr. George Hillgaertner, who were then making a tour through the Untied States. Though Sander had arrived only a few hours before he was taken to the meeting and there met the most prominent Germans in the city.

During the first year of his residence here he gave language lessons. A year later, 1853, he established a drugstore on Second Street between Elm and Myrtle Street, but in the following year he transferred it to the Barnum Hotel, corner of Second and Walnut Street. In 1865 he opened another drug store in the just completed Southern Hotel. In 1868 he established a laboratory for the preparation of chemicals for wholesale trade on Myrtle, between Second and Third Streets. This he operated till 1873, in which year he also sold his two drug stores, in order to devote himself to the production of mineral waters. With what success, was sufficiently shown above.

Dr. Sander was one of the most enthusiastic members of the local academy of science, whose secretary and treasurer he was for many years. In the St. Louis College of Pharmacy, whose organization he supported with much enthusiasm, he lectured for three years on materia medica. He is the author of the state law which requires an examination of druggists who want to do business in towns of seven hundred and more inhabitants. In 1871 he was honored by an election to the presidency of the American Society of Pharmacists. He is held in high esteem by experts in his own field, and he is one of the best representatives of the German element.

Southern Roller Mills

What a far cry from the mill in which French settlers in St. Louis had their grain ground some one hundred and twenty-five years ago, and the complicated machinery by which, in our days, in the steam-driven mills, wheat, corn and barley are transferred into flour, groats, and grits. What a difference also between the mills of three or four decades ago and the mills of today, for which science and technology has done so much.

Two mills stood on the bank of Chouteau pond during the last third of the century. One of these was water driven. The motive power of the other was a horse that went around and around in a circle. How many sacks or shall we say, how many pounds of flour these mills produced in a day is not known and hard to guess. For the last quarter of a century a mill has been operating a few blocks from the former Chouteau pond, that produces eighteen hundred barrels per day.

The Southern Roller Mills, whose capacity has just been cited, was begun in 1860 by John Engelke and Frank Feiner under the firm name of Southern Mills. After a number of years it gave up the grinding of wheat, and devoted itself to the grinding of corn, producing cornmeal, hominy, and grits. Immediately from its start it enjoyed good patronage, not only in the city but also in territory which it provided with food stuffs made of corn. It had a particularly heavy sale in the south, where the year round great quantities of its products were shipped. In 1881 the mill produced 214,709 barrels of cornmeal, 25,923 barrels of hominy and grits, and 1892 a total of 350,000 barrels. The mill obtains its corn mainly from Missouri, Illinois and other western states. It uses only the best quality of grain, for which reason it is preferred by the consumers, resulting in large sales.

In 1883 a large part of the mill was destroyed by fire. The owners had a much larger building built, and equipped it with the most modern machinery which increased its capacity. Just to mention one item of the new equipment, there were forty double rollers and the parts belonging to them. Later a dynamo was added which furnished the electricity to illumine the rooms with more than a hundred electric lights.

The buildings on South Broadway, between Gratiot and Papin Street, have a front of one hundred and seventy-five feet, and extend to the next street, Fourth Street. This provides convenient room for unloading grain and for shipping. The main building is five stories high and the storage building two stories high, all substantially made of brick.

After John Engelke's death in 1889, Frank Feiner became the sole owner of the business, to which he devoted all his attention.

John Engelke came to America from Bavaria in 1849. Like so many others the gold mines of California attracted him. After ten years he came to St. Louis and made this city his home. He has now been in the milling business for thirty-three years. He is a member of the Merchants Exchange, highly respected in business as in other circles. His mill is the largest in this part of the country which devotes itself entirely to the milling of corn.

J. H. Conrades Chair Manufacturing Company

During the first half of this century St. Louis and the territory in the west and southwest, which this city now supplies with goods, got its furniture from Cincinnati and other places in the east. Those factories seemed indeed to have a monopoly. For a long time it was very difficult to break through and win the territory which was tributary to St. Louis. It is, therefore, worth noting that at the beginning of the fifties a move was inaugurated which opened the field for the furniture industry here. For various reasons our city was in a position of advantage, particularly because of its geographic location and the convenience of easy procurement of most of the types of wood.

From the very start when furniture was made here on a large scale for the retail trade it became clear what an important branch of business this was for our city. There is no more suitable place for this industry in the west of the United States than St. Louis, with the Mississippi at its very door and numerous other river connections and the many railroad lines that terminate here. It is true that it required a number of years to combat the competition, but finally it was overcome, and for some time now our city has been considered the center of furniture manufacture west of the Mississippi. How much this industry has developed in the course of time became evident from the fact that three of the largest chair factories alone require an operating capital of more than a million dollars. In the report of the St. Louis Furniture Board of Trade, (which is the official name of the local organization of furniture manufacturers), for the year 1892 we read as follows: "In so far as accurate data could be obtained, the production of all the local furniture factories has, during 1892, exceeded the output of the preceding year, and has reached a total value of nearly six million dollars. The number of factories has increased, so that there are now ninety-five of them, and the oldest establishments have enlarged their plants considerably. The number of workers employed in the factories amounts to four thousand five hundred."

The first who deserve mention for transplanting this industry here are J. H. Conrades and F. L. Logemann, who, from the outset, devoted themselves to the manufacture of chairs. They formed a partnership in 1854 and built a workshop on North Sixth Street, between Carr and Biddle Streets. At first they required the assistance of only three workers, but by and by they increased this number. In the course of time their little shop was exchanged for an extensive factory business. In 1882 the partnership was dissolved, and Conrades soon thereafter built a new factory which occupies the city block between North Second, Main, Tyler and Chamber Streets. The building is five stories high and contains the required machinery of the newest design to assure the greatest practical operation. The factory has its own tracks which connect with the main line of the Wabash railroad, and so also with freight stations of the other railroads. The lumber yard of the factory, where throughout the year enormous supplies of lumber are stacked up, since only thoroughly dry wood is used, is close to the factory, near the river, which naturally is of great advantage for obtaining the raw material and shipping the finished wares.

It is an established fact that concentration on one single article of manufacture assures the greatest proficiency. The Conrades factory furnishes the most striking proof of this fact. From it more than two hundred different types of chairs have found a permanent demand in all parts of the United States, where they are preferred because of their style, solid workmanship and durability. The price list of the firm, which is supplied with illustrations, shows, as we have said, over two hundred types, which indicates the great variety which is offered the retail dealer. Of the kinds of wood that are used in the factory we mention only walnut, elm, ash, cherry and hickory. If one wanders through the rooms of the factory, where there is the activity of a bee hive, one can see the product in various stages of manufacture. The products are of the most varied shape and kind, from the simplest kitchen chairs to the most elegant parlor chairs. The wood is chiefly obtained from Missouri, Illinois and Tennessee, while certain kinds come from Arkansas and other places.

Of the extent of the business one can get an approximate idea if he knows that it requires the work of three hundred and fifty workers. Since the total number of workers in all furniture factories, according to the report of the secretary of the above-cited Furniture Board of Trade, is four thousand five hundred, the Conrades factory alone employs three-tenths of them. In addition to the already mentioned catalogs, which are sent all over the Union, the customers are waited upon at regular intervals by traveling representatives of the firm. Moreover, special agents are sent if it is a question of making an especially large contract.

Since 1888 the business is incorporated under the laws of the State of Missouri. The following officials head the corporation: J. H. Conrades as president, Theodore H. Conrades as vice president, Edwin H. Conrades as treasurer, and J. H. Conrades, Jr. as secretary. The latter three are the sons of the founder of this extensive business, whose management is handled jointly by them.

John H. Conrades came in 1852 to St. Louis from Cincinnati, where he had worked for some time. He was born in Bremen, where he had learned the carpenter trade. He enjoys a position of high esteem among the business men, and takes an active part in all things that are for the common good. Among other things he is one of the directors of the company that built the Germania Theater. This year he was chosen first vice president at the national convention of the American Furniture Workers Association. By this election not he alone, but his firm, was highly honored.

St. Louis Iron and Machine Works

The above is the name of a corporation that, being one of the largest and best-equipped machine factories of the west, has contributed to make St. Louis one of the greatest industrial cities of the country. The works grew from modest beginnings. In 1854, Gerhard (or Gerhardt) H. Timmermann began to make machines in his shop on Myrtle Street near Second Street. Presently he was able to add a foundry and to make further extensions. Since he required more room for the additions, he transferred his works in 1864 to Main and Chouteau Avenue. The proximity of the river and railroad tracks made this location a preferred one. From year to year his business grew, so that now for some time his factory occupies the whole plot between Main and Second Street, as also a large part of the block south of this site. The main front, on Chouteau Avenue, contains the foundry, the machine shops and the rooms for the making of the forms, as also for the storing of same, and the finished machines, of which always a suitable supply is kept on hand. The forges and boiler rooms are to the south, behind the main buildings. The firm has two tracks connecting the factory whith the different railroads. On one of these tracks the raw material comes direct into the yard, while on the otehr the finished product is hauled away. Both can, therefore, be operated without interfering with each other.

Gerhard H. Timmermann came as a young man to St. Louis in 1844. In ten years he had made himself independent, and when in 1875 the business was incorporated under the name of St. Louis Iron and Machine Works, the principal employees, in recognition of their services, wre given shares. After the expiration of forty years, a complete rebuilding and new construction was undertaken, to enlarge the factory considerably and to bring the whole factory, in all its parts, to the highest state of completeness. To this end the newest types of machinery were installed, and for the handling of heavy machine parts, an elevated traveling crane was put in place, not to mention many other modern and practical arrangements to facilitate the work of the plant.

Among the machines manufactured by the firm, the St. Louis Corliss Engine heads the list. It is constructed in all sizes up to two thousand horsepower, either for simple high pressure, with or without condensor, or so called triple expansion machines. These are made with specially constructed machinery, and constitute a specialty of this St. Louis facotry. The single parts are always of the same dimensions, so that any on hand. In all the machines that come from the St. Louis Iron and Machine Works, especial attention is paid to careful work, sensible construction, having in mind economy of operation and power, and dependability, accurate regulation of speed of revolution under varying conditions, a solid, heavily constructed bed, to avoid vibration, and carefuly arranged and constructed cross head to make the operation and control uniform.

Another specialty of the firm is the Lion Dry Press Brick Machine, with all the apparatus that belong to it for the pulverizing and preparation of the clay. In the dry press brick machine the clay is put in the machine in the form of dry powder, without the addition of water. Under a pressure of about forty tons per brick the clay is pressed into the usual brick form. These are then, without further drying, placed in the kiln where they are fired. In this manner more beautiful, regularly formed and sharp-edged bricks are produced in a cheap way. The firm builds these machines in three sized. The smallest presses two bricks at a time and is known as "Baby Lion," the next is the "Lion which presses five bricks at a time, and the largest, called "Jumbo Lion" makes six bricks at a stroke.

The factory, moreover, makes machines, ammonia condensers, for the manufacture of artificial ice and for other refirgeration purposes. These are made in sizes of three-ton capacity to two hundred ton. Then, too, the firm takes contracts for cotton machinery, for compresses of a great variety, and plate glass machinery.

The size of the plant can be understood if it is known that its annual sales amount to two million dollars, and that the number of permanently employed workers numbered nearly two hundred. The operating capital which was paid in full at the time of incorporation in 1875 was two hundred thousand dollars.

The men at present in charge of this business are: G. H. Timmermann as president, who in spite of advanced age is still active, Hermann Krutsch, as vice president and general manager, who was educated as a technical engineer in a German polytechnic institute, and then gained practical experience in Germany and England, which knowledge he applies, and has since 1871, to the work in the factory, John H. Timmermann, the son of the founder, who grew up in the factory and so is thoroughly familiar with every detail, is the secretary. These three head one of the most extensive establishments in this branch of industry.

Bauer-Walter Buggy and Carriage Company

The importance and extent, which the wagon construction industry has attained in St. Louis in the course of the years is best shown by the fact that in 1892 the total value of vehicles built here amounted to eight million dollars. Of this sum more than seven million were for coaches and buggies. The number of factories and workshops in this branch has reached an astonishing number, but of really large establishments of this kind there are not many. Among the most outstanding firms in this industrial branch must be named the Bauer-Walter Buggy and Carriage Company, whose history will follow here briefly.

In the year 1891 Ferdinand Bauer passed away.

At the beginning of the seventies Bauer assumed a responsible position with the firm of William Koenig, agricultural implements. Then he became a partner in the business. In 1883 he established a similar business under the firm name of Ferdinand Bauer and Company. In this concern Jacob Walter was for a year a silent partner, after he had held the post of bookkeeper and correspondent in the firm of Koenig and Company since 1873. After expiration of that year the young firm took the name of Bauer and Walter. A year later the firm made an agreement with Parlin, Ohrendorf and Company of Canton, Illinois, which managed a factory for the manufacture of agricultural implements. As the local representative of the above concern the firm took the name of Bauer, Walter and Company. In 1886 Walter left the connection with Parlin, Ohrendorf and Company and together with George W. Hoffman and Ferdinand Bauer established the wagon factory of which we are speaking, while Bauer continued his connection with the Canton firm.

The factory was first located on Seventh Street and Clark Avenue. Soon a second factory was necessary. It was built on Sixteenth and Poplar Streets. In one of these, only buggies, phaetons and surreys were manufactured. In the other, wagons and heavy vehicles were built. This division of operation was, of course, accompanied with disadvantages, and the firm found it necessary to provide more space in order to have everything under one roof. The building which it moved into occupies the entire eastern half of the block which is located between Third and Fourth, Papin Street and Chouteau Avenue. This new location met the requirements splendidly. It is equipped with all the facilities necessary, and the business is growing from year to year. In the first year at this location, 1670 wagons of various types were made. In 1892 a bit more than five thousand were produced. There is every reason to believe that the total of seven thousand vehicles will be reached. During the months in which the factory is busiest, that is from February to September, thirty-five to forty-five wagons are made each day.

The product of the Bauer-Walter Buggy and Carriage Company is sold over an enormous territory, extending from Indiana to the coast of the Pacific, from Minnesota to the Gulf of Mexico. This enormous area can be attributed in part to the connection with the Parlin-Ohrendorf Agricultural Company, with the latter's branch business in St. Louis, Minneapolis, Omaha, Kansas City, and Dallas and its many traveling salesmen, who look after the sales of both concerns. The Bauer-Walter Buggy and Carriage Company sends its agents to those states that are not covered by the Canton firm. Moreover, it sends out illustrated catalogs which make the product known in extensive circles.

The quick and extensive sale of their vehicles was due to the use of the best material and the best workmanship.

The founder and manager of an industrial establishment, that in such a relatively short time has assumed such dimensions, deserves a statement pertaining to himself.

Ferdinand Bauer, who passed away in the spring of 1891, was born in Alsace. As a small boy he came to St. Louis with his parents. He was the youngest of seven brothers, who received their education in the public schools of their home country, since their father could not afford a higher education. Ferdinand was only fourteen years old when he had the opportunity of learning basic principles of American retail business in a grocery store. After a few years he became a bookkeeper in the wholesale liquor business of Perry and Schenk. Later he entered the employment of William Koenig and Company. Here he also served a bookkeeper, and became still better acquainted with business ways. He established a firm of his own that handled agricultural implements.

Jacob Walter's birthplace is Edenkoben in the Bavarian Rhenish Palatinate. Here he finished the Latin school. As a youth of eighteen he came to St. Louis. During the first seven years of his residence here he was occupied in various businesses. In turn he learned to become a type setter, cigar maker, and telegrapher. But till then he had not gotten a proper start. In 1873 he secured an appointment with the Koenig firm, where he became acquainted with his later partner, Bauer, and they became friends. The business connection which followed, has already been told.

George W. Hoffmann was born of German parents in the state of New Jersey. He is now forty-eight years old. From youth he grew up in an environment that fitted him exactly for the work of this life. At that time this business was just in the first stages of development. Everything was made by hand, but that gave the eager young man ample opportunity to learn his trade in detail, something that came him in good stead. In enabled him to serve as superintendent in several wagon factories, until in partnership with F. Bauer and J. Walter he founded the establishment which we have described. Much of the success of the business is due to Hoffmann's technical knowledge and energy, while the leading force in the office and contact man with outside interests is his associate Walter and so contributed so much to the success of the Bauer-Walter Buggy and Carriage Company.

William Homann Saddlery Company

In 1812 John Chandler and Company announced in the only local paper, the *Missouri Gazette*, that they made and had in stock, saddles and harnesses. They also told that their workshop and store were on Main Street. Four years later, in 1816, John Jacoby announced that he had moved from Lexington, Kentucky, and had opened a saddlery business on Front Street, as the Levee was then called. After four more years the newspaper announced that Grimsley and Starch operated the saddlery hitherto managed by Jacoby. That was the beginning of this branch of industry which has become one of the most important and most extensive businesses in St. Louis, for since the fifties our city has become the center of the saddle and harness manufacture in the west. From here not only Missouri but Kentucky, Tennessee, Mississippi, Louisiana, Texas, Arkansas, Kansas, Colorado, New Mexico, Montana, North and South Dakota, Arizona and the Indian Territory are supplied with this commodity. During the war, enormous amounts of these articles were made for the cavalry of the Union army. However, a considerable increase of the larger businesses in this line did not come until the second half of the sixties.

At this time occurred the founding of the business which has been incorporated under the above firm name, but which has existed since 1865.

William Homann was born in 1842 in Dissen in what was at that time in the kingdom of Hanover. He was fourteen years old when he came to St. Louis, and here learned the saddlery business. After he had spent nine whole years to prepare himself in detail for this line of business, he, with Henry Hotze, formed their own firm under the name of Homann and Hotze. For a number of years they were located near the corner of Third Street and Washington Avenue. In the middle of the seventies they were on Fourth, between Lucas Avenue and Morgan Street, where it is still situated. In 1885 the business came into Homann's sole possession, as he bought out his partner. For five years he continued the business alone. In 1890 his two brothers, who had learned the business under William Hoffmann, became partners in the business, after which the firm was called the William Homann Saddlery Company.

There are at this time about twelve big saddle factories in St. Louis, and the Homann Company is one of them. What scope the operation in this branch of business has assumed in the course of time is shown in the report of the secretary of the Merchant's Exchange for the year 1892, according to which the sale of saddle goods amounted to three and a half million dollars for that year. This means an increase of ten percent over that of the year 1891.

The firm of Homann endeavors to furnish only the wares prepared by the best workmen. It speaks well for this concern that during all these years there has never been a strike or any other labor disturbance. Such things occurred frequently in some of the other businesses of this branch. The goods of Homann enjoy a good reputation. A large stock of wares affords good selection of various articles, in which are included also all sorts of metal goods which belong to the caption of saddlery hardware. The long years of practical experience which all three members of the firm have had in the saddlery business, are the basis of its great commercial success. This it owes to the sound business management, that has characterized it from the beginning, and which has given it such a good name among its customers.

The ever-increasing amount of business through the years has made imperative an enlargement of the plant. This was accomplishment by the purchase of the adjoining building. The two buildings at 716 and 718 North Fourth Street provide the necessary room. Since the incorporation mentioned above, William Homann serves as president and treasurer, Rudolph Homann as vice president and Henry J. Homann as secretary of the company. All three are well-known and respected, not only in the local business world but also in social circles.

William Prufrock's Parlor Furniture and Furniture Frame Factory

In general the American homes have greater comforts than those in most other countries. The entire arrangement of the houses here is designed to give the greatest possible convenience. The fact that all who can possibly afford it, live in their own homes, in itself contributes much to home comfort. Even in the more recent times, flats have not brought an essential change in these things on this side of the ocean, for here, the flats, in most cases, have separate entrances from the street, so that every family is alone and does not have to come into contact with other renters. The interior arrangement is in harmony with this idea. This is particularly true since people have discarded the idea that a certain room must be set aside for state occasions. These rooms had their windows tightly closed by window shutters which kept out all light and air, and whose doors were only opened when the guests were already close to the house. As long as this custom was tolerated, the parlor, for that is what we are talking about, was a most uncomfortable place, upon which the visitor was glad to turn his back as soon as possible. Just like the atmosphere that prevailed there, so also the furniture seemed chilly, as it stood cold and stiff along the walls. This has become essentially different during the last decades. The parlor today presents a pleasing appearance. It is a pleasure to be in it. One feels comfortable in it, thanks to the furnishings which it contains.

The furniture deserves most credit for this change. Fashion plays a prominent role in this matter, though obviously much depends on the taste of the owner, but still more upon the cabinet-maker and the paper-hanger, whose art and skill are in most cases the deciding factors. The increased luxury of our day demands progress also in this field. For this reason the making of parlor furniture has become an important branch of industry. St.

Louis has a number of firms which are devoted entirely to this line of work. The best known among these is that of William Prufrock, which has existed since the end of the sixties, therefore, for nearly a quarter of a century.

The business, which is now so great, started on a very small scale. William Prufrock learned upholstering and paper-hanging in a Pommeranian town, where he was born. Then he worked for several years in Berlin, which next to Paris and Vienna, is famous for the products of this branch. In various workshops there he gained knowledge and experience which he brought with him across the ocean, to make himself independent. He established his first shop on Sixteenth Street and Franklin Avenue. After two years he transferred it to Fourth Street near Franklin Avenue, where he added a salesroom and made the manufacture of parlor furniture and lounges his specialty. At first he worked alone. Then he employed two helpers, and now he has for some time employed two hundred and twenty-five helpers in the two factories which have grown from such humble beginnings.

In 1876 he moved to North Sixth Street and Cass Avenue. There he developed the factory which now occupies seven building sites. No cheap goods are made here. The finer kinds of parlor furniture make up the majority of the products made in this plant. Since pleasing form is one of the main requirements, the most skilled draftsmen are entrusted to make the designs. Some designs are also obtained from Europe. In this manner new and stylish patterns are provided. Among the types of wood used are mahogany, cherry, walnut, birch, ample and poplar. Among the various articles made in this factory are easy chairs, library chairs, studio chairs, rocking chairs, church pews, sofas, divans, lodge and theater chairs, settees, ottomans, chairs with adjustable backs for dentists and barbers, piano stools, etc. To these must be added the most varied parlor tables, most of which have tops made of onyx or fine marble.

The coverings of the upholstered furniture shows the greatest variety conceivable. Among these are brocatel, damasks, tapestry of silk and wool, all sorts of plush, everything in the most modern colors and designs. Not only is the Prufrock furniture characterized by attractive forms, but also by neat workmanship, for in spite of the exclusive use of the best material, this would not attract attention if the greatest care were not exercised in every step of the manufacture. This is done in the most complete manner, as one can convince himself by an examination of the sample room which the firm has at 1104 and 1106 Olive Street.

The factory in which the furniture frames are made is located on North Eighth Street between Cass Avenue and Mullanphy Street. It consists of four buildings adjoining one another and connected with one another. They are completely equipped to meet the growing demand. The sales territory for the frames and the finished furniture is in addition to Missouri and adjoining states, Nebraska, Iowa, Minnesota, Montana, Utah, California, New Mexico, Colorado, Tennessee, Kentucky, Ohio, Alabama, Georgia, Virginia, Texas, Mexico and Cuba. These regions are regularly visited by traveling salesmen. Illustrated catalogs keep the customers informed of the newest styles. The owner of this great business is untiringly active in both factories from early to late, always on the alert to preserve the good name of his firm. William Prufrock is truly a self-made man who richly deserves the success which he has attained.

The Gast Wine Company: Badenheim and St. Louis

It is now nearly sixty years ago that a small group of German settlers established themselves in what is now Gasconade county and founded the town of Hermann. After some time this place was called the German wine town of Missouri, since a part of the new arrivals came with the intention of practicing viniculture for their livelihood. The pioneer of the Hermann grape culture was Michael Poeschel, who passed away a short while ago, at an advanced age. He, more than anyone else, is to be credited with the successful development of the Hermann grape culture, and securing suitable markets for the products of the vineyards. Even four decades ago, Poeschel's vineyards were known far and wide. But few strangers came to Hermann who did not visit them. In the course of time they, indeed, constituted one of the sights worth seeing in this region.

It was in these vineyards that Paulus Gast, the founder and manager of the Gast Wine Company, learned vineculture from the ground up, and familiarized himself with every detail, theoretically and practically, and thus laid the foundation for his professional activity.

Paulus Gast came from Berlin. In 1848, as a seven-year-old boy, he came with his parents to America, and at once proceeded to St. Louis. His father, Leopold Gast, was the co-founder of the lithographic institute, which is known everywhere, and which is today bearing the name of Gast. (In another place in this book this concern will be discussed in full.) Mr. Gast provided an excellent education for his son. He attended a private school, then the public schools and then Washington University. At the age of nineteen he became a student of Michael Poeschel. A pronounced preference for country life, an early-manifested liking for the cultivation of the soil and especially for the care of the grape vines induced him to take up this calling. The attentive reading of the works of Frederick Muench, the well-known writer and raiser of wine. Muench's pen name was Far West. That was in 1860, and the author of this book at that time edited the *Hermanner Volksblatt*. He was often in the hospitable house of the Poeschels, and at that time got acquainted with the future owner of Badenheim.

In the following year came the war, and when President Lincoln issued the second call for the preservation of the Union, young Paulus Gast threw aside the hoe and the spade and hurried to arms. He entered the First Regiment of Missouri Engineers, commanded by Colonel Flad, as a private. In succession he became sergeant and finally lieutenant. Most of the time the regiment was a part of General Sherman's army. When, in October 1864, after the surrender of Atlanta, the time of service of most men in the regiment had expired, young Gast also left the army.

Having returned to St. Louis he did not hesitate to realize his favorite plan. For this purpose he bought a piece of land in what is now the suburb of Baden. At that time it was still in the county of St. Louis. Here he planned to start a vineyard. The plot consisted of a few acres, densely overgrown with trees and hazel brush. He cleared the land with his own hand, being assisted by his young wife, whom he had learned to honor in Hermann, and whom he had married in 1865. When his neighbors heard that he was going to plant grape vines, they advised him that it would be much wiser to plant potatoes. However, he insisted on carrying out his purpose. When his undertaking proved a success, he had the satisfaction of seeing that those who had shaken their heads most vigorously were the very ones that emulated his example first and also raised grapes.

In 1868 Gast could harvest his first small crop of grapes. The yield increased from year to year, and 1880 he also began to buy the grapes which his neighbors raised. He found that he did not have enough land, so he bought a tract in North St. Louis. It was a splendid location, well suited for viniculture. This new site he called Badenheim. At the same time he organized the Gast Wine Company. Associated with him in this enterprise were his uncle August Gast, Michael Poeschel and the latter's long-time partner, John Scherer. None of the last three are now living.

At Badenheim twenty-five acres are planted to grapes. These vineyards are considered models of viniculture in the whole Mississippi valley. They are now under the direct supervision of the oldest son of the owner, Ulysses S. Gast, who a few years ago completed his professional training in the famous school of viniculture of the Freiherr von Babo at Klosterneubau near Vienna. He is at the same time the master of the cellars of the firm, which cellars have a capacity of two hundred thousand gallons.

Since good wine can be made only from good grapes, only the newest and best varieties are cultivated at Badenheim. In the fall of 1892 the harvest amounted to one hundred thousand pounds. In addition the firm bought two hundred tons of grapes in Ohio, Illinois and Missouri. Special brands of wine, which the company has put on the market are the Badenheimer, a popular light wine, the Black Oak, an excellent red wine, which is mainly produced from Cynthiana grapes, that give it the fine aroma. Moreover, the company produces Gast's Extra Dry and Grand Monopole which are most carefully made champagnes. The company's light-colored wines are replacing to a large extent the wines that come from the other side of the ocean. The sales territory extends south to Florida and east to Boston. Five traveling salesmen are continually on the road visiting customers. The superior management of the concern, which was incorporated in 1883, is in the hands of the founder, who is at the same time president and manager of the company. U. S. Gast is the superintendent, and A. T. Gast, a younger son of Paulus Gast is the secretary. The city storage rooms, business office and sample rooms are at 919 North Sixth Street, between Franklin Avenue and Wash Street, therefore, in the center of the business part of St. Louis.

St. Louis Stamping Company

If all the housewives and cooks in the United States should be asked to vote on the kind of cooking and kitchen dishes they consider the best, the majority would vote in favor of enameled ware, which is made by the St. Louis Stamping Company. The chances are that there are but few households in this country in which there is not at least one or another of these enameled dishes, which, during the last decades, have come into common use. These articles are sold not only in this country but also in South America, Australia and even Europe.

The beginning of this business, that has assumed such great proportions, dates back to 1859. In a work shop and store, twenty-five by fifty in size, F. G. and W. F. Niedringhaus, in that year, opened their tin shop. From these small beginnings grew an establishment that developed into a new branch of industry, and into one of the largest industrial plants of our time. The firm was first called Niedringhaus and Brother. In 1862 they began to make flat tinware by the pressing stamping method. The demand for these goods increased so that in 1864 the manufacture on a large scale was begun. In the following year it was decided to also make deep dishes in addition to the flat type by the stamping process. Success was so great that it was decided to form the St. Louis Stamping Company and to expand its operation.

In 1873 the company began the manufacture of the type of enameled ware which was in used in Europe. But it soon was seen that it required a different method of manufacture to make it suitable for local use. The American cookstoves and the speed with which meals are prepared makes necessary greater durability and resistance. After much experimentation, a process was found which gave the product the desired properties. It was on April 10, 1874 that the manufacture of Granite Iron Ware was begun. The enamel is a glassy covering, which covers the metal completely, protects it from heat and vegetable acids, and with regard to cleanliness can be compared with porcelain and glass. To these properties must be added the great durability and the handsome appearance of the vessels.

The sheet iron, used in the manufacture, was for a long time obtained from England. It was generally assumed that it could not be made here in as good quality. How baseless the assumption was became manifest when the St. Louis Stamping Company established its own roller mills, and proceeded to make its own sheet iron instead of importing it. The buildings of the roller mills were begun in 1870. These cover almost six acres. They are located near the river, so that the raw material intended for the smelters can be brought conveniently to the site either by water or by rail. The daily output of sheet iron is forty tons.

The factory is also situated in the northern part of the city and the buildings occupy about three city blocks. The sample rooms are in one of the buildings on Cass Avenue and Second Street. There are branch offices of the firm at 69 Beekman Street in New York, 184 North Street in Boston and 143 Lake Street in Chicago.

In the rolling mills, seven hundred and fifty and in the factory eight hundred and fifty persons are employed. At this time new factory buildings are being erected by the Niedringhaus firm in Granite City, a town recently laid out in Illinois, directly opposite St. Louis. The plant will cover ten acres and will contain four hundred thousand square feet of floor space. It is the intention to employ twelve hundred workers. The location of the new city is unusually well suited for factory purposes since it is connected with several railroad lines and is only a mile and a half from the Merchant Bridge, which connects Illinois and Missouri. The new town is also close to the Illinois coal region.

What the St. Louis Stamping Company manufactures is sufficiently well-known. To enumerate them would make a list of several pages. It needs here only to be mentioned that its products include all sorts of cooking and kitchen utensils and the most varied household vessels

The superior officials of the corporation are the two founders of the firm: F. G. Niedringhaus as president, and William F. Niedringhaus as vice president. A son of the former, Thomas K. Niedringhaus, has for some time been the secretary.

Tinplated Sheet Iron

Till 1890 all tinplated sheet iron was imported from England because the view was held here that it could not be produced as good here, if at all. The English manufacturer had a real monopoly which they used to the limit. It was to the credit of the St. Louis Stamping Company that this prejudice was put an end to, and that the manufacture of tinplated sheet iron was transplanted to American soil.

The president of the company, F. G. Niedringhaus, had made a study of this subject on repeated visits in Europe. He was convinced that one could make tinplated sheet iron of just as good quality here as abroad. After overcoming certain opposition and hindrances, the firm of Niedringhaus introduced this branch of industry in America and established it permanently. Its example was soon emulated, and it is now only a question of time when the competition with English kitchenware and tinplated sheet iron will be completely overcome.

From the report of the special agent, Ayres, of the Treasury Department regarding tinplated sheet iron, it appears that during the time from July, 1891 to March 31, 1893 the production of rolled plates of tinplated sheet iron amounted to 34,632,032 pounds. The sheet iron that was imported and tinplated here amounted to 39,290,282 pounds. Ten firms used their own sheet iron exclusively, thirteen firms used domestic and foreign sheet iron, and nine firms used only foreign sheet iron. These data, according to agent Ayres, are based on the sworn statement of the manufacturers. In the quarter of the year, expiring on March 31, 1893, as the report states in conclusion, there were produced 29,565,399 pounds, of which 40% were of American sheet iron. The agent estimates the production, as of the quarter ending in June, at 35,000,000 pounds, and for the fiscal year 1892-1893 at more than 100,000,000.

Emil F. Seidel –Office, Bank, Store and House Interiors Mantels, Etc.

A refined taste, increasing sense of art and more desire for luxury have made themselves felt to a marked degree during the last decades. Formerly these desires were felt only to a limited degree. There have been some expensively equipped banks, drug stores and offices before this time, but this sort of equipment became general only in recent times. Artistic cabinet making and related branches of industry have gained a wide field of operation, and American metropolises show in their business houses what can be accomplished in this regard. One need only to compare the offices of newspapers, banks, insurance companies and stores of various kinds of our day with these same institutions as they were in former times, to note the difference between then and now, and observe the progress that has been made in this direction.

St. Louis has only a few firms which are engaged exclusively with work of this kind under consideration. One of these is that of Emil F. Seidel, whose place of business is on South Broadway at numbers 210, 212, and 214 between Elm Street and Clark Avenue. Erastus Wells had this four-story building erected in 1880 solely for the Seidel factory. Prior to this date the factory and store rooms had been for ten years on Third Street near Washington Avenue. Here E. F. Seidel established himself at the end of the sixties. The quality of his goods soon attracted customers. Seidel had learned cabinet making in Germany (he came from Silesia at Annaber in the Saxonian Ore Mountains), had emigrated to America in 1857, and had settled in Chicago, where he plied his trade till 1865 when he came to St. Louis to make his home.

The manufacture of office and store equipment still constitutes a great part of the work of the factory, though for some time other branches have been added. Among the innovations are fireplace mantels, and wall facings in living rooms, whose elegant furnishing require such work. The manufacture of parqueted floors and balustrades which are in harmony with the remaining, stylish arrangements of such dwellings. In more recent time the arrangement of bath rooms in the manner of Roman and Pompeiian baths has been added.

The types of wood that are mainly used for the above are red and white mahogany, prima vera from South America, birdseye maple, and satinwood from Santo Domingo.

There are many private homes in which Seidel's artistic work can be seen. This work appears in the most varied modern styles, including the rococo (white with gold), Empire, with rich wood carving. Among others the homes of the following contain work by Seidel: Erastus Wells, Daniel Catlin, Adolphus Busch, H. C. Pieree (of the Water-Pieree Oil Co.), Samual Kennard, William J. Lemp, William H. Dittmann, O. L. Hagan, and J. T. Drummond.

The firm makes a specialty of the fine furniture for drug stores. A particularly fine piece of work can be seen in the drug store of Alexander, Kirkbride and Riley.

Several local banks also have equipment from the Seidel factory, as for example, the Fourth National Bank in its new building on the southeast corner of Fourth and Olive.

The reputation of the Seidel factory has reached distant places. So, for instance, a complete drug store equipment was shipped to Tasmania (former Van Diemens Land), about whose beauty the local newspapers gave a full report at the time.

The owner of this extensive and in certain respects unique business, has a right to look with justified satisfaction at the results which were attained by perseverance, untiring diligence and endeavor.

Medart Patent Pulley Company

The most important part of a machine is the motive power and the utilization of the same, which depends upon the distribution from the driven power to the driven mechanism. The efficiency of the driving force depends upon its power and its distribution, in other words upon the transmission of power. What would the spinning mill and weaver's establishment with its thousands of spindles amount to, what in general all the great factories with their hundreds of working parts which are distributed in many rooms, indeed in many buildings, be without transmission, that is the contrivance to carry the driving force of the motor to the operating machines? And how would it be with the economy of operation, with the economic application and sufficient utilization of steam or other power, if there were no transmission? The visitor who steps into a factory for the first time, and has never before seen a machine at work, let us say, for example, a Jacquard loom, will observe with surprise how countless threads are joined together before his eyes into a splendid and vari-colored pattern. But he will hardly cast a glance at the large and small metal discs over which run broad and narrow belts, which form an actual network with the short and long shafts way up under the ceiling. And yet it is these discs and their appurtenances which keep all the machines in continuous activity. If such a pulley or a single shaft by accident should be moved by the smallest fractional part of an inch from its prescribed position, many machines would have to stop till repairs were made.

From the above it must be obvious what an important role transmission plays in a factory. For this reason it is understandable that improvements are constantly striven for in machine construction. Factories owe a great number of valuable inventions and improvements in this field to a German American, who for nearly a quarter of a century has lived in our midst.

Philip Medart was by training a pattern maker. With his brother, Fritz Medart, he pursued his business during the seventies on Market Street, near Second Street. Their workshop was small, and was in one of the rooms of Rauth's printing shop. The latter had formerly worked without steam power. This the Medart brothers supplied, and in this way paid for the rent. Fritz Medart continued to make designs for furniture to which he added the making of apparatus for Turner societies. Philip Medart turned to another field. In 1880 he applied himself to the making of apparatus for the transmission of. That same year he was granted a patent for an invention that he had made. From then on he devoted himself with much zeal and perseverance to the perfecting of pulleys manufactured by him, and to other essential parts required for power transmission. In the course of time he secured about fifty different patents for the Medart Pulley Company.

At the time when Fritz Medart left the concern, a younger brother, William Medart became a partner of the company. For thirteen years the factory was on Main, between Biddle and O'Fallon Streets. The reputation of the products of this company spread quickly in industrial circles of the country, so that today there are probably not many factories in the United States in which Medart's pulleys, etc. are not installed. In addition there are also many sales in South America and Europe.

Five years ago Philip Medart invented a machine. Its purpose is to draw round iron rods perfectly straight. By the use of this machine, workshops and factories are saved an unbelievable amount of time.

Increase in business necessitated a larger plant. After the purchase of the block that is bordered by DeKalb and Kosciusko, Potomac and President Streets, factory buildings were erected in 1892-1893. These have a frontal length of seven hundred and sixty-two feet. In the adjoining block, close to the Mississippi, in a separate building is the foundry. The entire equipment includes the newest and most complete machinery and every conceivable facility for the operation of the plant. The factory is the largest in the United States and employs nearly three hundred men, or thirty times as many as at the time when Philip and William Medart began to manufacture their now famous pulleys.

St. Louis Cooperage Company

The works of the St. Louis Cooperage Company are situated in the southern part of the city on Main and Arsenal Street, hence close to the river and also near the tracks of the St. Louis, Iron Mountain and Southern railroad. The buildings, lumber yards, etc. occupy three acres, and the number of employees is more than two hundred and fifty.

The incorporation of the firm took place in 1884, however, the beginning of the concern dates back fourteen years earlier. At the head of this extensive business is George F. Meyer as president, Harold H. Tittmann as secretary and manager.

When the firm began to devote itself to this branch of industry almost all types of barrels were made by hand. Trade, however, required even at that time, a large number of barrels in the shortest time possible. To meet this demand the investment of great amounts of capital for machines and for the equipment for the drying of the required wood, and for the accumulation of this material for a long time service became an absolute necessity. Containers such as have been used for a decade by brewers and distillers for vinegar, all sorts of oil and all other fluids, must now be made in an entirely different manner from that formerly employed, particularly in so far as the wood used is concerned. Formerly the matter of the dryness of the wood was considered far less important. The consumers demanded far less exacting work, and were satisfied with partially dry wood. And so it had continued till an actual revolution set in which demanded a new process of barrel manufacture.

In order to put barrels on the market such as trade and industry began to demand, a more careful treatment of wood was necessary than the large and small cooperages had previously given it. The drying of the wood was the first step in this treatment. The owners of the works under discussion correctly understood the situation from the outset, and built their factory to meet the need, not only for the moment but with a view into the future, and the results have shown how correct they were. They were the first in the field and have since then held the field, for the sale of their product extends form Boston to San Francisco, from St. Paul to New Orleans. While the demand is great everywhere, it is particularly great in those parts of the country in which climatic and temperature conditions cause the drying and shrinking of the wood, as for example in the region of the Pacific Ocean and the mountain states of the west. The new process offsets the disadvantageous effect of dry atmosphere. The artificially dried barrel staves preclude shrinkage completely and make possible the production of absolutely tight barrels. The company uses eight day kilns to dry its wood.

The product of the St. Louis Cooperage Company is of a very varied sort. It consists mainly of beer kegs, of whiskey barrels, wine barrels, cinder barrels, and vinegar barrels, moreover, barrels for pickles, kraut, coal oil, etc., also barrels for syrup and lard. Then, too, there are barrels not intended for liquids, but for flour, nails, etc. In addition there are made containers for groceries, bottled beer, mineral water and the like.

The employment of the best material, fine machinery and expert workmen have made this concern one of the largest of its kind in the United States and Canada.

Ferdinand Meszmer Manufacturing Company

On the east side of South Seven Street, between Sidney and Lynch Streets stands the stately factory of the Meszmer Manufacturing Company about whose founder and chief owner we shall speak immediately. It stands there as tangible evidence as to what can be made of the conceivably smallest undertaking if industry and perseverance have a hand in the undertaking.

In 1855 a plain blacksmith apprentice, an honest Bavarian came from Watterdingen am Enger to St. Louis. He came from a family of blacksmiths. His grandfather, his father and his brothers followed the trade. After his arrival in America Ferdinand Meszmer spent a short while in Pittsburgh before coming here. In St. Louis he immediately found employment in the machine shops and foundry of Palm and Robertson (Palm's foundry). Then he worked in the shops of Schinckle, Howard and Harrison. In 1859 he helped to place the cupola on the courthouse. At first it was made of cast iron, but was found to be much too heavy, and so another was made of wrought iron. Soon after that he worked as a locksmith. In 1883 he received a contract from a saddler firm on Main Street to make bridle bits for the United States cavalry. In the following year he opened a locksmith shop on the east side of Third Street, between Market and Chestnut Street. It was a very narrow room with only one window but it was large enough for the work that was done in it. The amount of work did not increase till 1867 when Meszmer moved to Market Street between Fifth and Sixth Street, where the workshop was larger. Here Meszmer worked only incidentally at lock smithing, and devoted himself mainly to work with brass, especially for manufacturers of coaches. This he continued to do for a number of years, until in 1875 he succeeded in making a faucet for beer kegs, which he protected by a patent and which formed the foundation for his later success. After a three year stay on market Street he moved in 1880 to Third Street between Elm and Myrtle Street. Here he was for the first time enabled to use steam power. Since he was now able to produce a greater quantity of articles the Meszmer faucets became known far and wide. They acquired a real reputation and were sold in all parts of the United States and were also shipped to Germany and England. The demand rose to such an extent that twenty thousand of them were placed on the market at the time when the manufacture of this article constituted only a subordinate part of the factory's production.

The rooms on South Third Street proved too small with the increase of business and a change became imperative. A new building site was bought in 1888 and the construction of a new factory was undertaken immediately. This factory on South Seventh Street has a front of sixty feet and a depth, to South Broadway, of one hundred and forty-two feet. In the three story building are the foundry, the grinding room, the polishing room and cabinet maker's room. The numerous machines needed for the operations are all of the newest construction, the tools of the best type and the whole equipment as complete as it can be had.

Among the various products that come from this establishment are to be mentioned, in addition to the faucets, in the first place brass work for electric streetcars, for breweries and distilleries, moreover, all sorts of sanitary contrivances, which are only sold to plumbers, also beer coolers, barrel stands, copper drains, bolts and locks for refrigerators, tavern bars and ice boxes, baggage markers and all sorts of brass checks for baker and tavern keepers, the most varied corkscrews, bottle cleaners, ice picks and the like. Since the factory is rather far from the center of the business part, the firm has a sales room at 106 South Fourth Street opposite the Southern Hotel. Traveling salesmen and illustrated price lists advertise the products of the company.

The Ferdinand Meszmer Manufacturing Company has been incorporated for years. Its founder, Ferdinand Meszmer, senior, is president and treasurer. His son-in-law, Frederick Werner is vice president. Ferdinand Meszmer, junior, is secretary, and the remaining sons and sons-in-law are likewise active in the business which continually employs more than thirty workers.

Anthony Ittner's Press and Ornamental Brick Works

In a metropolis in which new buildings for every imaginable purpose seem to spring up from the ground each day, it is obvious that good building material must be available. In the matter of the production of brick, St. Louis occupies third place in the United States. It would be entitled to second place if the products of brickyards in its immediate neighborhood were included in the count. During the last few years a number of ten and twelve-story buildings have been erected in the business part of the city. Of late some structures have been built that are still taller, as for example that of the Union Trust Company, on the corner of Seventh and Olive Street, which has seventeen stories. In so far as the building of dwelling houses is concerned, it need only to be mentioned that the city is expanding constantly and whole new divisions spring into being. So a great quantity of bricks is used here, not to mention the fact that many are used elsewhere.

Anthony Ittner, the owner of two of the largest brickyards in America, in recognized head of the representatives of this branch of industry. By profession and training Mr. Ittner is a master builder. In the middle of the fifties he began to devote himself to this profession, but as early as 1859 he also began to manufacture bricks. He was so successful in this business that after thirty years he decided to give up building operations entirely, and since 1890 has applied all his energy and activity to the manufacture of bricks. In 1859 he started brick making operations on a large scale on Eighteenth, between Papin and Gratiot Street. In the first twelve months this plant produced ten million bricks. The continually increasing market demanded greater production and so he established a much larger plant in 1870, which was located on Park and Ewing Avenue. This, too, could not supply the demand, so the magnificent yard on California Avenue and Sidney Street was established. The buildings alone of this plant cost forty thousand dollars. The most modern machinery is used. Since the time of opening this plant fifteen million bricks per year have been made in it. But even this enormous quantity in time failed to meet the requirements. Since the existing plant could not be sufficiently enlarged, the erection of a second plant became necessary. With this in mind Ittner bought, in 1890, seventy acres of land in the neighborhood of Belleville, Illinois. This land is situated close to the Louisville and Nashville railroad and is particularly well suited for brick production. Without delay the buildings for a large scale operation were erected, and equipped with modern machinery, among which is a Hamilton Corliss steam engine. Eight kilns of the best construction (Alsip patent) and several Andrew's Dry Clay Press-Brick

Machines were installed. The whole thing cost one hundred thousand dollars, and the plant is complete and may be called the best of its kind in the country. Each year twelve million bricks are made here, among them two million for ornamental purposes. For both plants this makes a total production of twenty-seven million bricks.

The Ittner brick is of a splendid dark red color and in this respect is not surpassed by any other product. They are noted for the fact that they never contain stripes, so-called granulations, and that they have sharp edges and corners, an advantage which is due to a frequent replacement of the press forms. This, of course, increases the value of the product. The prejudice against the making of brick by the dry method has long been dispelled. One of those who brought about this change in attitude was Ittner himself, who after thoroughly testing the dry process found it to be the best, and introduced this type of goods on the market.

The best argument for these bricks is the fact that architects and builders who once have used them recommend them over all others. Their use is not restricted to St. Louis and its environment. They are also shipped to other parts of Missouri, to Illinois, Nebraska, Minnesota, Iowa, Arkansas, Texas, Louisiana and Mississippi. The convenience of shipping by water as well as by railroad naturally plays an important role, moreover the fact that at all times a great supply of brick is on hand which makes possible the quick filling of orders, even in large quantities.

Anthony Ittner belongs to one of the oldest families in the state, and his name is known far beyond the borders of Missouri. His industrial career began when in 1856 he and several of his brothers undertook the building of houses. They had so much to do that it seemed advisable to form several firms from the one. Anthony Ittner formed a partnership with his brother, George. In the course of time he also had other members of his family as associates but never had he a partner who was not a member of his family. Of the many large buildings in whose erection he participated in the brickwork, only a few need be mentioned: the Southern Hotel, the Lindell Hotel, the Stock Exchange, the Exhibition Building, Belcher's Sugar Refinery, which with its thirteen stories was the first building that was taller than eight stories. He was one of the first members of Mechanics Exchange, (from which developed the Builder's Exchange), which was organized in the second half of the fifties. He was one of the most zealous advocates of this organization, and held the most varied offices in it.

Furthermore, he was chosen president of the Nation Builders Convention, and of the Nation Union of American Brick Manufacturers.

His fellow-citizens offered him various offices during the years, but he declined them all, with one exception, when he allowed them to elect him to the state senate, during the first half of the seventies.

The main office of the firm is in the Telephone Building, corner of Tenth and Olive Streets.

The Pauly Jail Building and Manufacturing Company

The statement that everyone must forge his own fortune is often only spoken as a platitude, and yet there are many cases where this is literally true. It is indeed true of Peter J. Pauly who in a double and literal sense forged his own fortune. With hammer and anvil, the fire of his forge, together with perseverance and honorable dealing he built for himself an establishment which is one of the largest and best known in the country. It began on a very small scale and the story of its development is, therefore, so much the more interesting.

Christian Pauly, the father of Peter J. and John Pauly, came from his Rhenish homeland near Coblenz, direct to St. Louis during the second half of the forties, to find for himself and his family a new home. In the old country he had followed the trade of a blacksmith. When his sons had reached the proper age they were placed as apprentices in Galy's smithy and foundry, which was at that time the largest in the city. In 1856 they started their own shop on Main and Wash Street. Their first customer was an Irish woman who lived in the neighborhood and who wanted to have a handle put on an old iron pot. Peter J. Pauly didn't want to charge her anything, but his father said that they would have to start sometime, so the first work netted them ten cents. This income was at once entered in the account book of the company. Even today, after nearly forty years, it is safely kept as valuable memorial in the fire-proof vault for future generations to contemplate. The first entries were made in the German language, till P. J. Pauly's wife, a young American, instructed her husband sufficiently in English orthography.

The proximity of the river brought it about that they soon did all sorts of work on steamboats. The extremely lively traffic on the river at that time induced them to devote themselves entirely to this kind of work. In a short time the Paulys were considered the best blacksmiths and had very much work to do. But times changed. In 1857 came a financial crisis over all of the United States. Paper money became badly devaluated. Then came the war which brought most businesses to a halt. Steamboating to the south was almost entirely suspended. At the close of the war conditions changed, and P. J. Pauly and Brother again had abundant work and looked cheerfully into the future. They took on large contracts but had to give too much credit and then could not raise the money to meet their expenses. Their own creditors pressed them for payment till there was nothing to do but to either declare themselves bankrupt or come to some agreement with their creditors to make complete payment after an extension of time. Somebody suggested that they should make settlement of payment of 25% of their obligation. This they indignantly rejected. In the course of ten years they paid all their obligations with accumulated interest to a cent. It may be added that this debt amounted to more than seventy thousand dollars.

In the meantime the constantly increasing number of railroads encroached considerably on steamboat traffic. The number of boats coming to and leaving the local landing became fewer from year to year. So Peter J. Pauly decided to make iron cells for county jails. The old cells were neither safe nor sanitary. It was in 1870 that the Paulys decided to make the change and from then on have devoted themselves entirely to this new branch of industry. Improvements have been continually added. His son, P. J. Pauly, Jr., was assigned to study architecture under the excellent St. Louis architect, Barnett, and young Pauly's ideas are incorporated in thousands of county jails from Maine to the Pacific Ocean and from Minnesota to the Gulf of Mexico and far up in Canada.

There is no state in the Union in which a number of counties have not entrusted the Pauly Jail Building and Manufacturing Company with the building or reconstruction or the inner arrangement of their prisons. Good work and good material brought their reward, so that at various times enlargement of the plant became necessary. The most telling proof of the acceptability of the product of this company is the number of contracts it received. In many states as many as fifty counties have installations from this organization. The state of Texas has one hundred and fifty such installations.

The factory is situated in the southern part of the city. It is close to the tracks of the Iron Mountain railroad, and since it is only two squares from the river, it has all desired facilities for receiving the iron and for shipping the finished articles to all parts of the United States. The factory buildings occupy half a block. All machines, tools and equipment are of the most modern construction. The supervision of the work is in charge of technical experts and only able workers are employed.

In 1880 P. J. Pauly, Jr. became a partner. However, his health had suffered from too close and continuous work that a change of climate seemed indicated. For this reason he spent almost eight years in the pure air of the Rocky Mountains. His absence imposed double duty on his father. This and the increase in business induced the firm in 1885 to proceed to become incorporated. From then on it was officially called The Pauly Jail Building and Manufacturing Company. Till 1889 P. J. Pauly, Sr. remained president of the company. Then he retired and his son became his worthy successor in office. Since 1885 J. J. Liggon has been vice president, though he was for many years prior to this date identified with the house. John Pauly is treasurer and E. C. Blackmar is secretary.

Peter J. Pauly must be considered a pioneer of a specialized branch of industry, in which he and his partners have achieved great success. He was also an inventor as a number of patents attest. His son, too, has been granted several patents on valuable inventions. Mr. Pauly, Sr. has not entirely retired to private life. He still spends a part of his time in his factory, and every year when his son must be absent from St. Louis for the summer months because of his health, the older man looks after the business with every detail of which he is still quite familiar. He is a highly respected citizen. He takes an active interest in all public affairs, and for four years was a member of our city council.

Griesedieck Artificial Ice Company

Geographic location, climate and conditions of temperature of St. Louis make the use of ice a necessity during the greater part of the year. From the middle of April to the beginning of November, ice is a real need which is dictated not only be the requirements of comfort but also by the demands of health. It is, therefore, to be regretted that in the use of ice the public in general manifests so little caution that they use a product which is actually injurious to health. Of the enormous quantity of ice which a metropolis uses the year through, only a relatively small amount is actually pure and wholesome, that is free of all impurities that injure health. Particularly harmful is the organic matter contained in the ice. Most of the ice sold here does not come from the lakes, but from the stagnant water of ponds or from pools full of all sorts of impurities. Such ice is put in pitchers filled with water. The ice dissolves and so all organisms contained in it are consumed.

In view of these facts the manufacture of artificial ice must be regarded a blessing to humanity. The inventors of the process are benefactors of the commonwealth. The method of producing such ice affords the most complete guarantee for its sanitary condition. Whoever wishes to convince himself of this fact needs only to visit the Griesedieck ice factory, which is in operation since 1890. The buildings are situated on the corner of Thirteenth and Papin Street. They cover an area of one hundred and sixty-four by one hundred and seventy-nine feet.

Two De la Vergne ice machines of newest construction furnish one hundred and fifty to one hundred and sixty tons of ice per day. The steam engine of eight hundred horsepower that serves the plant requires one and a half carloads of coal each day. In the summer months they are almost continually in use, in order to meet the ever increasing demand for the product of this factory. The water used for the ice is first distilled in giant boilers. The heat produced in this operation destroys every trace of organisms in the water. The ice that forms on rivers and ponds by natural cold contains germs of every sort, which are not killed by the freezing of the water, but are only in a state of suspended animation, which ceases the moment the ice melts, and are now ready to take up their battle against health, producing diseases of the most varied sort, and not infrequently causing death. Artificial ice is made from water that is boiled and evaporated. The steam is re-converted into water, which then is once more carefully filtered. In this way it cannot contain anything harmful to health. We speak of lake ice as being crystal clear. This expression is even more applicable to artificial ice.

The Griesedieck Artificial Ice Company was originally incorporated under the laws of the state of Missouri with a capital of one hundred thousand dollars. Since the operation increased very soon, an increase in capital was necessary. It was raised to two hundred thousand dollars and the expansion of the plant was at once undertaken. In order to simplify the work the ice is not delivered directly from the factory to the consumer, but is sold exclusively to ice dealers who at all times can obtain any amount of ice they desire thanks to the efficiency of the establishment.

Participants in the business are Anton Griesedieck and his sons Bernhard, Joseph and Henry Griesedieck and his son-in-law Robert Bauer. Anton Griesedieck is the president, R. Bauer is the vice president and B. Griesedieck is the treasurer.

Anton Griesedieck has been here for more than three decades. For many years he was head of a brewery. He is one of the best known and most respected German citizens of St. Louis.

In closing this ice chapter it is perhaps not amiss to point out a rather widely spread misunderstanding, and to correct same. Many people believe that the water used in the making of artificial ice comes in contact with chemicals in the process of freezing. But that is by no means the case, for the water is contained in tightly closed cases that are made of zinc. The fluid which produces the cold is in iron tubes, and even the cases and tubes do not come in direct contact with each other. The above assumption is therefore entirely without foundation.

Charles Ehlermann Hop and Malt Company

Malting is of course most closely associated with the brewing industry. As the latter industry increased, the former also grew. The number of malt-houses which did not belong to a brewery, and which sold their product to breweries in general, was in former times greater than it has been in the last decades. Now, with enlargement of the brewing establishments their requirement of malt is entirely or in great part provided by their own malt houses and their own personnel. But there are still a good many breweries that are dependent on the independent malt houses. As a result the latter continue to flourish.

The largest of the local malt firms is that of Ehlermann and has been such for a long time. Its founder, Charles Ehlermann, came to St. Louis near the end of the fifties. He came here as a very young man. After completing the course in one of the local business colleges he entered the service of Wattenberg, Busch and Company for practical mercantile experience. This firm dealt in hops. Under the guidance of such an experienced businessman, as his uncle, Ernest Wattenberg, young

Ehlermann in a short time gained extensive knowledge of things pertaining to the office as also the store rooms. His practical knowledge and experience was still further increased when, in 1862, the firm undertook the operation of a malt house located on Third and Plum Street (behind what was then Busch or Buena Vista Garden). In the middle of the sixties Wattenberg moved to New York, where since then he has headed a hop importing concern. From the time of Wattenberg's departure, Adolphus Busch and Company carried on the business, including the malt business, till in 1868 it was taken over by Charles Ehlermann and Company. In this new firm Charles Rueppele, who had been a bookkeeper with Busch and Company, became a partner. The new concern bought the malt house from the just mentioned company and operated it for thirteen years, from 1868 to 1881 in which latter year there occurred the construction of the present establishment and the transfer to it. Up to that time the office and storage of hops and brewing utensils had been on the west side of Main, between Market and Walnut Streets. A few years later Rueppele left the company and Philipp Karl acquired an interest in the firm. However, he severed his connection with it early, and since that time Charles Ehlermann has been the sole owner.

The move to the large new plant on Twenty-second and Scott Avenue, therefore close to the many tracks near the Union Depot, assured the required storing space, and necessary facilities, including those of receiving barley, hops, etc. and the shipment of malt, thus saving time and money.

In the six-story building, with its well-lighted airy rooms, the malt is carefully prepared from barley of the best quality. This grain comes from the most preferred barley regions of the west. Nine hundred bushels of barley are each day converted into malt. The trade territory of this firm for malt, as well as the hops which the firm handles, includes, of course, St. Louis and the state of Missouri, but also all western, southern and northern states, and toward the east its business extends as far as Pennsylvania, moreover to British Columbia, Old Mexico and some South American states. The hops are obtained from Oregon, the state of New York and Germany, particularly Bavaria, and from Bohemia.

The business of the Charles Ehlermann Hop and Malt Company has increased from year to year, and has required continual expansion of its facilities. Charles Ehlermann is untiringly busy in his plant, but also finds time to be interested in public affairs, and is a delightful companion.

Dodson-Hils Manufacturing Company

In no country in the world is the consumption of variously prepared pickles, catsup, mustard, horseradish and other table condiments so great as in America. This is definitely due to conditions of climate and temperature, since the consumption of most of these articles are especially beneficial to health in countries with this kind of climate. It is, therefore, not merely a matter of taste.

Since the Dodson-Hils Manufacturing Company is the largest establishment of this kind, not only in St. Louis but in the United States, a sketch of its development, its progress, accomplishment and expansion will be of more than ordinary interest.

The company was formed in 1881. From its origin the concern had only one aim –to make better goods than any other company which put such a product on the market.

At an early date it was seen that more space would be required by the company, so a three-story building was built which covers half a block. This plant is located on Third and Cedar Street. It is provided with the best equipment and most complete machinery. A special advantage, that can scarcely be valued too highly, is the fact that the elevated railway of the Merchants Terminal Company passes through the building.

The company manufactures every type of pickle in English and American style, as the market demands. Its vinegar factory, on Gratiot and Sixth Streets, has a capacity of twenty-thousand barrels a year. Its extensive salting establishments are located in Canton, Illinois and Carlinville, Illinois. Its grocery ware department includes catsups, mustard, spices, baking power, flavoring extracts, washing bluing, table and fruit syrup, honey and candies. These goods go to thirty-eight different states of the Union, and many are exported, particularly to South America.

The company employs two hundred and fifty workers, which draw a weekly total salary of two thousand dollars. Twenty traveling salesmen are continually on the road. The company's sales amounted to three quarters of a million dollars last year.

To acquaint the general public with its goods, the company arranges an elegant and attractive display each year at our great St. Louis exposition.

The officials of the company are: John Dodson, president; Edward Hils, secretary-treasurer. These two, together with Marquard Forster, Jr., and

William W. Price, constitute the directors. These men are assisted by Frederick C. Meyer, chief of the grocery-ware department, and Albert Hils and A. Dodson as superintendents of the extensive salting establishments in Canton and Carlinville.

Grone and Company, Sodawater, etc.

On this side of the ocean, soda water is such a popular beverage that many thousand factories in large and small cities are engaged in its manufacture. Here in St. Louis the largest and at the same time oldest sodawater factory is that of Grone and Company. It was established in 1851 by Henry Grone, on the very site where it is today, namely on South Eleventh, between Market and Walnut Street. Having started on a very small scale, it now prepares for sale during its busy season, that is from May to October, twelve hundred cases, each holding two dozen bottles, hence a total of twenty-eight thousand and eight hundred bottles per day. The plant works ten hours per day.

The factory building has a breadth of seventy feet and a depth of two hundred and ten feet. Its entire output is consumed in St. Louis, and so provides a considerable part of the local need. In addition to soda water other beverages are also made, as for example, sarsaparilla, cream soda, phosphates, ginger ale and others. For the delivery to customers, which, as already indicated, is limited to the city, eight teams and wagons are needed.

The owners of the business are Henry Grone and his two sons, Edward and Hermann.

Welle-Boettler Bakery Company

It is obvious that in a metropolis with a population such as St. Louis has, the bakery industry is very extensive. The number of local bakeries is very large. It is safe to say that there are two thousand of them. Among these are some really large establishments. One of the largest in St. Louis and in the entire west of the United States is the Welle-Boettler Bakery Company. Its business exceeds that of all other steam bakeries of the city.

Albert F. Welle, the founder, came here in 1867. Soon he was engaged in selling flour to retailers. He was quite successful. In his daily business he met with the owners of bakeries in all parts of the city, observed them at work, and presently decided to open a bakery on a large scale. To this end he bought in 1874 an already operating bakery on Twenty-second and Biddle Street. Five years later he disposed of this bakery to continue operations at a new site, on Morgan, between Seventh and Eighth Street. This change proved to be advantageous. He now sold to retailers, grocers, wholesalers, and his own retail business in the immediate surroundings also increased.

From the outset Adolph Boettler and H. Ruhe had been employed by Welle. After the move to Morgan Street they became partners and from 1879 the firm was known as the A. F. Welle and Company.

The concern operates with the best of machinery. Two large gas engines furnish the power. The two-story building covers six building lots. All the operations are under one roof. The plant which is situated at 708 to 718 Morgan Street, has a front of one hundred and twenty-five feet and a depth of one hundred and five feet.

In 1884 the company was incorporated with fully paid up capital of thirty-five thousand dollars. The original organization with A. F. Welle as president, H. Ruhe as vice president and A. Boettler as secretary-treasurer has continued unchanged.

Albert F. Welle was only nineteen years old when he came to St. Louis from Dissen near Osnabrueck. Prior to emigrating he had been employed in a mercantile concern in Bielefeld. Adolph Boettler, his brother-in-law, came here in 1865 from Rhenish Bavaria. He was then eleven years old. With A. Wiebusch and Company he learned the book-binding business, and worked at it till twenty years ago he exchanged that trade for the bakery business. Henry Ruhe came from Westphalia. By trade he was a cabinet maker. Soon after his arrival here he gave up that occupation, and in 1874 began to work for the concern in question.

Postscript: The preceding was already in the printer's hands when on August 8 of this year (1893) Albert F. Welle died after a brief illness. He was only forty-five years old. The Welle-Boettler Bakery Company will continue as before.

R. H. Follenius Marble Works

From time immemorial people have erected memorials for their dead. A metropolis like St. Louis with its many cemeteries naturally gives employment to many workshops that make gravestones. One of these, the one owned by Reinhold H. Follenius, we wish to discuss briefly here.

Reinhold H. Follenius is the descendent of one of the oldest German families that emigrated to Missouri. He is the son of the well-known Paul Follenius who was born in Giessen in 1799, who, in spite of his youth, participated in the war of liberation in 1814 and 1815, then studied law in his native city and practiced his profession, till in 1831 he organized the Giessen Emigration Society. In 1834 he emigrated for the United States with a company that had among its numbers such men as Frederick Muench and Gert Goebel. He settled at once in Missouri, where he died on his farm near Marthasville in 1844. As a pronounced anti-slavery man, he published a unique paper, called *Die Waage* (*The Balance*). However, it appeared only for a short time. Early in life his son had manifested pronounced aptitude for drawing. In the first half of the sixties he established a business of his own. Till 1870 he had his workshop on the southwest corner of Fifth Street and Chouteau Avenue. In that year he moved it a bit farther west to 508 and 510 Chouteau Avenue, where it has remained.

The inscriptions of the gravestones are exceptionally fine. It does not make any difference in what language they are desired. Of the many monuments that have come from the Follenius workshop at least a few may be mentioned: that of A. O'Sullivan, the former Grand Secretary of the Free Masons of Missouri, in the Belle fountain cemetery, which was ordered by the Missouri Grand Lodge; that at the grave of Pastor Dr. Hugo Krebs in the old Picker Cemetery; that of the dentist, Dr. Dienst, and of Dr. Fritz in the new Picker cemetery; that of George Fritz, and the Schumacher family vault in St. Mark's cemetery; that of August Reimler and Gustav F. Haenschen in St. Matthew's; that of the A. B. Maier family, of Albert Fischer, of B. Heyfinger and others in the Mt. Sinai cemetery.

Upon the insistence of Colonel Charles G. Stifel, who was an eager advocate of cremation, lately a columbiarium of special beauty in style and execution is being constructed. It is made entirely of Italian marble and eastern granite. All the work is under the personal supervision and active participation of the owner.

Mr. Follenius recently made an invention after long experimentation. This is likely to bring about a complete revolution in the making of inscriptions on gravestones, etc. He discovered a method of making inscriptions which are completely protected from the weather. Neither heat nor cold, moisture nor dust, nor time can have an effect on such inscriptions. This invention consists of glass plates, inside of which are the inscriptions that are produced by a method known only to the inventor. It is protected by another glass plate superimposed on it. This is of the greatest transparency and suitable thickness. Thus it protects the inscription from atmospheric influences. The letters are in this manner contained in a completely air tight space. They can be made in any desired color, gold, silver, etc. A reflector placed between the two glass plates causes the whole to shine in indescribable brilliance. This art of inscription is also excellently suited for advertising signs. They can be put at low cost and without any trouble, on the wood, stone or metal of a wall, where they are tightly held by a metal frame. The inventor has secured a patent and there is every reason to expect good returns from the invention.

August Gast Banknote and Lithographing Company

The series of eminent representatives of various branches of industry to which the preceeding pages are devoted, can certainly have no worthier conclusion than by giving the story of the August Gast Banknote and Lithographing Company from its origin to the present time.

The brothers Leopold and August Gast, the founders of the business that can justly claim to be the largest of its kind, came to St. Louis in 1852. They came from the principality of Lippe Detmold, had received a good education in the Detmold Gymnasium, and then had been trained to become lithographers. They understood their work thoroughly. In 1848 they decided to emigrate to America where they hoped they might have a better chance to follow their trade. That same year they arrived in New York where they stayed a short while. Then they worked for a few years in Pittsburgh, after which they turned to St. Louis where they made their permanent home. They had only small means, but Leopold Gast brought with him a lithographing press and the necessary accessories for the profession. His brother, on the other hand, brought only his skill and professional knowledge. Where today the Southern Hotel stands, they opened a small business on Fourth Street. The work they did was of good quality and soon the number of customers increased. Now they moved to larger quarters on Fourth near Olive Street. After some time they transferred their business to the upper story on the northeast corner of Third and Olive Street. In 1866 Leopold sold his share in the business to his brother, August, and from this time on the firm was known as the August Gast and Company. Once more the concern moved. This time to Third Street on the corner of Walnut Street. It was in the year 1876 that the great development of the business really began.

In the just-cited year, E. F. Wittler, who till then had been a traveling salesman, and L. J. W. Wall, who had grown up in the business, became partners of the concern. The energy and activity which these men manifested made itself felt immediately. They devoted much energy to securing new customers in the city as well as out of the city. An increase of facilities had to be provided and this was found at 216 and 218 Locust Street. At this time the firm employed twenty-six persons. Two years later, in 1878, the number had been increased to a hundred. In the same year James McKittrick and Company were compelled to give up their extensive business. This gave Gast and Company the opportunity, not only to buy their entire lithographic equipment, but also to move into their large place of business on the east side of Third Street, between Olive and Locust Street. Here the prosperity of the firm increased rapidly. However, in 1880 a fire destroyed the whole establishment. In spite of this the work of the firm was interrupted only for three days, when it was resumed in a leased location. Four weeks later the firm moved into a three-story building at 217 and 219 Pine Street. This, too, did not prove large enough, so two stories were added, while in the three stories below business was transacted as usual. But here also the demon of fire inflicted injury another time. In 1882 practically the entire interior of the building was destroyed. Fortunately the adjoining five-story building was available. Operations were transferred into this while the other building was repaired.

In 1885 August Gast withdrew from the business, having sold his share to his two partners, Wittler and Wall. The following year Wittler also withdrew, selling his share. He moved to Seattle, Washington, where he became a street railway magnate.

The products of the firm were sold to all states of the west and the south. As business increased it was decided to build a plant that was specifically designed for lithographic and steel engraving work. This building on the south side of Morgan Street, corner of Twenty-first Street was moved into in 1887. The business has been there ever since. The number of employees is more than two hundred and fifty. The firm has the most complete equipment and modern machinery. It furnishes every kind of engraving in stone or steel, from the largest picture to the smallest etiquette, from a bond with so and so many coupons, to a visiting card, any kind of work. It is all done most carefully and at the same time in the best of taste. The firm has established a branch business in New York City, which branch has assumed the same dimensions as the St. Louis house. The growth can be attributed to the business acumen of President Wall.

The company has a paid-up capital of two hundred and seventy-five thousand dollars. The officials are L. J. W. Wall, president; O. D. Gray, vice president; P. F. Van der Lippe, secretary.

Of the original founders of the business, August Gast passed away at the age of seventy. His older brother, Leopold Gast still enjoys good health. Both were without doubt able in their profession, but it was younger forces that joined the business, which gave the impulse that made the firm great.

St. Louis Agricultural and Mechanical Association

Expositions at which local industrialists and manufacturers showed their goods all under one roof were known in St. Louis as early as the thirties and forties. However, these occurred at irregular intervals, often several years apart, and now in this and then in that building. There were also agricultural and livestock exhibits. This was known as the St. Louis County Fair. In the middle of the fifties the first steps were taken to hold the two exhibits in the future at the same time, and every year. For this purpose a company was formed, which in 1855 received its charter from the state legislature, under the name of the St. Louis Agricultural and Mechanical Association. It was organized with the following directors: Andrew Harper, Thomas T. January, Henry C. Hart, John Whitnell, Thornton Grimsley, Frederick Dings, James M. Hughes, Henry S. Turner, Charles L. Hunt, John M. Chambers, Henry T. Blow, Norman J. Coleman and J. R. Barret. The following were chosen officers of the board of directors: J. R. Barret as president, Th. Grimsley, A. Harper and H. C. Hart as vice presidents, Henry S. Turner as treasurer, A. W. Collet as corresponding secretary and G. O. Kalb as recording secretary and business manager. The latter continued in this position for nearly thirty years, and the great success of the St. Louis Fair, (by which name it is known in the whole United States) may justly be ascribed to him. In addition to serving as secretary, Kalb is also superintendent of the zoological garden. Sixty thousand dollars of stock found ready buyers. So many desired to buy that on the average only two shares, each at fifty dollars, were sold to a buyer. The income from the sale of shares was used in large part for the erection of buildings and landscaping of fifty acres that were bought for the fairgrounds. The land did not have to be paid for at once but payments were made over a series of years.

The land was situated on Grand Avenue and the Natural Bridge Plankroad, and formed the nucleus of the present fairgrounds, which were considerably enlarged by the further purchases of land, and the race track with the fairgrounds club buildings adjoining. The first fair was held in October 1856. Financially it was very successful. In fact it became better from year to year, till the war brought an unwished-for interruption. The fairgrounds were changed to a military camp, especially for the cavalry. Among others Benton's Hussars were encamped there for some time. For five years there was no fair, and not until 1866 was the old order restored. Since then the fair has been held each year during the first week of October. Each year there is a migration of people to attend the fair. On each of the six days an average of some forty thousand people attend. During the first years the exposition buildings consisted of one structure which was used for the display of the products of the soil, including fruit, one for machines and agricultural implements, and a third for the products of industry, and there were also a few smaller buildings. At the very outset an arena was arranged which is surrounded by an amphitheater which had a circumference of nine hundred feet. The arena serves for the display of flowers and potted plants, etc. Also a hall for carriages was added, moreover, a poultry hall, which contained ninety compartments for birds. There was also an administration building and another with parlors for ladies. The proximity of the city waterwork was one of the factors that was decisive in the choice of this particular piece of land. For, in the first place, there had to be sufficient water for the watering of the livestock, and then also on account of the plantings and the landscape gardening, which constituted one of the main attractions. The terrain for these plantings was very advantageous. It presented a very great variety, and what nature had not done that the skill of the landscape gardener did, which by and by created a little paradise.

It was not the intention of the stockholders to derive dividends from the investment. Rather it was the purpose to apply all income from the investment to further improvement and beautifying of the place. This maxim has since been adhered to. The stockholders were content to have free admission to the grounds for their families throughout the year. In this manner almost all the income, most of which came from gate admissions, could be expended for the expansion and beautifying of the grounds. In harmony with this plan, in the course of time, a new amphitheater, much larger than the original one, was built. Its circumference is fifteen hundred feet. The race track adjoining is a half-mile long. Also a much larger industrial hall, and an arts building with twenty-thousand square feet of space, and also more room for other industrial branches were provided. The building of the House of Comfort contributed much to make the fairgrounds an attractive place to come to at other times than during fair week. In 1876 it was decided to add a zoological garden. This plan was put into action without delay. Secretary Kalb was entrusted with its supervision. He corresponded with Hagenbeck in Hamburg, the dealer in animals, and personally looked after the transportation of the animals from New York here. The buildings for the housing of the animals, the bear pit, etc. were planned and constructed without consideration of cost. The result was that they became a permanent ornament of the place.

Thursday had always been considered the main day of the fair. A proclamation of the mayor made it an official holiday, on which all city offices, the courts, the banks, most factories and businesses, and also the schools were closed. In some years the number of visitors on this day exceeded seventy thousand. On fair Thursday in 1860 the then-very-young Prince of Wales was among the visitors.

By further purchases of land the original fifty acres were increased to eighty-three, at a total cost of one hundred thousand dollars, and the improvements in the form of buildings, parking and landscaping, etc., from the time of organization have cost an expenditure of one and a half million dollars. The presidents of the association have in turn been: J. R. Barret, A. Harper, Charles Todd, Arthur B. Barret, Julius S. Walsh and Charles Green, whose successor is the present incumbent, Rolla Wells, who has headed the organization since 1891.

Rolla Wells, of whom we have spoken in another chapter in connection with the street railways which he managed, took over the management of the Fair Association with the determination to expand the field of operation as much as possible. And that is exactly what he succeeded in doing. In the first place he proceeded to make the fairgrounds an even more popular meeting place of the public by arranging really good concerts, as for example those of the Symphony Society under director Otten. The main interest, however, was the horse races which were held on the race track of the fairgrounds under the auspices of the St. Louis Fairground Club which was closely allied with the association. The spring races, which begin in the middle of June and continue for forty-eight days, and the fall races that begin at the end of August and extend through the week of the fair. The strictest adherence to the rules of the turf, the conscientious business management and the maintenance of the strictest order have created for these races an honorable name in the whole country, and assures the regular participation of the most prominent race horse owners on this side of the ocean. The number of spectators which come from great distances has increased from year to year, and from the city itself thousands flock to the grounds on days when races are scheduled. The club house is regarded as the most beautiful of its kind in the whole Union. The members and their families (sons only to their twenty-first year) have at all times free admission to the fairgrounds, to the club rooms and to all races. Among the roster of members are the most prominent names, not only of the city, but also of the state, and the quota of members is nearly full.

The present directors of the Fair Association and of the Fairground Club are: Rolla Wells, president, L. M. Rumsey, Ellis Wainwright, Alvah Mansur, first, second and third vice presidents, respectively, A. B. Ewing, treasurer, Julius S. Walsh, C. C. Maffitt, Richard Kerens, C. H. Turner, W. F. Nolker, D. R. Francis, Charles Green, and John W. Turner. William M. Lockwood is the secretary of the association and of the club.

The St. Louis Agricultural and Mechanical Association has rendered great service to agricultura and industry during nearly forty years of its existence by awarding of premiums, medals and diplomas, by which it has again and again stimulated competition among exhibitors, and it has brought benefit to the whole city by attracting large numbers of strangers during the fair week. There is indeed nothing in the United States like the

St. Louis Fair, and it is one of the most worthwhile institutions in this great country.

St. Louis Exposition and Music Hall Association

St. Louis is the only city in the United States in which each year an industrial and art exposition of the highest caliber takes place, for which purpose a special and magnificent building has been provided. The geographic location of St. Louis, its river and railroad connections make it the trade center of the Mississippi valley, the focus for the extensive commercial traffic with the west, the southwest, and a great part of the south. This extensive territory is supplied from here with goods of every kind. This alone would make our city the most suitable place for such an exposition. With the erection of an exposition building, therefore, the industrialists of this part of the country were given the opportunity to meet an already existing demand.

The St. Louis Exposition and Music Hall Association was organized in 1882, but it required considerable time till all doubts were removed that Missouri Park, which was selected for the proposed building, could be used for anything else but for park purposes. The park had been given to St. Louis by James H. Lucas. It required the consent of the city and also that of Lucas' heirs to use it for any other purpose. This consent was finally obtained in the summer of 1883. The park which was bordered by Thirteenth, Fourteenth, Olive and St. Charles Streets disappeared and on its site there is now one of the most imposing buildings that St. Louis has to exhibit. Ground was broken on August 22, 1883, and in less than a year the structure and its inner arrangement was completed.

A correct notion of the massive buildings can be obtained from the following facts. Sixty thousand cubic yards of earth had to be excavated for the foundation. The front of the building is three hundred and thirty-eight feet wide and the depth is four hundred and thirty-eight feet and the height is one hundred and eight feet. Nine million bricks and six hundred tons of iron were used in the construction which exhibits the greatest solidity in all its parts. The building stands unobstructed on all sides. Its front, with its wide steps stands far enough back from the street to allow the building to appear in its entire beauty.

The exhibition rooms extend over the two two-storied wings and over the entire ground floor, and have a surface of two hundred and eighty square feet. Moreover, the building contains one large and one small music hall. The dimensions of the former are two hundred feet in length, one hundred and twenty feet in width and eighty feet in height. It has a seating capacity of four thousand while the stage has room for fifteen hundred persons. The smaller hall, which has a separate entrance from the outside, is one hundred and sixty feet long and sixty-four feet wide. It has seats for fifteen hundred. Vestibule and corridors are of suitable dimensions. The stairways on the interior are wide and comfortable, all rooms are high, well-lighted and airy. In the evening they can be illuminated with more than three thousand electric bulbs and one hundred and sixty arc lights, all of which are supplied with electricity from a dynamo in the building. As a precaution against fire and explosions the boiler house is on the other side of the street and the steam is conducted to the exposition building in conduits that pass under the street.

Since most of the exhibited machinery is shown in actual operation, the necessary power has to be provided. This is furnished by a large, two hundred and fifty horsepower Corliss steam engine, moreover by a Watertown Automatic Machine of one hundred horsepower, and eight others that have between twenty-five to one hundred and fifty horsepowers. For the distribution of power contrivances are provided which transmit the fifteen hundred horsepowers. The above-mentioned boiler house has four Heine Safety Boilers with a normal capacity of two hundred and fifty horsepowers each, but which can be considerably increased, and which can change thirty-six hundred gallons of water into steam every hour. In order to be able to show visitors how the pumps on exhibition actually work, there is in the machine room of the exhibition hall a basin that holds thirty thousand gallons of water.

The first board of directors under whose management the building was erected consisted of the following members: Charles H. Turner, R. S. Brookings, John T. Davis, E. O. Stanard, Joseph Franklin, R. S. Hayes, D. M. Houser, E. C. Simmons, Samuel Kennard, H. V. Lucas, R. M. Scruggs, Ellis Wainwright, and A. D. Brown. The officers were: S. M. Kennard - president, E. O. Stanard - vice president, R. M. Scruggs - treasurer, and H. V. Lucas - secretary. These men had the satisfaction, that, in spite of the relatively short time of preparation, the exposition which opened on

September 3, 1884, was a distinct success, and clearly demonstrated that the undertaking met with the approval of exhibitors as well as the public at large. The various branches of trade and industry were so well represented at the exposition that every inch of space was taken. The great variety which the exhibit contained drew the visitors in such decisive a manner that the public eagerly looked forward to the next exposition. Since then the company has very wisely been able to keep this interest alive. Great care was taken to provide for the comfort of visitors. As an added attraction it was decided to furnish excellent concerts on every afternoon and evening in the great music hall. During the first year the arsenal band from the Jefferson Barracks was engaged. The next year Gilmore's famous band was hired and for years it formed one of the real attractions, so that when this great director unexpectedly died, after one day's illness, at the 1892 exposition, there was great anxiety regarding his successor. Last spring Sousa's new Marine Band, whose director had for twelve years conducted the United States Marine Band in Washington, D. C. gave a few concerts here while on tour through the west. Because this band was so well received here, as everywhere else, it was engaged for the next exposition. Now there is no doubt that no wiser choice could have been made, and that the concerts in the future will meet with the same approval as in the past, and that the concerts will continue to be an essential contribution to the exposition.

In the matter of the development of machinery, as everyone knows, America leads all other countries, in construction as well as application. In keeping with this fact, the exhibit of machinery from the outset has been most extensive and interesting. This applies not only to the expert but to the layman as well. The greater part of the machines are in actual operation and so are especially interesting to the visitors. During the first years, farm machinery and farm tools were not included in the exhibition, because the management felt that the manufacturers would prefer to show them on the fairgrounds. But interested parties desired to have a part in the exposition, and since then agricultural machinery and implements are a part of the exhibit.

Especially it was the aim to make the exposition attractive by offering the best in music. How successfully this has worked out from the first to the last day of the exposition is shown by the fact that the large music hall was each evening filled to the last seat.

In this great hall which offers more space than any other auditorium in the city, during the other times of the year, German and American operas by New York companies have been sung. This has shown all music lovers of what great value the exposition building is also in the matter of music. This was fully recognized by local music organizations such as the Musical Union, the Choral Society, and by the Symphony Society. The smaller entertainment hall likewise renders valuable service in this direction.

It was the happy choice on the part of the directors when they, in 1889, made Frank Gaiennie the general manager, and thus assured for the undertaking a businesslike head. He proved to be quite equal to the difficult task, and applies his immense energy to maintaining the exposition at a high level, giving new attractions and continually making it known in the widest circles. The success that has been attained is an eloquent testimonial to his circumspection and energy.

During the past forty years St. Louis has become the gathering place of thousands of visitors of this state, from neighboring states from the west and southwest, who come to its exposition, to its unique autumn festival, which consists of the unique illumination of his principal streets, its procession and ball of the Veiled Prophet, also its fair, and various other entertainments of this season. There is no other city in the United States that can show anything like it.

The exposition attracts the interest of strangers more than anything else. They can stay in the exposition building the whole day long, from the hour of opening at eight o'clock in the morning till ten-thirty in the evening, all for the one admission price of twenty-five cents. They can attend the afternoon and evening concerts. In Tony Faust's restaurant which is in the basement, they can have a meal any hour of the day. This is something that many St. Louisans are accustomed to do.

The present directors have E. O. Stanard as their president; T. B. Boyd as their first and C. H. Turner as their second vice-president; Richard M. Scruggs as their treasurer; Charles Nagel as their secretary and E. P. Davis as assistant secretary. Other directors are Samuel M. Kennard, L. D. Kingland, L. Methudy, C. H. Sampson, B. Nugent, Ellis Wainwright, H. C. Townsend, and D. M. Houser. The undertaking, so important for St. Louis and the whole Mississippi Valley is in the best of hands. It is a permanent institution, or as the Americans say: "It has come to stay."

IV. Selective Bibliography

I. The following bibliographies deal with German-American history and should be consulted for additional works dealing with the German element and heritage of St. Louis:

Arndt, Karl J. R. and May E. Olson. *The German Language Press of the Americas*. (Munchen: K. G. Saur, 1973ff).

Pochmann, Henry. *Bibliography of German Culture in America to 1940*. Rev. and corrected edition by Arthur R. Schultz. (Milwood, NY: Kraus, 1982).

Schultz, Arthur R. *German-American Relations and German Culture in America: A Subject Bibliography, 1941-1980*. (Millwood, NY: Kraus, 1984).

Tolzmann, Don Heinrich. *Catalog of the German-Americana Collection, University of Cincinnati*. (Munchen: K. G. Saur, 1990).

_____ *German-Americana: A Bibliography*. (Metuchen, NJ: Scarecrow Pr., 1975).

II. The following is a selection of various works dealing with various aspects of the German heritage of St. Louis and Missouri:

Bachhuber, Claire Marie. *The German-Catholic Elite: Contributions of a Catholic Intellectual and Culture Elite of German-American Background in Early Twentieth Century St. Louis*. (Ph.D. Diss., St. Louis University, 1984).

Baepler, Walter August. *A Century of Grace: A History of The Missouri Synod, 1847-1947*. (St. Louis: Concordia Publishing House, 1947).

Blumenthal, Fred A. *The German Romantic Movement in Music in St. Louis*. (Ph.D. Diss., Washington University, 1983).

Boernstein, Heinrich. *Memories of a Nobody: The Missouri Years of an Austrian Radical, 1848-1866.* Translated and edited by Steven Rowan. (Columbia: Missouri Historical Society, 1997).

_____. *The Mysteries of St. Louis: A Novel,* Translated by Friedrich Munch and edited by Steven Rowan and Elizabeth Sims. (Chicago: Kerr, 1990).

Burnett, Robyn & Ken Luebbering. *German Settlement in Missouri: New Land/Old Ways.* (Columbia: University of Missouri Pr., 1996).

Detjen, David W. *The Germans in Missouri, 1900-1918: Prohibition, Neutrality and Assimilation.* (Columbia; University of Missouri Pr., 1985).

Engle, Stephen Douglas. *The Yankee Dutchman: The Life of Franz Sigel.* (Fayetteville: University of Arkansas Pr., 1993).

Graebner, Alan N. *The Acculturation of an Immigrant Lutheran Church: The Lutheran Church-Missouri Synod, 1917-1929.* (Ph.D., Diss., 1965).

Hernon, Peter. *Under the Influence: The Unauthorized Story of the Anheuser-Busch Dynasty.* (New York: Simon & Schuster, 1991).

Hofacker, Erich. *German Literature as Reflected in the German-Language Press of St. Louis Prior to 1898.* (St. Louis: Washington University Pr., 1946).

Kampfhoefner, Walter D. *The Westfalians: From Germany to Missouri* (Princeton: Princeton University Pr., 1987).

Krebs, Roland. *Making Friends Is Our Business: 100 Years of Anheuser-Busch.* (St. Louis, 1953).

Mallinckrodt, Anita M. *From Knights to Pioneers: One German Family in Westphalia and Missouri.* (Carbondale: Southern Illinois University Pr., 1994).

_____. *How They Came: German Immigration from Prussia to Missouri.* (Augusta, MO: Mallinckrodt Communications Research, 1988).

Muhl, Eduard. *Travels of a German-American Newspapers Man: Eduard Muhl's Letters to His Wife, Pauline, 1842 and 1848.* (Iowa City, 1977).

Olson, Aubrey L. *St. Louis Germans, 1850-1920: The Nature of an Immigrant Community and Its Relations to the Assimilation Process.* (New York: Arno Pr., 1980).

Padberg, Daniel L. *German Ethnic Theater in Missouri: Cultural Assimilation.* (Ph.D. Diss., Southern Illinois University, 1980).

Rothensteiner, John Ernest. *Die literarische Wirksamkeit der deutsch-amerikanischen Katholiken: eine literarische Skizze.* (St. Louis: Herausgegeben von der Schriftleitung der "Amerika," 1922).

Rowan, Steven, ed. *Germans for A Free Missouri: Translations from the St. Louis Radical Press, 1857-1862.* (Columbia: University of Missouri Pr., 1983).

Schroeder, Adolf E. and Carla Schulz-Geisberg, eds., *Hold Dear, As Always: Jette, A German Immigrant Life in Letters.* (Columbia; University of Missouri Pr., 1988).

Tolzmann, Don Heinrich. *German-American Literature.* (Metuchen, NJ: Scarecrow Pr., 1977).

Tucker, Marlin T. *Political Leadership in the Illinois-Missouri German Community, 1836-1872.* (Ph.D. Diss., University of Illinois, 1968).

Index

Abbath, Theodore, 163, 176
Abeles, Adolph, 207, 250
Able, B., 241
Able, Barton, 235
Abt, Franz, 170
Achenbach, Hermann, 111, 178
Acuzena, 62, 85
Adam, Mrs., 197
Adam, Paul, 116
Addicks, Dick, 10
Adelmann, Carl, 220
Adler, Julia, 127
Ahlfeld, 183
Ahrens, Thomas, 227
Ahrens, William, 225
Alexander, 114, 134, 305
Allen, Thomas, 20, 49, 65, 100, 129, 146, 150, 246, 247, 250
Allerhausen, August, 223
Alles, Henry J., 120, 121
Allison, Brainard, 251
Amann, Jacob, 161
Amberg, 188
Ambs, Peter, 110, 150
Amelung, John H., 138, 145
Ames, Henry, 108
Anderson, 162
Andrew, John H., 119
Angelbeck, 34
Angelbeck, Frederick, 197, 198
Angelrodt, 6, 156
Angelrodt, Ernest, 248
Anheuser, Eberhard, 58, 146, 189

Anheuser-Busch, 146
Anschuetz, Carl, 166
Anton, Gottlieb, 173
Anton, Lina, 170, 173
Anton, P. G., 66, 158, 161, 173, 174
Archer, James, 102
Arendes, Frederick, 131
Arendes, Fritz, 113, 136
Arendes, Joseph, 113
Armstrong, D. H., 244
Arndt, Karl J. R., 335
Arnold, 65, 78
Arnold, Henry, 78
Arnot, Andrew, 101, 103
Arnot, Jesse, 101, 103
Ascher, Julius, 181
Ashley, O. D., 254
Aszmannshaeuser, 12
Auer, Andrew, 152
Augst, G. A. W., 30
Augustin, Edward, 139
Auler, 194
Avery, 66
Axt, 114
Axtmann, 186
Babo, A. Freiherr von, 281
Babo, Freiherr von, 301
Bach, A. W., 175
Bach, Louis, 28
Bachhuber, Claire Marie, 335
Bachmann, Hermann, 150
Backer, George H., 265
Backer, Mathias, 264, 265
Bacon, 93

Baepler, Walter August, 335
Baer, 138, 189
Baer, Isaak, 138
Baerens, A. F., 167
Baerndorf, von, 182
Bailey & Co., 98
Balatka, Hans, 47, 173
Ballmann, Max, 162
Balmer, Charles, 53, 54, 155-161, 168, 195
Balmer, Mrs. Charles, 155, 156
Baltzer, 200, 201
Bamberger, Georg, 51
Bamberger, John, 22, 99
Bamberger, Phillip, 99, 106
Bandissin, 13
Bang, Adolph, 7, 131
Bang, Charles, 79, 135
Bang, George, 191
Bang, William, 131
Bar, Ben de, 54, 88, 95, 96, 112, 156, 162, 166, 169, 178
Barada, 98
Barclay, 218
Bardenheier, Philipp, 37
Barlow, Stephen D., 153, 250
Barnes, Robert A., 244
Barnett, 73, 256, 314
Barney, 69
Barney, Ludwig, 55, 188
Barnum, Hotel, 17, 52, 85, 286
Barnum, Phineas, 13, 82, 115, 116, 158
Barnum, Theron, 13
Barr, 55, 73, 90, 134
Barr, William, 55
Barret, Arthur B., 327

Barret, J. R., 325, 327
Barry, James G., 100
Bartels, 199
Barth, Mrs. Robert, 156
Barth, Robert, 5, 6, 196
Barthels, Louis, 217
Bartmann, S., 18
Bartram, 132
Baston, 255
Bates, Julian, 68
Bauchholz, 199
Bauer, 293
Bauer, Charles, 94
Bauer, Ferdinad, 293-295
Bauer, Ferdinand, 293
Bauer, Joseph A., 122
Bauer, Robert, 317
Bauer-Walter, 294
Baumann, L., 61, 113
Baumeister, Billy, 85
Baumgaertner, 68
Baumgarten, 120, 189
Bausemer, Anna, 169
Bausemer, Franz, 169
Bechtner, William, 71
Beck, Dr., 190
Beck, Frederick, 218
Beck, Louis, 111
Beck, Sylvester, 114
Becker, Carl, 162
Becker, Charles, 222
Becker, Emil A., 228
Becker, Francis P., 128, 221, 222
Becker, Fritz, 145
Becker, G., 166
Becker, John, 127
Becker, Louis, 222

Becker-Grahn, Antonie, 11, 48, 181
Beckmann, Charles, 127
Beckmann, Edward, 47
Beckmann, William, 47
Beckwith, 144
Beckwith, Tullia, 144
Beecher, Henry Ward, 69
Beets, 184
Behne, Ernest, 119
Behr, 17
Behrens, C., 171
Behrens, Frederick S., 109, 210
Behringer, John, 25
Beinert, Frederick, 166
Bek, William G. , v
Belcher, 312
Belcher, William H., 249
Bell, Henry, 68
Bellstedt, Bernhard, 44
Belt, 98
Bemisch, 46
Bender, 6, 128
Bender, George, 10
Bender, P. A., 166
Benecke, 114
Benig, L., 227
Benkendorf, Oswald, 142, 178
Bennecke, Robert, 284
Bennet, L. A., 217
Benson, 94
Benton, 326
Bentzen, U. F. W., 207, 211, 212, 216
Benz, 196
Benzinger, Conrad, 18
Berg, Nicholaus, 225, 226
Berg, Peter W., 135
Berg, Prof., 164
Berger, Peter, 43
Bergesch, 196
Bergesch, Frederick, 207
Bergesch, J. F., 196
Bergg, S., 166
Bergner, Walter, 114
Bermann, Carl, 160
Bernays, Carl Ludwig, 25, 173
Bernays, George, 120, 193, 285
Berne, G. J., 163
Bernecker, J. L., 228
Berthold, 67, 68
Besch, 152
Beschestobil, 197
Bessehl, Emil, 70, 106
Beyer, 44
Biddle, 33, 204
Biddle, Anna, 204
Biebinger, F. W., 28, 30
Biebinger, Oscar L., 271
Biedenstein, 127
Biedermann, 137
Biermann, H. H., 210
Bierwirth, 194
Binder, Henry, 110, 112
Bircher, Rudolph, 107
Birkmann, Frank, 223
Bischoff, Ferdinand, 106
Bishop, Anna, 160
Bismarck, Chancellor, 195
Bismarck, Leo, 195
Bissing, Theodore, 222, 225
Blackmar, E. C., 315
Blair, Frank P., 86, 88, 93, 217
Blakesly, 23

Blanche, 95
Blank, Oscar, 194
Blanke, 118
Blankenhorn, Jacob, 18
Blattau, Charles F., 134
Blattner, Jacob, 116, 196
Blind, Charles, 137
Block, Fritz, 227
Block, H., 119
Block, J. C. H. D., 30, 196
Block, John C. H. D., 4
Bloebaum, 198
Bloebaum, H., 198
Bloecher, Christian, 225
Blow, Henry T., 92, 325
Blow, Susie, 92
Blumenthal, Fred A., 335
Blumentritt, 33
Boatmen, 7, 20, 56, 94
Bode, Karl, 169
Bodemann, Henry, 11
Bodemann's Grove, 11
Boeck, Adam, 76
Boeckler, 34
Boehl, 52
Boehl, E., 172
Boehm, Christoph, 164
Boehm, Frank, 38, 133, 163, 164
Boehme, John, 173, 174
Boehmen, Franz, 162, 163, 176
Boehmer, 197
Boehnz, Frank, 38
Boernstein, 160
Boernstein, August Siegmund, 117
Boernstein, Heinrich, 336

Boernstein, Henry, 24, 25, 39, 93, 95, 113, 117, 179, 180, 188, 190
Boernstein, Lina, 179
Boernstein, Marie, 179
Boesewetter, 192
Boesewetter, R., 210, 225
Boetger, F., 227
Boettler, Adolph, 321
Bogy, Julia, 62
Bogy, Lewis V., 62, 249, 250
Bohlen, John, 171
Bohlmann, H., 174
Bohn, H., 7
Boisliniere, 108
Boll, 196
Bolland, John, 14, 217
Bollinger, J. R., 225, 228, 229
Bollmann, 66, 161
Bondi, Rudolph, 176
Bonnet, 52, 179
Bonnet, Frederich, 163
Booth, 98
Booth, J. W., 95
Borch, Edward, 171, 172
Bordogni, 175
Borgia, Lucretia, 60, 85, 169
Borgmann, Henry, 224
Bork, 216
Bornmueller, Albert, 165, 225
Boshold, 103
Bosse, Louis, 193
Botz, Johann, 187
Boyd, T. B., 332
Boyle, 270
Brachvogel, Udo, 39, 44, 173
Brady, Vicar General, 75

Braeutigam, 199
Brambilla, Emily, 185
Bramsch, C. W., 198
Brandt, 71, 77
Brandtstetter, 127
Braschler, 201
Brauer, 202
Braun, 110, 204
Braun, Henry, 143, 220
Braun, John, 226
Brecht, G. V., 77
Breckenridge, Sam H., 105
Bredell, Edward, 153
Breidenbach, Henry, 152
Breitenstein, Edward, 209
Breitinger, John, 225
Bremermann, 7
Bremermann, George, 207
Brickwirth, 34
Bridge, Hudson E., 244, 247
Brignoli, 160
Brinkmann, 199
Brinkmann, F. H., 223, 224
Britton, James H., 5, 241
Brock, Stephen, 241
Brockmann, Bernhard, 145
Brockmeyer, Henry C., 28
Broderick and Bascom, 242
Brookings, R. S., 330
Brotherton, Marshall, 238
Brown, A. D., 330
Brown, B. Gratz, 243
Brown, Joseph, 140, 172
Bruch, Max, 173
Bruck, Carl, 223
Brueggemann, A. H., 222
Brueh, 176

Bruening, 111
Brummer (or Brunner), Carl, 139, 260
Brunner, Carl, 139, 260
Bruno, Charles, 227
Bruns, 199
Brunschweiler, B., 165
Buchroeder, F. A., 107
Buddecke, 127, 199
Buechel, 173
Buechel, Edward C., 188
Buechel, Julius, 37, 178
Buehler, Charles, 48
Buehler, Edward, 49
Buehrle, 199
Buelow, Hans von, 175
Buenger, 203
Buesching, Frederick, 89, 94, 99
Buff, 49
Buhlert, E., 188
Bull, Ole, 156
Bulte, 7, 265
Bunding, 6
Bunsen, 270
Burdeau, James P., 236
Burg, Henry, 157, 161
Burg, Phillip, 157, 161
Burgh, Phillip, 127
Burnett, Robyn, 336
Busch, 47, 317
Busch, Adolphus, 5, 58, 305, 318
Busch, Isidor, 48, 59, 109, 280, 281
Busch, Raphael, 281
Buschberg, 280, 281
Buschmann, C. L., 30, 31
Buschmann, K., 196

Bush, 132
Bush, Isidor, 208-210
Butler, 88
Byrne, 58
Cabot, 70
Caesar, 21
Cafferatta, Angelo, 60
Cairns, John, 121
Cajacob, 17
Califf, A. H., 251
Campbell, James, 242
Canissa, 96
Capen, Samuel D., 237
Caradori-Allen, 155
Careno, Clara, 175
Carl, Emily, 135
Carl, Phillip, 128
Carlmueller, 186
Carpenter, 7
Carroll, Billy, 118
Cary, Louise, 96
Case, 238
Casper, George, 85
Cassel, Ferdinand, 135
Castelhuhn, John, 192, 229
Catlin, Daniel, 239, 240, 305
Cavender, John S., 241, 249
Cavizel, 200
Chambers, John M., 325
Chandler, F., 254
Chandler, John, 295
Chapman, H., 171
Chase, 70
Chester, E. L., 279
Chouteau, Charles P., 90, 112, 118
Chouteau, Mrs., 118
Chouteau, Pierre, 118, 124, 248, 265
Christian, 142, 161
Christmann, Jacob, 159
Clabes, A. J., 224
Clark, George A., 261
Clark, James, 239
Clark, S. H. H., 237
Clarner, Henry, 165, 213, 216
Claussen, Johanna, 65, 181, 182, 184
Clover, Henry A., 104
Coelln, C. V., 139
Cohn, 50
Coleman, Norman J., 325
Collet, A. W., 325
Collier, George, 248
Collmer, 186
Companini, 60
Compton, 54, 152
Comrade, Christ, 174
Comstock, 67
Conrad, 10
Conrad House, 118
Conrad, Adam, 28, 196
Conrad, J. F., 228
Conrad, J. J., 227
Conrad, Julius, 210
Conrad, Karl, 48
Conrad, Mrs. Carl, 169
Conrades, 34
Conrades, Edwin H., 290
Conrades, H., 188, 288
Conrades, J. H., 289, 290
Conrades, Theodore H., 290
Conried, 188
Conzelmann, John, 191

Cook, John, 34
Copp, 20, 100
Cordes, 199
Cordes, A. C., 4
Cornelius, 43
Cornet, 31
Cornet, Francis, 30, 31
Cortambert, Louis, 110
Coste, Felix, 5, 21, 44, 139, 156
Cotrelly, 185
Cotrelly, Mathilde, 186
Cotting, 204
Cottrelly, 185
Cottrelly< Mathilde, 186
Couzins, Phoebe, 107
Cramer, Ernest, 284
Cramer, Gustav, 127, 188, 282-284
Crawford, Joseph, 78
Crawfords, 76
Cremer, J. E., 220
Creswold, 175
Crittenden, H., 241
Cronenbold, F. W., 129, 133, 145
Crow, 70
Crow, Wayman, 5
Cullen, 62
Cunningham, 102
Cuno, Charles A., 4, 6
Cushman, Charlotte, 95
Daenzer, Carl, 25, 112
Dahlmann, 114
Dahmen, Louis, 162, 165, 200
Damen, L., 162, 164, 165, 200
Danjen, 20
Darby, John F., 89

Darguth, August, 51
Dauernheim, H., 228
Dauernheim, Philipp, 14, 15, 159
Dauth, Ferdinand, 137
Davis, E. P., 332
Davis, John T., 330
Davis, Samuel C., 70
de Ahna, 11
De la Vergne, 316
de Meyer, Lepold, 157
Deagle, George, 73
Dean, Edwin, 70
Dean-Lowe, Edwina, 161, 162, 174
DeBar, 65, 112
Decker, Jacob, 134
Degenau, 217
Degenhardt, John, 136, 261
DeGreck, Charles, 9
Derlitz, 45
Detjen, David W., 336
Detmerin, Frederick, 166
Deubach, Henry, 166
Deutsch, Gustav von, 64, 161, 167, 170
Dickens, Charles, 69
Dickinson, E., 237
Dickmann, 49
Dickmann, Otto, 168
Dieckeriede, 21
Dieckriede, C. B., 217
Diegle, George, 118
Diehm, JFerdinand, 170, 172
Dienst, Dr., 91, 322
Dierberger, John, 227, 228
Diesz, 18
Dietrich, 144

Dietz, A., 225
Dietz, Frank H., 221
Dietz, H., 179
Dingert, Leopold, 162
Dings, 108
Dings, F., 6
Dings, Frederick, 196, 325
Distelhorst, 196
Dittmann, George, 110
Dittmann, William H., 305
Doddridge, W. B., 251
Dodson, John, 319
Doehn, Rudolph, 213, 216
Doerner, August, 167
Doerr, Charles J., 223
Doerr, P. J., 131
Dollner, Henry, 102
Dombrowski, 183
Don Juan, 96
Donald, Gustav, 185
Donk, 101
Donk, Emil, 173
Donna Anna, 96
Dorguth, August, 49
Dorris, 91
Dorris, Tom, 91
Dorsten, W., 27
Drack, Charles A., 101
Drechsler, William, 225
Dreckmann, Henry W., 207
Dreigus, Arthur, 220
Dremmel, Alwine, 179
Dreyer, 19
Dreyer, Gustavus W., 103
Driscoll, Patrick, 72
Droege, 127
Drucker, Louis, 23
Druhe, William, 121
Drummond, 46
Drummond, J. T., 305
Dryer, Gustavus, 58, 241
Duchouquette, 124
Dudly, 64
Dueber, Phillip, 174
Duenkel, 26
Duestrow,, Louis, 5
Duncan, 55
Dunker, A., 56
Duprez, 184
Durand, H., 254
Dusenberry, Judge, 105
Dziuba, Sophie, 184
D'Oench, Guido, 31
D'Oench, William, 4, 14, 196
Eads, James B., 83, 93, 245
Eber, Louis P., 14
Eberhard, J. G., 196, 197
Eckerle, Theobald, 137, 138
Eckhardt, Carl, 162
Eckhof, 34
Edison, 64
Eggers, Charles, 12
Eggers, Edward, 5, 6, 207, 211
Ehlermann, Charles, 317, 318
Ehlers, Adolph, 26
Ehling, Victor, 176
Eisenhardt, H., 21, 28, 65, 210
Eisenhardt, Otto, 170
Eisenlohr, 196
Elleard, 63
Ellerbeck, F., 166
Ellermann, John, 37
Elliot, Dr., 91
Elliot, Pastor, 174

Elsner, Hermann, 163
Emanuel, 127
Endres, 54
Engelke, John, 43, 287, 288
Engelmann, A. O., 111
Engelmann, Dr., 192, 216
Engle, Stephen Douglas, 336
Enslin, Charles, 5, 20
Entzeroth, L., 229
Epstein, 176
Epstein, Marcus, 171, 177
Erard, 157
Erdmannsdoerfer, 176
Erfort, 21
Esher, 66
Espenschied, Louis, 34
Essig, Louis, 165
Essiposs, Anna, 175
Estel, 6
Eszmueller, Frederick, 226
Etten, 204
Etzel, 6
Etzel, Fritz, 10
Evers, F. H., 216
Evers, Henry, 30
Everts, Charles, 5, 277, 279
Ewald, Phillip, 194
Ewald, R., 196
Ewing, A. B., 242, 328
Eyser, John, 38
Faber, 131
Fabian, George C., 110
Fabri-Mulder, Inez, 56
Fabricius, Henry P., 76
Faerber, Rev., 41, 205
Falstaff, 89
Fanchon, 95

Far West, 300
Fath, Valentine, 127
Faust, 60, 85, 169, 181
Faust, Tony, 138, 332
Fehringer, Antoinette, 182
Feigenbutz, Emil, 169
Feikert, 22, 23
Feiner, Frank, 43, 143, 287, 288
Feldmann, 222
Fellerer, 158, 161
Felsing, 38
Ferrenbach, Thomas, 261
Feuerbacher, Max, 18, 146
Feustel, Robert, 159, 218
Filley, Chauncey J., 145
Filley, Oliver D., 73
Filley, Oliver D. , 100
Fink, J. C., 260
Finkelnburg, G. A., 107, 111, 219, 220
Finkelnburg, Rudolph, 111
Finn, John, 72
Fisch, John, 39
Fischer, 47, 204
Fischer, Adolph, 137, 145, 146
Fischer, Albert, 66, 110, 111, 209, 210, 322
Fischer, Gustav, 132, 193
Fischer, William, 119
Fishback, George W., 84
Fisher, 177
Fisher, Richard, 225
Fisse, John H., 130, 135, 196
Fitzgerald, Mollie, 64
Flad, Henry, 83, 300
Flattich, 144
Fleischmann, Henry, 63

Fleitz, John P., 263
Fleitz, Peter J., 42
Fletcher, 115
Flohr, 6
Florence, Bernard Canlin, 95
Florenz, 37
Florissant, 126
Flotow, 60, 161, 170
Foellger, A., 179, 181
Foelsing, Henry, 164
Foerg, Henry, 142
Foerstel, Julius, 171
Follenius, Paul, 322
Follenius, R. H., 127, 321, 322
Forepaugh, 82
Formes, Carl/Karl, 11, 96, 166, 184
Forster, Marquard, 34, 75, 319
Forthmann, F., 213
Foster, 93
Fox, 91
Fox, Patrick, 36
Foy, Peter L., 84, 241
Francis, Charles W., 144
Francis, D. R., 328
Francis, Mayor, 255
Frankenberg, von, 184
Frankenthal, A., 82, 113
Franklin, Joseph, 330
Franosch, 184
Franz, Bernard, 19
Franzmueller, 182
Frederick, 151
Freiligrath, 175
Fremont, 114, 164
Freuger, George W., 224

Freund, Christian, 68, 91, 115, 116
Frey, Henry, 168
Friedhold, Malwine, 186
Frings, 48, 183
Friton, Julius, 220
Fritsch, C. R., 28, 209, 210
Fritsch, G. R., 210
Fritsch, von, 65
Fritsche, C., 225
Fritz, 142, 190, 322
Fritz, George, 188, 322
Froebel, August, 61
Froehlich, Carl, 171, 176
Froehlich, E., 163, 169, 170, 172, 175, 177
Froehlich, F. W., 223
Froelich, Egmont, 168
Frost, D. M., 217, 218
Fuchs, Ferdinand, 12, 89, 172
Fuchs, Helen, 89
Fuchs, Major, 89
Fuchs, Reinhard, 158, 159
Fuchs, Robert, 27
Fuerth, Josephine, 127
Fuerth, Julia, 127
Fuhrmann, 103
Fusz, 21, 265
Fusz, Louis, 264, 265
Gades, 176
Gaertner, 186
Gaffron, Walther, 224
Gaiennie, Frank, 332
Gallmeyer, Josephine, 188
Gamble, Archibald, 48, 256
Gamble, Hamilton R., 48
Ganahl, John J., 42, 56, 262, 263

Ganahl, Louis J., 263
Garrell, 137
Garrison, C. K., 248
Gast, 299
Gast, A. T., 301
Gast, August, 88, 301, 323-325
Gast, Leopold, 88, 299, 300, 323, 325
Gast, Paulus, 299-301
Gast, Ulysses S, 301
Gattung, C., 221
Gauger, Jacob, 35
Gausz, C. W., 6, 70
Gauszmann, 78
Gay, Edward J., 47
Gebser, 193
Gecks, Jr., Frank, 176
Gecks, Sr., Frank, 161, 164
Gehner, August, 108
Gehrke, George, 133
Gehrmann, William, 220
Geisel, Andrew, 131
Geistinger, 186
Geistinger, Marie, 91, 188
Gempp, 131
Gempp, Henry C., 132, 189, 207
Gené, 186
Genee, Ottilie, 65, 181, 186, 188
Genoro, 85
Gentles, 72
Gerber, Mrs., 199
Gerber, Theodore, 137, 197, 198
Gerber, Valentine, 113
Gerhart, P. G., 85
Gerichten, Jacob von, 143, 221, 222
Gericke, 168, 173
Gerster, Etelka, 60
Gescheid, Charles, 224
Geszner, F., 164
Geyer, 120
Giebermann, Rudolph, 227
Giesecke, Hermann, 111
Giesecke, W. F., 6
Giesecke, William, 111
Gietner, Charles, 142
Gildehaus, Charles, 188
Gildehaus, Henry, 10, 21
Gilmore, 331
Glaeser, F., 163
Glaeser, William, 137
Godron, Adolph, 143
Goebel, Gert, 59, 145, 322
Goedde, C. C., 225, 226
Goeden, Max, 111
Goerlich, 79
Goethe, 179
Goettler, Michael, 127, 210
Goetz, Gustav L., 139
Goetz, J. L., 261
Goldstein, S., 227
Goldsticker, Carrie, 62
Goller, Franz, 205
Gollmer, Hugo, 220
Gottschalk, Ferdinand, 196
Gottschalk, Charles W., 109, 133, 145, 159, 160, 163
Gottschalk, F. A., 211, 212, 216
Gottschalk, Ferdinand, 133
Gottschalk, Louis, 145, 188, 190, 209
Gottschalk, W., 163
Gough, 69
Gould, George J., 251

Gould, Jay, 248, 250
Graebner, Alan N., 336
Graff, 22
Graffmann, C. H. L., 225
Grahl, William, 217
Grant, 21
Grant, President, 98
Gratiot, 124
Grau, Henry, 170
Grau, Jacob, 169
Grauer, A., 163
Gray, O. D., 325
Green, Charles, 241, 242, 327, 328
Green, James J., 261
Greiner, Otto, 47, 173, 194
Grell, 175
Grenzenbach, 10
Grether, 76
Griesedick, Anton, 152
Griesedieck, 315, 316
Griesedieck, Anton, 317
Griesedieck, Bernhard, 317
Griesedieck, Henry, 317
Griesedieck, Joseph, 317
Griesediek, 34
Griesediek, Anton, 188
Griesmayer, 18
Grimm, Valentine, 220
Grimminger, 118
Grimsley, Thornton, 110, 295, 325
Groffmann, C. F., 225
Groll, 205
Grone, Edward, 320
Grone, Henry, 121, 320
Grone, Hermann, 320

Grossman, 179
Grosz, Julius, 127, 283
Groszenheider, Julius, 120
Grover, Leonard, 96, 165, 166
Grube, 187
Gruen, 58, 142
Gruen, Jacob M., 116
Gruenwald, G., 174
Grumme, W., 166
Gruner, 199
Gruner, Philipp, 34
Guenther, E., 225
Guerdan, Adam, 19
Guerdan, Franz, 143
Guerdan, John, 145
Guerdan, Nick, 110
Guether, Oscar H., 131
Gundelfinger, William, 85
Gundlach, 118
Gutberlet, John, 197, 198
Guthart, 146
Guye, Paul, 6
Haake, 31
Haar, L., 164
Haarstick, H. C., 237
Haarstick, Henry C., 235
Haarstick, William T., 236, 237
Haas, 31
Haas, Eugene, 175
Haas, J. G., 78
Haas, J. P., 57
Haase, A. C. L., 18
Haase, Friedrich, 186, 188
Haase, Louise, 65, 182, 183
Habelmann, Theodore, 60, 96, 166, 184
Haber, Louis, 114

The German Element in St. Louis 351

Haberstroh, Frederick, 174
Habicht, 94
Hackmann, 21
Hadnett, 37
Haenschen, 8
Haenschen, Gustav F., 322
Haerting, Edward, 181
Haeseler, Albert H., 223
Haeseler, Charles, 223
Haeusgen, 162
Haeuszler, Ferdinand W., 193
Hafkemeier, 55
Hafkemeir, 197
Hagan, 305
Hage, Carl, 162
Hagemann, W., 197, 204
Hagenbeck, 327
Hahn, William, 226
Hamilton, D. G., 243, 244
Hammel, 116
Hammer, 12, 17, 58, 74, 117, 120, 135, 141, 146, 158, 172, 192
Hammer, L. K., 223
Hammer, Louis, 223
Hammerstein, 7
Hanck, Fritz, 138
Hanck, Karl, 17
Hannemann, 34
Hanpeter, 34
Hansen, 10
Hansen, Gustav, 226
Hanser, Otto, 202
Haquett, Philipp, 58
Harchert, Erwin, 224
Hardt, 199
Haren, Edward, 250
Haren, William A., 142
Harless, 162, 173
Harlesz, Adolph, 31, 47
Harlow, 258
Harney, 48, 49
Harper, Andrew, 325, 327
Harris, Lloyd G., 279
Harrison, 309
Harrison, James, 250, 265
Harrsen, F., 188
Harrsen, Mrs. F., 96
Hart, 102, 103
Hart, Henry C., 325
Hartmann, 98
Hartmann, John, 98, 183, 188, 190
Hasse, Edward, 193
Hassendeubel, Franz, 105
Hathaway, Charles, 238
Hauck, C., 163
Hauck, Carl, 190
Hauck, Fritz, 189
Hauer, August W., 157
Haumeier, 197
Haus, Friederich, 22
Hauschulte, Bernhard, 261
Hauser, 66
Hauser, Miska, 160
Hausmann, 191
Haws, 37
Haydn, 170
Hayes, Katharine, 157
Hayes, R. S., 237, 330
Hazard, 119
Heckler, 85
Heerich, George, 176
Hehrlein, 144

352 *The German Element in St. Louis*

Heidacker, Bernhard, 130
Heidbreder, 34
Heidenreich, Albert, 225
Heidsich, 31
Heidsick, 24
Heil, William, 174
Heimbach, John, 132
Heinecke, 6
Heinrich, J. P., 228
Heinrichshofen, 7, 157, 210
Heitkamp, Fritz, 43, 151
Heitmann, C., 197
Heitz, 14
Helfensteller, 79
Helgenberg, John, 89
Heller, 34
Hellmann, J., 94
Hellmann, Louis M., 94
Hellmich, Anton, 89
Helmbacher, Michael, 131, 139, 259, 260
Helmbacher, Peter, 139, 259, 260
Helmer, 184
Helmich, Julius, 12, 13
Helmkampf, 58
Helmrich, G., 113
Hemann, Ernest W., 112, 114
Hembold, William, 223
Hengelsberg, G. H., 198
Henkler, 102
Hennig, Robert, 207
Henrich-Wilhelme, Mrs. Hedwig, 216
Henry, Alfred, 122
Henry, Frank R., 240
Henry, William D., 239

Henze, F. W., 228
Herche, 197
Hergesell, 76
Hergesell, Carl, 159
Herkenroth, 162
Hermann, 125, 135, 153, 172
Hermann, John, 194
Hermann, Julius, 183, 184
Hermann, Mathias, 223
Herminghaus, 173
Hernon, Peter, 336
Herold, Ferdinand, 107, 152
Herold, Frederick, 39
Herrmann, 173
Hers, Henry, 158
Herter, J. H., 210
Hertig, Edward, 65
Herting, Hugo, 220
Hertle, Daniel, 12, 110
Hertter, Julius H., 109
Hertwig, Christian, 227-229
Hertwig, Gustav, 227
Hertwig, Phillip, 227
Hertz, Julius, 162, 163
Herwig, 164
Herz, 158
Herzog, 199
Herzog, Henry, 164
Hesse, Hedwig, 65, 181
Hetlage, 196
Heuer, F. W., 222
Heuer, Henry, 27, 106
Heyer, O. W., 77
Heyfinger, B., 322
Heynold, Alwine, 186
Hickey, 120
Hiemenz, 131

Hiemenz, Henry, 116
Hiemez, Jacob D., 135
Hildebrandt, Theodore, 217
Hilgard, Theodore, 191
Hill, 116
Hill, Britton, 88, 89
Hill, Clara, 152
Hill, Frederick, 116
Hillegeist, 191
Hillgaertner, George, 12, 25, 139, 286
Hils, Edward, 319
Hinsmann, H., 227
Hirschberg, Louis C., 5
Hirschberg, Salo, 66
Hirschfeld, Julius, 228
Hirt, William, 121, 218
Hischberg, Louis C., 157
Hobicht, Charles, 10
Hodgman, M. M., 238
Hoeber, Gustav, 21
Hoefer, Oscar, 226
Hoefl, 183
Hoefl, Auguste, 183
Hoegemann, W., 197
Hoel, Theodore, 174
Hoelke, 114
Hoelzle, C., 146
Hofbauer, 204
Hoffer, Charles, 18
Hoffman, 173
Hoffman, George W., 293
Hoffmann, 34, 176
Hoffmann, August, 165, 213, 216
Hoffmann, B., 213, 216
Hoffmann, George, 216, 295
Hoffmann, M., 166
Hofmann, E. G., 227
Hofmann, Karl, 226
Hofstetten, 182
Hogan, John, 84
Holthaus, Anton, 78
Holthaus, Arnold, 78
Holthaus, L. J., 210, 228
Holz, William, 210
Holzman, Joseph, 159
Homann, Henry J., 297
Homann, Rudolph, 297
Homann, William, 30, 168, 295-297
Hoppe, 5, 6, 79
Hoppe, Charles, 7, 138
Horn, 49
Horn, Charles W., 109
Hornbostel, 21
Horskotter, A., 164
Horskotter, William, 164
Horwitz, 50
Hospes, Gustav, 64
Hospes, Richard, 5
Hoster, H., 229
Hotze, 30
Hotze, Henry, 296
Houser, Dan, 84, 330, 332
How, James F., 255
How, John, 100, 139, 250
Howard, 309
Hoym, Elise, 183
Hoym, Otto von, 11, 48, 181, 183
Huber, A., 174
Hufnagel, Charles, 136
Hughes, James M., 325

Humboldt Institute, 117, 120
Humbolt Institute, 117, 120
Humbser, 183
Humphrey, 68
Hunicke, 8, 10, 70, 75
Hunicke, William, 156
Hunt, Charles L., 325
Hurst, John H., 54, 107
Husman, George, 280
Husmann, George, 47
Hutzler-Kainz, Sarah, 191
Ibermeyer, F., 163
Imbs,, 21, 265
Indermark, W. H., 223
Irrsehick, Magda, 186
Isenstein, 186
Ittner, Anthony, 59, 310-312
Ittner, George, 312
Jaccard, 70, 107
Jaccard, D. C., 55, 58
Jaccard, Eugene, 54, 55, 68
Jackson, Claiborne, 85
Jacoby, 21-23
Jacoby, John, 295
Jacoby, L. S., 203
Jacoby, S., 113
Jaeger, 151, 163, 172
Jaeger (Schueler), 184
Jaeger, Anna, 183
Jael, Alfred, 160
Jaentsch, Frederick, 210
Jaeschke, 199
Jahn, 222
Jahreisz, Theodore, 114
Janauscheck, Fanny, 95, 182
Janauschek, Fanny, 95, 182
January, Thomas T., 325

Jecko, Joseph, 64
Jefferson, 28, 34, 65, 119, 200, 331
Jefferson, Thomas, 25
Jenks, Mrs. Doctor, 168
Jochim, Jack, 225
Johannsen, 96
Johler, L., 166
John, 201
Johnson, Chalres P., 104
Johnson, John D., 63
Jonas, 199
Jonas, J. F., 198
Jorgensen, 31
Juch, Emma, 177
Juengst, Albert, 218
Kahle, George, 220, 275-277
Kaime, 90
Kaiser, Henry, 196
Kaiser, J. H., 30
Kaiser, Philipp, 221
Kalb, Guido, 14, 28, 325-327
Kalb, Theodore, 17
Kalbfleisch, Henry, 139
Kalisch, 177
Kallmeier, A., 225
Kallmeier, O., 225
Kaltmeyer, Frederick, 120
Kaltwasser, H. W., 165
Kampfhoefner, Walter D., 336
Kankemeier, B., 166
Kanne, 21
Kargau, Ernst D., i, v, vi, ix, 209, 210
Karguth, R. A., 163
Karl, Phillip, 318
Karst, 161

Karst, Mrs. Eugene, 62
Kassing, John H., 221, 222
Kauck, Carl, 193
Kaufmann, 121, 122
Kayser, Henry, 249
Keevil, 31, 158
Kehr, Adolph, 26, 196, 210
Kehr, Edward C., 26, 145
Kehrmann, Statius, 63, 79, 157
Keil, Mrs. Otto, 229
Keil, Otto, 174, 229
Keiler, 56
Keiler, William, 51
Keiser, George W., 21
Keiser, John P., 21
Keisker, Ernest, 168
Keisker, Herman, 168
Keller, 161
Keller, George, 279
Keller, Joseph, 162
Kellermann, 150
Kellermann, Francis, 249
Kellogg, 107
Kellogg, Clara Louise, 96
Kendel, 74
Kennard, Samuel, 330
Kennard, Samuel M., 332
Kennett, Luther M., 100, 250
Kennett, Mayor, 247
Keppler, Joseph, 39, 44, 110, 173, 182
Kerens, Richard, 328
Kerksiek, 197
Kern, Jacob, 109
Kern, John, 41, 109
Kerner, Otto, 127
Kerzinger, 95
Kerzinger, Franz, 153, 211
Kielholz, Bernhard, 52
Kieselhorst, 161, 170
Kingland, L. D., 332
Kinkel, Gottfried, 217, 286
Kinner, Hugo, 112, 144, 209, 210
Kinsalla, 154
Kircher, Charles E., 223
Kirkbride, 305
Kirschner, Franz, 185
Kiselhorst, 62
Kittlaus, Louis, 226
Klassing, August, 210
Kleemann, C., 211
Klein, 118
Klein, J., 166
Kleinecke, Adolph, 111, 112, 168
Klickermann, Franz, 226
Klier, 189
Klipstein, Gustav A., 79
Klipstein, Theodore, 222, 228, 229
Klotz, 186
Kluender, 102
Kluender, Frederick, 16, 162, 179
Kluever, 176
Klymann, 94
Knapp, George, 116
Knapp, John, 22
Knecht, 123
Knepper, J. H., 164
Knickmeyer, 199
Knoblauch, 141
Knorr, Ludwig, 181

Koch, 116, 182, 184, 191
Koch, August, 59
Koch, Christian, 34
Koch, F., 163
Koch, Golconda, 191
Koch, Julius, 181
Koch, M., 229
Koch, Mastodon, 191
Koch, W., 226
Kochn, Theodore, 35
Koehler, A. W., 165
Koehler, Caspar, 123, 146
Koehler, Charles, 123
Koehler, Henry, 146
Koehler, Julius, 123
Koeln, Christian, 227
Koenig, 52, 293, 295
Koenig, Marie, 186
Koenig, William, 21, 293, 294
Koenigsberg, Frederick, 163, 164
Koerner, 152
Koetter, 48, 65
Kohlberg, Charles, 223
Kohlberg, Louis L., 223
Kohler, 145
Kohlhund, Christian, 136
Koken, William, 222
Kolbe, 270
Kolbenheyer, 10
Koperlick, J., 128
Kopf, J. M, 202
Koppe, 184
Korn, August, 12
Korndoerffer, 194, 195
Kortjohn, 132, 199
Kortkamp, H., 28, 77
Kortkamp, William E., 77
Koser, William, 48, 116, 181, 182
Kossak, William, 131
Kossuth, Ludwig, 115
Kost, 182
Kost, Alexander, 182, 183
Kost, Jacob, 133
Kraft, 197
Kramer, G., 174
Kraul, 123
Krausnick, 153
Krausnick, Edward C., 154
Krebs, Hugo, 111, 195, 196, 322
Krebs, Roland, 336
Kreling, D., 227
Krell, 196
Kreming, 119
Krending, Franz H., 197
Krenning, 196, 197
Krenning, F. H. W., 198
Kretschmar, Frederick, 104, 159
Kretzer, 156
Kreuter, E., 166
Kreuter, H., 166
Kribben, Christian, 26, 156, 178
Kribben, William, 26, 178
Krieckhaus, A., 8, 116, 172, 221
Krieger, Philipp, 32
Krippen, 102
Krite, 6
Kroener, 184
Krone, John W., 162
Kroschel, Theodore, 114
Krueer, M., 220
Krueger, Ferdinand, 14, 182-185, 198

Kruer, A., 134
Kruer, Mazzini, 134, 220
Krug, Andrew, 207
Krug, Louis, 11
Krug,, Mrs. Louis, 178
Krumm, John M., 100
Krutsch, Hermann, 19, 292
Kuchn, E., 50
Kuhs, Henry W., 37
Kuhse, 186
Kunkel, Charles, 61, 62, 175
Kunkel, Jacob, 61, 62, 175
Kunsemueller, 56
Kunsemueller, G., 168
Kunz, 150
Kupferle, 22
Kurlbaum, 211
Kurst, Emil, 157
Kurth, Louis, 182, 183, 190
Kurtzeborn, A., 165
Kurtzekorn, 211
Kurzeborn, 113
Kurzeborn, Jacob, 196
Kuttner, 205, 206
Labadie, 124
Lack, Frederick, 204
Laclede, 20, 66, 74, 107
Laclede, Pierre, 83
Ladue, R. S., 20
Lafayette, 124
Lafontaine, Fritz, 184
Lager, 127
Lager, D., 171
Lahmann, 197
Lahrmann, William, 168
Laibold, Bernhard, 38
Lammersick, Frederick, 225

Lammert, Martin, 72
Landesoberst, 114
Lang, 65
Lang, Henry, 222
Lange, 34, 111, 225
Lange, Charles F., 77
Lange, Christian, 139
Lange, Emil, 128
Lange, Henry, 222, 225, 229
Lange, William C., 111, 120, 130, 210
Langeloth, Moritz, 94, 95
Lanham, Judge, 98
Lappe, C., 166
LaSalle, 124
Laser, 170
Laszwitz, Emil, 65, 143, 182, 183
Laumann, Frederick, 79, 210
Laumeier, Henry, 196
Lauth, John N., 261
Lawall, Fritz, 27
Lawitzky, Hermann, 171
Leach, Henry B., 238
Leathe, S. H., 188
Lebrecht, John, 189
Leffingwell, 98
Lehman, Lillie, 177
Lehmann, Catherine, 199
Lehmann, W., 198
Leichsenring, Charles, 106, 151
Leinberger, Charles, 10, 11, 46
Leisse, Albrecht, 43
Leisse, August, 42, 131
Leitch, Alexander, 54
Lemp, 268
Lemp, Adam, 14, 266

Lemp, Louis F., 268
Lemp, William J., 151, 188, 225, 226, 266, 268, 305
Lenz, 6
Lenz, August, 162
Lenz, Hermann, 30
Lenze, E., 166
Leonhard, Conrad A., 114
Leopold, M., 225
Lepique, 197
Lerch, H., 171
Leser, Fritz, 130
Lesperance, 124
Leuszler, A., 139
Leuszler, Robert, 210
Lewens, Hannes, 181-184
Lewis, 82
Liebig, Justus von,, 270
Liedertafel, Louis, 166
Liggon, J. J., 315
Lightner, H., 241
Lilliger, Adam, 229
Limberg, Hermann, 13
Limberg, Rudolph, 123
Linck, 137
Lincoln, President, 68, 84, 92, 103, 162, 300
Lind, Jenny, 115, 158, 159
Linde, Hermann, 56
Lindell, 312
Lindell, Peter, 81, 93
Lindemann, Caroline, 179, 181, 182, 184
Lindenschidt, 122
Lingenau, Ferdinand, 12
Link, Julius, 119, 223
Lionberger, John R., 239-241

Lippe, P. F. Van der, 325
Lippmann, M. J., 22
Lips, 16-18
Lischer, Henry, 112, 178
Livingston, 5
Lockwood, William M., 328
Lodlow, N. M., 87
Loebs, 152
Loebs, George, 222
Loehr, Adalbert, 12, 134, 178
Loeschhorn, 175
Loewe, 161
Loewenstein, 55, 116, 128
Logemann, 34
Logemann, F. L., 289
Lohmann, 33
Lohmeyer, H., 196
Lohrum, C., 225
Loker, 20
Lolmann, Charles T., 49
Looney, Jack, 71
Loos, Louis, 49
Lord, Judge, 105
Lorentzen, 197
Lorle, 95
Loth, 6
Loyd, H. A., 255
Lube, Josephine, 184
Lube, Max, 184
Lucas, 92
Lucas, H. V., 330
Lucas, James H., 92, 97, 98, 120, 142, 248, 329
Lucca, Pauline, 96, 169
Lucus, James H., 256
Ludovika, 181, 182
Ludwig, Johannes, 6

Luebbering, Ken, 336
Luecken, 199
Luedeking, Carl, 211-216, 229
Lungstras, Eugene, 273, 274
Luthy, Jacob, 121
Luyties, Dietrich, 68, 191
Lynch, B. M., 57, 58
Lynch, Henry C., 146
Lyon, Nathaniel, 93, 140
L'Arronge, Theodore, 11, 182
Mack, 138, 145
Mackwitz, Rudolph, 102, 168
Mackwitz, William, 178
MacPherson, William M., 250
Mader, Leopold, 181
Madison, John F., 244
Maffitt, C. C., 328
Maffitt, Dr., 90
Maffitt, Julia, 90
Maffitt, P. C., 239, 240
Magius, 184
Magnus, L., 127
Maguire, Charles J., 242
Maguire, Mayor, 144
Mahler, Albert, 26, 27, 154, 174
Mahoney, John, 242
Maier, A. B., 322
Mallinckrodt, 34, 270, 271, 337
Mallinckrodt, Anita M., 336
Mallinckrodt, Edward, 271
Malmene, Waldemar, 175
Mandelbaum, 110
Mansur, Alvah, 328
Mapleson, 60, 169
Maretzek, Max, 169
Marquard, Henry, 196
Marx, Prof., 146

Mathey, C. F., 55
Matthews, George, 88
Mauch, Albert, 226
Mauntel, 7, 265
Mauro, Charles G., 104
Maximilian, Emperor, 10
Mays, Charles M., 255
McClelland, 55
McDonald, A., 139, 260
McDonough, 85
McDowell, 19, 58, 142
McGrath, Michael K., 104
McHose, Abe, 18
McKee, Billy, 84
McKee-Rankin, 66
McKeen, 85
McKittrick, James, 324
McLean, James H., 24, 50, 167
McPherson, William M., 238
Medart, Fritz, 306, 307
Medart, Phillip, 306
Medart, William, 307
Meersmann, Joseph, 30
Mehl, Carl, 132
Mehling, Anna, 175
Mehrkens, William, 222
Meier, Adolphus, 7, 153, 248, 261
Meier, C. F., 142
Meier, E. F. W., 6
Meier, Hermann H., 207
Meier, Thomas J., 207
Meinhold, A., 197
Meiniger, Thomas, 111
Meininger, 188
Meis, John, 77
Meisenbach, Gustav, 162

360 *The German Element in St. Louis*

Meister, F. W., 5, 237
Meiszner, Gustav E., 281
Meiszner, L., 166
Melcher, Rev., 41, 204
Mendelssohn, 176
Mense, 5, 6
Mentrup, 128
Merkel, 68
Merkel, Louis C., 132
Mermod, August S., 55, 70, 107
Messing, 205
Meszmer, Ferdinand, 25, 224, 309, 310
Methua-Scheller, 184
Methudi, Leopold, 10, 177
Methudy, L., 332
Methudy, Leopold, 10, 177
Mette, Louis, 21
Mettelmann, J., 216
Mettlemann, 199
Metzger, 127
Meunch, Hugo, 223
Meuschke, 184
Meyer, 6, 21, 30, 47, 94, 110, 128, 197, 265
Meyer, Charles F., 4, 9, 14, 197
Meyer, F. W., 14
Meyer, Frederick C., 320
Meyer, George, 217, 307
Meyer, Henry, 277
Meyer, Henry J. G., 222, 277
Meyer, Henry P., 5
Meyer, J. H., 174
Meyer, John C., 207
Meyer, Julius, 7
Meyer, Louis, 173
Meyer, Max, 226

Meyer, Tamm, 277
Meyerbeer, 175
Meylert, William, 12, 13
Meyrer, Louis, 45
Michel, 44, 152
Michel, Anton, 43, 171
Michel, Jean, 37
Michenfelder, Franz, 110
Milfeil, W., 198
Milges, Catherine, 199
Miller, 284
Miller, Henry, 261
Miller, Madison, 250
Mills, 66
Miltenberger, Eugene, 94, 157
Mitchell, 96
Mitchell, Maggie, 95
Mitterwurzer, 188
Moeller, H., 49
Moeller, Mrs., 49
Mohrstadt, J. C., 221
Moll, A., 77
Moll, Adolph, 24
Moll, W., 217
Moller, Christoph, 26
Mols, Franz, 44, 139
Monelius, Karl, 15
Monschein, A., 225
Monschein, G., 225
Moor, Karl, 177
Moore, Austin R., 236, 237
Moritz, 127
Moser, Josef, 102
Moskop, Lorenz, 136
Mozart, 96, 160
Muegge, August, 228
Muegge, Charles, 207

Muegge, George, 222, 223, 225
Muehlsiepen, Rev., 41, 205
Mueller, 156, 197
Mueller, A., 172
Mueller, Conrad, 182, 183
Mueller, Cornelius, 45, 47, 53
Mueller, Emil, 172, 218
Mueller, Florian, 113
Mueller, Gustav, 207
Mueller, John, 43
Mueller, Marie, 137
Mueller, Phillip, 42
Muench, Frederick, 59, 280, 300, 322
Muhl, Eduard, 337
Mullally, John, 242
Mullanphy, 126
Myer, William, 217
Nacke, 35
Nacke, Anthony, 223
Naeusche, 222
Naeusche, Albert, 223
Nagel, 194
Nagel, Charles, 332
Nagel, Robert, 165
Naldauer, A., 176
Napa & Sonoma, 88
Nast, William, 203
Nauer, H. N., 14
Nedderhuth, 7, 12, 268-270
Nedderhuth, August, 269, 270
Nedderhuth, Charles O., 269
Nedderhuth, Emil A., 269
Nedderhuth, Frederick, 171
Nega, 285
Neidmann, 184
Nelson, Dr., 86

Nennstil, Edward, 176
Neuer, Ernest, 157
Neuhaus, 6
Neumann, Bernhard, 41
Neun, Henry, 128
Neun, John, 128
Neusche, Albert, 220, 222, 223
Nicholson, David, 50, 61
Niebert, R., 171
Niederwieser, Tony, 37, 38, 48, 152, 153
Niederwiesser, Tony, 48, 181
Niedringhaus, 34, 302, 303
Niedringhaus, Charles, 79
Niedringhaus, F. G., 79, 302, 303
Niedringhaus, Thomas K., 303
Niedringhaus, William F., 79, 302, 303
Niemann, Christian, 135
Niemann, Hermann H., 71
Niemetz, A., 132
Niermeyer, John H., 207
Nies, 76
Nies, John, 120, 228
Niese, Julius, 141
Nilsson, Christina, 95
Nisbet, 20, 100
Nischwitz, Frederick, 137, 163
Noel, 132
Nofstetter, 185
Nohl, Charles, 30
Nohl, Karl, 165
Nolker, 34
Nolker, W. F., 328
Nollau, E. L., 117, 200, 201
Nollau, John, 201
Nollau, Louis, 201

Norden, H., 283
Norsch, F. W., 169, 174
Nuelsen, John C., 4, 30
Nuernberger, Phillip, 118
Nugent, B., 332
Nunz, Christian, 149
Obear, 98
Obenhaus, 199
Obermoeller, Henry, 31, 164
Oberreider, J., 174
Obert, Franz, 157, 158
Oblicke, S., 166
Ochsner, 111
Ocker, H. W., 225-227
Oebicke, 17
Oerters, O., 196, 197
Oeters, O., 196, 197
Ofenstein, Adam, 80
Ohe, Adele aus der, 177
Ohm, William, 171
Olshausen, Arthur, 109, 112, 207, 209, 210
Olshausen, Theodore, 110, 112
Olson, Aubrey L., 337
Olson, May E., 335
Orthwein, 8
Orthwein, Charles F., 188
Osten, Emil von der, 182, 185
Osten, Louise von der, 182
Osten, Otto von der, 185
Osterheld, D., 225
Ostermann, Gustav, 179, 182
Osthoff Nau, 11
Otten, Joseph, 176, 328
Ottenad, 137
Ottenad, Louis, 137, 138
Otto, 183, 186, 187
Otto, Dr., 173
Otto, Mrs., 185
Otto, Rohardine, 179
Otto, William, 122
Overstolz, Ferdinand, 207
Overstolz, Henry, 35
O'Blennis, Robert, 238
O'Brien, 102
O'Fallon, 31, 32, 43
O'Fallon, John, 108, 199, 248, 249
O'Fallon, Polytechnic Institute, 108
O'Leary, F. L., 255
O'Sullivan, 64
O'Sullivan, A., 322
Padberg, Daniel L., 337
Page, 93
Page, Daniel D., 248
Palm, William, 5, 41, 156, 309
Palmer, 173
Panse, Hermann, 207
Pappenheim, Eugenia, 170
Parepa, 54
Parker, E. A., 251
Parodi, 160
Parodi, Theresa, 160
Parsons, Charles, 239, 240
Partenheimer, F., 165-167, 174
Paschall, Nathaniel, 22, 86
Pate, Robert C., 51
Patti, 54
Patti, Adelina, 60, 158, 159
Patti, Amelia, 159
Paul, George, 227
Paul, John, 130, 135
Pauli, P. J., 8, 315

Pauly, Christian, 313
Pauly, John, 313, 315
Pauly, P. J., 8, 313-315
Pauly, Peter J., 313
Paust, 173
Peck, Charles H., 73
Peipers, Constantine, 6
Pellitz, 196
Pelosi, 181, 183-186
Penney, 72
Peper, Christian, 30, 121, 244
Perry, 294
Pestalozzi, 144
Peteler, Charles, 25
Peters, 8, 34
Peters, Edward, 225
Peters, F., 164
Petersen, 34
Petersen, Adam, 196
Petersen, H., 225
Petersen, W., 213, 216
Petri, 191
Petzold, Carl, 225
Peyer, J., 110
Pfaff, George, 229
Pfau, Theodore, 44
Pfeifer, Carl, 83
Pfeiffer, Alexander, 111, 179, 180
Pfeiffer, Ludovika, 181, 182
Pfeil, 197
Pfisterer, Frederick, 222
Picker, 159, 190, 218
Picker, Charles, 134, 197
Picker, Frederick, 195, 197
Pieree, H. C., 305
Pierson, 55

Pins, H., 198, 225
Pitzmann, Julius, 106
Plate, Theodore, 61, 112, 141
Plochmann, 94
Ploehn, Henry, 222
Pluesz, Theodore, 164
Pochmann, Henry, 335
Poeschel, Michael, 299-301
Pollack, 88
Polster, 197
Pommer, Gustav, 176
Pommer, W., 170
Pope, Charles, 91, 141
Pope, Dr., 91, 189
Porberg, 164
Porcher, 60, 61, 91
Porter, 89
Possart, Ernest, 188
Poten, 10
Prang, 34
Preetorius, Emil, 46, 59, 112, 140, 188, 214-216
Preusz, E., 89
Price, Stirling, 116
Price, Thomas L., 116
Price, William W., 320
Priest, 98
Priest, John G., 22
Primm, Wilson, 104
Prince of Wales, 327
Prufrock, 34
Prufrock, William, 297-299
Pulitzer, Joseph, 39, 139
Puls, 186
Raacke, 173
Rachow, Henry, 43
Racowitza, Helene von, 185, 188

Rainau, Franz, 186
Rammekamp, Rudolph, 213
Rammelkamp, R., 216
Rapp, Julius, 163
Raschid, Harun al, 100
Rashcoe, 5, 13
Rassieur, Leo, 107, 218, 220
Rathmann, C. G., 209, 210
Rau, 49
Rau, Henry, 224
Raum, Louis A., 134
Raupach, 183
Rauschbach, 106
Ravold, 68
Rea, George H., 235
Rebenack, Christopher, 137
Rebenak, 199
Reber, Samuel, 105
Rebstocky, Charles, 17
Reichard, George, 178, 208, 210
Reichelt, Charles, 163
Reif, Theodore, 218
Reimler, August, 322
Reinder, A., 159
Reinhard, Charles, 225
Reipschlaeger, August, 78
Reipschlaeger, William, 78
Reis, Bartholomew, 130
Reisse, Adolph William, 46
Reisse, Karl, 46
Reisse, William, 163
Reitzel, Robert, 216
Remenyi, 175
Remnitz, 199
Renick, R. M., 241
Rethwilm, Edward F., 76
Retzer, Carl, 220
Reusz, F. A., 6
Ricci, Bertha, 85
Richardson, 47
Richter, Carl, 162
Richter, John, 161
Rieckhoff, 185, 186
Riedel, Adam, 223
Rieken, 222
Ries, 200
Riggin, John, 98
Riley, 305
Riley, C. V., 280
Rimberger, 191
Ringeling, Francis, 4
Ringen, John, 275, 276
Ringhoff, 203
Rinkel, 80
Riotte, Hermann, 187, 188
Rist, Albert, 226
Ristori, Adelaide, 95
Ritter, Hermann W., 220, 226
Ritterskamp, Louis, 7
Rittig, J., 39, 173
Rive-King, Julia, 175
Rives, 14
Robbins, 56
Robertson, 309
Robyn, 102, 161, 336
Robyn, Alfred, 157
Robyn, Henry, 156, 157
Robyn, William, 155-158
Roche, La, 65
Roe, John J., 66
Roeder, 198, 201
Roemer, Bertha, 184
Roemich, 49
Roemmich, Dr., 91

Roentgen, 98
Roepenack, 181
Roepenak, 179
Roepke, William, 79
Roesch, Carl, 17, 189
Roeser, Carl, 112
Roeslein, 102
Roeslein, Frederick, 49
Roesler, Anton, 10
Roever, Frederick, 217
Rohlke, F., 220
Rohrer, Louis, 46
Rolf, 184
Roman, Alexander, 89
Rombauer, 107
Rombauer, Robert J., 112, 129
Roos, 201
Roos, Leonhard, 57
Rosa, 54
Rosa, Karl, 175
Rosa, Parepa, 96
Rose, 17
Rose, Conrad, 171
Rose, Edward, 193
Rose, William, 18
Rosebaum, 211
Rosenfeld, Jr., Isaac, 5
Rosenheim, 82
Rosewell, 22
Ross, A. U., 178
Rossini, 158
Rothensteiner, John Ernest, 337
Rothhan, 8
Rothweiler, George, 136
Rotteck, C., 112
Rottman, J. H., 31
Rowan, Steven, 337

Rubelmann, 35
Rubelmann, George A., 35
Rubelmann, John G., 35
Rubens, Harry, 39, 110
Rubinstein, 175
Rueckert, George, 144
Ruempler, Theodore, 281
Rueppele, Charles, 5, 318
Ruesse, 205
Ruff, Franz, 50
Ruhe, Henry, 321
Rumsey, L, M., 328
Ruppelt, H., 111, 227, 229
Ruppius, Otto, 39
Rusch, George, 40
Russell, 150
Rust, John C., 7, 153
Ruther, O., 225
Sabatzki, 163
Saeger, Henry, 164
Saettele, Max, 131
Sale, 206
Saler, 42, 134
Saler, Franz, 5
Salm Salm, 10
Salomon, C. L., 213
Salomon, E., 106
Salomon, Karl, 165, 216
Salorgne, Theodore, 237
Samesreuther, F, 10
Sampson, C. H., 332
Sander, Enno, 12, 13, 16, 17, 61, 62, 284-287
Sarner, Hugo, 186, 187
Sarner, Victor, 186
Sarpi, Jean Baptiste, 90
Sarti, 65

Satter, Gustav, 175
Sauret, 175
Saussenthaler, Peter, 123
Sauter, Severin Robert, 40, 48, 150, 160, 161, 170
Schacht, 114
Schacht, Hermann, 220
Schade, 145
Schaefer, Frederick, 24
Schaefer, Louis, 174, 228
Schaefer, Otto, 225
Schaeffer, 83, 146
Schaeffer, Nicolaus, 261
Schaller, G., 202
Schallert, 56
Scharmann, George, 115
Scharwitz, Franz, 10, 127
Schatzmann, 66
Scheele, Fritz, 145
Schenk, 294
Schenk, A., 228
Scheufler, A., 165
Schierenberg, E., 112
Schiffmann, John, 14, 133
Schild, 7, 162, 173
Schiller, Anna, 41
Schiller, Friedrich, 180, 182-184
Schiller, Louis, 14, 24, 36, 75, 177
Schilliger, 161
Schilliger, F., 165, 167
Schilling, 60
Schilling, Moritz, 151
Schilling, W., 174
Schillinger, 161
Schillinger, F., 165, 167
Schinckle, 309

Schinkowsky, F. M., 210
Schleiffarth, Charles, 114
Schloehaum, 197
Schloszstein, 139
Schloszstein. Louis, 18, 146
Schloszstein, George, 111
Schlueter, 53
Schlulenburg, Rudolph, 167
Schmid, Adam, 223
Schmid, F. L., 12
Schmid, John, 223
Schmidt, Ernest, 37, 120
Schmidt, Franz, 211-213
Schmidt, Hermann, 223
Schmidt, Jack, 226
Schmidt, Mrs., 197
Schmidt, Otto, 120, 159
Schmieding, F. E., 30, 31
Schmitz, Edward, 187
Schmitz, Friedrich, 187
Schmoll, Oscar, 165, 169
Schnaider, 153, 172
Schnaider, Joseph, 153, 171
Schneeberger, John H., 88
Schneider, 146
Schneider, A., 7
Schneider, Charles F., 13, 60, 153
Schneider, F. A. H., 134
Schneider, George, 140, 159
Schneider, Joseph, 18, 153
Schneider, Julius, 175
Schneider, L., 28
Schneider, Louis, 72
Schnell, 161
Schnell, Keller, 164
Schnell, Louis, 157

Schnerr, Constantine, 152
Schoen, 31
Schoenfeld, 199
Schoenle, John, 228
Schoenthaler, Frederick, 105
Schoenthaler, J., 172
Scholten, John A., 90, 91, 127, 151, 283
Schopp, Valentine, 161
Schotten, Christian, 37
Schotten, William, 37
Schramm, Carl, 173, 183
Schramm-Rolff, 183
Schratt, Katie, 186
Schraubenbach, K., 226
Schraubstaedler, 47
Schray, 44
Schreiber, 184
Schreiber, William, 34, 188, 223
Schreiner, 22
Schreiner, E. F., 225, 226
Schrick, Julius, 207
Schroeder, 197
Schroeder, Adolf E., 337
Schroeder, C., 199
Schroeder, Julius, 62
Schroth, 127
Schroth, Peter J., 37
Schueler, Otto, 184
Schuenemann-Pott, 216
Schuermann, August, 227, 228
Schuetz, Frederick, 216
Schuetze, John, 6, 23, 31
Schuh, 138
Schulenburg, 34
Schulenburg, F., 211, 249, 250
Schulenburg, Rudolph, 63

Schuler, 170
Schulter, 21
Schultz, Arthur R., 335
Schulz, C., 28, 156
Schulz-Geisberg, Carla, 337
Schumacher, 322
Schumacher, George, 85
Schumann, 176
Schuricht, 41
Schuricht, F. W., 144
Schurz, Carl, 217
Schuster, Florentine, 13
Schuster, Mortiz, 16, 49
Schwaerzel, H., 229
Schwan, 179
Schwanecke, Frederick, 168
Schwarner, Henry, 165
Schwartz, Anton, 137
Schwartze, H., 223
Schwarz, Caroline, 127
Schwedel, Henry, 218
Schweickhardt, Bernard, 16
Schweickhardt, Bernhard, 16
Schweickhardt, Carl, 162
Schweickhardt, Henry, 11, 12, 16, 99
Schweikard, Charles, 168
Scott, 102, 103
Scroka, Ernest, 166
Scruggs, 55, 69
Scruggs, R. M., 330, 332
Seebach, Marie, 44, 182
Seemann, E., 194, 222
Seibert, John A., 65
Seidel, 86, 199
Seidel, Emil F., 304, 305
Seifert, Martin, 110

Seisl, 204
Seitz, Louis, 79
Sellers, 170
Sembrich, Marcella, 60
Senden, 21
Sennewald, F. W., 17, 111, 120
Senter, 37
Sessinghaus, 34
Sessinghaus, G., 213
Sessinghaus, Theodore, 165
Sessinghaus, William, 225
Seybold, 201
Shakespeare, 62, 89
Shaler, 67
Shaw, Henry, 248
Shepard, Elihu, 218
Sherman, 300
Sherman, W. T., 244
Sichers, William, 127
Sickels, J. B., 241
Siebel, 85
Siedler, F., 163
Siegrist, 205
Sigel, Franz, 38, 93, 336
Simmons, E. C., 330
Simon, Ferdinand, 138
Simonds, John, 120
Simone, C., 225
Simpson, 183
Simpson, Robert, 255
Singer, 6, 69, 86
Singer, Ferdinand, 111
Smith, A. J., 255
Smith, D. S. H., 237, 251
Smith, Elon G., 40
Smith, Mark, 87
Smith, Solon, 87, 276

Sobolewski, Edward, 161, 168
Sobolewski, Miss, 170
Soeding, Casper, 122
Soeding, Charles, 122
Soest, William, 220
Soldon, 141
Solia, Clara, 184
Sommerfruechte, Dietrich, 33
Sonneschein, 206
Sonntag, Karl, 186
Sostmann, Ernest, 165
Soulard, 124
Soulard, Henry, 134
Sousa, 331
Spaeter, Anna, 169
Spahn, 186
Spakler, H., 168
Spannagel, H., 167, 211
Spaunhorst, 21
Spaunhorst, H. J., 4
Spaunhorst, Henry J., 4, 59, 89
Speck, 10
Speck, Charles, 135, 217, 218, 221
Speck, Louis, 207
Spengel, Tobias, 34
Spengler, Tobias, 223
Spiegelhalter, Joseph, 47, 72, 173
Spiegelthal, Caesar, 224
Spiering, Ernest, 173, 174
Spilker, 92
Spilker, August, 132
Spindler, 274
Spinzig, 192
Spitz, 206
Spoeri, Mathias, 227

Sprague, Charles C., 88
Springer, Charles, 274
St. John, 47
StaehlinChristian, 152
Stahl, 270
Stamm, Hermann, 26, 226
Stammwitz, Elizabeth von, 188
Stanard, 122
Stanard, E. O., 145, 330, 332
Stange, Julius, 15
Starck, Charles, 171
Starck, Christian, 171
Stark, 197
Starke, 153
Starkloff, H. H., 227
Stauff, Conrad, 261
Stecher, W. A., 220
Stegemann, J. D., 198
Steger, 177
Steidel, 182
Steigerwalt, Frederick, 56
Stein, Martin, 227
Steinberg, M. J., 52
Steiner, Charles W., 223, 224
Steiner, Frederick L., 224
Steinhauer, Adrian L., 162
Steinmeyer, 132
Steins, Oscar, 172
Steinway, 61
Steitz, Mathias, 19
Steller, 122
Steller, Louis, 51
Steller, Philipp, 222
Stelzleni, 189
Stephanie, 184, 186
Stickel, Otto, 218
Stickels, A., 217
Stickney, Benjamin, 52
Stiefel, August C., 43
Stiefel, L., 165
Stierlin, 179
Stiesmeyer, 173
Stiesmeyer, Mrs. Charles, 96
Stifel, Charles G., 34, 76, 94, 140, 188, 322
Stifel, Christian A., 209, 210, 218, 220, 221
Stifel, Christoph A., 122
Stifel, Frederick, 122
Stinde, C. R., 6
Stock, Stephan, 144
Stockstrom, 275
Stockstrom, Charles A., 275
Stockstrom, Louis, 275
Stoecker, Robert, 162
Stoffregen, 127
Stolle, Casper, 28, 30
Stracke, 21
Strakosch, Maurice, 158, 160
Strakosch, Max, 54, 85, 96, 169
Strasser, 178
Straszacker, William, 229
Straszburger, 101
Straszburger, A. F., 10
Strattmann, 197
Straub, A. W., 122, 209, 210, 228
Straus, 8
Strechmann, Gerhard, 207
Stremmel, Philipp, 35
Strittmatter, Charley, 137
Stroka, Ernest, 166
Strothotto, Mrs. Doctor, 176
Struve, Frederick, 284

Struve, Gustav Adolf, 285
Stueck, Jacob, 163
Stuermann, 199
Stuesser, F., 225
Stumpf, Charles, 42, 85
Stumpf, Frederick, 150, 151
Stumpf, Jacob, 128
Stumpf, William, 207
Sturgeon, Isaac H., 258
Suesz, 6
Surry, Hedwig, 182
Sutter, Christoph, 136
Sutter, John J., 109, 227, 228
Sutter, Mike, 112, 238
Tamm, Jacob, 5, 208, 277, 278
Tamm, Theodore, 5, 277, 279
Tamm, William B., 278, 279
Tausig, William, 161
Taussig, Charles, 4, 5
Taussig, William, 83, 107, 144, 168
Taussing, 132
Taylor, Daniel G., 22
Taylor, George R., 58
Tebbe, 211
Teichmann, Charles H., 7, 209, 210
Teichmann, Otto L., 7
Temme, Charles, 216
Tentsch, 186
Tesson, 144
Tessone, 20
Teuteberg, J., 213
Teuteberg, L. W., 223
Thalberg, 160
Thalmann, B., 171
Thamer, Julius, 28

Thannberger, Louis, 15, 16
Theummler, T., 109
Thias, 78
Thiebes, 162
Thielemann, 178
Thiemann, Ernest, 78
Thiet, Charles, 44
Thole, Bernhard, 69
Thomann, Aloys, 88
Thomas, 54
Thomas, James S., 100
Thomas, Mayor, 40, 127
Thomas, Rev. M., 198
Thomas, Theodore, 166
Thonssen, B. E., 90
Thul, Peter, 141
Thumb, Tom, 56, 69
Ticknor, Edwin, 56
Tiedemann, F. C. P., 221, 222
Timmermann, 120
Timmermann, Gerhardt H.,, 19, 291, 292
Timmermann, John H., 19, 292
Tittmann, 63
Tittmann, Harold H., 307
Todd, Albert, 76
Todd, Charles, 327
Toensfeldt, 220, 222
Toeppen, Hugo, 226
Tolle, John F., 76, 122
Tolzmann, Don Heinrich, i, vi, 335, 337
Tomlinson, 162
Torlina, 31, 197
Townsend, H. C., 251, 332
Trask, George, 238
Trauernicht, Theodore, 78

Trautmann, Ida von, 186
Trebus, Charles J., 223
Trexler, 199
Trieselmann, Henry, 77
Trimbe, 174
Troll, Henry, 222
Trorlicht, J. H., 56, 228
Trovatore, 62, 85, 169
Tschieder, 204
Tschirpe, 17
Tucker, Marlin T., 337
Tuerk, Hermann, 10
Turner, C. H., 328, 332
Turner, Charles H., 330
Turner, Henry S., 325
Turner, John W., 328
Twain, Mark, 69
Tyler, 50, 66
Ubsdell, 55
Uhland, 205
Uhlmann, C. Theodore, 111, 210
Uhrig, Joseph, 123, 149, 228
Ullman, 49
Ulrich, Louis, 223
Ulrici, 19
Ulrici, C., 196
Ulrici, Emil, 130
Ulrici, Rudolf, 50, 58
Ungar, Karl, 226
Unger, Champaign, 143
Unger, Richard, 143
Unrath, H., 223
Upmeyer, H. C., 167
Urso, Camilla, 160
Vahlkamp, Henry, 268
Valentin, Sarah, 191
Vallat, Carl, 119, 218

Valle, Amade, 58
Van Diemens, 305
Vandervoort, 55, 69
Varrelmann, H. A., 31
Velguth, 186
Vellguth, 183, 186
Verdi, 62, 176
Vidaver, 205
Vierling, 176
Vieuxtemps, Henri, 156
Visseur, Louis, 44
Vogel, 45, 150, 153
Vogel, Benjamin, 46, 48
Vogel, Charles F., 105, 226
Vogel, Henry, 138, 150, 153, 161
Vogel, Jacob, 133
Vogel, John C., 109, 196, 238
Vogel, William, 210
Vogeler, Julius, 24
Vogelsang, 169
Vogt, Charles, 225
Vogt, Frank, 197
Vogt, Julius, 223
Vogtmann, Gustav F., 70
Voigt, 6
Volkening, 17
Volkening, Louis, 57
Volkmann, 13, 14
Vordtriede, E. H., 146, 152
Vortriede, Henry E., 221
Wachtel, Joseph, 111
Wachter, Emil, 131
Wagemann, Louis, 227
Wagner, Anna, 186
Wagner, Edward, 225
Wagner, Franz, 207

Wagner, Louis, 225
Wagner, Mrs., 183
Wagner, Rudolph, 27
Wahl, 171
Wahl, John, 7
Waif of Lowood, 95, 182
Wainwright, Ellis, 142, 328, 330, 332
Waite, Joseph, 94, 112
Waldauer, 45, 150, 153
Waldauer, August, 27, 156, 160, 161, 164, 168, 171
Waldecker, 78, 197
Waldemar, 187
Waldemar, Carl, 188
Walker, Ely, 70
Wall, 195, 201, 324
Wall, L. J. W., 324, 325
Wall, Louis J., 88
Wall, Rev., 195, 200, 201
Wallstab, C., 165
Walsh, D. E., 241
Walsh, Edward, 248
Walsh, Julius S., 241, 243, 327, 328
Walter, Frederick, 68
Walter, Fritz, 111
Walter, Jacob, 41, 293-295
Walther, 203
Walther, C. F. W., 202
Walther, Hermann, 202
Walther, Jak, 226
Walther, William K., 117
Waltke, Louis H., 273
Waltke, William, 272, 273
Wamsganz, John, 127
Wangelin, Baron von, 157

Ward, Artemus, 69
Ward, Robert E., v
Warner, C. G., 251
Warren, Minnie, 69
Wartenburg, Rink von, 174
Wartenburg, Snyder von, 174
Washington Hall, 37, 38, 163, 178
Wattenberg, 317
Wattenberg, Ernest, 5
Weber, Charles G., 53, 54, 224
Weber, George, 136
Weber, Henry, 155, 156, 204
Weber, Peter, 78
Weber, Sergeant, 136
Weber, Theresa, 155
Weckes, A., 187
Wedig, Charles, 224, 225
Wedig, Louis, 224
Wedig, William, 224, 225
Wehrkamp, 111
Weidmann, 182
Weidner, E., 229
Weig, Arthur, 224
Weigel, Philipp, 16, 58
Weil, J., 6
Weil, Joseph, 66
Weinbrecht, Julius, 226
Weinhagen, 21
Weisz, Mathias, 138
Weisz, Peter, 129, 131
Weizenecker, Peter, 152
Welker, 36
Welker, Fritz, 37
Welle, Albert F., 320, 321
Welle-Boettler, 320
Welles, Edgar T., 254

Wells, Erasmus, 103, 122, 237, 238, 304, 305
Wells, Erastus, 239
Wells, Rolla, 239, 327, 328
Wendl, Franz, 120
Wenzel, Adam, 78
Werber, Phillip, 114
Werner, Frederick, 310
Werner, Kuno, 226
Wertz, H., 166
Werz, 199
Wesseling, George, 78
Wesseling, Rudolph, 78
Westermann, H., 6
Weszling, Rudolph, 28
Wette, John, 227
Wetteroth, 199
Wettle, 200
Wetzel, Charles, 18
Wetzler, Charles, 17
Whedon, 66
White, 89
Whitnell, John, 325
Whitnell, W. W., 242
Wichmann, 144
Wiebusch, 45
Wiebusch, A., v, 44, 321
Wiebusch, August, 44
Wiebusch, Henry, 44
Wieden, Frederick, 229
Wiedmann, Emily, 96
Wiegand, George, 118
Wiemann, J., 224
Wiese, F., 174
Wiesler, L., 174
Wiggins, 245
Wilde, Henry T., 79, 209, 210
Wilhelmy, 175
Will, 201
Willhartitz, A., 173, 180
Williams, 171
Willich, Louis, 110, 114
Wilson, 119
Wilucky, Ernst von, 6
Windmueller, Alexander, 134
Winiawski, 175
Winkelmeyer, 122
Winkelmeyer, Christiane, 122, 197
Winkelmeyer, Julius, 122
Winklee, 86
Winter, Carl, 188
Wintergarten, Gregory, 48, 103
Winzer, George, 114
Wippern, Adolph, 76
Wippold, F. J., 220
Wisemann, Anton, 57, 74
Wislizenus, 58, 192, 193
Wist, 8, 10, 75
Wiszmann, 21
Wiszmann, Christian, 113, 197
Witte, C. G., 45
Witte, Ernest, 78
Witte, F. A., 31
Witte, L. Edward, 223
Witter, Conrad, 12, 13
Wittgenstein, Prince, 164
Wittich, George, 222
Wittler, E. F., 324
Woerner, J. G., 26, 114, 141, 184, 188
Wolf, 5, 6, 79, 179, 199
Wolf, C. D., 136
Wolf, Christian, 45

Wolf, Dorthea, 9, 10
Wolf, Gustav, 109
Wolf, Ignatz, 181-183
Wolf, J., 110
Wolf, John, 196, 207
Wolf, Louis, 10, 11
Wolf, Marie, 185, 186
Wolf, Stout, 12
Wolfarth, H., 79
Wolfenstein, 206
Wolff, 5, 79
Wolff, Daniel, 139, 260
Wolff, Ignaz, 181
Wolff, John, 196
Wollbrecht, George, 48
Woltmann, G., 8
Wotke, F. W., 132
Wright, Uriel, 84
Wulfind, 21
Wurpel, Moritz, 165, 216
Wurster, Alexander, 185-187
Wyman, 158
Wyman, Edward, 116
Wymann, 115, 191
Wymann, Henry P., 236
Wyneke, Frederick, 202
Xaupi, 26, 111
Yeatman, 91
Yeatman, James E., 92, 162
Young, Dorothy, vi
Young, John M., 71
Zallee, 90
Zandt, William van, 238
Zell, 31
Zepp, 137
Zepp, Louis, 141
Zerboni, Alfons von, 182, 190

Zerboni, Mrs. von, 65
Zerbonie, Mrs., 65
Zerlina, 96
Zettlage, Edwin, 224
Zeuchlodons, 116
Ziegenheim, 105
Zimmer, Charles, 78
Zimmerer, John, 18
Zimmermann, 94, 187
Zimmermann, Gustav A., v
Ziock, 6
Ziock, William, 6
Zisemann, John F., 7, 9
Zott, Armin, 173
Zuendt, E. A., 188, 227, 229
Zurstraszen, 211

www.ingramcontent.com/pod-product-compliance
Lightning Source LLC
Chambersburg PA
CBHW070009010526
44117CB00011B/1477